Java® Programming for Android™ Developers

FOR DUMMIES®

A Wiley Brand

Java® Programming for Android™ Developers

FOR DUMMIES®

A Wiley Brand

by Barry Burd

FOR
DUMMIES®
A Wiley Brand

Java® Programming for Android™ Developers For Dummies®

Published by: **John Wiley & Sons, Inc.,** 111 River Street, Hoboken, NJ 07030-5774, www.wiley.com

Copyright © 2014 by John Wiley & Sons, Inc., Hoboken, New Jersey

Published simultaneously in Canada

No part of this publication may be reproduced, stored in a retrieval system or transmitted in any form or by any means, electronic, mechanical, photocopying, recording, scanning or otherwise, except as permitted under Sections 107 or 108 of the 1976 United States Copyright Act, without the prior written permission of the Publisher. Requests to the Publisher for permission should be addressed to the Permissions Department, John Wiley & Sons, Inc., 111 River Street, Hoboken, NJ 07030, (201) 748-6011, fax (201) 748-6008, or online at http://www.wiley.com/go/permissions.

Trademarks: Wiley, For Dummies, the Dummies Man logo, Dummies.com, Making Everything Easier, and related trade dress are trademarks or registered trademarks of John Wiley & Sons, Inc. and may not be used without written permission. Java is a registered trademark of Oracle America, Inc. Android is a trademark of Google, Inc. All other trademarks are the property of their respective owners. John Wiley & Sons, Inc. is not associated with any product or vendor mentioned in this book.

LIMIT OF LIABILITY/DISCLAIMER OF WARRANTY: THE PUBLISHER AND THE AUTHOR MAKE NO REPRESENTATIONS OR WARRANTIES WITH RESPECT TO THE ACCURACY OR COMPLETENESS OF THE CONTENTS OF THIS WORK AND SPECIFICALLY DISCLAIM ALL WARRANTIES, INCLUDING WITHOUT LIMITATION WARRANTIES OF FITNESS FOR A PARTICULAR PURPOSE. NO WARRANTY MAY BE CREATED OR EXTENDED BY SALES OR PROMOTIONAL MATERIALS. THE ADVICE AND STRATEGIES CONTAINED HEREIN MAY NOT BE SUITABLE FOR EVERY SITUATION. THIS WORK IS SOLD WITH THE UNDERSTANDING THAT THE PUBLISHER IS NOT ENGAGED IN RENDERING LEGAL, ACCOUNTING, OR OTHER PROFESSIONAL SERVICES. IF PROFESSIONAL ASSISTANCE IS REQUIRED, THE SERVICES OF A COMPETENT PROFESSIONAL PERSON SHOULD BE SOUGHT. NEITHER THE PUBLISHER NOR THE AUTHOR SHALL BE LIABLE FOR DAMAGES ARISING HEREFROM. THE FACT THAT AN ORGANIZATION OR WEBSITE IS REFERRED TO IN THIS WORK AS A CITATION AND/OR A POTENTIAL SOURCE OF FURTHER INFORMATION DOES NOT MEAN THAT THE AUTHOR OR THE PUBLISHER ENDORSES THE INFORMATION THE ORGANIZATION OR WEBSITE MAY PROVIDE OR RECOMMENDATIONS IT MAY MAKE. FURTHER, READERS SHOULD BE AWARE THAT INTERNET WEBSITES LISTED IN THIS WORK MAY HAVE CHANGED OR DISAPPEARED BETWEEN WHEN THIS WORK WAS WRITTEN AND WHEN IT IS READ.

For general information on our other products and services, please contact our Customer Care Department within the U.S. at 877-762-2974, outside the U.S. at 317-572-3993, or fax 317-572-4002. For technical support, please visit www.wiley.com/techsupport.

Wiley publishes in a variety of print and electronic formats and by print-on-demand. Some material included with standard print versions of this book may not be included in e-books or in print-on-demand. If this book refers to media such as a CD or DVD that is not included in the version you purchased, you may download this material at http://booksupport.wiley.com. For more information about Wiley products, visit www.wiley.com.

Library of Congress Control Number: 2013948033

ISBN 978-1-118-50438-3 (pbk); ISBN 978-1-118-61212-5 (ebk); ISBN 978-1-118-61214-9 (ebk)

Manufactured in the United States of America

10 9 8 7 6 5 4 3 2 1

Contents at a Glance

Table of Contents

Introduction

• •

A ndroid is everywhere. In mid-2013, Android ran on 53 percent of all smartphones in the United States and on 80 percent of all smartphones worldwide.[1] In a study that spans the Americas, Europe, Asia, and the Middle East, GlobalWebIndex reports that Android tablets outnumber iPads by 34 million.[2] More than a million apps are available for download at the Google Play store (double the number of apps that were available in May 2012).[3] And more than 9 million developers write code using Java, the language that powers Android devices.[4]

If you read this book in a public place (on a commuter train, at the beach, or on the dance floor at the Coyote Ugly saloon, for example), you can read proudly, with a chip on your shoulder and with your head held high. Android is hot stuff, and you're cool because you're reading about it.

How to Use This Book

You can attack this book in either of two ways: go from cover to cover or poke around from one chapter to another. You can even do both (start at the beginning, and then jump to a section that particularly interests you). This book was designed so that the basic topics come first, and the more-involved topics follow them. But you may already be comfortable with some basics, or you may have specific goals that don't require you to know about certain topics.

[1]See www.kantarworldpanel.com/global/News/news-articles/ Samsung-nears-50-share-across-Europe-as-Apple- powers-back-in-the-US and http://www.idc.com/getdoc. jsp?containerId=prUS24257413.

[2]See www.globalwebindex.net/android-tablets-dominate-q1- mobile-market.

[3]See www.androidguys.com/2013/07/24/sundar-pichai-there-are- now-more-than-1-million-android-apps.

[4]See www.java.com/en/about.

In general, my advice is this:

✔ If you already know something, don't bother reading about it.

✔ If you're curious, don't be afraid to skip ahead. You can always sneak a peek at an earlier chapter if you need to do so.

Conventions Used in This Book

Almost every technically themed book starts with a little typeface legend, and *Java Programming For Android Developers For Dummies* is no exception. What follows is a brief explanation of the typefaces used in this book:

✔ New terms are set in *italics*.

✔ If you need to type something that's mixed in with the regular text, the characters you type appear in bold. For example: "Type **MyNewProject** in the text field."

✔ You also see this `computerese` font. I use computerese for Java code, filenames, onscreen messages, and other such things. Also, if something you need to type is really long, it appears in computerese font on its own line (or lines).

✔ You may need to change certain things when you type them on your own computer keyboard. For instance, I may ask you to type

```
public void Anyname
```

which means that you type **public void** and then a name that you make up on your own. Words that you need to replace with your own words are set in *italicized computerese*.

What You Don't Have to Read

Pick the first chapter or section that has material you don't already know and start reading there. Of course, you may hate making decisions as much as I do. If so, here are some guidelines you can follow:

✔ **If you already know what kind of an animal Java is and you don't care what happens behind the scenes when an Android app runs:** Skip Chapter 1 and go straight to Chapter 2. Believe me — I won't mind.

✔ **If you already know how to get an Android app running:** Skip Part I and start with Part II.

- ✔ **If you have experience writing computer programs in languages other than C and C++:** Start with Part II. You'll probably find Part II to be easy reading. When you get to Part III, it'll be time to dive in.

- ✔ **If you have experience writing computer programs in C or C++:** Skim Part II and start reading seriously in Part III. (Java is a bit different from C++ in the way it handles classes and objects.)

- ✔ **If you have experience writing Java programs:** Come to my house and help me write *Java Programming For Android Developers For Dummies,* 2nd Edition.

If you want to skip the sidebars and the paragraphs with Technical Stuff icons, please do. In fact, if you want to skip anything at all, feel free.

Foolish Assumptions

In this book, I make a few assumptions about you, the reader. If one of these assumptions is incorrect, you're probably okay. If all these assumptions are incorrect . . . well, buy the book anyway.

- ✔ **I assume that you have access to a computer.** Access to an Android device is helpful but not absolutely necessary! All the software you need in order to test Android apps on a laptop or desktop computer is freely available. You simply download, install, and get going.

- ✔ **I assume that you can navigate your computer's common menus and dialog boxes.** You don't have to be a Windows, Linux, or Macintosh power user, but you should be able to start a program, find a file, put a file into a certain directory — that sort of thing. Much of the time, when you follow the instructions in this book, you're typing code on the keyboard, not pointing and clicking the mouse.

  On those occasions when you need to drag and drop, cut and paste, or plug and play, I guide you carefully through the steps. But your computer may be configured in any of several billion ways, and my instructions may not quite fit your special situation. When you reach one of these platform-specific tasks, try following the steps in this book. If the steps don't quite fit, consult a book with instructions tailored to your system. If you can't find such a book, send me an e-mail. (My address appears later in the Introduction.)

- ✔ **I assume that you can think logically.** That's all there is to application development — thinking logically. If you can think logically, you've got it made. If you don't believe that you can think logically, read on. You may be pleasantly surprised.

✔ **I make very few assumptions about your computer programming experience (or your lack of such experience).** In writing this book, I've tried to do the impossible: make the book interesting for experienced programmers yet accessible to people with little or no programming experience. This means that I don't assume any particular programming background on your part. If you've never created a loop or indexed an array, that's okay.

On the other hand, if you've done these things (maybe in Visual Basic, COBOL, or C++), you'll discover some interesting plot twists in Java. The creators of Java took the best ideas from object-oriented programming, streamlined them, reworked them, and reorganized them into a sleek, powerful way of thinking about problems. You'll find many new, thought-provoking features in Java. As you find out about these features, many of them will seem quite natural to you. One way or another, you'll feel good about using Java.

How This Book Is Organized

This book is divided into subsections, which are grouped into sections, which come together to make chapters, which are lumped, finally, into five parts (like one of those Russian *matryoshka* dolls). The parts of the book are described here.

Part 1: Getting Started with Java Programming for Android Developers

Part I covers all the nuts and bolts. It introduces you to the major ideas behind Java and Android software development and walks you through the installation of the necessary software products. You also run a few simple Java and Android programs.

The instructions in these chapters cover both Windows and Macintosh computers. They cover many computer configurations, including some not-so-new operating system versions, the differences between 32-bit systems and 64-bit systems, and situations in which you already have some form of Java on your computer. But installing software is always tricky, and you might have a few hurdles to overcome. If you do, check the end of this chapter for ways to reach me (the author) and get some quick advice. (Yes, I answer e-mails, tweets, Facebook posts, and notes sent by carrier pigeons.)

Part II: Writing Your Own Java Programs

Chapters 5 through 8 cover Java's basic building blocks. These chapters describe the things you need to know so that you can get your computer humming along.

If you've written programs in Visual Basic, C++, or in any another language, some of the material in Part II may be familiar to you. If so, you can skip some sections or read this stuff quickly. But don't read *too* quickly. Java is a little different from some other programming languages, especially in the features I describe in Chapter 6.

Part III: Working with the Big Picture: Object-Oriented Programming

Part III has some of my favorite chapters. This part covers the all-important topic of object-oriented programming. In these chapters, you find out how to map solutions to big problems. (Sure, the examples in these chapters aren't big, but the examples involve big ideas.) You discover, in bite-worthy increments, how to design classes, reuse existing classes, and construct objects.

Have you read any of those books that explain object-oriented programming in vague, general terms? I'm very proud to say that *Java Programming for Android Developers For Dummies* isn't like that. In this book, I illustrate each concept with a simple-yet-concrete program example.

Part IV: Powering Android with Java Code

If you've tasted some Java and want more, you can find what you need in this part of the book. This part's chapters are devoted to details — the things you don't see when you first glance at the material. This part includes some fully functional Android apps. So, after you read the earlier parts and write some programs on your own, you can dive in a little deeper by reading Part IV.

Part V: The Part of Tens

In The Part of Tens, which is a little Java candy store, you can find lists — lists of tips for avoiding mistakes, tracking down resources, and finding all kinds of interesting goodies.

More on the web!

You've read the *Java Programming For Android Developers* book, seen the *Java Programming For Android Developers* movie, worn the *Java Programming for Android Developers* T-shirt, and eaten the *Java Programming for Android Developers* candy. What more is there to do?

That's easy. Just visit this book's website: `www.allmycode.com/Java4 Android`. There you can find updates, comments, additional information, and answers to commonly asked questions from readers. You can also find a small chat application for sending me quick questions when I'm online. (When I'm not online, you can contact me in other ways. See the end of this chapter for more info.)

Icons Used in This Book

If you could watch me write this book, you'd see me sitting at my computer, talking to myself. I say each sentence in my head. Most of the sentences I mutter several times. When I have an extra thought, a side comment, or something else that doesn't belong in the regular stream, I twist my head a little bit. That way, whoever's listening to me (usually nobody) knows that I'm off on a momentary tangent.

Of course, in print, you can't see me twisting my head. I need some other way to set a side thought in a corner by itself. I do it with icons. When you see a Tip icon or a Remember icon, you know that I'm taking a quick detour.

Here's a list of icons that I use in this book:

A tip is an extra piece of information — helpful advice that the other books may forget to tell you.

Everyone makes mistakes. Heaven knows that I've made a few in my time. Anyway, when I think people are especially prone to make a mistake, I mark the text with a Warning icon.

Question: What's stronger than a tip but not as strong as a warning?

Answer: A Remember icon.

"If you don't remember what *such-and-such* means, see *blah-blah-blah*," or "For more information, read *blahbity-blah-blah*."

This icon calls attention to useful material that you can find online. (You don't have to wait long to see one of these icons. I use one at the end of this introduction!)

Occasionally, I run across a technical tidbit. The tidbit may help you understand what the people behind the scenes (the people who created Java) were thinking. You don't have to read it, but you may find it useful. You may also find the tidbit helpful if you plan to read other (geekier) books about Java and Android.

Beyond the Book

We have written a lot of extra content that you won't find in this book. Go online to find the following:

- **Dummies.com online articles:** Be sure to check out www.dummies. com/extras/javaprogrammingforandroiddevelopers for additional online content dealing with Java and Android app development. Here you'll find examples of delightfully weird code, a disquisition on classes and objects, a quick look at using Android Asset Studio, an additional Parts of Ten chapter, and much more. And, if we have to post any updates to this edition of *Java Programming for Android Developers For Dummies*, here's where you'd find them.
- **The Cheat Sheet for this book is at** www.dummies.com/cheatsheet/ javaprogrammingforandroiddevelopers

Where to Go from Here

If you've gotten this far, you're ready to start reading about Java and Android application development. Think of me (the author) as your guide, your host, your personal assistant. I do everything I can to keep things interesting and, most importantly, to help you understand.

If you like what you read, send me a note. My e-mail address, which I created just for comments and questions about this book, is java4android@ allmycode.com. If e-mail and chat aren't your favorites, you can reach me instead on Twitter (@allmycode) and on Facebook (/allmycode). And don't forget — for the latest updates, visit this book's website. The site's address is www.allmycode.com/java4android.

Part I
Getting Started with Java Programming for Android Developers

In this part . . .

- Downloading the software
- Installing Java and Android
- Testing Android apps on your computer

Chapter 1

All about Java and Android

In This Chapter

▶ The consumer's view of the Android ecosystem

▶ The ten-cent tour of Java and Android technologies

*U*ntil the mid-2000s, the word *android* represented a mechanical, humanlike creature — a root'n-toot'n officer of the law with built-in machine guns or a hyperlogical space traveler who can do everything except speak using contractions. And then in 2005, Google purchased Android, Inc. — a 22-month old company creating software for mobile phones. That move changed everything.

In 2007, a group of 34 companies formed the Open Handset Alliance. Its task is "to accelerate innovation in mobile and offer consumers a richer, less expensive, and better mobile experience"; its primary project is *Android,* an open, free operating system based on the Linux operating system kernel.

Though HTC released the first commercially available Android phone near the end of 2008, in the United States the public's awareness of Android and its potential didn't surface until early 2010.

As I sit and write in mid-2013, Mobile Marketing Watch reports more than 50 billion downloads from the Google Play app store.[1] Android developers earned more from their apps in the first half of 2013 than in all of 2012. And according to *Forbes*, Google paid approximately $900 million to Android developers during the 12-month period starting in mid-2012.[2] The pace is accelerating.

[1]See www.mobilemarketingwatch.com/google-play-tops-50-billion-app-downloads-34516/.

[2]See www.forbes.com/sites/tristanlouis/2013/08/10/how-much-do-average-apps-make/.

The Consumer Perspective

A consumer considers the alternatives:

- **Possibility #1: No mobile phone.**

  Advantages: Inexpensive; no interruptions from callers.

  Disadvantages: No instant contact with friends and family; no calls to services in case of emergencies.

- **Possibility #2: A feature phone.**

  This type of mobile phone isn't a smartphone. Though no official rule defines the boundary between feature phone and smartphone, a feature phone generally has an inflexible menu of Home screen options compared with a smartphone's "desktop" of downloaded apps.

  Advantage: Less expensive than a smartphone.

  Disadvantages: Less versatile than a smartphone, not nearly as cool as a smartphone, and nowhere near as much fun as a smartphone.

- **Possibility #3: An iPhone.**

  Advantages: Great-looking graphics.

  Disadvantages: Little or no flexibility with the single-vendor iOS operating system; only a handful of models to choose from.

- **Possibility #4: A Windows phone, a BlackBerry, or another non-Android, non-Apple smartphone**

  Advantage: Having a smartphone without having to belong to a crowd.

  Disadvantage: The possibility of owning an orphan product when the smartphone wars come to a climax.

- **Possibility #5: An Android phone**

  Advantages: Using a popular, open platform with lots of industry support and powerful market momentum; writing your own software and installing it on your own phone (without having to post the software on a company's website); publishing software without having to face a challenging approval process.

  Disadvantages: Security concerns when using an open platform; dismay when iPhone users make fun of your phone.

For me, Android's advantages far outweigh its possible disadvantages. And you're reading a paragraph from *Java Programming For Android Developers For Dummies*, so you're likely to agree with me.

The Many Faces of Android

Version numbers can be tricky. My PC's model number is T420s. When I download the users' guide, I download one guide for any laptop in the T400 series. (No guide specifically addresses the T420, let alone the T420s.) But when I have driver problems, knowing that I have a T420s isn't good enough. I need drivers that are specific to my laptop's seven-digit model number. The moral to this story: What constitutes a "version number" depends on who's asking for the number.

With that in mind, you can see a history of Android versions in Figure 1-1.

A few notes on Figure 1-1 are in order:

✔ **The platform number is of interest to the consumer and to the company that sells the hardware.**

   If you're buying a phone with Android 4.2.2, for example, you might want to know whether the vendor will upgrade your phone to Android 4.3.

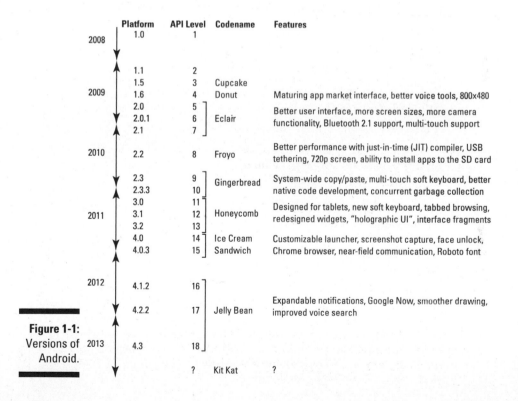

	Platform	API Level	Codename	Features
2008	1.0	1		
2009	1.1	2		
	1.5	3	Cupcake	
	1.6	4	Donut	Maturing app market interface, better voice tools, 800x480
	2.0	5		Better user interface, more screen sizes, more camera
	2.0.1	6	Eclair	functionality, Bluetooth 2.1 support, multi-touch support
	2.1	7		
2010	2.2	8	Froyo	Better performance with just-in-time (JIT) compiler, USB tethering, 720p screen, ability to install apps to the SD card
	2.3	9	Gingerbread	System-wide copy/paste, multi-touch soft keyboard, better native code development, concurrent garbage collection
	2.3.3	10		
2011	3.0	11	Honeycomb	Designed for tablets, new soft keyboard, tabbed browsing, redesigned widgets, "holographic UI", interface fragments
	3.1	12		
	3.2	13		
	4.0	14	Ice Cream	Customizable launcher, screenshot capture, face unlock, Chrome browser, near-field communication, Roboto font
	4.0.3	15	Sandwich	
2012	4.1.2	16		Expandable notifications, Google Now, smoother drawing,
	4.2.2	17	Jelly Bean	improved voice search
2013	4.3	18		
		?	Kit Kat	?

Figure 1-1: Versions of Android.

✔ **The API level (also known as the SDK version) is of interest to the Android app developer.**

For example, the word MATCH_PARENT has a specific meaning in Android API Levels 8 and higher. You might type MATCH_PARENT in code that uses API Level 7. If you do (and if you expect MATCH_PARENT to have that specific meaning), you'll get a nasty-looking error message.

You can read more about the Application Programming Interface (API) in Chapter 2. For more information about the use of Android's API levels (SDK versions) in your code, see Chapter 4.

✔ **The code name is of interest to the creators of Android.**

A *code name* refers to the work done by the creators of Android to bring Android to the next level. Picture Google's engineers working for months behind closed doors on Project Cupcake, and you'll be on the right track.

An Android version may have variations. For example, plain-old Android 2.2 has an established set of features. To plain-old Android 2.2 you can add the Google APIs (thus adding Google Maps functionality) and still be using platform 2.2. You can also add a special set of features tailored for the Samsung Galaxy Tab.

As a developer, your job is to balance portability with feature-richness. When you create an app, you specify a target Android version and a minimum Android version. (You can read more about this topic in Chapter 4.) The higher the version, the more features your app can have. But on the flip side, the higher the version, the fewer devices that can run your app.

The Developer Perspective

Android is a multifaceted beast. When you develop for the Android platform, you use many toolsets. This section gives you a brief rundown.

Java

James Gosling of Sun Microsystems created the Java programming language in the mid-1990s. (Sun Microsystems has since been bought by Oracle.) Java's meteoric rise in use stemmed from the elegance of the language and its well-conceived platform architecture. After a brief blaze of glory with applets and the web, Java settled into being a solid, general-purpose language with a special strength in servers and middleware.

In the meantime, Java was quietly seeping into embedded processors. Sun Microsystems was developing Java Mobile Edition (Java ME) for creating small apps to run on mobile phones. Java became a major technology in Blu-ray disc players. So the decision to make Java the primary development language for Android apps is no big surprise.

An *embedded processor* is a computer chip that is hidden from the user as part of a special-purpose device. The chips in cars are now embedded processors, and the silicon that powers the photocopier at your workplace is an embedded processor. Pretty soon, the flower pots on your windowsill will probably have embedded processors.

Figure 1-2 describes the development of new Java versions over time. Like Android, each Java version has several names. The *product version* is an official name that's used for the world in general, and the *developer version* is a number that identifies versions so that programmers can keep track of them. (In casual conversation, developers use all kinds of names for the various Java versions.) The *code name* is a more playful name that identifies a version while it's being created.

Year	Product Version	Developer Version	Codename	Features
1995	(Beta)			
1996	**JDK* 1.0**	1.0		
1997	**JDK 1.1**	1.1		Inner classes, Java Beans, reflection
1998	**J2SE* 1.2**	1.2	Playground	Collections, Swing classes for creation of GUI interfaces
1999				
2000	**J2SE 1.3**	1.3	Kestrel	Java Naming and Directory Interface (JNDI)
2001				
2002	**J2SE 1.4**	1.4	Merlin	New I/O, regular expressions, XML parsing
2003				
2004	**J2SE 5.0***	1.5	Tiger	Generic types, annotations, enum types, varargs, enhanced
2005				for statement, static imports, new concurrency classes
2006	**Java SE* 6**	1.6	Mustang	Scripting language support, performance enhancements
2007				
2008				
2009				
2010				
2011	**Java SE 7**	1.7	Dolphin	Strings in switch statement, catching multiple exceptions
2012				try statement with resources, integration with JavaFX
2013	**Java SE 8**	1.8		Lambda expressions

Figure 1-2:
Versions of
Java.

The asterisks in Figure 1-2 mark changes in the formulation of Java product-version names. Back in 1996, the product versions were *Java Development Kit 1.0* and *Java Development Kit 1.1*. In 1998, someone decided to christen the product *Java 2 Standard Edition 1.2*, which confuses everyone to this day. At the time, anyone using the term *Java Development Kit* was asked to use *Software Development Kit* (SDK) instead.

In 2004 the *1.* business went away from the platform version name, and in 2006 Java platform names lost the *2* and the *.0.*

By far the most significant changes for Java developers came about in 2004. With the release of J2SE 5.0, the overseers of Java made changes to the language by adding new features — features such as generic types, annotations, varargs, and the enhanced `for` statement.

To see Java annotations in action, go to Chapter 10. For examples of the use of generic types, varargs, and the enhanced for statement, see Chapter 12.

If you compare Figures 1-1 and 1-2, you might notice that Android entered the scene when Java was in version Java SE 6. As a result, Java is frozen at version 6 for Android developers. When you develop an Android app, you can use J2SE 5.0 or Java SE 6. You cannot use Java SE 7 with strings in its `switch` statements or use Java SE 8 with its lambda expressions. But that's okay: As an Android developer, you probably won't miss these features.

XML

If you find View Source among your web browser's options one day and decide to use it, you'll see a bunch of HyperText Markup Language (HTML) tags. A *tag* is some text, enclosed in angle brackets, that describes something about its neighboring content.

For example, to create boldface type on a web page, a web designer writes

```
<b>Look at this!</b>
```

The b tags in angle brackets turn boldface type on and off.

The *M* in HTML stands for *Markup* — a general term describing any extra text that annotates a document's content. When you annotate a document's content, you embed information about the content into the document itself. For example, in the previous line of code, the content is `Look at this!` The markup (information about the content) consists of the tags <b> and </b>.

The HTML standard is an outgrowth of Standard Generalized Markup Language (SGML), an all-things-to-all-people technology for marking up documents for use by all kinds of computers running all kinds of software and sold by all kinds of vendors.

In the mid-1990s, a working group of the World Wide Web Consortium (W3C) began developing the eXtensible Markup Language, commonly known as *XML.* The working group's goal was to create a subset of SGML for use in transmitting data over the Internet. They succeeded. XML is now a well-established standard for encoding information of all kinds.

For an overview of XML, see the sidebar that describes it in Chapter 4.

Java is good for describing step-by-step instructions, and XML is good for describing the way things are (or the way they should be). A Java program says, "Do this and then do that." In contrast, an XML document says, "It's this way and it's that way." Android uses XML for two purposes:

✔ **To describe an app's data**

An app's XML documents describe the layout of the app's screens, the translations of the app into one or more languages, and other kinds of data.

✔ **To describe the app itself**

Every Android app has an `AndroidManifest.xml` file, an XML document that describe features of the app. A device's operating system uses the `AndroidManifest.xml` document's contents to manage the running of the app.

For example, an app's `AndroidManifest.xml` file describes code that the app makes available for use by other apps. The same file describes the permissions that the app requests from the system. When you begin installing a new app, Android displays these permissions and asks for your permission to proceed with the installation. (I don't know about you, but I always read this list of permissions carefully. Yeah, right!)

For more information about the `AndroidManifest.xml` file, see Chapter 4.

Concerning XML, I have bad news and good news. The bad news is that XML isn't always easy to compose. At best, writing XML code is boring. At worst, writing XML code is downright confusing. The good news is that automated software tools compose most the world's XML code. As an Android programmer, the software on your development computer composes much of your app's XML code. You often tweak the XML code, read part of the code for information from its source, make minor changes, and compose brief additions. But you hardly ever create XML documents from scratch.

Linux

An *operating system* is a big program that manages the overall running of a computer or a device. Most operating systems are built in layers. An operating system's outer layers are usually in the user's face. For example, both Windows and Macintosh OS X have standard desktops. From the desktop, the user launches programs, manages windows, and does other important things.

An operating system's inner layers are (for the most part) invisible to the user. While the user plays Solitaire, for example, the operating system juggles processes, manages files, keeps an eye on security, and generally does the kinds of things that the user shouldn't have to micromanage.

At the deepest level of an operating system is the system's kernel. The *kernel* runs directly on the processor's hardware and does the low-level work required to make the processor run. In a truly layered system, higher layers accomplish work by making calls to lower layers. So an app with a specific hardware request sends the request (directly or indirectly) through the kernel.

The best-known, best-loved general purpose operating systems are Windows, Macintosh OS X (which is really Unix), and Linux. Both Windows and Mac OS X are the properties of their respective companies. But Linux is open source. That's one reason why your TiVo runs Linux and why the creators of Android based their platform on the Linux kernel.

As a developer, your most intimate contact with the Android operating system is via the command line, also known as the *Linux shell*. The shell uses commands such as `cd` to change to a directory, `ls` to list a directory's files and subdirectories, `rm` to delete files, and many others.

Google's Android Market has plenty of free terminal apps. A *terminal* app's interface is a plain-text screen on which you type Linux shell commands. And by using one of Android's developer tools, the Android Debug Bridge, you can issue shell commands to an Android device via your development computer. If you like getting your virtual hands dirty, the Linux shell is for you.

From Development to Execution with Java

Before Java became popular, running a computer program involved one translation step. Someone (or something) translated the code that a developer wrote into more cryptic code that a computer could actually execute. But then Java came along and added an extra translation layer, and then Android added another layer. This section describes all those layers.

What is a compiler?

A Java program (such as an Android application program) undergoes several translation steps between the time you write the program and the time a processor runs the program. One of the reasons is simple: Instructions that are convenient for processors to run are not convenient for people to write.

People can write and comprehend the code in Listing 1-1.

Listing 1-1: Java Source Code

```
public void checkVacancy(View view) {
    if (room.numGuests == 0) {
        label.setText("Available");
    } else {
        label.setText("Taken :-(");
    }
}
```

The Java code in Listing 1-1 checks for a vacancy in a hotel. You can't run the code in this listing without adding several additional lines. But here in Chapter 1, those additional lines aren't important. What's important is that, by staring at the code, squinting a bit, and looking past all its strange punctuation, you can see what the code is trying to do:

```
If the room has no guests in it,
    then set the label's text to "Available".
Otherwise,
    set the label's text to "Taken :-(".
```

The content of Listing 1-1 is *Java source code.*

The processors in computers, phones, and other devices don't normally follow instructions like the instructions in Listing 1-1. That is, processors don't follow Java source code instructions. Instead, processors follow cryptic instructions like the ones in Listing 1-2.

Listing 1-2: Java Bytecode

```
 0 aload_0
 1 getfield #19 <com/allmycode/samples/MyActivity/room
Lcom/allmycode/samples/Room;>
 4 getfield #47 <com/allmycode/samples/Room/numGuests I>
 7 ifne 22 (+15)
10 aload_0
11 getfield #41 <com/allmycode/samples/MyActivity/label
Landroid/widget/TextView;>
14 ldc #54 <Available>
```

(continued)

Listing 1-2 *(continued)*

```
16 invokevirtual #56
   <android/widget/TextView/setText
   (Ljava/lang/CharSequence;)V>
19 goto 31 (+12)
22 aload_0
23 getfield #41 <com/allmycode/samples/MyActivity/label
 Landroid/widget/TextView;>
26 ldc #60 <Taken :-(>
28 invokevirtual #56
   <android/widget/TextView/setText
   (Ljava/lang/CharSequence;)V>
31 return
```

The instructions in Listing 1-2 aren't Java source code instructions. They're *Java bytecode instructions*. When you write a Java program, you write source code instructions (refer to Listing 1-1). After writing the source code, you run a program (that is, you apply a tool) to the source code. The program is a *compiler*. It translates your source code instructions into Java bytecode instructions. In other words, the compiler translates code that you can write and understand (again, refer to Listing 1-1) into code that a computer can execute (refer to Listing 1-2).

At this point, you might ask "What will I have to do to get the compiler running?" The one-word answer to your question is "Eclipse." All the translation steps described in this chapter come down to using Eclipse — a piece of software that you download for free using the instructions in Chapter 2. So when you read in this chapter about compiling and other translation steps, don't become intimidated. You don't have to repair an alternator in order to drive a car, and you won't have to understand how compilers work in order to use Eclipse.

No one (except for a few crazy developers in isolated labs in faraway places) writes Java bytecode. You run software (a compiler) to create Java bytecode. The only reason to look at Listing 1-2 is to understand what a hard worker your computer is.

If compiling is a good thing, compiling twice may be even better. In 2007, Dan Bornstein at Google created *Dalvik bytecode* — another way to represent instructions for processors to follow. (To find out where some of Bornstein's ancestors come from, run your favorite map application and look for Dalvik in Iceland.) Dalvik bytecode is optimized for the limited resources on a phone or a tablet device.

Listing 1-3 contains sample Dalvik instructions.

* To see the code in Listing 1-3, I used the Dedexer program. See dedexer. sourceforge.net.

Listing 1-3:   Dalvik Bytecode

```
.method public checkVacancy(Landroid/view/View;)V
.limit registers 4
; this: v2 (Lcom/allmycode/samples/MyActivity;)
; parameter[0] : v3 (Landroid/view/View;)
.line 30
    iget-object
    v0,v2,com/allmycode/samples/MyActivity.room
    Lcom/allmycode/samples/Room;
; v0 : Lcom/allmycode/samples/Room; , v2 :
    Lcom/allmycode/samples/MyActivity;
    iget     v0,v0,com/allmycode/samples/Room.numGuests I
; v0 : single-length , v0 : single-length
    if-nez    v0,14b4
; v0 : single-length
.line 31
    iget-object
    v0,v2,com/allmycode/samples/MyActivity.label
    Landroid/widget/TextView;
; v0 : Landroid/widget/TextView; , v2 :
    Lcom/allmycode/samples/MyActivity;
    const-string    v1,"Available"
; v1 : Ljava/lang/String;
    invoke-virtual
    {v0,v1},android/widget/TextView/setText
    ; setText(Ljava/lang/CharSequence;)V
; v0 : Landroid/widget/TextView; , v1 : Ljava/lang/String;
14b2:
.line 36
    return-void
14b4:
.line 33
    iget-object
    v0,v2,com/allmycode/samples/MyActivity.label
    Landroid/widget/TextView;
; v0 : Landroid/widget/TextView; , v2 :
    Lcom/allmycode/samples/MyActivity;
    const-string    v1,"Taken :-("
; v1 : Ljava/lang/String;
    invoke-virtual
    {v0,v1},android/widget/TextView/setText ;
    setText(Ljava/lang/CharSequence;)V
; v0 : Landroid/widget/TextView; , v1 : Ljava/lang/String;
    goto     14b2
.end method
```

When you create an Android app, Eclipse performs at least two compilations:

✔ **One compilation creates Java bytecode from your Java source files.**
The source filenames have the .java extension; the Java bytecode
filenames have the .class extension.

✔ **Another compilation creates Dalvik bytecode from your Java bytecode files.** Dalvik bytecode file names have the .dex extension.

But that's not all! In addition to its Java code, an Android app has XML files, image files, and possibly other elements. Before you install an app on a device, Eclipse combines all these elements into a single file — one with the .apk extension. When you publish the app on an app store, you copy that .apk file to the app store's servers. Then, to install your app, a user visits the app store and downloads your .apk file.

To perform the compilation from source code to Java bytecode, Eclipse uses a program named javac, also known as the Java compiler. To perform the compilation from Java bytecode to Dalvik code, Eclipse uses a program named dx (known affectionately as "the dx tool"). To combine all your app's files into one .apk file, Eclipse uses a program named apkbuilder.

What is a virtual machine?

In the section "What is a compiler?" earlier in this chapter, I make a big fuss about phones and other devices following instructions like the ones in Listing 1-3. As fusses go, it's a nice fuss. But if you don't read every fussy word, you may be misguided. The exact wording is ". . . processors follow cryptic instructions *like* the ones in Listing *blah-blah-blah.*" The instructions in Listing 1-3 are a lot like instructions that a phone or tablet can execute, but computers generally don't execute Java bytecode instructions, and phones don't execute Dalvik bytecode instructions. Instead, each kind of processor has its own set of executable instructions, and each operating system uses the processor's instructions in a slightly different way.

Imagine that you have two different devices: a smartphone and a tablet computer. The devices have two different kinds of processors: The phone has an ARM processor, and the tablet has an Intel Atom processor. (The acronym ARM once stood for Advanced RISC Machine. These days, *ARM* simply stands for ARM Holdings, a company whose employees design processors.) On the ARM processor, the *multiply* instruction is 000000. On an Intel processor, the *multiply* instructions are D8, DC, F6, F7, and others. Many ARM instructions have no counterparts in the Atom architecture, and many Atom instructions have no equivalents on an ARM processor. An ARM processor's instructions make no sense to your tablet's Atom processor, and an Atom processor's instructions would give your phone's ARM processor a virtual headache.

What's a developer to do? Does a developer provide translations of every app into every processor's instruction set?

No. Virtual machines create order from all this chaos. Dalvik bytecode is similar to the code in Listing 1-3, but Dalvik bytecode isn't specific to a single kind of processor or to a single operating system. Instead, a set of Dalvik bytecode instructions runs on any processor. If you write a Java program and compile that Java program into Dalvik bytecode, your Android phone can run the bytecode, your Android tablet can run the bytecode, and even your grandmother's supercomputer can run the bytecode. (To do this, your grandmother must install *Android-x86,* a special port of the Android operating system, on her Intel-based machine.)

You never have to write or decipher Dalvik bytecode. Writing bytecode is the compiler's job. Deciphering bytecode is the virtual machine's job.

Both Java bytecode and Dalvik bytecode have virtual machines. With the Dalvik virtual machine, you can take a bytecode file that you created for one Android device, copy the bytecode to another Android device, and then run the bytecode with no trouble. That's one of the many reasons why Android has become popular quickly. This outstanding feature, which lets you run code on many different kinds of computers, is called *portability*.

Imagine that you're the Intel representative to the United Nations Security Council, as shown in Figure 1-3. The ARM representative is seated to your right, and the representative from Texas Instruments is to your left. (Naturally, you don't get along with either of these people. You're always cordial to one another, but you're never sincere. What do you expect? It's politics!) The distinguished representative from Dalvik is at the podium. The Dalvik representative speaks in Dalvik bytecode, and neither you nor your fellow ambassadors (ARM and Texas Instruments) understand a word of Dalvik bytecode.

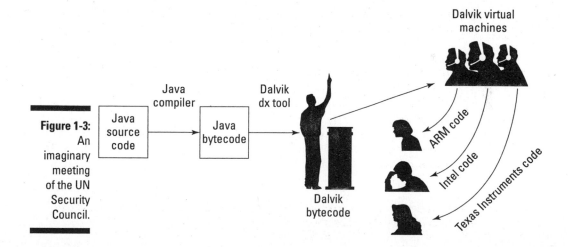

Figure 1-3: An imaginary meeting of the UN Security Council.

But each of you has an interpreter. Your interpreter translates from Dalvik bytecode to Intel instructions as the Dalvik representative speaks. Another interpreter translates from bytecode to "ARM-ese." And a third interpreter translates bytecode into "Texas Instruments-speak."

Think of your interpreter as a virtual ambassador. The interpreter doesn't really represent your country, but the interpreter performs one important task that a real ambassador performs: It listens to Dalvik bytecode on your behalf. The interpreter does what you would do if your native language were Dalvik bytecode. The interpreter, pretending to be the Intel ambassador, endures the boring bytecode speech, taking in every word and processing each one in some way or another.

You have an interpreter — a virtual ambassador. In the same way, an Intel processor runs its own bytecode-interpreting software. That software is the Dalvik virtual machine — a proxy, an errand boy, a go-between. The _Dalvik virtual machine_ serves as an interpreter between Dalvik's run-anywhere bytecode and your device's own system. As it runs, the virtual machine walks your device through the execution of bytecode instructions. It examines your bytecode, bit by bit, and carries out the instructions described in the bytecode. The virtual machine interprets bytecode for your ARM processor, your Intel processor, your Texas Instruments chip, or whatever kind of processor you're using. That's a good thing. It's what makes Java code and Dalvik code more portable than code written in any other language.

Java, Android, and Horticulture

"You don't see the forest for the trees," said my Uncle Harvey. To which my Aunt Clara said "You don't see the trees for the forest." This argument went on until they were both too tired to discuss the matter.

As an author, I like to present both the forest and the trees. The "forest" is the broad overview, which helps you understand why you perform various steps. The "trees" are the steps themselves, getting you from Point A to Point B until you complete a task.

This chapter shows you the forest. The rest of this book shows you the trees.

Chapter 2

Getting the Tools That You Need

***e*rgaliophile** /ɜr gə li ə faɪ əl/ *noun* 1. A lover of tools. 2. A person who visits garage sales for rusty metal implements that might be useful someday but probably won't. 3. A person whose computer runs slowly because of the daily, indiscriminate installation of free software tools.

Several years ago, I found an enormous monkey wrench (more than a yard long and weighing 35 pounds) at a nearby garage sale. I wasn't a good plumber, and to this day any pipe that I fix starts leaking again immediately. But I couldn't resist buying this fine piece of hardware. The only problem was, my wife was sitting in the car about halfway down the street. She's much more sensible than I am about these matters, so I couldn't bring the wrench back to the car. "Put it aside and I'll come back for it later," I told the seller.

When I returned to the car empty-handed, my wife said, "I saw someone carrying the world's largest pipe wrench. I'm glad you weren't the one who bought it." And I agreed with her. "I don't need more junk like that."

So of course I returned later that day to buy the monkey wrench, and to this day the wrench sits in our attic, where no one ever sees it. If my wife ever reads this chapter, she'll be either amused or angry. I hope she's not angry, but I'm taking the risk because I enjoy the little drama. To add excitement to my life, I'm turning this trivial secret into a public announcement.

The Stuff You Need

This book tells you how to write Java programs, and before you can write them, you need some software tools. Here's a list of the tools you need:

✓ **A Java virtual machine**

Cool people refer to this item as the *JVM* or simply as *Java*.

✓ **The Java code libraries**

These code libraries are known affectionately as the *Java Runtime Environment* (JRE) or simply as *Java*.

✓ **An integrated development environment**

You can create Java programs using geeky, keyboard-only tools, but eventually you'll tire of typing and retyping commands. An *integrated development environment* (IDE), on the other hand, is a little like a word processor: A word processor helps you compose documents (memos, poems, and other works of fine literature); in contrast, an IDE helps you compose computer programs.

For composing Java programs, I recommend using the Eclipse IDE.

You should also gather these extra goodies:

✓ **Some sample Java programs to help you get started**

All examples in this book are available for download from www.all mycode.com/Java4Android.

✓ **The Android Software Development Kit**

The Android *Software Development Kit (SDK)* includes lots and lots of prewritten, reusable Android code and a bunch of software tools for running and testing Android apps.

The prewritten Android code is the Android *Application Programming Interface (API)*. The API comes in several versions — versions 9 and 10 (both code-named Gingerbread), versions 11, 12, and 13 (Honeycomb), versions 14 and 15 (Ice Cream Sandwich), and so on.

✓ **Android-oriented add-ons for the integrated development environment**

By using add-ons, you customize the Eclipse IDE to help you compose, run, and test your Android apps. The set of Eclipse add-ons for working with Android apps is the *Android Development Toolkit (ADT)*.

All these tools run on the *development computer* — the laptop or desktop computer you use to develop Java programs and Android apps. After you create an Android app, you copy the app's code from the development computer to a *target device* — a phone, a tablet, or (someday soon) a refrigerator that runs Android.

Here's good news: You can download from the web all the software you need to run this book's examples for free. The software is separated into three downloads:

- This book's website (www.allmycode.com/Java4Android) has a link to all code in the book.

- When you visit www.java.com, you can click a button to install the Java virtual machine.

- A button at the page http://developer.android.com/sdk gives you the big Android SDK download. In spite of its name, it includes more than simply the Android code libraries. The download includes all the ingredients you didn't already collect from www.allmycode.com or www.java.com.

The websites I describe in this chapter are always changing. The software programs you download from these sites change, too. A specific instruction such as "Click the button in the upper-right corner" becomes obsolete (and even misleading) in no time at all. So in this chapter, I provide explicit steps, but I also describe the ideas behind them. Browse the suggested sites and look for ways to get the software I describe. When a website offers you several options, check the instructions in this chapter for hints on choosing the best option. If your computer's Eclipse window doesn't look quite like the one in this chapter's figures, scan your computer's window for whatever options I describe. If, after all that effort, you can't find the elements you're looking for, check this book's website (www.allmycode.com/Java4Android) or send an e-mail to me at Java4Android@allmycode.com.

If You Don't Like Reading Instructions . . .

I start this chapter with a brief (but useful) overview of the steps required in order to get the software you need. If you're an old hand at installing software, and if your computer isn't quirky, these steps will probably serve you well. If not, you can read the more detailed instructions in the next several sections.

1. **Visit** www.allmycode.com/Java4Android **and download a file containing all the program examples in this book.**

2. **Visit** www.java.com **and download the Java Runtime Environment (if you don't already have a recent version of Java on your computer).**

   Choose a version of the software that matches your operating system (Windows, Macintosh, or whatever) and your operating system's word length (32-bit or 64-bit).

3. **Visit** http://developer.android.com/sdk **and download the Android Software Development Kit (SDK).**

   The downloaded bundle is a .zip archive file.

4. **Extract the contents of the downloaded archive file to your local hard drive.**

   On my Windows computer, I extract the `.zip` file's contents to a new folder, named `c:\Users\`*MyUserName*`\adt-bundle-windows-x86`. So I have the folders shown in Figure 2-1.

Figure 2-1:
My
Windows
computer's
`adt-`
`bundle`
folder.

On my Mac, I extract the `.zip` file's contents into my existing `Applications` folder, as shown in Figure 2-2.

Figure 2-2:
My Mac's
`adt-`
`bundle`
folder.

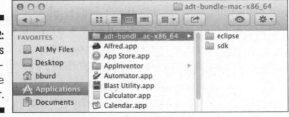

WARNING!

If the Android SDK `.zip` file contains more than one folder, don't separate the folders when you extract the `.zip` file's contents. Extract all content inside the `.zip` file to the same place on your hard drive.

5. **Launch the Eclipse app.**

   The first time you run a fresh, new copy of Eclipse, the Welcome screen appears.

6. **Dismiss the Welcome screen.**

   For most versions of Eclipse, you can dismiss the Welcome screen by clicking the little *x* icon that appears on a tab above the screen.

7. **Import the code that you downloaded in Step 1.**

In Eclipse, choose File⇨Import⇨Existing Projects into Workspace. Then browse for this book's sample code — the `.zip` file from Step 1. (If the web browser automatically expanded the `.zip` archive, browse for the folder containing the files that were in the archive.)

8. **Create an Android virtual device.**

   You can test Android programs on a phone or a tablet. But, for convenience, you might test on an *emulator* — a program that behaves like a phone or a tablet but runs on the development computer.

   To run an emulator, you need an *Android Virtual Device (AVD)*, which is a set of specs for a device (processor type, screen size, screen resolution, and Android version, for example). In Eclipse, you create an AVD by choosing Window⇨Android Virtual Device Manager and filling in the blanks. For more info, see the later section "Creating an Android Virtual Device."

For details about any of these topics, see the next several sections.

Those pesky filename extensions

The filenames displayed in My Computer or in a Finder window can be misleading. You may browse a directory and see the name `Mortgage`. The file's real name might be `Mortgage.java`, `Mortgage.class`, `Mortgage.somethingElse`, or plain old `Mortgage`. Filename endings such as `.zip`, `.java`, and `.class` are *filename extensions*.

The ugly truth is that, by default, Windows and Macs hide many filename extensions. This awful feature tends to confuse programmers. If you don't want to be confused, change your computer's systemwide settings. Here's how to do it:

✔ **In Windows XP:** Choose Start⇨Control Panel⇨Appearance and Themes⇨Folder Options. Then skip to the fourth bullet.

✔ **In Windows 7:** Choose Start⇨Control Panel⇨Appearance and Personalization⇨

Folder Options. Then skip to the fourth bullet.

✔ **In Windows 8:** On the Charms bar, choose Settings⇨Control Panel. In the Control Panel, choose Appearance and Personalization⇨Folder Options. Then proceed to the following bullet.

✔ **In all versions of Windows (XP and newer):** Follow the instructions in one of the preceding bullets. Then, in the Folder Options dialog box, click the View tab. Look for the Hide File Extensions for Known File Types option. Make sure that this check box is *not* selected.

✔ **In Mac OS X:** In the Finder application's menu, select Preferences. In the resulting dialog box, select the Advanced tab and look for the Show All File Extensions option. Make sure that this check box *is* selected.

Getting This Book's Sample Programs

To get copies of this book's sample programs, visit `www.allmycode.com/Java4Android` and click the link to download the programs in this book. Save the download file (`Java4Android_Programs.zip`) to the computer's hard drive.

 In some cases, you can click a download link all you want but the web browser doesn't offer you the option to save a file. If this happens to you, right-click the link (or control-click on a Mac). From the resulting contextual menu, select Save Target As, Save Link As, Download Linked File As, or a similarly labeled menu item.

Most web browsers save files to the `Downloads` directory on the computer's hard drive. But your browser may be configured a bit differently. One way or another, make note of the folder containing the downloaded `Java4Android_Programs.zip` file.

Compressed archive files

When you visit `www.allmycode.com/Java4Android` and you download this book's examples, you download a file named `Java4Android_Programs.zip`. A *zip* file is a single file that encodes a bunch of smaller files and folders. For example, my `Java4Android_Programs.zip` file encodes folders named `06-01`, `06-02`, and so on. The `06-02` folder contains subfolders, which in turn contain files. (The folder named `06-02` contains the code in Listing 6-2 — the second listing in Chapter 6.)

A `.zip` file is an example of a *compressed archive* file. Other examples of compressed archives include `.tar.gz` files, `.rar` files, and `.cab` files. When you *uncompress* a file, you extract the original files stored inside the larger archive file. (For a `.zip` file, another word for uncompressing is *unzipping*.) Uncompressing normally re-creates the folder structure encoded in the archive file. So after uncompressing my `Java4Android_Programs.zip` file, the hard drive has folders named `06-01`, `06-02`, with subfolders named `src` and `bin`, which in turn contain files named `TypeDemo1.java`, `TypeDemo1.class`, and so on.

When you download `Java4Android_Programs.zip`, the web browser may uncompress the file automatically for you. If not, you can see the `.zip` file's contents by double-clicking the file's icon. (In fact, you can copy the file's contents and do other file operations after double-clicking the file's icon.) One way or another, don't worry about uncompressing my `Java4Android_Programs.zip` file. When you follow this chapter's instructions, you can import the contents of the file into the Eclipse IDE. And behind the scenes, the Eclipse import process uncompresses the `.zip` file.

Gathering Information

For many people (including some inexperienced people), the installations of Java and the Android SDK are routine tasks. Visit a few websites, click some buttons, and then take a coffee break. But as you follow this chapter's instructions, you might have a question, experience a difficulty, or encounter a fork in the road. In that case, it helps to know your computer — which entails jotting down the answers to a few questions.

Are you running a 32-bit or 64-bit operating system?

In this chapter, you install Java and the Android SDK on your computer. Java comes in two flavors: 32-bit and 64-bit. The Android SDK comes in the same two flavors, and in order for the Android SDK to work with Java, the Java flavor must match the Android SDK flavor. In this section, you find out which flavor is best for your computer.

The steps in this section are all optional. If you don't want to perform this section's fact-finding missions, try visiting www.java.com and http://developer.android.com/sdk to download whichever versions of Java and the Android SDK are offered to you by these two websites. If either site makes you choose between 32-bit and 64-bit software, be consistent. That is, get the 32-bit versions of both Java and the Android SDK, or get the 64-bit versions of both Java and the Android SDK. (For Windows, the 32-bit versions are the safest choice. For Mac, the 64-bit versions are the safest.)

For Windows 8, Windows 7, and Windows Vista:

1. **Press the Windows key.**

   In Windows 8, the Start screen appears. In Windows 7 and Windows Vista, the Start menu appears.

2. **In Windows 8, type the words** Control Panel, **and then press Enter. In Windows 7 or Windows Vista, click the Control Panel item on the Start menu.**

   The Control Panel appears.

3. **In the Control Panel, select System and Security (Windows 8 and Windows 7) or System and Maintenance (Windows Vista).**

The System window appears. To recognize the System window, look for the words `View basic information about your computer` near the top of the window.

4. In the System window, look for the words `System type`.

The system type is either 32-bit or 64-bit, as shown in Figure 2-3.

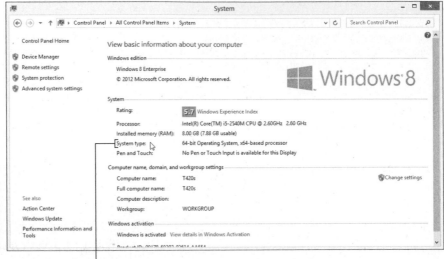

System type

Figure 2-3:
Determining
the system
type.

For Windows XP

1. Press the Windows key.

The Start menu appears.

2. Click the My Computer item on the Start menu.

Windows Explorer opens.

3. In Windows Explorer, navigate to Drive C.

4. In Drive C, look for folders named `Program Files` **and** `Program Files (x86)`.

If you find `Program Files` but not `Program Files (x86)` folders, you're running 32-bit Windows. If you find both `Program Files` and `Program Files (x86)` folders, you're running 64-bit Windows.

For Macintosh OS X

1. Choose Apple⇨About This Mac.

The About This Mac window appears.

How many bits does your computer have?

As you follow this chapter's instructions, you may be prompted to choose between two versions of a piece of software — the 32-bit version and the 64-bit version. What's the difference, and why do you care?

A *bit* is the smallest piece of information that you can store on a computer. Most people think of a bit as either a zero or a one, and that depiction is quite useful. To represent almost any number, you pile several bits next to one another and do some fancy things with powers of two. The numbering system's details aren't showstoppers. The important thing to remember is that each piece of circuitry inside the computer stores the same number of bits. (Well, some circuits inside the computer are outliers with their own particular numbers of bits, but that's not a big deal.)

In an older computer, each piece of circuitry stores 32 bits. In a newer computer, each piece of circuitry stores 64 bits. This number of bits (either 32 or 64) is the computer's *word length*. In a newer computer, a word is 64 bits long.

"Great!" you say. "I bought my computer last week. It must be a 64-bit computer." Well, the story may not be that simple. In addition to a computer's circuitry having a word length, the operating system on it also has a word length. An operating system's instructions work with a particular number of bits. An operating system with 32-bit instructions can run on either a 32-bit computer or a 64-bit computer, but an operating system with 64-bit instructions can run only on a 64-bit computer. And to make things even more complicated, each program that you run (a web browser, a word processor, or one of your own Java programs) is either a 32-bit program or a 64-bit program. You may run a 32-bit web browser on a 64-bit operating system running on a 64-bit computer. Alternatively, you may run a 32-bit browser on a 32-bit operating system on a 64-bit computer. (See the figure that accompanies this sidebar.)

When a website makes you choose between 32-bit and 64-bit software versions, the main consideration is the word length of the operating system, not the word length of the computer's circuitry. You can run a 32-bit word processor on a 64-bit operating system, but you can't run a 64-bit word processor on a 32-bit operating system (no matter what word length the computer's circuitry has). Choosing 64-bit software has one primary advantage: 64-bit software can access more than 3 gigabytes of a computer's fast random access memory. And in my experience, more memory means faster processing.

How does all this information about word lengths affect Java and Android SDK downloads? Here's the story:

- If you run a 32-bit operating system, you run only 32-bit software.

- If you run a 64-bit operating system, you probably run some 32-bit software and some 64-bit software. Most 32-bit software runs fine on a 64-bit operating system.

- On a 64-bit operating system, you might have two versions of the same program. For example, on my Windows computer, I have two versions of Internet Explorer: a 32-bit version and a 64-bit version.

Normally, Windows stores 32-bit programs in its `Program Files (x86)` directory and stores 64-bit programs in its `Program Files` directory.

- A chain of word lengths is as strong as its weakest link. For example, when I visit `www.java.com` and click the site's Do I Have Java? link, the answer depends on the match between my computer's Java

(continued)

(continued)

version and the web browser that I'm running. With only 64-bit Java installed on my computer, the Do I Have Java? link in my 32-bit Firefox browser answers, `No working Java was detected on your system`. But the same link in my 64-bit Internet Explorer answers, `You have the recommended Java installed`.

✔ Here's the most important thing to remember about word lengths: When you follow this chapter's instructions, you install Java software and Android SDK software on the computer. The Java software's word length must match the Android SDK's word length. In other words, 32-bit Android SDK software runs with 32-bit Java, and 64-bit Android SDK runs with 64-bit Java. I haven't tried all possible combinations, but when I try to run the 32-bit Android SDK with 64-bit Java, I see the misleading error message `No Java virtual machine was found`.

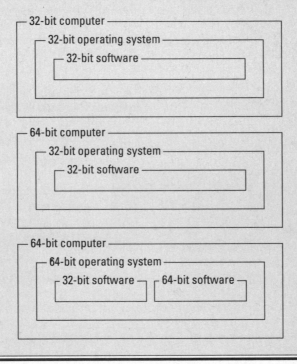

2. **In the About This Mac window, look for the word *Processor*.**

If your processor is an Intel Core Solo or Intel Core Duo, you have a 32-bit Mac. All other Intel processors, including Intel Core 2 Duo, are 64-bit Macs. (See Figure 2-4.)

Figure 2-4:
Displaying
the Mac
processor
type.

Here's an alternative (geeky) way to find out whether your Mac is a 32-bit or 64-bit operating system: In the Spotlight, type the word **Terminal**, and then press Enter. Then when the Terminal app opens, type **uname -a** and press Enter. If the Mac's response includes i386, you have a 32-bit system. If the Mac's response includes x86_64 instead, you have a 64-bit system.

If you're a Mac user, which version of Mac OS X do you have?

To answer a burning question about the Macintosh operating system, follow these steps:

1. **Choose Apple⇨About This Mac.**

   The About This Mac window appears.

2. **In the About This Mac window, look for the word *Version*.**

   You see Version 10.8 (or something like that) in very light gray text. (Refer to Figure 2-4.)

The Android development software for the Mac requires OS X 10.5.8 or later, and an Intel processor. If the About This Mac window reports that you have a PowerPC processor or that your version of OS X is older than OS X 10.5, you'll have a hard time developing Android apps. (For versions such as OS X 10.5.1, you can try updating the system to version 10.5.8. For systems before OS X 10.5, and for systems running on PowerPC processors, you can search the web for hacks and workarounds. Of course, if you use hacks and workarounds, I make no promises.)

If you don't regularly apply software updates, choose Software Update from the Apple menu. In the resulting window, look for OS X updates and for items with the word *Java* in them. Select the relevant items, and then click the appropriate Install or Update button (or buttons). In addition, you can follow the instructions in the next section to find out whether the www.java.com website recommends updates.

Is a recent version of Java installed on your computer?

Android development requires Java 5.0 or later. Java 6 is recommended (but not absolutely required). Java 7 and beyond are overkill.

You might see *Java 1.5* and *Java 1.6* rather than *Java 5.0* and *Java 6.* Some people understand the differences these names make, but few people care. (If you're one of the people who care, see Chapter 1.)

Follow these steps to check for a recent version of Java on your computer:

1. **Visit** www.java.com.

2. **On the main page at** www.java.com, **click the Do I Have Java? link.**

3. **On the Do I Have Java? page, click the Verify Java Version button.**

After a brief pause, the java.com site reports that you have Java Version 7 Update 9, or something like that.

- ✔ If you have Java version 6 or higher, you're good to go. You don't have to install any other Java version. You can skip this chapter's later section "Setting Up Java."

- ✔ If the java.com site doesn't report that you have Java 6 or later, don't fret. The java.com site might be wrong!

  After all, a 32-bit web browser can't detect a 64-bit version of Java, and (as of early 2013) no browser running in Windows 8 mode can even detect Java. The potential pitfalls are endless.

  Anyway, if java.com doesn't report that you have Java 6 or later, I suggest following the instructions in the section "Setting Up Java." If you accidentally install a second version of Java (or a third or fourth version of Java), you'll probably be okay.

Setting Up Java

You can get the latest, greatest version of Java by visiting www.java.com. The site offers several alternatives.

- ✔ **(Recommended) Click the big Free Java Download button on the site's main page.**

  For most computers, clicking this Free Java Download button gives you all the Java you need for this book's examples. So if you're unsure what to do when you visit www.java.com, click the Free Java Download button and move to the section "Setting Up the Android SDK," later in this chapter.

   If you're running Mac OS X 10.6 or earlier (or if you're running OS X 10.7 and you haven't upgraded to OS X 10.7.3 or later), clicking the Free Java Download button opens a "Sorry, Charlie!" page that tells you to download Java directly from Apple. Follow the instructions on that page to install Java on your computer.

- ✔ **(Optional) Follow the Do I Have Java? link.**

  When you follow this link, the web browser scans the computer for Java installations. For this book's examples, I recommend Java 6 (also known as Java 1.6) or later (Java 7, Java 8, or whatever). If your version of Java is older than Java 6 (or if the scan doesn't find Java on the computer), I recommend clicking one of the Download buttons at www.java.com.

- ✔ **(Optional) Pick and choose among Java versions.**

  If you click the All Java Downloads link at www.java.com, you can pick and choose from among several versions of Java — 32-bit and 64-bit versions for Windows, Mac, Linux, and Solaris computers.

  This alternative is useful for overriding the default Free Java Download button's choice. For example, you want the 64-bit version of Java even though the Free Java Download button gives you the 32-bit version. (See the sidebar "How many bits does your computer have?" earlier in this chapter.) Later, you might visit www.java.com with a Windows computer to download Java for your Macintosh.

- ✔ **(Optional) Cleanse your computer of all but the latest version of Java.**

  At www.java.com, the Remove Older Versions link promises to clean up any Java clutter you've collected over time. I've had some good luck and some bad luck in keeping multiple Java versions on a computer. In my opinion, this Remove Older Versions step is optional.

Visit the Remove Older Versions link if you're having trouble that you suspect is Java related. But if you've read several chapters of this book and the examples are running nicely, don't worry about an impending disaster from not having followed the Remove Older Versions link.

Setting Up the Android SDK

In this section, you get four useful tools in one download. Here's how:

1. **Visit** `http://developer.android.com/sdk`.

2. **Click the Download button on the web page.**

3. **Agree to all the legal mumbo-jumbo.**

4. **Choose between the 32-bit and 64-bit downloads.**

   For sage advice, see the earlier section "Are you running a 32-bit or 64-bit operating system?"

   After you make a choice, one last Download button appears. (At least, that's what happens early in 2013.)

5. **Click the last Download button and save the download to the local hard drive.**

   The downloaded file is one big `.zip` archive.

6. **Extract the contents of the downloaded archive file to the local hard drive.**

   On my Windows computer, I extract the `.zip` file's contents to the new folder `c:\Users\`*MyUserName*`\adt-bundle-windows-x86`. On my Mac, I extract the `.zip` file's contents to my existing `Applications` folder. (Refer to Figures 2-1 and 2-2.)

For help with archive files, see the earlier sidebar "Compressed archive files."

In Windows, the blank space in the name `Program Files` confuses some Java software. I don't think any of this book's software presents this problem, but I can't guarantee it. If you want, extract the `.zip` file's contents to the `C:\Program Files` or `C:\Program Files (x86)` folder. But make a mental note about your choice (in case you run into any trouble later).

The `.zip` archive that you download from `http://developer.android.com/sdk` contains these two components:

✔ **The eclipse component:** It contains a customized version of the popular Eclipse integrated development environment (IDE). You can compose, run, and debug Java applications in the Eclipse environment. This customized version of Eclipse includes the Android Development Toolkit (ADT) — extra plug-ins for working with Android apps.

✔ **The sdk component:** (Yes, only half of the large Android SDK download is the SDK component. If the names are misleading, don't blame me.) The SDK component contains the Android software library (one or more versions of the Android API). This component also contains a bunch of software tools for running and testing Android apps.

While you're still in the mood to follow my advice, note the location on the hard drive where the sdk component lands. (For example, in Figure 2-1, the SDK folder is `c:\Users\Barry\adk-bundle-windows-x86_64\sdk`.) I have a name for this location: the `ANDROID_HOME` folder.

Running Eclipse for the First Time

The first time you launch Eclipse, you perform a few extra steps. To get Eclipse running, follow these steps:

1. **Launch Eclipse.**

    In Windows, the Start menu may not have an Eclipse icon. In that case, look in Windows Explorer (it's File Explorer in Windows 8) for the folder containing the extracted Eclipse files. Double-click the icon representing the `eclipse.exe` file. (If you see an `eclipse` file but no `eclipse.exe` file, check the sidebar "Those pesky filename extensions," earlier in this chapter.)

    On the Mac, go to the Spotlight and type **Eclipse** in the search field. When *Eclipse* appears as the Top Hit in the Spotlight's list, press Enter.

    When you launch Eclipse, you see the Workspace Launcher dialog box, as shown in Figure 2-5. The dialog box asks where, on the computer's hard drive, you want to store the code that you will create using Eclipse.

2. **In the Workspace Launcher dialog box, click OK to accept the default (or don't accept the default).**

    One way or another, it's no big deal.

    Because this is your first time using a particular Eclipse workspace, Eclipse starts with a Welcome screen, as shown in Figure 2-6.

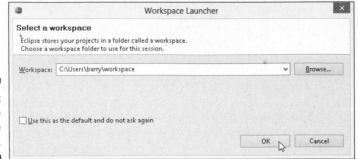

Figure 2-5:
The Eclipse
Workspace
Launcher.

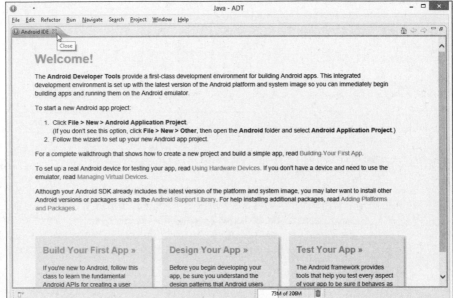

Figure 2-6:
The
Welcome
screen for
Android's
customized
version of
Eclipse.

3. **Dismiss the Welcome screen.**

In most versions of Eclipse, you can dismiss the Welcome screen by clicking the little *x* icon that appears on a tab above the screen.

A view of the main screen, after opening Eclipse with a brand-new workspace, is shown in Figure 2-7.

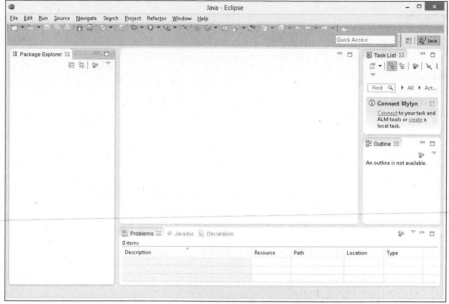

Figure 2-7:
The Eclipse
workbench
with a
brand-new
workspace.

Dude, where's my Android SDK?

When you launch Eclipse, the Eclipse IDE looks on the hard drive for the prewritten, reusable Android code files. (After all, Eclipse uses these files to help you write and run Android apps.) If Eclipse has trouble finding these files, you see a nasty-looking Could Not Find SDK Folder message. To tell Eclipse where to install the Android SDK files, follow these steps:

1. **In Windows, in the Eclipse main menu, choose Window⇨Preferences. On the Mac, in the Eclipse main menu, choose Eclipse⇨Preferences.**

   The Eclipse Preferences dialog box opens.

2. **In the tree list on the left side of the Preferences dialog box, select Android.**

   Don't expand the Android branch of the tree. Simply click the word *Android.*

   The SDK Location field appears in the main body of the Preferences dialog box, as shown in Figure 2-8.

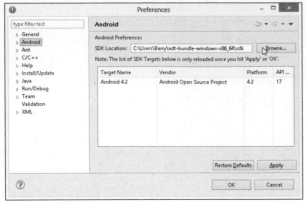

Figure 2-8:
Telling
Eclipse
about the
location of
the Android
SDK.

3. **Click the Browse button and (of course) browse to the** `ANDROID_HOME` **directory.**

   For example, in Figure 2-1, the `ANDROID_HOME` directory is `c:\Users\Barry\adt-bundle-windows-x86_64\sdk`.

4. **Click Apply and OK, and all those good things to return to the main Eclipse workbench.**

Look again at Figure 2-8 and notice the text box in the window's upper-left corner — the box containing the words *type filter text*. The text box is for filtering the names of Eclipse preferences. Figure 2-8 displays only 11 preferences (such as General, Android, Ant, and C++). But this list of preferences expands to a tree with approximately 150 branches. Each branch refers to its own set of choices in the main body of the Preferences window. If you want to see a bunch of Eclipse preferences related to font (for example), type **font** in the little text box. Eclipse then displays only branches of the tree containing the word *font*.

Eclipse, meet Java!

Eclipse normally looks on the computer for Java installations and selects an installed version of Java to use for running your Java programs. The computer may have more than one version of Java, so double-check Eclipse's Java version selection. The steps in this section show you how.

The steps in this section are optional. Follow them only if you suspect that Eclipse isn't using your computer's favorite version of Java.

1. *In Windows:* **From the Eclipse main menu, choose Window⇨ Preferences.** *On the Mac:* **From the Eclipse main menu, choose Eclipse⇨Preferences.**

   As a result, the Eclipse Preferences dialog box appears. (You can follow along in Figure 2-9.)

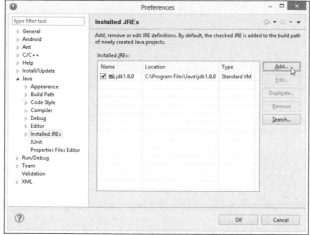

Figure 2-9: The Installed JREs page of the Eclipse Preferences dialog box.

2. **In the tree on the left side of the Preferences dialog box, expand the Java branch.**

3. **Within the Java branch, select the Installed JREs subbranch.**

4. **Look at the list of Java versions (Installed JREs) in the main body of the Preferences dialog box.**

   In the list, each version of Java has a check box. Eclipse uses the version whose box is checked. If the checked version isn't your preferred version (for example, if it isn't version 6 or later), you have to make changes.

5. **If your preferred version of Java appears in the Installed JREs list, select that version's check box.**

6. **If your preferred version of Java doesn't appear in the Installed JREs list, click the Add button.**

   When you click the Add button, the JRE Type dialog box appears, as shown in Figure 2-10.

Figure 2-10:
The JRE
Type dialog
box.

7. In the JRE Type dialog box, double-click Standard VM.

As a result, the JRE Definition dialog box appears, as shown in
Figure 2-11. What you do next depends on a few different factors.

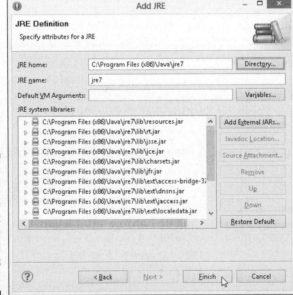

Figure 2-11:
The JRE
Definition
dialog box
(after you've
followed
Steps 8
and 9).

8. **Fill in the JRE Home field in the dialog box.**

   How you do this depends on the operating system:

   - *In Windows:* Browse to the directory in which you've installed your preferred Java version. On my many Windows computers, the directory is either `C:\Program Files\Java\jre7`, `C:\Program Files\Java\jdk1.7.0`, `C:\Program Files (x86)\Java\jre8`, or something of that sort.

   - *On the Mac:* Use the Finder to browse to the directory in which you've installed your preferred Java version. Type the name of the directory in the dialog box's JRE home field.

     My Mac has one Java directory, named `/System/Library/Java/Java Virtual Machines/1.6.0jdk/Contents/Home`, and another Java directory named `/Library/Java/JavaVirtualMachines/JDK 1.7.0.jdk/Contents/Home`.

      Directories such as `/System` and `/Library` don't normally appear in the Mac's Finder window. To browse to one of these directories (to the `/Library` directory, for example) choose Go⇨Go to Folder on the Finder's menu bar. In the resulting dialog box, type **/Library** and then press Go.

      As you navigate toward the directory containing your preferred Java version, you might encounter a `JDK 1.7.0.jdk` icon, or another item whose extension is `.jdk`. To see the contents of this item, control-click the item's icon and then select Show Package Contents.

   You might have one more thing to do back in the JRE Definition dialog box.

9. **Look at the JRE Name field in the JRE Definition dialog box; if Eclipse hasn't filled in a name automatically, type a name (almost any text) in the JRE Name field.**

10. **Dismiss the JRE Definition dialog box by clicking Finish.**

    The Preferences dialog box in Eclipse returns to the foreground. Its Installed JREs list contains the newly added version of Java.

11. **Select the check box next to the newly added version of Java.**

    You're almost done. (You have a few more steps to follow.)

12. **Within the Java branch on the left side of the Preferences dialog box, select the Compiler subbranch.**

    In the main body of the Preferences dialog box, you see the Compiler Compliance Level drop-down list, as shown in Figure 2-12.

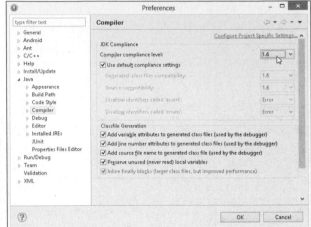

Figure 2-12:
Setting the
compiler
compliance
level.

13. **In the Compiler Compliance Level drop-down list, select 1.5 or 1.6.**

    Android works with only Java 1.5 or 1.6.

14. **Whew! Click the Preferences dialog box's OK button to return to the Eclipse workbench.**

Importing this book's sample programs

This import business can be tricky. As you move from one dialog box to the next, you see that many of the options have similar names. That's because Eclipse offers many different ways to import many different kinds of items. Anyway, if you follow these instructions, you'll be okay:

1. **Follow the steps in this chapter's earlier section "Getting This Book's Sample Programs."**

2. **On the Eclipse main menu, choose File⇨Import, as shown in Figure 2-13.**

    As a result, Eclipse displays the Import dialog box.

3. **In the tree in the Import dialog box, expand the General branch.**

4. **In the General branch, double-click the Existing Projects into Workspace subbranch, as shown in Figure 2-14.**

    As a result, the Import Projects dialog box appears.

5. **In the Import Projects dialog box, choose the Select Root Directory or the Select Archive File radio button, as shown in Figure 2-15.**

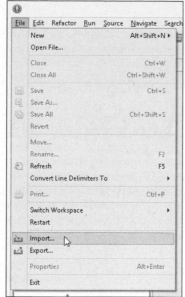

Figure 2-13:
Starting to
import this
book's code.

Figure 2-14:
Among all
the options,
select
Existing
Projects into
Workspace.

Figure 2-15:
The Import
Projects
dialog box.

This book's code lives in a folder named Java4Android_Programs or in an archive file named Java4Android_Programs.zip.

Safari on a Mac generally uncompresses .zip archives automatically, and Windows browsers (Internet Explorer, Firefox, Chrome, and others) do not uncompress .zip archives automatically. For the complete scoop on archive files, see the earlier sidebar "Compressed archive files."

6. **Click the Browse button to find the** Java4Android_Programs.zip **file or the** Java4Android_Programs **folder on the computer's hard drive.**

   If you're unsure where to find these items, look first in a folder named Downloads.

   After you find Java4Android_Programs, the Import Projects dialog box in Eclipse displays the names of the projects inside the file. (Refer to Figure 2-15.)

7. **Click the Select All button.**

   This book's examples are so exciting that you'll want to import all of them!

8. **Click the Finish button.**

   As a result, the main Eclipse workbench reappears. The left side of the workbench displays the names of this book's Java projects, as shown in Figure 2-16.

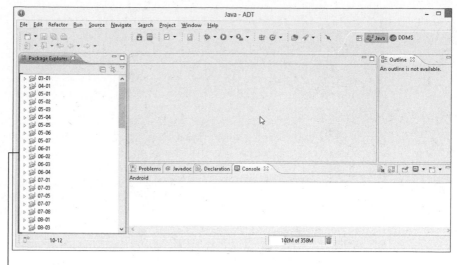

Figure 2-16: Eclipse displays a bunch of Java projects.

Listing of Java projects

After importing the code from this book, you may see lots of red error markers indicating trouble with the book's projects. If you do, stay calm. The markers might disappear after several seconds. If they don't, check the lower area of the Eclipse workspace for a message similar to `Unable to resolve target 'android-15'`.

If you see such a message, it means that my book's code insists on an API level that you haven't installed on your computer. To fix the problem, do the following:

1. **On the Eclipse main menu, choose Window⇨Android SDK Manager.**

   As a result, the computer displays the Android SDK Manager. (No surprise here!)

2. **Select the check box labeled Android 4.0.3 (API 15) or in whichever box is labeled with the missing API level number.**

3. **Click the Install button in the lower-right corner of the Android SDK Manager window.**

4. **Wait for installation to finish.**

5. **Close the Android SDK Manager.**

6. **Restart Eclipse.**

When Eclipse restarts, you see the red error markers for a few seconds. But after a brief (and possibly tense) waiting period, the error markers go away. You're ready to roll.

Creating an Android Virtual Device

You might be itching to run some code, but first you must have something that can run an Android program. By *something*, I mean either an Android device (a phone, a tablet, an Android-enabled toaster — whatever) or a virtual device. An *Android Virtual Device* (AVD) is a test bed for Android code on the development computer.

The Android SDK comes with its own *emulator* — a program that behaves like a phone or a tablet but runs on the development computer. The emulator translates Android code into code that the development computer can execute. But the emulator doesn't display a particular phone or tablet device on the screen. The emulator doesn't know what kind of device you want to display. Do you want a camera phone with 800-x-480-pixel resolution, or have you opted for a tablet device with its own built-in accelerometer and gyroscope? All these choices belong to a particular AVD. An AVD is simply a bunch of settings, telling the emulator all the details about the device to be emulated.

Before you can run Android apps on your computer, you must first create at least one AVD. In fact, you can create several AVDs and use one of them to run a particular Android app.

To create an AVD, follow these steps:

1. **In the Eclipse main menu, choose Window⇨Android Virtual Device Manager.**

   The Android Virtual Device Manager window opens.

2. **In the Android Virtual Device Manager window, click New, as shown in Figure 2-17.**

   The Create New Android Virtual Device (AVD) window opens. That's nice!

3. **In the AVD Name field, type a new name for the virtual device.**

   You can name your device My Sweet Petunia, but in Figure 2-18, I name my device Nexus7_Android4.2. The name serves to remind me of this device's capabilities.

4. **In the Device drop-down menu, select a device type.**

   In Figure 2-18, I select Nexus 7 (7.27", 800 x 1280: tvdpi).

5. **Determine the kind of secure digital (SD) card your device has.**

   In Figure 2-18, I choose an SD card with a modest 1000 MiB, which is roughly 1 gigabyte. Alternatively, I could have selected the File radio button and specified the name of a file on my hard drive. That file would be storing information as though it were a real SD card on a real device.

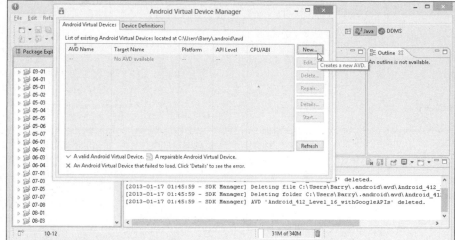

Figure 2-17:
The Android
Virtual
Device
Manager.

Recently, my department hired a new person. We offered a salary of $50K, which (we thought) meant $50,000 per year. Little did we know that the new person expected to be paid $51,200 each year. Computer scientists use the letter *K* (or the prefix *Kilo*) to mean 1,024 because 1,024 is a power of 2 (and powers of 2 are quite handy in computer science). The trouble is, the formal meaning of *Kilo* in the metric system is 1,000, not 1,024. To help clear things up (and to have fun creating new words), a commission of engineers created the *Kibibyte* (KiB) meaning 1,024 bytes, the *Mebibyte* (MiB) which is 1,048,576 bytes, and the *Gibibyte* (GiB), meaning 1,073,741,824 bytes. Most people (computer scientists included) don't know about KiBs or MiBs, and they don't worry about the difference between MiBs and ordinary megabytes. I'm surprised that the creators of the Android Virtual Device Manager thought about this issue.

6. **Leave the other choices at their defaults (or don't, if you don't want to) and click the Create AVD button.**

    The computer returns you to the Android Virtual Device Manager window, where you see a brand-new AVD in the list, as shown in Figure 2-19.

And that does it! You're ready to run your first Android app. I don't know about you, but I'm excited. (Sure, I'm not watching you read this book, but I'm excited on your behalf.) Chapter 3 guides you through the run of a standard Oracle Java program, and Chapter 4 does the same for an Android application. Go for it!

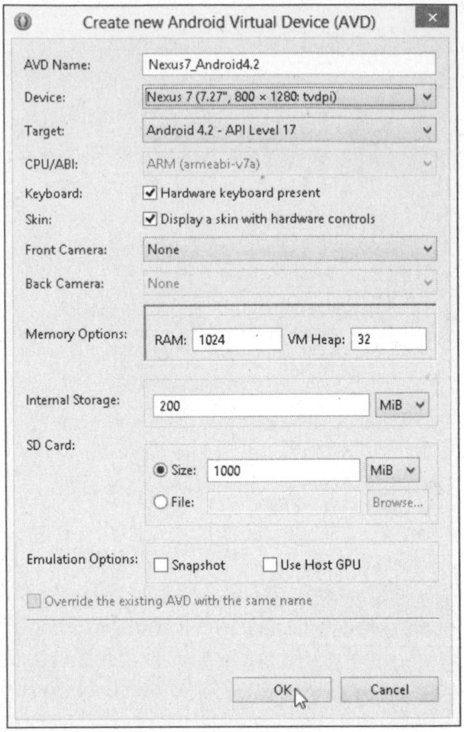

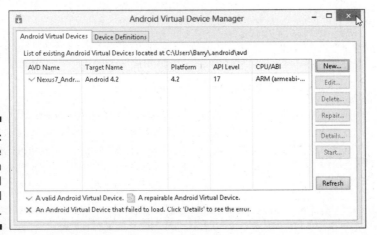

Figure 2-18:
Creating
a new
Android
virtual
device.

Figure 2-19:
You've
created an
Android
virtual
device.

Chapter 3

Running Standard Java Programs

*I*f you're a programming newbie, running a program probably means, for you, clicking the mouse. You want to run Internet Explorer, so you double-click the Internet Explorer icon. That's all there is to it. As far as you're concerned, Internet Explorer is a black box. How the program does whatever it does is none of your concern.

But when you create your own program, the situation is a bit different. You start with no icon to click, and possibly no well-defined notion of what the program should (and should not) do.

So how do you create a brand-new Java program? Where do you click? How do you save your work? How do you get the program to run? What do you do if, at first, the program doesn't run correctly?

This chapter tells you what you need to know.

The example in this chapter is a *standard Oracle* Java program. A standard Oracle Java program runs only on a desktop or laptop computer. The example cannot run on an Android device. For an example that runs on Android devices, see Chapter 4.

Running a Canned Java Program

The best way to get to know Java is to "do Java," by writing, testing, and running your own Java programs. This section prepares you by describing how to run and test a program. Rather than write your own program, you run one that I've already written for you. The program calculates the monthly payments on a home mortgage loan, as shown in Figure 3-1.

Figure 3-1:
A run of the mortgage program in this chapter.

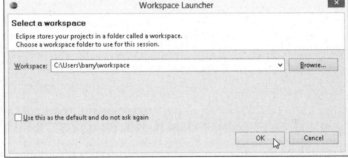

Here's how to run the mortgage program:

1. **First, follow the instructions in Chapter 2 for installing Java, installing and configuring Eclipse, and downloading this book's sample programs.**

    Thank goodness! You don't have to follow those instructions more than once.

2. **Launch Eclipse.**

    The Workspace Launcher dialog box in Eclipse appears, as shown in Figure 3-2.

Figure 3-2:
The Workspace Launcher in Eclipse.

For a complete how-to on launching Eclipse, see Chapter 2.

A *workspace* is a folder on the computer's hard drive. Eclipse stores Java programs in one or more workspace folders. Along with these Java programs, each workspace folder contains some Eclipse settings. These settings store information such as the version of Java that you're using, the colors you prefer for words in the editor, the size of the editor area when you drag the area's edges, and other preferences. You can have several workspaces with different programs and different settings in each workspace.

By default, the Workspace Launcher offers to open whatever workspace you opened the last time you ran Eclipse. In this example, you open the workspace that you use in Chapter 2, so don't modify anything in the Workspace field.

3. In the Workspace Launcher dialog box, click OK.

The big Eclipse workbench stares at you from the computer screen, as shown in Figure 3-3.

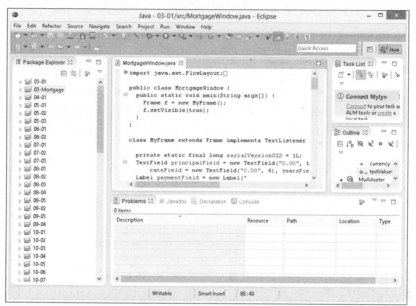

Figure 3-3:
The Eclipse
workbench.

In Figure 3-3, the leftmost part of the workbench is the Eclipse Package Explorer, which contains numbers such as 03-01, 04-01, and so on. Each number is the name of an Eclipse *project*, which is, formally, a collection of files and folders inside a workspace. Intuitively, a project is a basic work unit. For example, a self-contained collection of Java program files to manage a CD collection (along with the files containing the data) may constitute a single Eclipse project.

Looking again at the Package Explorer in Figure 3-3, you see projects named 03-01, 04-01, and so on. My project 03-01 holds the code in Listing 3-1. Project 04-01 contains the Android app whose code begins in Listing 4-1 (the first code listing in Chapter 4 of this book). Project 05-03 contains the code in Listing 5-3. The project named 03-Mortgage is a slight anomaly because the code for this chapter's Mortgage example isn't in any of the listings.

Eclipse project names can include letters, digits, blank spaces, and other characters; for the names of this book's examples, I stick with digits and dashes.

To read more about topics such as the Eclipse Package Explorer, see the later section "What's All That Stuff in the Eclipse Window?"

When you launch Eclipse, you may see different elements than the ones shown in Figure 3-3. You may see the Eclipse Welcome screen with only a few icons in an otherwise barren window. You may also see a workbench like the one shown in Figure 3-3, but with no list of numbers (03-01, 04-01, and so on) in the Package Explorer. If so, you may have missed some instructions in Chapter 2 for configuring Eclipse. Alternatively, you may have modified the workspace name in the Eclipse Workspace Launcher dialog box.

In any case, make sure that you see numbers like 03-01 and 04-01 in the Package Explorer. Seeing these numbers ensures that Eclipse is ready to run the sample programs from this book.

4. **In the Package Explorer, click the 03-Mortgage branch.**

   As a result, the 03-Mortgage project appears highlighted.

To see a sneak preview of the Java program you're running in Project 03-Mortgage, expand the 03-Mortgage branch in the Package Explorer. Inside the 03-Mortgage branch, you find the src branch, which in turn contains a (default package) branch. Inside the (default package) branch, you find the MortgageWindow.java branch. This MortgageWindow.java branch represents my Java program. Double-clicking the MortgageWindow.java branch makes my code appear in the Eclipse editor, as shown in Figure 3-4.

```
MortgageWindow.java ⊠
20  class MyFrame extends Frame implements TextListener {
21
22    private static final long serialVersionUID = 1L;
23    TextField principalField = new TextField("0.00", 15),
24       rateField = new TextField("0.00", 6), yearsField = new TextField("0", 3);
25    Label paymentField = new Label("                    ");
26    double principal, rate, ratePercent;
27    int years;
28    final int paymentsPerYear = 12;
29    final int timesPerYearCalculated = 12;
30    double effectiveAnnualRate, interestRatePerPayment;
31    double payment;
32
33    public MyFrame() {
34      setTitle("Mortgage Payment Calculator");
35      setLayout(new GridLayout(4, 2));
36
37      Label principalLabel = new Label("Principal $"), rateLabel = new Label(
38        "Rate (%)"), yearsLabel = new Label("Years"), paymentLabel = new Label(
39        "Payment $");
40      Panel principalLabelPanel = new Panel(new FlowLayout(FlowLayout.RIGHT)), rateLabelPane
41        new FlowLayout(FlowLayout.RIGHT)), yearsLabelPanel = new Panel(
42        new FlowLayout(FlowLayout.RIGHT)), paymentLabelPanel = new Panel(
43        new FlowLayout(FlowLayout.RIGHT));
44      Panel principalFieldPanel = new Panel(new FlowLayout(FlowLayout.LEFT)), rateFieldPanel
```

Figure 3-4:
Java code in the Eclipse editor.

5. **Choose Run⇨Run As⇨Java Application from the main menu, as shown in Figure 3-5.**

   When you choose Run As⇨Java Application, the computer runs the project's code. (In this example, the computer runs a Java program that I wrote.) The program displays the Mortgage Payment Calculator window on the screen, as shown in Figure 3-6.

Figure 3-5:
One way to
run the code
in Project
03-Mortgage.

Figure 3-6:
The
Mortgage
Payment
Calculator
begins
its run.

6. **Type numbers into the fields in the Mortgage Payment Calculator window. (Refer to Figure 3-1.)**

   When you type a principal amount in Step 6, don't include the country's currency symbol and don't group the digits. (U.S. residents: Omit dollar signs and commas.) For the percentage rate, omit the % symbol. For the number of years, don't use a decimal point. If you break any of these rules, the Java code can't read your number, and my Java program displays nothing in the *Payment* row.

   Disclaimer: Your local mortgage company charges more (a lot more) than the amount that my Java program calculates.

   If you follow this section's instructions and you don't see the results I describe, you can try these three strategies, listed in order from best to worst:

   ✔ Double-check all steps to make sure that you followed them correctly.

   ✔ Contact me at `Java4Android@allmycode.com` via e-mail, `@allmycode` on Twitter, or `/allmycode` on Facebook If you describe what happened, I can probably figure out what went wrong and tell you how to correct the problem.

   ✔ Panic.

Typing and Running Your Own Code

The earlier section "Running a Canned Java Program" is all about running someone else's Java code (code that you download from this book's website). But, eventually, you'll write code on your own. This section shows you how to create code by using the Eclipse IDE.

Separating your programs from mine

You can separate your code from this book's examples by creating a separate workspace. Here are two (distinct) ways to do it:

✔ **When you launch Eclipse, type a new folder name in the Workspace field of the Workspace Launcher dialog box in Eclipse.**

If the folder doesn't already exist, Eclipse creates the folder. If the folder already exists, the Eclipse Package Explorer lists any projects that the folder contains.

✔ **In the main menu in the Eclipse workbench, choose File⇨Switch Workspace, as shown in Figure 3-7.**

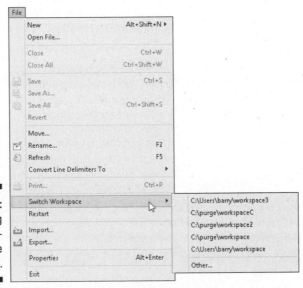

Figure 3-7: Switching to a different Eclipse workspace.

When you choose File⇨Switch Workspace, Eclipse offers you a few of your previously opened workspace folders. If your choice of folder isn't in the list, select the Other option. In response, Eclipse reopens its Workspace Launcher dialog box.

Writing and running your program

Here's how to create a new Java project:

1. **Launch Eclipse.**

2. **From the Eclipse menu bar, choose File⇨New⇨Java Project.**

   The Create a Java Project dialog box appears.

3. **In the Create a Java Project dialog box, type a name for the project and then click Finish.**

   In Figure 3-8, I type the name `MyFirstProject`.

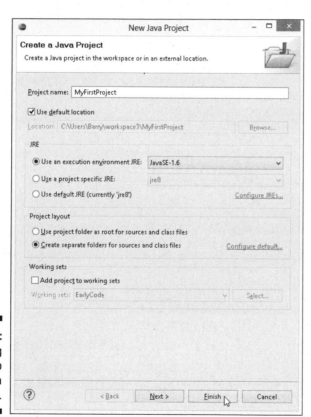

Figure 3-8: Getting Eclipse to create a new project.

If you click Next instead of Finish, you see other options that you don't need right now. To avoid confusion, just click Finish.

Clicking Finish returns you to the Eclipse workbench, with `MyFirst Project` in the Package Explorer, as shown in Figure 3-9.

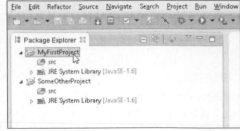

Figure 3-9:
Your project
appears in
the Package
Explorer in
Eclipse.

The next step is to create a new Java source code file.

4. Select the newly created project in the Package Explorer.

To create Figure 3-9, I selected `MyFirstProject` instead of
`SomeOtherProject`.

5. In the Eclipse main menu, choose File⇨New⇨Class.

The Eclipse Java Class dialog box appears, as shown in Figure 3-10.

Figure 3-10:
Getting
Eclipse to
create a
new Java
class.

Like every other windowed environment, Eclipse provides many ways to accomplish the same task. Rather than choose File➪New➪Class, you can right-click MyFirstProject in the Package Explorer in Windows (or control-click MyFirstProject in the Package Explorer on a Mac). In the resulting context menu, choose New➪Class. You can also start by pressing Alt-Shift+N in Windows (or Option-Command-N on a Mac). The choice of clicks and keystrokes is up to you.

6. **In the Name field in the Java Class dialog box, type the name of the new class.**

   In this example, I use the name MyFirstJavaClass, with no blank spaces between the words in the name. (Refer to Figure 3-10.)

   The name in the Java Class dialog box cannot have blank spaces, and the only allowable punctuation symbol is the underscore character (_). You can name the class MyFirstJavaClass or My_First_Java_Class, but you can't name it My First Java Class, and you can't name it JavaClass,MyFirst. Finally, you can't start a class name with a digit. For example, you can name the class Go4It but not 2bOrNot2b.

7. **In the Package field in the Java Class dialog box, type a package name. (Refer to Figure 3-10.)**

   In Java, you group code into bunches called *packages*. And in the Android world, each app comes in its own package.

   Don't worry much about making up package names. If you have your own domain name (allyourcode.org, for example), you should reverse the domain name (resulting in org.allyourcode) and then add a descriptive word. For example, org.allyourcode.myfirst project is a good package name. If you don't have a domain name, any words (separated from one another by dots) will work.

   The package name contains one or more words. Each word can be any combination of letters, digits, and underscores (_) as long as the word doesn't start with a digit. A package name is a bunch of these words, separated from one another by dots. For example, org.allyourcode. Go4It is a valid package name, but org.allyourcode. 2bOrNot2b is not. (You can't start the third part of the package name with the digit 2. For that matter, you can't start any of the three words in a name like org.allyourcode.myfirstproject with a digit.)

8. **Put a check mark in the** public static void main(String[] args) **check box.**

   The check mark tells Eclipse to create some boilerplate Java code.

9. **Accept the defaults for everything else in the Java Class dialog box. (In other words, click Finish.)**

Clicking Finish brings you back to the Eclipse workbench. Now `MyFirstProject` contains a file named `MyFirstJavaClass.java`. For your convenience, the `MyFirstJavaClass.java` file already has some code in it. The Eclipse editor displays the Java code, as shown in Figure 3-11.

```
MyFirstJavaClass.java ⊠
 1   package org.allyourcode.myfirstproject;
 2
 3   public class MyFirstJavaClass {
 4
 5⊖     /**
 6       * @param args
 7       */
 8⊖     public static void main(String[] args) {
 9           // TODO Auto-generated method stub
10
11       }
12
13   }
14
```

Figure 3-11:
Eclipse
writes some
code in the
editor.

10. **Replace an existing line of code in the new Java program.**

Type a line of code in the Eclipse editor. Replace the line

```
// TODO Auto-generated method stub
```

with these lines:

```
javax.swing.JOptionPane.showMessageDialog
                        (null, "Hello");
```

Any program containing these lines of code runs only on a desktop (or laptop) computer. The code `javax.swing.JOptionPane.show MessageDialog` belongs to standard Oracle Java, but not to Android Java.

Copy the new lines of code exactly as you see them in Listing 3-1.

• Spell each word exactly the way I spell it in Listing 3-1.

• Capitalize each word exactly the way I do in Listing 3-1.

• Include all the punctuation symbols — the dots, the quotation marks, the semicolon — everything.

When you're done, the code in the Eclipse editor should look exactly like the code in Listing 3-1.

Do I see formatting in my Java program?

When you use the Eclipse editor to write a Java program, you see words in various colors. Certain words are always in blue. Other words are always in black. You even see some bold and italic phrases. You may think you see formatting, but you don't. Instead, what you see is *syntax coloring* or *syntax highlighting*.

No matter what you call it, the issue is this:

✔ In Microsoft Word, elements such as bold formatting are marked inside a document. When you save MyPersonalDiary. doc, the instructions to make the words *love* and *hate* bold are recorded inside the MyPersonalDiary.doc file.

✔ In a Java program editor, elements such as bold and coloring aren't marked inside

the Java program file. Instead, the editor displays each word in a way that makes the Java program easy to read.

For example, in a Java program, certain words (such as class, public, and void) have their own, special meanings. So the Eclipse editor displays class, public, and void in bold, reddish letters. When I save my Java program file, the computer stores nothing about bold, colored letters in my Java program file. But the editor uses its discretion to highlight special words with reddish coloring.

Another editor may display the same words in a blue font. Another editor (such as Windows Notepad) displays all words in plain, old black.

Listing 3-1: A Program to Display a Greeting

```
public class MyFirstJavaClass {

  /**
   * @param args
   */
  public static void main(String[] args) {
    javax.swing.JOptionPane.showMessageDialog
                             (null, "Hello");
  }

}
```

Java is *case-sensitive*, which means that Showmessagedialog isn't the same as showMessageDialog. If yOu tyPe Showmessagedialog, your progrAm won't worK. Be sUre to cAPItalize your codE eXactLy as it is shown in Listing 3-1.

Some people notice the difference between "curly" quotation marks and "straight" quotation marks. Is the distinction between the two types useful? (Do you see the difference?) Is it even appropriate to use the words *curly* and *straight* for the two kinds of quotation marks? In a Java program, a word like `"Hello"` (surrounded by straight quotation marks) stands for a string of characters. In fact, the code in Listing 3-1 makes the letters `Hello` appear on the user's screen. Here's the rule:

In Java, to denote a string of characters, always use straight quotation marks; never curly quotation marks.

In practice, if you copy code from a Kindle or from another electronic medium, you're probably copying curly quotation marks, and the code is incorrect. Fortunately, when you use the computer keyboard to type code in the Eclipse editor, you automatically type straight quotation marks. That's nice.

In a Java program, almost none of the spacing and indentation matters. In Listing 3-1, I don't need all the blank spaces before `(null, "Hello")`, but the blank spaces help me to remember that `(null, "Hello")` is a continuation of the `showMessageDialog` stuff. In other words, all the characters between the word `javax` and the word `"Hello"` are part of one big Java command. I separate the command into two lines because if I didn't, the command would run off the edge of the page.

If you type everything correctly, you see the information shown in Figure 3-12.

```
MyFirstJavaClass.java ☒
 1   package org.allyourcode.myfirstproject;
 2
 3   public class MyFirstJavaClass {
 4
 5⊖      /**
 6        * @param args
 7        */
 8⊖      public static void main(String[] args) {
 9          javax.swing.JOptionPane.showMessageDialog
10                              (null, "Hello");
11      }
12
13   }
14
```

Figure 3-12:
A Java program in the Eclipse editor.

If you don't type your part of the code exactly as it's shown in Listing 3-1, you may see jagged red underlines, tiny rectangles with X-like markings inside them, or other red marks in the Editor, as shown in Figure 3-13.

The red marks in the Eclipse editor refer to compile-time errors in the Java code. A *compile-time* error (also known as a *compiler* error) is an error that prevents the computer from translating the code. (See the talk about code translation in Chapter 1.)

```
MyFirstJavaClass.java ⋈                                    − ⬚
 1  package org.allyourcode.myfirstproject;
 2
 3  public class MyFirstJavaClass {
 4
 5⊖     /**
 6       * @param args
 7       */
 8⊖     public static void main(String[] args) {
 9          javax.swing.JOptionPane.shoWmESsaGediAlog
10                                  (null, "Hello");
11      }
12
13  }
14
```

Figure 3-13: A Java program, typed incorrectly.

Here, the error markers in Figure 3-13 appear on line 9 of the Java program. Line numbers are designed to appear in the editor's left margin, but they do not appear by default. To make the Eclipse editor display line numbers, choose Window⇨Preferences (in Windows) or Eclipse⇨Preferences (on a Mac). Then choose General⇨Editors⇨Text Editors. Finally, add a check mark in the Show Line Numbers check box.

To fix compile-time errors, you must become a dedicated detective and join the elite squad known as *Law & Order: JPU (Java Programming Unit)*. You seldom find easy answers. Instead, comb the evidence slowly and carefully for clues. Compare everything you see in the editor, character by character, with my code in Listing 3-1. Don't miss a single detail, including spelling, punctuation, and uppercase versus lowercase.

Eclipse has a few nice features to help you find the source of a compile-time error. For example, you can hover over the jagged red underline. When you do, you see a brief explanation of the error along with suggestions for repairing the error — some *quick fixes,* in other words. See Figure 3-14.

In Figure 3-14, a pop-up message tells you that Java doesn't know what the word shoWmESsaGediAlog means — that is, shoWmESsaGediAlog is "undefined." Near the bottom of the figure, one quick-fix option is to repair the incorrect capitalization by changing shoWmESsaGediAlog to showMessageDialog.

When you click the Change to `'showMessageDialog' (..)` option, the Eclipse editor replaces `shoWmESsaGediAlog` with `showMessage Dialog`. The editor's error markers disappear, and the incorrect code shown in Figure 3-13 changes to the correct code shown in Figure 3-12.

11. **Make any changes or corrections to the code in the Eclipse editor.**

    When at last you see no jagged underlines or blotches in the editor, you're ready to try running the program.

12. **Select** `MyFirstJavaClass` **either by clicking inside the editor or by clicking the** `MyFirstProject` **branch in the Package Explorer.**

13. **In the Eclipse main menu, choose Run⇨Run As⇨Java Application.**

    That does the trick. The new Java program runs, and you see the `Hello` message shown in Figure 3-15. It's like being in heaven!

What can possibly go wrong?

Ridding the editor of jagged underlines is cause for celebration. Eclipse likes the look of your code, so from that point on, it's smooth sailing. Right?

Well, it ain't necessarily so. In addition to some conspicuous compile-time errors, the code can have other, less obvious errors.

Imagine someone telling you to "go to the intersection, and then *run tight*." You notice immediately that the speaker has made a mistake, and you respond with a polite "Huh?" The nonsensical *run tight* phrase is like a compile-time error. Your "Huh?" is like the jagged underlines in the Eclipse editor. As a human being who listens, you may be able to guess what *run tight* means, but the Eclipse editor never dares to fix the mistakes in your code.

In addition to compile-time errors, other kinds of gremlins can hide inside a Java program:

✔ **Unchecked runtime exceptions:** You see no compile-time errors, but when you run the program, the run ends prematurely. Somewhere in the middle of the run, the instructions tell Java to do something that can't be done. For example, while you're running the Mortgage program in the earlier section "Running a Canned Java Program," you type 1,000,000.00 instead of 1000000.00. Java doesn't like the commas in the number, so the program crashes and Eclipse displays a nasty-looking message, as shown in the first figure.

This example shows an *unchecked runtime exception* — the equivalent of someone telling you to turn right at the intersection when the only thing to the right is a big, brick wall. The Eclipse editor doesn't warn you about an unchecked runtime exception because, until you run the program, the computer can't predict that the exception will occur.

✔ **Logic errors:** You see no error markers in the Eclipse editor, and when you run the code, the program runs to completion. But the answer isn't correct. Instead of $552.20 in the second figure, the payment amount is $551,518,260.38. The program incorrectly tells you to pay thousands of times what your house is worth and tells you to pay this amount each month! It's the equivalent of being told to turn right rather than turn left. You can drive in the wrong direction for quite a long time.

Logic errors are the most challenging errors to find and to fix. And worst of all, logic errors often go unnoticed. In March 1985, I got a monthly home heating bill for $1,328,932.21. Clearly, a computer had printed the incorrect amount. When I called the gas company to complain, the telephone service representative said, "Don't be upset. Pay only half that amount."

✔ **Compile-time warnings:** A warning isn't as severe as an error message. So when Eclipse notices suspicious behavior in a program, the editor displays a jagged yellow underline, an exclamation point enclosed in a tiny yellow icon, and a few other not-so-intrusive clues.

For example, in the third figure, you can see that, on Line 9, I added material related to amount = 10 to the code from Listing 3-1. The problem is, I never make use of the amount or of the number 10 anywhere in my program. With its faint, yellow markings, Eclipse effectively tells me "Your amount = 10 code isn't bad enough to be a showstopper. Eclipse can still manage to run the program. But are you sure you want amount = 10 (this material that seems to serve no purpose) in your program?"

(continued)

(continued)

A subtle hint

```
MyFirstJavaClass.java  ⊠
 1  package org.allyourcode.myfirstproject;
 2
 3  public class MyFirstJavaClass {
 4
 5⊖     /**
 6       * @param args
 7       */
 8⊖     public static void main(String[] args) {
 9          int amount = 10;
10          javax.swing.JOptionPane.showMessageDialog
11                                  (null, "Hello");
12      }
13
14  }
```

Imagine being told, "Turn when you reach the intersection." The direction may be just fine. But if you're suspicious, you ask, "Which way should I turn? Left or right?"

When you're sure that you know what you're doing, you can ignore warnings and worry about them later. But a warning can be an indicator that the code has a more serious problem. My sweeping recommendation is this: Pay attention to warnings. But if you can't figure out why you're seeing a particular warning, don't let the warning prevent you from moving forward.

Icon yellow?

Your code is mellow.

Icon red?

Your code is dead!

What's All That Stuff in the Eclipse Window?

Believe it or not, an editor once rejected one of my book proposals. In the margin, the editor scribbled "This is not a word" next to text such as *can't, it's,* and *I've.* To this day, I still do not know what this editor did not like about contractions. My own opinion is that language always needs to expand. Where would we be without a few new words — words such as *dotcom, infomercial,* and *vaporware*?

Even the *Oxford English Dictionary* (the last word in any argument about words) grows by more than 4,000 entries each year. That's an increase of more than 1 percent per year — about 11 new words per day!

The fact is, human thought resembles a high-rise building: You can't build the 50th floor until you've built at least part of the 49th. You can't talk about *spam* until you have a word such as *e-mail*. In these fast-paced, changing times, you need verbal building blocks. That's why this section contains a bunch of new terms.

In this section, each newly defined term describes an aspect of the Eclipse IDE. Before you read all this Eclipse terminology, I provide these disclaimers:

- **This section is optional reading.** Refer to this section if you have trouble understanding some of this book's instructions. But if you have no trouble navigating the Eclipse IDE, don't complicate things by fussing over the terminology in this section.

- **This section provides explanations of terms, not formal definitions of terms.** Yes, my explanations are fairly precise; but no, they're not airtight. Almost every description in this section has hidden exceptions, omissions, exemptions, and exclusions. Take the paragraphs in this section as friendly reminders, not as legal contracts.

- **Eclipse is a useful tool.** But Eclipse isn't officially part of the Java ecosystem. Although I don't describe details in this book, you can write Java programs without ever using Eclipse.

Understanding the big picture

Your tour of Eclipse begins with the big Burd's-eye view:

- **Workbench:** The Eclipse desktop (refer to Figure 3-3). The workbench is the environment in which you develop code.

- **Area:** A section of the workbench. The workbench shown in Figure 3-3 contains five areas. To illustrate the point, I've drawn borders around each area, as shown in Figure 3-16.

- **Window:** A copy of the Eclipse workbench. In Eclipse, you can have several copies of the workbench open at a time. Each copy appears in its own window.

   To open a second window, go to the main Eclipse menu bar and choose Window➪New Window.

- **Action:** A choice that's offered to you, typically when you click something. For example, when you choose File➪New from the Eclipse main menu bar, you see a list of new elements you can create. The list usually includes Project, Folder, File, and Other, but it may also include items such as Package, Class, and Interface. Each of these things (each item on the menu) is an *action*.

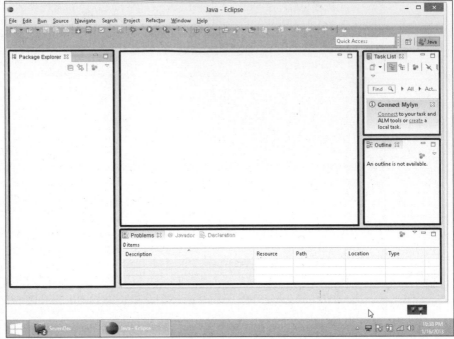

Figure 3-16:
The work-bench is divided into areas.

Views, editors, and other stuff

The next bunch of terms deals with things called views, editors, and tabs.

You may have difficulty understanding the difference between views and editors. (A *view* is like an *editor*, which is like a *view*, or something like that.) If views and editors seem the same to you, and you're not sure whether you can tell which is which, don't be upset. When you're an ordinary Eclipse user, the distinction between views and editors comes naturally as you gain experience using the workbench. You rarely have to decide whether the thing you're using is a view or an editor.

Anyway, if you ever have to distinguish between a view and an editor, here's what you need to know:

✔ **View:** A part of the Eclipse workbench that displays information for you to browse. In the simplest case, a view fills up an area in the workbench. For example, in Figure 3-3, earlier in this chapter, the Package Explorer view fills up the leftmost area.

Many views display information as lists or trees. For example, in Figure 3-9, the Package Explorer view contains a tree.

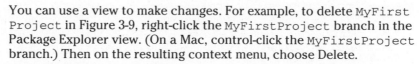

You can use a view to make changes. For example, to delete `MyFirst Project` in Figure 3-9, right-click the `MyFirstProject` branch in the Package Explorer view. (On a Mac, control-click the `MyFirstProject` branch.) Then on the resulting context menu, choose Delete.

When you use a view to change something, the change takes place immediately. For example, when you choose Delete in the Package Explorer's context menu, whatever item you've selected is deleted immediately. In a way, this behavior is nothing new. The same kind of thing happens when you recycle a file using Windows Explorer or trash a file using the Macintosh Finder.

✔ **Editor:** A part of the Eclipse workbench that displays information for you to modify. A typical editor displays information in the form of text. This text can be the contents of a file. For example, an editor in Figure 3-11 displays the contents of the `MyFirstJavaClass.java` file.

When you use an editor to change something, the change doesn't take place immediately. For example, look at the editor shown in Figure 3-11. This editor displays the contents of the `MyFirstJavaClass.java` file. You can type all kinds of things in the editor. Nothing happens to `MyFirstJavaClass.java` until you choose File⇨Save from the Eclipse menu bar. Of course, this behavior is nothing new. The same kind of thing happens when you work in Microsoft Word or in any other word processing program.

Like other authors, I occasionally become lazy and use the word *view* when I mean *view or editor* instead. I also write "the Eclipse editor" when I should write "an Eclipse editor" or "the Editor area of the Eclipse workbench." When you catch me blurring the terminology this way, just shake your head and move onward. When I'm being careful, I use the official Eclipse terminology. I refer to views and editors as *parts* of the Eclipse workbench. Unfortunately, this "parts" terminology doesn't stick in peoples' minds.

An area of the Eclipse workbench might contain several views or several editors. Most Eclipse users get along fine without giving this "several views" business a second thought (or even a first thought). But if you care about the terminology surrounding tabs and active views, here's the scoop:

✔ **Tab:** Something that's impossible to describe except by calling it a "tab." That which we call a tab by any other name would move us as well from one view to another or from one editor to another. The important thing is, views can be *stacked* on top of one another. Eclipse displays stacked views as though they're pages in a tabbed notebook. For example, Figure 3-17 displays one area of the Eclipse workbench. The area contains six views (Problems view, Javadoc view, Declaration view, Search view, Console view, and LogCat view). Each view has its own tab.

Figure 3-17:
An area
containing
several
views.

```
Problems  Javadoc  Declaration  Search  Console  LogCat
Android
[2013-01-18 15:19:03 - RandomColorGlowAPI10]  HOME is up on device 'emulator-5554'
[2013-01-18 15:19:03 - RandomColorGlowAPI10]  Uploading RandomColorGlowAPI10.apk onto devic
[2013-01-18 15:19:03 - RandomColorGlowAPI10]  Installing RandomColorGlowAPI10.apk...
[2013-01-18 15:19:20 - RandomColorGlowAPI10]  Success!
[2013-01-18 15:19:20 - RandomColorGlowAPI10]  Starting activity com.allmycode.randomcolorgl
[2013-01-18 15:19:21 - RandomColorGlowAPI10]  ActivityManager: Starting: Intent ( act=andro
```

The Console view is shown in Figure 3-17, but it doesn't always appear as part of the Java perspective. Normally, the Console view appears automatically whenever the program crashes. If you want to force the Console view to appear, choose Window⇨Show View⇨Other. In the resulting Show View dialog box, expand the General branch. Finally, within that General branch, double-click the Console item.

A bunch of stacked views is a *tab group*. To bring a view in the stack to the forefront, you click that view's tab.

By the way, all this information about tabs and views holds true for tabs and editors. The only interesting thing is the way Eclipse uses the word *editor*. In Eclipse, each tabbed page of the Editor area is an individual editor. For example, the Editor area shown in Figure 3-18 contains three editors (not three tabs belonging to a single editor). The three editors display the contents of three files: `MyFirstJavaClass.java`, `MortgageWindow.java`, and `activity_main.xml`.

Figure 3-18:
The Editor
area
contains
three
editors.

```
MyFirstJavaClass.java    MortgageWindow.java    activity_main.xml
  1  package org.allyourcode.myfirstproject;
  2                                          Android04-01/res/layout/activity_main.xml
  3  public class MyFirstJavaClass {
  4
  5    /**
  6     * @param args
  7     */
  8    public static void main(String[] args) {
  9      javax.swing.JOptionPane.showMessageDialog
 10                          (null, "Hello");
 11    }
 12
 13  }
 14
```

✔ **Active view or active editor:** In a tab group, the active view or editor refers to the view or editor that's in front.

In Figure 3-18, the `MyFirstJavaClass.java` editor is the active editor. The `MortgageWindow.java` and `activity_main.xml` editors are inactive. (The `activity_main.xml` looks as though it's active, but that's because, in Figure 3-18, I'm hovering the mouse over that editor's tab.)

Looking inside a view or an editor

The terms in this section deal with individual views, individual editors, and individual areas:

✔ **Toolbar:** The bar of buttons (and other little items) at the top of a view, as shown in Figure 3-19.

Figure 3-19: The toolbar in the Package Explorer view.

✔ **Menu button:** A downward-pointing arrow on the toolbar. When you click the menu button, a drop-down list of actions appears, as shown in Figure 3-20. Which actions you see in the list vary from one view to another.

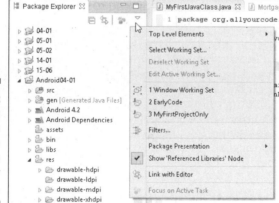

Figure 3-20: Clicking the menu button in the Package Explorer view.

✔ **Close button:** A button that eliminates a particular view or editor, as shown in Figure 3-21.

Figure 3-21:
An editor's
Close
button.

✔ **Chevron:** A double arrow indicating that other tabs should appear in a particular area (but that the area is too narrow). The chevron shown in Figure 3-22 has a little number 2 beside it. The 2 tells you that, in addition to the two visible tabs, two tabs are invisible. Clicking the chevron opens a hover tip containing the labels of all the tabs. (See Figure 3-22.)

Figure 3-22:
The chevron
indicates
that two
editors are
hidden.

✔ **Marker bar:** The vertical ruler on the left edge of the editor area. Eclipse displays tiny alert icons, called *markers*, inside the marker bar. (Refer to Figure 3-13.)

Returning to the big picture

The two terms in this section deal with the overall look and feel of Eclipse:

✔ **Layout:** An arrangement of certain views. The layout shown in Figure 3-3, for example, has seven views, four of which are active:

- *Package Explorer view:* You see it on the far left side.

- *Task List view and Outline views:* They're on the far right side.

- *Problems, Javadoc, Declaration, and Console views:* They're near the bottom. In this area of the workspace, the Problems view is the active view.

Along with all these views, the layout contains a single *editor area.* Any and all open editors appear inside this editor area.

✔ **Perspective:** A useful layout. If a particular layout is truly useful, someone gives that layout a name. And if a layout has a name, you can use the layout whenever you want. For example, the workbench shown in Figure 3-3 displays Eclipse's *Java perspective*. By default, the Java perspective contains six views in an arrangement much like the arrangement shown in Figure 3-3.

Along with all these views, the Java perspective contains an editor area. (Sure, the editor area has several tabs, but the number of tabs has nothing to do with the Java perspective.)

You can switch among perspectives by choosing Window➪Open Perspective on the Eclipse main menu bar. This book focuses almost exclusively on Eclipse's Java perspective. But if you like poking around, visit some of the other perspectives to get a glimpse of the power and versatility of Eclipse.

Chapter 4

Creating an Android App

C hapter 3 describes the writing and running of a dirt-simple Java program. Like many Java programs, the one in Chapter 3 runs on a plain-old desktop or laptop computer. Behind the scenes, the code in Chapter 3 uses the powerful features of standard Oracle Java. But the two kinds of Java (standard Oracle Java for desktops and laptops, and Android's Java for mobile devices) are slightly different animals, for these reasons:

▸ **Standard Java uses the power and speed of desktop and laptop computers.**

Android Java is streamlined to run on smaller devices with less memory.

▸ **Standard Java uses some features that aren't available in Android Java.**

For example, the `javax.swing.JOptionPane.showMessageDialog` call in the program in Chapter 3 isn't available in Android Java.

▸ **Android Java uses some features that aren't available in standard Java.**

For example, the `Activity` class in this chapter's program isn't available in standard Java.

▸ **Creating a basic Android app requires more steps than creating a basic standard Java app.**

This chapter covers the steps that are required in order to create a basic Android app, though the app doesn't do much. (In fact, you might argue that it does nothing.) But the example shows you how to create and run a new Android project.

Creating Your First Android App

A gadget typically comes supplied with a manual. The manual's first sentence is "Read all 37 safety warnings before attempting to install this product." Don't you love it? You can't get to the pertinent material without wading through the preliminaries.

Well, nothing in this chapter can set your house on fire or even break your electronic device. But before you follow this chapter's instructions, you need a bunch of software on your development computer. To make sure you have this software, and that it's properly configured, see Chapter 2. (Do not pass Go; do not collect $200.)

When at last you have all the software you need, you're ready to start Eclipse and create a real, live Android app.

Creating an Android project

To create your first Android application, follow these steps:

1. **Launch Eclipse.**

   For details on launching Eclipse, see Chapter 2.

2. **From the main menu in Eclipse, choose File⇨New⇨Android Application Project.**

   As a result, Eclipse fires up its New Android Application dialog box, as shown in Figure 4-1.

3. **In the Application Name field, type a name for the app.**

   In Figure 4-1, I type the boring words `My First Android App`. Ordinary folks such as Joe and Jane User, however, will see this name under the app's icon on the Android launcher screen. If you're planning to market your app, make the name short, sweet, and descriptive. You can even include blank spaces in the name.

   The next several steps involve lots of clicking, but you primarily accept the default settings.

4. **(Optional) In the Project Name and Package Name fields, change the name of the project and the name of the Java package containing the project.**

   Eclipse automatically fills in the Project Name and Package Name fields (guided by whatever text you type in the Application Name field). In

Figure 4-1, Eclipse creates the project name `MyFirstAndroidApp` and the package name `com.example.myfirstandroidapp`. Eclipse uses the project name to label this app's branch in the Package Explorer tree.

Figure 4-1:
The first
New
Android
Application
dialog box.

For practice apps, you can cheat by using the package name that Eclipse creates. But if you plan to publish an app, give the app its own package name, using the rules described in Chapter 3.

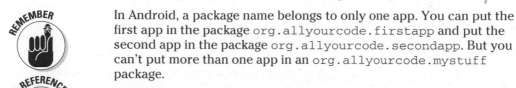

In Android, a package name belongs to only one app. You can put the first app in the package `org.allyourcode.firstapp` and put the second app in the package `org.allyourcode.secondapp`. But you can't put more than one app in an `org.allyourcode.mystuff` package.

For the lowdown on Java packages and package names, see Chapter 5.

5. (Optional) Choose values from the drop-down boxes in the dialog box.

To find out what you're promising when you select Minimum Required SDK API 8 and Target SDK API 16, see the nearby sidebar, "Using Android versions."

In Figure 4-1, I accept the defaults offered to me — API 8, API 16, and API 17. You can select any values from the drop-down boxes as long as you've created an Android Virtual Device (AVD) that can run the target's projects. (For example, an Android 2.3.3 AVD can run projects targeted to earlier versions of Android, such as Android 2.3.1, Android 2.2, and Android 1.6. The project target doesn't have to be an exact match with an existing AVD.)

Using Android versions

Android has a few different uses for version numbers. For example, in Figure 4-1, the minimum required SDK is API 8 and the target SDK is API 16. What's the difference?

You design an Android app to run on a range of API versions. You can think informally of the minimum SDK version as the lowest version in the range, and the target version as the highest. So if you select API 8 as the minimum SDK and select API 16 as the target, you design an app to run on API levels 8 through 16.

But the lowest-to-highest-version idea needs refining. The official Android documentation reports that " . . . new versions of the platform are fully backward-compatible." So an app that runs correctly on API 8 should run correctly on all versions higher than API 8. (I write "*should run correctly*" because, in practice, full backward compatibility is difficult to achieve. Anyway, if the Android team is willing to promise full backward compatibility, I'm willing to take my chances.)

The *target version* (it's API 16 in Figure 4-1) is the version for which you test the app. When you run this chapter's example, Eclipse opens an emulator with API 16 or higher installed. (For example, if you've created an AVD whose API is level 17 but you have no AVD whose API is level 16, Eclipse opens the emulator with API 17.) To the extent that your app passes your testing,

the app runs correctly on devices that run API 16 (also known as Android 4.1). What about devices that run other versions of Android? This list provides an explanation:

- *The app's target version is API 16, but the app uses only features that are available in API 8 and earlier:* In that case, you can safely enter the number 8 in the Minimum Required SDK field in Eclipse.

- *The app uses some features available only in API 16 and later, but the app contains workarounds for devices that run API 8:* (The app's code can detect a device's Android version and contains alternative code for different versions.) In that case, you can safely put the number 8 in the Minimum Required SDK field.

- *The app's target version is API 16:* In 2019, someone installs your app on a device running API 99 (code-named Zucchini Bread). Because of backward compatibility, the app runs awkwardly but correctly on the API 99 device. Then the app's target version (API 16) isn't truly the upper limit.

When you select a target version and a minimum SDK version, Android stores these numbers in the project's `AndroidManifest.xml` file. You can see the `AndroidManifest.xml` file in the project's tree in the Package Explorer in Eclipse.

If you mistakenly select a target for which you have no AVD, Eclipse hollers at you when you try to run the project. (Though Eclipse hollers, it also offers to help you create the necessary AVD, so everything turns out just fine.)

For help with creating an AVD, see Chapter 2.

6. Click Next.

As a result, the New Android Application dialog box reappears. (See Figure 4-2 — okay, originality in naming dialog boxes may not be Eclipse's strong suit.)

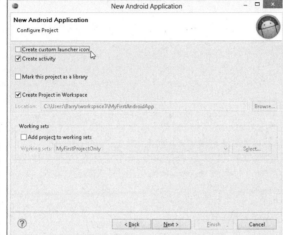

Figure 4-2:
The
second New
Android
Application
dialog box.

7. (Optional) Tweak the settings in the latest incarnation of the New Android Application dialog box.

For a practice app, I recommend deselecting the Create Custom Launcher Icon check box and leaving untouched the other settings in this New Android Application dialog box. In particular, keep the Create Activity option selected.

8. Click Next.

As a result, the Create Activity dialog box appears, as shown in Figure 4-3.

For the truth about activities in Android, see Chapter 5.

9. Click Next again. (In other words, accept the defaults in the Create Activity dialog box.)

The next box in the sequence is the New Blank Activity dialog box, as shown in Figure 4-4.

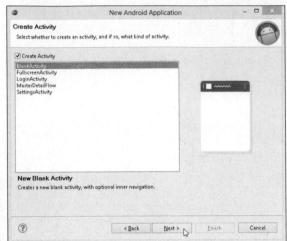

Figure 4-3:
Creating a
new activity.

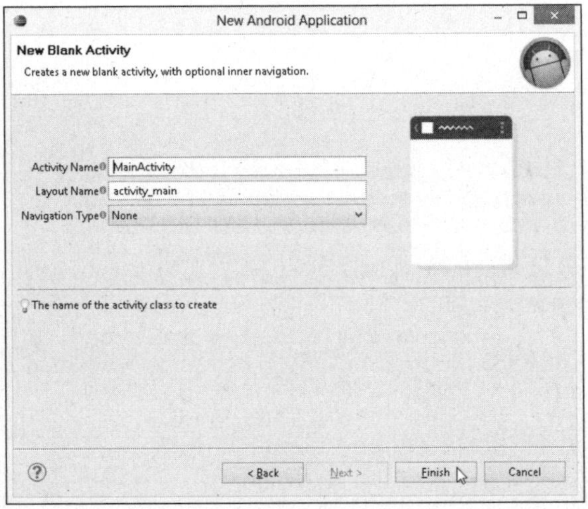

Figure 4-4:
Creating a
blank
activity.

10. **Click Finish. (That is, accept the defaults.)**

As a result, the New Blank Activity dialog box closes, and the Eclipse workbench moves to the foreground. The Package Explorer tree in Eclipse has a new branch. The branch's label is the name of the new project, as shown in Figure 4-5.

Your new Android project

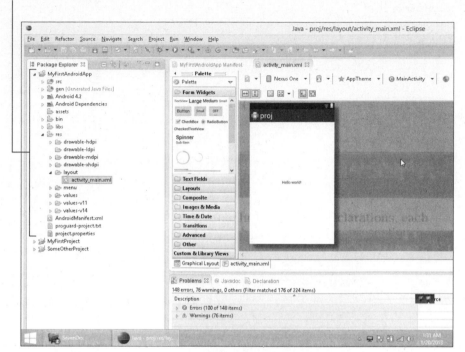

Figure 4-5:
A new
MyFirst
Android
App
branch.

Congratulations — you've created an Android application.

Running your project

To kick your new app's tires and take your app around the block, do the following:

1. **Select the app's branch in the Package Explorer in Eclipse.**

   (Refer to Figure 4-5.)

2. **In the main menu, choose Run➪Run As➪Android Application.**

   As a result, the Console view displays several lines of text. Among them, you might find the phrases Launching a new emulator, Waiting for HOME, and (as shown in Figure 4-6) my personal favorite, Success!

Figure 4-6:
The Console
view
during the
successful
launch of
an app.

Success!

If you don't see the Console view, you have to coax it out of hiding. For details, see Chapter 3.

In the lingo of general app development, a *console* is a text-only window that displays the output of a running program. A console might also accept commands from the user (in this case, the app developer). A single Android run might create several consoles at a time, so the Console view in Eclipse can display several consoles at a time. If the material you see in the Console view in Eclipse is nothing like the text shown in Figure 4-6, the Console view may be displaying the wrong console. To fix this problem, look for a button showing a picture of a computer terminal in the upper-right corner of the Console view, as shown in Figure 4-7. Click the arrow to the right of the button. In the resulting drop-down list, choose Android.

Computer Terminal icon

Figure 4-7:
Choosing a
console.

3. **Wait for the Android emulator to display the Device Locked screen, a Home screen, or an app's screen.**

   First you see the word ANDROID as though it's part of a scene from *The Matrix,* as shown in Figure 4-8. Then you see the word ANDROID in shimmering, silvery letters, as shown in Figure 4-9. Finally, you see the Device Locked screen, a Home screen, or an app's screen, as shown in Figure 4-10.

Figure 4-8: The emulator starts running.

Figure 4-9: Android starts running on the emulator.

4. **I can't overemphasize this point: Wait for the Android emulator to display the Device Locked screen, a Home screen, or an app's screen.**

   The Android emulator takes a long time to start. For example, on my 2 GHz processor with 4GB of RAM, the emulator takes a few minutes to mimic a fully booted Android device. You need lots of patience when you deal with the emulator.

5. **Keep waiting.**

   While you're waiting, you can search the web for the phrase *Android emulator speed up*. Lots of people have posted advice, workarounds, and other hints.

Figure 4-10:
The Device Locked screen in Android 2.3.3 appears.

Oh! I see that the emulator is finally displaying the Device Locked screen. It's time to proceed. . . .

6. **If the emulator displays the Device Locked screen, do whatever you normally do to unlock an Android device.**

Usually, you unlock the device by sliding something from one part of the screen to another.

7. **See the app on the emulator's screen.**

Figure 4-11 shows the running of the Hello World app in Android. (The screen even displays `Hello World!`) Eclipse creates this tiny app when you create a new Android project.

The Hello World app in Android has no widgets for the user to push, and the app doesn't do anything interesting. But the appearance of an app on the Android screen is a good start. Following the steps in this chapter, you can start creating many exciting apps.

Don't close an Android emulator unless you know that you won't be using it for a while. The emulator is fairly reliable after it gets going. (It's sluggish, but reliable.) While the emulator runs, you can modify the Android code and choose Run➪Run As➪Android Application again. When you do, Android reinstalls the app on the running emulator. The process isn't speedy, but you don't have to wait for the emulator to start. (Actually, if you run a different app — an app whose minimum required SDK is higher than the running emulator can handle — Android fires up a second emulator. But in many developer scenarios, jumping between emulators is the exception rather than the rule.)

Figure 4-11:
The Hello
World app
in action.

What if . . .

You try to run your first Android app. If your effort stalls, don't despair. This section has some troubleshooting tips.

Error message: R cannot be resolved

Every Android app has an R.java file. The Android development tools generate this file automatically, so normally you don't have to worry about R.java. Occasionally, the file takes longer than average to be generated. In this case, Eclipse finds references to the R class in the rest of the project's code and complains that the project has no R class. My advice is to wait.

If one minute of waiting doesn't bring good results, follow these steps to double-check the project settings:

1. **Highlight the project in the Package Explorer in Eclipse.**
2. **From the main menu, choose Project.**

   A list of submenu items appears.
3. **Look for a check mark next to the Build Automatically menu subitem.**

4. **If you don't see a check mark, select the Build Automatically subitem to add one.**

   With any luck, the `R.java` file appears almost immediately.

If the project is set to Build Automatically and you still don't have an `R.java` file, try these steps:

1. **Highlight the project in the Package Explorer.**
2. **From the main menu, choose Project.**

   A list of submenu items appears.
3. **In the Clean dialog box in Eclipse, select the project that's giving you trouble along with the Clean Projects Selected Below radio button.**
4. **Click OK.**

Cleaning the project should fix the problem. But if the problem persists, close Eclipse and then restart it. (Eclipse occasionally becomes "confused" and has to be restarted.)

After copying Java code from one Android project to another, you might see the annoying message *Import cannot be resolved* near the top of the program. If so, you might have inadvertently told one project to fetch material from another project's `R.java` file. If the offending line of code is `import` *somethingOrOther*`.R`, try deleting that line of code. Who knows? Your deletion might just fix the problem.

Error message: No compatible targets were found

When you see this message, it probably means that you haven't created an Android Virtual Device (AVD) capable of running your project. If Eclipse offers to help you create a new AVD, accept it. Otherwise, choose Window➪Android Virtual Device Manager to create a new AVD.

For information about Android Virtual Devices, see Chapter 2.

The emulator stalls during start-up

After five minutes or so, you don't see the Device Locked screen or the Android Home screen. Try these solutions:

✔ **Close the emulator and launch the application again. (Or lather, rinse, repeat.)**

   Sometimes, the second or third time's a charm. On rare occasions, my first three attempts fail but my fourth attempt succeeds.

✔ **Start the emulator independently.**

That is, start the emulator without trying to run an Android project. Follow these four steps:

> a. *From the Eclipse main menu, choose Window⇨Android Virtual Device Manager.*
>
> The Android Virtual Device Manager window opens. It contains a list of AVDs that you've already created.
>
> For help creating an AVD, see Chapter 2.
>
> b. *In the Android Virtual Device Manager, select the AVD that you want to start.*
>
> c. *On the right side of the Android Virtual Device Manager, click Start.*
>
> As a result, Eclipse displays the Launch Options dialog box.
>
> d. *In the Launch Options dialog box, click Launch.*
>
> In other words, accept the default options and fire up the emulator.

When, at last, you see the new emulator's Device Locked screen or Home screen, follow Steps 1, 2, 6, and 7 in the earlier section "Running your project."

If you try the tricks in this section but the stubborn Android emulator still doesn't start, visit this book's website (`http://allmycode.com/Java4Android`) for more strategies to try.

✔ **Run the app on a phone, a tablet, or another real Android device.**

Testing a brand-new app on a real device makes me queasy. But the Android sandbox is fairly safe for apps to play in. Besides, apps load quickly and easily on phones and tablets.

For instructions on installing apps to Android devices, see the section "Testing Apps on a Real Device," later in this chapter.

Error message: The user data image is used by another emulator

If you see this message, a tangle involving the emulator prevents Android from doing its job. First try closing and restarting the emulator.

If a simple restart doesn't work, try these steps:

1. **Close the emulator.**

2. **From the main menu in Eclipse, choose Window⇨Android Virtual Device Manager.**

To read about the Android Virtual Device Manager, see Chapter 2.

3. **In the list of virtual devices, select an AVD that's appropriate to the project and click Start.**

4. **In the resulting Launch Options dialog box, select the Wipe User Data check box and click Launch.**

   As a result, Eclipse launches a new copy of the emulator — this time, with a clean slate.

   If you follow the steps in this section but you still see the message User data image is used by another emulator, visit this book's website (http://allmycode.com/Java4Android) for more help with this problem.

Error message: Unknown virtual device name

Android looks for AVDs in the home directory's .android/avd subdirectory, and occasionally the search goes awry. For example, one of my Windows computers lists my home directory on an i drive. My AVDs are in i:\Users\barry\.android\avd. But Android ignores the computer's home directory advice and instead looks in c:\Users\Barry. When Android doesn't find any AVDs, it complains.

You can devise fancy solutions to this problem by using either junctions or symbolic links. But solutions of this kind require special handling of their own. To keep it simple, I copy the contents of my i:\Users\barry\.android directory to c:\Users\barry\.android to fix the problem.

Error message: INSTALL_PARSE_FAILED_ INCONSISTENT_CERTIFICATE

This error message indicates that an app you previously installed conflicts with the app you're trying to install. So, on the emulator screen, navigate to the list of installed applications (which is usually an option on the Settings screen). In the list of applications, delete any apps that you installed previously.

Occasionally, you might have trouble finding previously installed apps from the Settings➪Applications menus in the emulator. If you do, visit this book's website (http://allmycode.com/Java4Android) for a geeky workaround solution.

The app starts, but the emulator displays the Force Close or Wait dialog box

The formal name of the Force Close or Wait dialog box is Application Not Responding (ANR). Android displays the ANR dialog box whenever an app takes too long to do whatever it's supposed to do. When the app runs on a real device (a phone or a tablet), the app shouldn't make Android display the ANR dialog box.

But on a slow emulator, seeing a few Force Close or Wait messages is par for the course. When I see the ANR dialog box in an emulator, I usually select Wait. Within about ten seconds, the dialog box disappears and the app continues to run.

Changes to your app don't appear in the emulator

Your app runs and you want to make a few improvements. So, with the emulator still running, you modify the app's code. But after choosing Run⇨Run As⇨Android Application, the app's behavior in the emulator remains unchanged.

When this happens, something is clogged up. Close and restart the emulator. If necessary, use the Wipe User Data trick that I describe in the earlier section "Error message: The user data image is used by another emulator."

The emulator's screen is too big

Sometimes, the development computer's screen resolution isn't high enough. (Maybe your eyesight isn't what it used to be.) This symptom isn't a deal breaker, but if you can't see the emulator's lower buttons, you can't easily test the app. You can change the development computer's screen resolution, though adjusting the emulator window is less invasive.

To change the emulator window size, follow these steps:

1. **Close the emulator.**

2. **From the Eclipse main menu, choose Window⇨Android Virtual Device Manager.**

3. **In the list of virtual devices, select an AVD that's appropriate to the project and click Start.**

4. **In the resulting Launch Options dialog box, select the Scale Display to Real Size check box.**

5. **Lower the value in the Screen Size field.**

    As you change the Screen Size value, the value in the Scale field changes automatically. The smaller the Scale value, the smaller the emulator appears on the development computer's screen.

6. **Click Launch.**

    As a result, Eclipse launches a new copy of the emulator — this time, with a smaller emulator window.

Testing Apps on a Real Device

You can bypass emulators and test apps on a phone, a tablet, or maybe an Android-enabled trash compactor. To do so, you have to prepare the device, prepare the development computer, and then hook the two together. This section describes the process.

To test an app on a real Android device, follow these steps:

1. **On the Android device, turn on USB debugging.**

   Various Android versions have their own ways of enabling (or disabling) USB debugging. You can poke around for the debugging option on your own device or visit this site for the procedures on some representative Android versions:

   ```
   www.teamandroid.com/2012/06/25/how-to-enable-usb-
             debugging-in-android-phones
   ```

   On my device, I keep USB debugging on all the time. But if you're nervous about security, turn off USB debugging when you aren't using the device to develop apps.

2. **In your project's branch of the Package Explorer, double-click the** `AndroidManifest.xml` **file.**

   Eclipse offers several ways to examine and edit this file.

3. **At the bottom of the Eclipse editor, click the Application tab.**

   Eclipse displays a form like the one shown in Figure 4-12.

4. **In the Debuggable drop-down list, choose True. (Refer to Figure 4-12.)**

   When Debuggable is set to True, Android tools can monitor the run of the app.

   The ability to debug is the ability to hack. Debugging also slows down an app. Never distribute an app to the public with Debuggable set to True.

5. **Choose File⇨Save to store the new** `AndroidManifest.xml` **file.**

6. **Set up the development computer to communicate with the device.**

   - *On Windows:* Visit `http://developer.android.com/sdk/oem-usb.html` to download the device's Windows USB driver. Install the driver on the development computer.

   - *On a Mac:* `/* Do nothing. It just works. */`

Figure 4-12:
The
Application
tab of a
project's
`Android`
`Manfest`
`.xml` file.

7. **Using a USB cable, connect the device to the development computer.**

   For ways to verify that the device is connected to the development computer, visit this book's website at `http://allmycode.com/Java4Android`.

8. **In Eclipse, run the project.**

   A connected device trumps a running emulator. So, if the Android version on the device can handle the project's minimum SDK version, choosing Run⇨Run As⇨Android Application installs the app on the connected device.

Eventually, you'll disconnect the device from the development computer. If you're a Windows user, you may dread reading `Windows can't stop your device because a program is still using it`. To disconnect the device safely, do the following:

1. **Open the Command Prompt window.**

   On Windows 7 or earlier: **Choose Start⇨All Programs⇨Accessories⇨ Command Prompt.**

   On Windows 8: **First press Windows+Q. Then type** Command Prompt **and press Enter.**

2. **In the Command Prompt window, navigate to the** `ANDROID_HOME/platform-tools` **directory.**

For example, if the `ANDROID_HOME` directory is

```
C:\Users\yourName\adt-bundle-windows-x86_64\sdk
```

type this command:

```
cd C:\Users\yourName\adt-bundle-windows-x86_64\sdk\platform-tools
```

3. **In the Command Prompt window, type** adb kill-server **and then press Enter.**

   The `adb kill-server` command stops communication between the development computer and any Android devices, real or virtual. In particular,

   - The development computer no longer talks to the device at the end of the USB cable.

   - The development computer no longer talks to any emulators it's running.

   After issuing the `adb kill-server` command, you see the friendly `Safe to Remove Hardware` message.

4. **Unplug the Android device from the development computer.**

   After unplugging the device, you might want to reestablish communication between the development computer and any emulators you're running. If so, follow Step 5.

5. **In the Command Prompt window, type** adb start-server **and then press Enter.**

Examining an Android App

In Figure 4-13, the Package Explorer in Eclipse shows the structure of a newly created Android project. Each branch of the tree represents a file or a folder, and if you expand all branches of the tree, you see even more files and folders. Why so many files and folders in an Android project? This section provides answers.

The src directory

The `src` directory contains the project's Java source code. Files in this directory have names such as `MainActivity.java`, `MyService.java`, `DatabaseHelper.java`, and `MoreStuff.java`.

Figure 4-13:
The
Package
Explorer
displays
an Android
app.

You can cram hundreds of Java files into a project's `src` directory. But when you create a new project, Android typically creates only one file for you. Earlier in this chapter, I accepted the default name `MainActivity` so that Android creates a file named `MainActivity.java`. (Refer to Figure 4-4.)

An Android activity is one "screenful" of components. For more information about Android activities, see Chapter 5.

Most of the material in this book is about files in the `src` directory. In this chapter, I focus on the other directories.

The res directory

A project's `res` directory contains resources for use by the Android application. In Figure 4-13, you see that `res` has a bunch of subdirectories: four `drawable` directories, a `layout` directory, a `menu` directory, and three `values` directories.

The drawable subdirectories

The `drawable` directories contain images, shapes, and other elements.

Each `drawable` directory applies to certain screen resolutions. For example, in the name `drawable-hdpi`, the letters `hdpi` stand for *h*igh number of *d*ots *p*er *i*nch. Files in the `drawable-hdpi` directory apply to devices whose resolutions are (roughly) between 180 and 280 dots per inch.

For more information about Android screen resolutions, visit `http://developer.android.com/guide/practices/screens_support.html`.

In Figure 4-13, the `drawable-hdpi` directory contains one file named `ic_launcher.png`. This file describes the image that appears on the app's icon on the Android launcher screen.

The values subdirectory

An app's `res/values` directory contains a file named `strings.xml`. (Refer to Figure 4-13.) Listing 4-1 shows the code in a simple `strings.xml` file.

Listing 4-1:   A Small strings.xml File

```
<?xml version="1.0" encoding="utf-8"?>
<resources>

    <string name="app_name">My First Android App</string>
    <string name="hello_world">Hello world!</string>
    <string name="menu_settings">Settings</string>

</resources>
```

The code in Listing 4-1 is XML code. For information about XML code, see the "All about XML files" sidebar, later in this chapter.

In the `strings.xml` file, you collect all the words, phrases, and sentences that the app's user might see. You lump together phrases such as *Hello world!* and *My First Android App* so that someone can translate them all into different languages. With all those phrases collected in the `strings.xml` file, a translator doesn't have to poke around to find phrases in the Java code. (Poking around in the code in any real programming language can be dangerous because program code is intricate, and it can be brittle. Believe me: If I were a translator, I'd much rather translate the phrases in a `strings.xml` file.)

Listing 4-1 describes a `"hello_world"` string containing the characters *Hello World!* So in the app's Java code, you refer to the words *Hello world!* by typing `R.string.hello_world`. To refer to the words *Hello world!* in another XML file (such as the one in Listing 4-2), you type `"@string/hello_world"`. Either way, the text `R.string.hello_world` or the text `"@string/hello_world"` stands for the words *Hello world!* in Listing 4-1.

The use of `strings.xml` files helps with *localization,* which, in the tech world, is what you do to adapt an app to a culture's local language and customs. To localize the app for French-speaking users, for example, you create an additional folder named `values-fr`. You add this folder to the tree shown in Figure 4-13. Inside the `values-fr` folder, you create a second `strings.xml` file, and the new `strings.xml` file contains a line such as this one:

```
<string name="hello_world">Bonjour tout le monde!</string>
```

For Romanian, you create a `values-ro` directory, containing a `strings.xml` file with this line:

```
<string name="hello_world">Salut lume!</string>
```

When Android sees either `R.string.hello_world` or `"@string/hello_world"` in the code, Android determines the user's country of origin and automatically displays the correct translation. This localization happens with no further effort on your part.

The layout subdirectory

The `layout` directory contains descriptions of the activities' screens.

A minimal app's `res/layout` directory contains an XML file describing an activity's screen. (Refer to the `activity_main.xml` branch in Figure 4-13.) Listing 4-2 shows the code in the simple `activity_main.xml` file.

Listing 4-2: A Small Layout File

```
<RelativeLayout xmlns:android=
        "http://schemas.android.com/apk/res/android"
    xmlns:tools="http://schemas.android.com/tools"
    android:layout_width="match_parent"
    android:layout_height="match_parent"
    tools:context=".MainActivity" >

    <TextView
        android:layout_width="wrap_content"
        android:layout_height="wrap_content"
        android:layout_centerHorizontal="true"
        android:layout_centerVertical="true"
        android:text="@string/hello_world" />

</RelativeLayout>
```

The code in Listing 4-2 specifies that the layout of the app's activity is a `RelativeLayout` (whatever that means) and, centered inside the `RelativeLayout`, you have a `TextView`. This `TextView` thingy is a little label containing the words *Hello world!* (Refer to Figure 4-11.)

All about XML files

Every Android app consists of some Java code, some XML documents, and some other information. (The acronym *XML* stands for eXtensible Markup Language.) You might already be familiar with HTML documents — the bread and butter of the World Wide Web.

Listings 4-1 and 4-2 contain XML documents. Like an HTML document, every XML document consists of tags (angle-bracketed descriptions of various pieces of information). But unlike an HTML document, an XML document doesn't necessarily describe a displayable page.

Here are some facts about XML code:

✔ **A *tag* consists of text surrounded by angle brackets.**

For example, the code in Listing 4-2 consists of three tags: The first tag is the `<RelativeLayout ... >` tag, the second tag is the `<Text View ... />` tag, and the third tag is the `</RelativeLayout>` tag.

✔ **An XML document may have three different kinds of tags: start tags, empty element tags, and end tags.**

A *start tag* begins with an open angle bracket and a name. A start tag's last character is a closing angle bracket.

The first tag in Listing 4-2 (the `<RelativeLayout ... >` tag on lines 1–6) is a start tag. Its name is `RelativeLayout`.

An *empty element tag* begins with an open angle bracket followed by a name. An empty element tag's last two characters are a forward slash followed by a closing angle bracket.

The second tag in Listing 4-2 (the `<TextView ... />` tag on lines 8–13 in the listing) is an empty element tag. Its name is `TextView`.

An *end tag* begins with an open angle bracket followed by a forward slash and a name. An end tag's last character is a closing angle bracket.

The third tag in Listing 4-2 (the `</RelativeLayout>` tag on the last line of the listing) is an end tag. Its name is `RelativeLayout`.

✔ **An XML *element* either has both a start tag and an end tag, or it has an empty element tag.**

In Listing 4-2, the document's `RelativeLayout` element has both a start tag and an end tag. (Both the start and end tags have the same name, `RelativeLayout`, so the name of the entire element is `RelativeLayout`.)

In Listing 4-2, the document's `TextView` element has only one tag: an empty element tag.

✔ **Elements are either nested inside one another or have no overlap.**

For example, in the following code, a `TableLayout` element contains two `TableRow` elements:

```
<TableLayout xmlns:android=
    "http://schemas.
android.com/apk/res/
android"
    android:layout_
width="fill_parent"
    android:layout_
height="fill_parent" >

<TableRow>

 <TextView
     android:layout_
width="wrap_content"
     android:layout_
height="wrap_content"
```

```
            android:text="@
    string/name" />

    </TableRow>

    <TableRow>

      <TextView
          android:layout_
    width="wrap_content"
          android:layout_
    height="wrap_content"
          android:text="@
    string/address" />

    </TableRow>

    </TableLayout>
```

The preceding code works because the first `TableRow` ends before the second `TableRow` begins. But the following XML code is illegal:

```
<!-- The following code isn't
    legal XML code. -->
<TableRow>

      <TextView
          android:layout_
    width="wrap_content"
          android:layout_
    height="wrap_content"
          android:text="@
    string/name" />
<TableRow>

    </TableRow>

      <TextView
          android:layout_
    width="wrap_content"
          android:layout_
    height="wrap_content"
          android:text="@
    string/address" />
    </TableRow>
```

With two start tags followed by two end tags, this new XML code doesn't pass muster.

✔ **Each XML document contains a** *root element* — **one element in which all other elements are nested.**

In Listing 4-2, the root element is the `RelativeLayout` element. The listing's only other element (the `TextView` element) is nested inside that `RelativeLayout` element.

✔ **Different XML documents use different element names.**

In every HTML document, the `<br />` element stands for *line break*. But in XML, the names `RelativeLayout` and `TextView` are particular to Android layout documents. And the names `portfolio` and `trade` are particular to financial product XML (`FpML`) documents. The names `prompt` and `phoneme` are peculiar to voice XML (`VoiceXML`). Each kind of document has its own list of element names.

✔ **The text in an XML document is case-sensitive.**

For example, if you change `RelativeLayout` to `relativelayout` in Listing 4-2, the app won't run.

✔ **Start tags and empty element tags may contain attributes.**

An *attribute* is a name-value pair. Each attribute has the form *name="value"*. The quotation marks around the *value* are required.

In Listing 4-2, the start tag (`RelativeLayout`) has five attributes, and the empty element tag (`TextView`) has five of its own attributes. For example, in the `TextView` empty element tag, the text `android:layout_width="wrap_content"` is the first attribute. This attribute has the name `android:layout_width` and the value `"wrap_content"`.

(continued)

(continued)

✔ **A non-empty XML element may contain content.**

For example, in the element `<string name="hello_world">Hello` world!`</string>` in Listing 4-1, the content `Hello world!` is sandwiched between the start tag (`<string name="hello_world">`) and the end tag (`</string>`).

The gen directory

The directory name `gen` stands for *gen*erated. The `gen` directory contains `R.java`. Listing 4-3 shows that part of the `R.java` file generated for you when you create a brand-new project.

Listing 4-3: Don't Even Look at This File

```
/* AUTO-GENERATED FILE.  DO NOT MODIFY.
 *
 * This class was automatically generated by the
 * aapt tool from the resource data it found.  It
 * should not be modified by hand.
 */

package com.example.myfirstandroidapp;

public final class R {
    public static final class attr {
    }
    public static final class drawable {
        public static final int ic_launcher=0x7f020000;
    }
    public static final class id {
        public static final int menu_settings=0x7f070000;
    }
    public static final class layout {
        public static final int activity_main=0x7f030000;
    }
    public static final class menu {
        public static final int activity_main=0x7f060000;
    }
    public static final class string {
        public static final int app_name=0x7f040000;
        public static final int hello_world=0x7f040001;
        public static final int menu_settings=0x7f040002;
    }
    // ... (There's more!)
```

The values in R.java are the jumping-off points for the resource management mechanism in Android. Android uses these numbers for quick and easy loading of the items you store in the res directory.

You can't make changes to the R.java file. Long after the creation of a project, Android continues to monitor (and, if necessary, update) the contents of the R.java file. If you delete R.java, Android re-creates the file. If you edit R.java, Android undoes the edit. If you answer Yes in the dialog box named Do You Really Want to Edit This File?, Eclipse accepts the change — but immediately afterward, Android clobbers your change.

The Android 4.2 branch

The tree shown in Figure 4-13 has an Android 4.2 branch, but it isn't a directory on the computer's file system. In the Package Explorer view, the Android 4.2 branch (or Android 3.0 branch or Android *whatever* branch) reminds you that the project includes prewritten Android code (the Android API).

A .jar file is a compressed archive containing a useful bunch of Java classes. In fact, a .jar file is a .zip archive. You can open any .jar file by using WinZip or StuffIt Expander or the operating system's built-in unzipping utility. (You may or may not have to change the filename from *whatever*.jar to *whatever*.zip.) Anyway, an android.jar file contains prewritten Android code (the Android API) for a particular version of Android. In Figure 4-13, a Package Explorer branch reminds you that your project contains a reference to another location on the hard drive (to one containing the .jar file for Android 4.2).

R.java and the legend of the two vaudevillians

According to legend, two friends named Herkimer and Jake once worked together for 50 years as a comedy team in vaudeville. Year after year, they practiced and refined their act, adding a new joke here and removing an old joke there. As time went on, they adopted a kind of shorthand to refer to the jokes in their act. "Let's move Joke Number 35 to the end of the first song," said Herkimer. And Jake responded, "I'd rather do Joke Number 119 when the song ends."

Eventually, both Herkimer and Jake retired to an old-age home. Day after day, they sat side by side in the TV room, staring at reruns of Milton Berle's show and *The Ed Sullivan Show.* Occasionally, something on the screen would remind Herkimer of one the team's old jokes. "Fifty-one," Herkimer would call out. And upon hearing this number, Jake would start laughing hysterically.

(continued)

(continued)

Many elements of the code in an Android app are numbered. For example, an item on the screen can be in one of three states: 0, 4, or 8. To help you (the developer) remember what the numbers mean, the creators of Android provide synonyms for each number. So rather than write 0 in your Java code, you can write View.VISIBLE. An item in this state is in plain sight on the user's screen. On the other hand, an item in state 4 (with the synonym View.INVISIBLE) occupies space on the screen but doesn't light up any pixels. The user doesn't see this item, but its spooky presence might force other items to move one way or another. Finally, an item in state 8 (with the synonym View.GONE) has no presence on the screen. This item might have once appeared in the center of the screen, and it might later appear again on the screen. But now, in the View.GONE state, this item has no influence on the layout of the screen.

When dealing with state numbers, and with other code numbers, the creators of Java use hexadecimal notation. In Java, numbers starting with 0x are hexadecimal (base 16) numbers. For example, the number 0x00000004 stands for 4×16^0 — which (in the conventional base 10 system) is plain old 4. And the number 0x00000024 stands for $2 \times 16^1 + 4 \times 16^0$ — which (in base 10) is 36. Finally, the number 0x0000001b stands for $1 \times 16^1 + 11 \times 16^0$ — which (in base 10) is 27. As an Android developer, I seldom have to convert a hexadecimal value into its conventional base 10 representation. So don't worry about doing it.

Anyway, the app you see in Figure 4-11 displays the text *Hello world!* When you create an Android app, you seldom put actual words such as "Hello World!" in the app's Java code. Instead, you refer to the words indirectly. You give the words *Hello World!* a number, and you put that number in the Java code. More precisely, these things happen:

- ✔ You have the line `<string name="hello_world">Hello world!</string>` in the strings.xml file, which is in the values subdirectory of the project's res directory.

- ✔ Eclipse generates a code number, such as 0x7f040001. (Refer to Listing 4-3.)

- ✔ Android associates the number 0x7f040001 with the synonym R.string.hello_world by having the text hello_world=0x7f040001 in the string portion of the R.java file. (Refer to Listing 4-3).

- ✔ You have the text R.string.hello_world in the Java code. Alternatively, you have the text @string/hello_world in the activity_main.xml file.

This indirect way to refer to the words *Hello world!* might seem to be needlessly complicated. But the indirectness is exactly what helps you create apps that appeal to people all over the world. Look at the discussion of localization in the earlier section "The res directory." By creating a new values-fr directory, you allow a user's device to automatically localize to another language, and to display *Bonjour tout le monde!* or *Hallo Welt!* or *Hej Verden!* instead of the Anglocentric *Hello world!* phrase.

The android.jar file contains code grouped into Java packages, and each package contains Java classes. Figures 4-14 and 4-15 show you the tip of the android.jar iceberg. The android.jar file contains classes specific to Android and classes that simply help Java do its job. Figure 4-14 shows some Android-specific packages in android.jar. Figure 4-15 displays some general-purpose Java packages in the android.jar file.

Figure 4-14:
Some pack-
ages and
classes in
android
.jar.

Figure 4-15:
The
android
.jar file
includes
general-
purpose
Java
packages.

The AndroidManifest.xml file

If you followed the instructions earlier in this chapter, you've already
tinkered with an `AndroidMaifest.xml` file. Keep in mind that every
Android app has an `AndroidManifest.xml` file. The `AndroidManifest.
xml` file provides information that a device needs in order to run the

app. The `AndroidManifest.xml` file in Listing 4-4 stores some options that you choose when you create a brand-new Android project. For example, the listing contains the package name, the minimum required SDK (the `android:minSdkVersion` attribute), and the target SDK (the `android:targetSdkVersion` attribute).

Listing 4-4:   An AndroidManifest.xml File

```xml
<?xml version="1.0" encoding="utf-8"?>
<manifest
  xmlns:android=
    "http://schemas.android.com/apk/res/android"
  package="com.example.myfirstandroidapp"
  android:versionCode="1"
  android:versionName="1.0" >

  <uses-sdk
    android:minSdkVersion="8"
    android:targetSdkVersion="16" />

  <application
    android:allowBackup="true"
    android:icon="@drawable/ic_launcher"
    android:label="@string/app_name"
    android:theme="@style/AppTheme" >
    <activity
      android:name=
        "com.example.myfirstandroidapp.MainActivity"
      android:label="@string/app_name" >
      <intent-filter>
        <action android:name=
          "android.intent.action.MAIN" />

        <category android:name=
          "android.intent.category.LAUNCHER" />
      </intent-filter>
    </activity>
  </application>

</manifest>
```

For my money, the most important items in an `AndroidManifest.xml` file are the `activity` elements. The code in Listing 4-4 has only one `activity` element. But a single Android app can have many activities, and each activity must have its own `activity` element in the app's `AndroidManifest.xml` file.

For the scoop on Android activities, see Chapter 5.

An Android activity is one "screenful" of components. (Refer to Chapter 5 for more about Android activities.) If you add an activity's Java code to an Android application, you must also add an `activity` element to the application's `AndroidManifest.xml` file. If you forget to add an `activity` element, you see an `ActivityNotFoundException` when you try to run the application. (Believe me. I've made this mistake many, many times.)

Within an `activity` element, an `intent-filter` element describes the kinds of duties that this activity can fulfill for apps on the same device. (Intent filters are complicated, so in this book I don't dare open that whole can of worms.) But to give you an idea, the action `android.intent.action.MAIN` indicates that this activity's code can be the starting point of an app's execution. And the category `android.intent.category.LAUNCHER` indicates that this activity's icon can appear on the device's Apps screen.

Part II
Writing Your Own
Java Programs

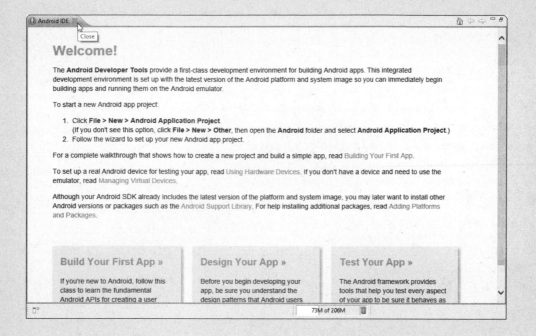

In this part . . .

- ✔ Writing your first Java programs
- ✔ Assembling Java's building blocks
- ✔ Changing course as your program runs

Chapter 5

An Ode to Code

- -

In This Chapter

▶ Reading the statements in a basic Java program

▶ Writing a Java console app

▶ Understanding the boilerplate Android activity

- -

"Hello, hello, hello, . . . hello!"

—*The Three Stooges in* Dizzy Detectives *and other short films*

To most people, the words *Hello World* form a friendly (or even sugary) phrase. Is *Hello World* a song title? Is it the cheery slogan of a radio deejay? Maybe so. But to computer programmers, the phrase *Hello World* has a special meaning.

A *Hello World app* is the simplest program that can run in a particular programming language or on a particular platform. Authors create Hello World apps to show people how to start writing code for particular systems.

To help you get started with Java and Android, I devote this chapter to explaining a few Hello World programs. The programs don't do much. (In fact, you might argue that they don't do anything.) But they introduce some basic Java concepts.

To see Hello World apps for more than 450 different programming languages, visit www.roesler-ac.de/wolfram/hello.htm.

Examining a Standard Oracle Java Program

Listing 5-1 is a copy of the example in Chapter 3.

Listing 5-1:   A Small Java Program

```
package org.allyourcode.myfirstproject;

public class MyFirstJavaClass {

    /**
     * @param args
     */
    public static void main(String[] args) {
        javax.swing.JOptionPane.showMessageDialog
                                   (null, "Hello");
    }

}
```

When you run the program in Listing 5-1, the computer displays the word *Hello* in a dialog box, as shown in Figure 5-1. Now, I admit that writing and running a Java program just to make `Hello` appear on a computer screen is a lot of work, but every endeavor has to start somewhere.

Figure 5-1: Running the program in Listing 5-1.

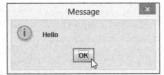

Figure 5-2 describes the meaning of the code in Listing 5-1.

The next several sections present, explain, analyze, dissect, and otherwise demystify the Java program shown in Listing 5-1.

> Inside of a package named
> `org.allyourcode.myfirstproject...`

> ...you create a class named `MyFirstJavaClass`
> And inside of `MyFirstJavaClass`...

```
package org.allyourcode.myfirstproject;

public class MyFirstJavaClass {

    /**
     * @param args
     */
    public static void main (String[] args) {
      javax.swing.JOptionPane.showMessageDialog
                                 (null, "Hello");

    }

}
```

> ...you create a list of instructions* named `main`.
> And inside that `main` list of instructions...

> ...you tell Java to show a dialog box
> containing the word _Hello_.

Figure 5-2:
What you
· do in
Listing 5-1.

* By the way, a list of instructions (such as
the list named `main`) is called a _method_.

The Java class

Java is an object-oriented programming language. As a Java developer,
your primary goal is to describe classes and objects. A _class_ is a kind of
category, like the category of all customers, the category of all accounts,
the category of all geometric shapes, or, less concretely, the category of all
`MyFirstJavaClass` elements, as shown in Listing 5-1. Just as the listing
contains the words `class MyFirstJavaClass`, another piece of code to
describe accounts might contain the words `class Account`. The `class`
`Account` code would describe what it means to be (for example) one of
several million bank accounts.

The previous paragraph contains a brief description of what it means to be a
class. For a more detailed description, see Chapter 9.

You may know what js meant by the phrases "the category of all customers"
and "the category of all geometric shapes," but you may wonder what "the
category of all `MyFirstJavaClass` things" means or in what sense a computer
program (such as the program in Listing 5-1) is a category. Here's my answer
(which, I admit, is somewhat evasive): A Java program gets to be a "class" for
esoteric, technical reasons and not because thinking of a Java program as a
category always makes perfect sense. Sorry about that.

Except for the first line, the entire program In Listing 5-1 is a class. When I create a program like this one, I get to make up a name for my new class. In the listing, I choose the name `MyFirstJavaClass`. That's why the code starts with `class MyFirstJavaClass`, as shown in Figure 5-3.

```
                    The package declaration
                              ↓
package org.allyourcode.myfirstproject;

public class MyFirstJavaClass {

  /**
   * @param args
   */
  public static void main (String[] args) {
    javax.swing.JOptionPane.showMessageDialog
                              (null, "Hello");

  }

}

The class MyFirstJavaClass
```

Figure 5-3:
A simple
Java
program
is a class.

The code inside the larger box in Figure 5-3 is, to be painfully correct, the *declaration* of a class. (This code is a *class declaration*.) I'm being slightly imprecise when I write in the figure that this code *is* a class. In reality, this code *describes* a class.

The declaration of a class has two parts: The first part is the *header,* and the rest — the part surrounded by curly braces, or {} —is the *class body,* as shown in Figure 5-4.

The word `class` is a Java *keyword*. No matter who writes a Java program, `class` is always used in the same way. On the other hand, `MyFirstJava Class` in Listing 5-1 is an *identifier* — a name for something (that is, a name that identifies something). The word `MyFirstJavaClass`, which I made up while I was writing Chapter 3, is the name of a particular class — the class that I'm creating by writing this program.

In Listing 5-1, the words `package`, `public`, `static`, and `void` are also Java keywords. No matter who writes a Java program, `package` and `class` and the other keywords always have the same meaning. For more jabber about keywords and identifiers, see the nearby sidebar, "Words, words, words."

The class header

```
package│org.allyourcode.myfirstproject;

public class MyFirstJavaClass │{

    /**
     * @param args
     */
    public static void main (String[] args) {
        javax.swing.JOptionPane.showMessageDialog
                                    (null, "Hello");

    }

}
```

Figure 5-4:
A class declaration's header and body.

The class body

To find out what the words `public`, `static`, and `void` mean, see Chapters 9 and 10.

tHE jAVA PROGRAMMING LANGUAGE IS cASe-sEnsITiVE. FOR EXAMPLE, iF YOU CHANGE A lowercase LETTER IN A WORD TO UPPERCASE OR CHANGE AN UPPERCASE WORD TO lowercase, YOU CHANGE THE WORD'S MEANING AND CAN EVEN MAKE THE WORD MEANINGLESS. iN THE FIRST LINE OF lISTING 5-1, FOR EXAMPLE, IF YOU TRIED TO REPLACE `class` WITH `Class`, THE WHOLE PROGRAM WOULD STOP WORKING.

The same holds true, to some extent, for the name of a file containing a particular class. For example, the name of the class in Listing 5-1 is `MyFirstJavaClass`, with 4 uppercase letters and 12 lowercase letters. So the code in the listing belongs in a file named `MyFirstJavaClass.java`, with exactly 4 uppercase letters and 12 lowercase letters in front of `.java`.

The names of classes

I'm known by several different names. My first name, used for informal conversation, is Barry. A longer name, used on this book's cover, is Barry Burd. The legal name that I use on tax forms is Barry A. Burd, and my passport (the most official document I own) sports the name Barry Abram Burd.

In the same way, elements in a Java program have several different names. For example, the class that's created in Listing 5-1 has the name `MyFirstJavaClass`. This is the class's *simple name* because, well, it's simple and it's a name.

Words, words, words

The Java language uses two kinds of words: keywords and identifiers. You can tell which words are keywords because Java has only 50 of them. Here's the complete list:

abstract	continue	for	new	switch
assert	default	goto	package	synchronized
boolean	do	if	private	this
break	double	implements	protected	throw
byte	else	import	public	throws
case	enum	instanceof	return	transient
catch	extends	int	short	try
char	final	interface	static	void
class	finally	long	strictfp	volatile
const	float	native	super	while

As a rule, a *keyword* is a word whose meaning never changes (from one Java program to another). For example, in English, you can't change the meaning of the word *if*. It doesn't make sense to say, "I think that I shall never *if* / A poem lovely as a riff." The same concept holds true in a Java program: You can type `if (x > 5)` to mean "If x is greater than 5," but when you type `if (x > if)`, the computer complains that the code doesn't make sense.

In Listing 5-1, the words `package`, `public`, `class`, `static`, and `void` are keywords. Almost every other word in that listing is an *identifier,* which is generally a name for something. The identifiers in the listing include the package name `org.allyourcode.myfirstproject`, the class name `MyFirstJavaClass`, and a bunch of other words.

In programming lingo, words such as *Wednesday, Barry,* and *university* in the following sentence are identifiers, and the other words (*If, it's, is,* and *at*) are keywords:

> *If it's Wednesday, Barry is at the university.*

(I'm undecided about the role of the word *the*. You can worry about it if you want.)

As in English and most other spoken languages, the names of items are reusable. For example, a recent web search turns up four people in the United States named Barry Burd (with the same uncommon spelling). You can even reuse well-known names. (A fellow student at Temple University had the name *John Wayne*, and in the 1980s two different textbooks were named *Pascalgorithms*.) The Android API has a prewritten class named `Activity`, but that doesn't stop you from defining another meaning for the name `Activity`.

Of course, having duplicate names can lead to trouble, so intentionally reusing a well-known name is generally a bad idea. (If you create your own thing named `Activity`, you'll find it difficult to refer to the prewritten `Activity` class in Android. As for my fellow Temple University student, everyone laughed when the teacher called roll.)

Listing 5-1 begins with the line `package org.allyourcode.myfirst project`. The first line is a *package declaration*. Because of this declaration, the newly created `MyFirstJavaClass` is inside a package named `org. allyourcode.myfirstproject`. So `org.allyourcode.myfirst project.MyFirstJavaClass` is the class's *fully qualified name*.

If you're sitting with me in my living room, you probably call me Barry. But if you've never met me and you're looking for me in a crowd of a thousand people, you probably call out the name Barry Burd. In the same way, the choice between a class's simple name and its fully qualified name depends on the context. For more information, see the later section "An import declaration."

Why Java methods are like meals at a restaurant

I'm a fly on the wall at Mom's Restaurant in a small town along Interstate 80. I see everything that goes on at Mom's: Mom toils year after year, fighting against the influx of high-volume, low-quality restaurant chains while the old-timers remain faithful to Mom's menu.

I see you walking into Mom's. Look — you're handing Mom a job application. You're probably a decent cook. If you get the job, you'll get carefully typed copies of every one of the restaurant's recipes. Here's one:

> Scrambled eggs (serves 2)
>
> 5 large eggs, beaten
>
> ¼ cup 2% milk
>
> 1 cup shredded mozzarella
>
> Salt and pepper to taste
>
> A pinch of garlic powder

In a medium bowl, combine eggs and milk. Whisk until the mixture is smooth, and pour into preheated frying pan. Cook on medium heat, stirring the mixture frequently with a spatula. Cook for 2 to 3 minutes or until eggs are about halfway cooked. Add salt, pepper, and garlic powder. Add cheese a little at a time, and continue stirring. Cook for another 2 to 3 minutes. Serve.

Before your first day at work, Mom sends you home to study her recipes. But she sternly warns you not to practice cooking. "Save all your energy for your first day," she says.

On your first day, you don an apron. Mom rotates the sign on the front door so that the word *Open* faces the street. You sit quietly by the stove, tapping four fingers in round-robin fashion. Mom sits by the cash register, trying to look nonchalant. (After 25 years in business, she still worries that the morning regulars won't show up.)

At last! Here comes Joe the barber. Joe orders the breakfast special with two scrambled eggs.

What does Mom's Restaurant have to do with Java?

When you drill down inside the code of a Java class, you find these two important elements:

- ✔ **Method declaration:** The "recipe"

  "If anyone ever asks, here's how to make scrambled eggs."
- ✔ **Method call:** The "customer's order"

  Joe says, "I'll have the breakfast special with two scrambled eggs." It's time for you to follow the recipe.

Almost every computer programming language has elements akin to Java's methods. If you've worked with other languages, you may recall terms like *subprogram*, *procedure*, *function*, *subroutine*, *subprocedure*, or PERFORM *statement*. Whatever you call a *method* in your favorite programming language, it's a bunch of instructions, collected in one place and waiting to be executed.

Method declaration

A *method declaration* is a plan describing the steps that Java will take if and when the method is called into action. A *method call* is one of those calls to action. As a Java developer, you write both method declarations and method calls. Figure 5-5 shows you the method declaration and the method call from Listing 5-1.

If I'm being lazy, I refer to the code in the outer box in Figure 5-5 as a method. If I'm not being lazy, I refer to it as a method declaration.

A method declaration is a list of instructions: "Do this, then do that, and then do this other thing." The declaration in Listing 5-1 (and in Figure 5-5) contains a single instruction.

To top it all off, each method has a name. In Listing 5-1, the method declaration's name is main. The other words — such as public, static, and void — aren't parts of the method declaration's name.

```
package org.allyourcode.myfirstproject;

public class MyFirstJavaClass {

    /**
     * @param args                          The main method's declaration
     */
    public static void main(String[] args) {

        javax.swing.JOptionPane.showMessageDialog
                                (null, "Hello");

    }

}
```

Figure 5-5:
A method
declaration
and a
method call.

The single instruction inside the main method.
This instruction is a call to another method (to the
javax.swing.JOptionPane.showMessageDialog method).

The words public, static, and void are *modifiers* (similar to adjectives, in the English language), For more information about modifiers, see Chapters 9 and 10.

A method declaration has two parts: the *method header* (the first line) and the *method body* (the rest of it, which is the part surrounded by {} — curly braces), as shown in Figure 5-6.

Method call

A method *call* includes the name of the method being called, followed by some text in parentheses. So the code in Listing 5-1 contains a single method call:

```
javax.swing.JOptionPane.showMessageDialog
                        (null, "Hello")
```

In this code, javax.swing.JOptionPane.showMessageDialog is the name of a method, and null, "Hello" is the text in parentheses.

A Java instruction typically ends with a semicolon, so the following is a complete Java instruction:

```
javax.swing.JOptionPane.showMessageDialog
                        (null, "Hello");
```

```
package org.allyourcode.myfirstproject;

public class MyFirstJavaClass {

    /**
     * @param args
     */

    public static void main (String[] args) {

        javax.swing.JOptionPane.showMessageDialog
                                (null, "Hello");

    }

}
```

The main method's header

Figure 5-6:
A method
header and
a method
body.

The main method (or more precisely, the main method's declaration)

The main method's body

This instruction tells the computer to execute whatever statements are inside the `javax.swing.JOptionPane.showMessageDialog` method declaration.

Another term for *Java instruction* is *Java statement*, or just *statement*.

The names of methods

Like many elements in Java, a method has several names, ranging from the shortest name to the longest name and with names in the middle. For example, the code in Listing 5-1 calls a method whose simple name is `showMessageDialog`.

In Java, each method lives inside a class, and `showMessageDialog` lives inside the API's `JOptionPane` class. So a longer name for the `showMessageDialog` method is `JOptionPane.showMessageDialog`.

A *package* in Java is a collection of classes. The `JOptionPane` class is part of an API package named `javax.swing`. So the `showMessageDialog` method's fully qualified name is `javax.swing.JOptionPane.show MessageDialog`. Which version of a method's name you use in the code depends on the context.

For more info on choosing between simple names and fully qualified names, see Chapter 9.

In Java, a package contains classes, and a class contains methods. (A class might contain other elements, too, but I tell you that story in Chapters 9 and 11.) A class's fully qualified name includes a package name, followed by the class's simple name. A method's fully qualified name includes a package name, followed by a class's simple name, followed by the method's simple name. To separate one part of a name from another, you use a period (or "dot").

Method parameters

In Listing 5-1, this call displays a dialog box:

```
javax.swing.JOptionPane.showMessageDialog
                        (null, "Hello");
```

The dialog box has the word *Message* in its title bar and an *i* icon on its face. (The letter *i* stands for *information*.) Why do you see the *Message* title and the *i* icon? For a clue, notice the method call's two parameters: `null` and `"Hello"`.

The effect of the values `null` and `"Hello"` depends entirely on the instructions inside the `showMessageDialog` method's declaration. You can read these instructions, if you want, because the entire Java API code is available for viewing — but you probably don't want to read the 2,600 lines of Java code in the `JOptionPane` class. (I'm sure you'd rather read the *CliffsNotes* version.)

Here's a brief description of the effect of the values `null` and `"Hello"` in the `showMessageDialog` call's parameter list:

✔ **In Java, the value `null` stands for "nothing."**

In particular, the first parameter `null` in a call to `showMessageDialog` indicates that the dialog box doesn't initially appear inside any other window. That is, the dialog box can appear anywhere on the computer screen. (The dialog box appears inside of "nothing" in particular on the screen.)

✔ **In Java, double quotation marks denote a string of characters.**

The second `"Hello"` parameter tells the `showMessageDialog` method to display the characters *Hello* on the face of the dialog box.

Even without my description of the `showMessageDialog` method's parameters, you can avoid reading the 2,600 lines of Java API code. Instead, you can examine the indispensable Java documentation pages. You can find these documentation pages by visiting

```
www.oracle.com/technetwork/java/javase/documentation
```

The main method in a standard Java program

Figure 5-7 shows a copy of the code from Listing 5-1 with arrows indicating what happens when the computer runs the code. The bulk of the code contains the declaration of a method named `main`.

Like any Java method, the `main` method is a recipe:

```
How to make scrambled eggs:
   Combine eggs and milk
   Whisk until smooth
   Pour into preheated frying pan
   Cook for 2 to 3 minutes while stirring the mixture
   Add salt, pepper, and garlic powder
   Add cheese a little at a time
   Cook for another 2 to 3 minutes
```

or

```
How to follow the main instructions for MyFirstJavaClass:
    Display "Hello" in a dialog box on the screen.
```

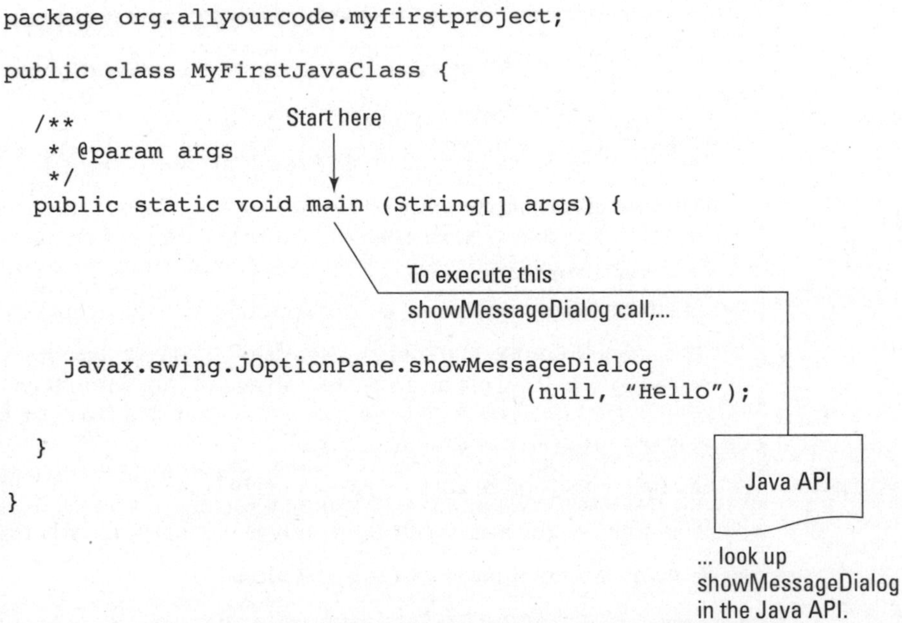

```
package org.allyourcode.myfirstproject;

public class MyFirstJavaClass {

    /**                          Start here
     * @param args
     */
    public static void main (String[] args) {

                                     To execute this
                                     showMessageDialog call,...

       javax.swing.JOptionPane.showMessageDialog
                                  (null, "Hello");

                                                    Java API

    }

}
```

Figure 5-7:
It all starts
with the
`main`
method.

... look up
showMessageDialog
in the Java API.

The word `main` plays a special role in Java. In particular, you never write code that explicitly calls a `main` method into action. The word `main` is the name of the method that's called into action when the program begins running.

When the `MyFirstJavaClass` program runs, the computer automatically finds the program's `main` method and executes any instructions inside the method's body. In the `MyFirstJavaClass` program, the `main` method's body has only one instruction. That instruction tells the computer to display *Hello* in a dialog box on the screen. So in Figure 5-1, `Hello` appears on the computer screen.

None of the instructions in a method is executed until the method is called into action. But if you give a method the name `main`, that method is called into action automatically.

Punctuating your code

In English, punctuation is vital. If you don't believe me, ask this book's copy editor, who suffered through my rampant abuse of commas and semicolons in the preparation of this manuscript. My apologies to her — I'll try harder in the next edition.

Anyway, punctuation is also important in a Java program. This list lays out a few of Java's punctuation rules:

✔ **Enclose a class body in a pair of curly braces.**

In Listing 5-1, the `MyFirstJavaClass` body is enclosed in curly braces.

The placement of a curly brace (at the end of a line, at the start of a line, or on a line of its own) is unimportant. The only important aspect of placement is consistency. The consistent placement of curly braces throughout the code makes the code easier for you to understand. And when you understand your own code, you *write* far better code. When you compose a program, Eclipse can automatically rearrange the code so that the placement of curly braces (and other program elements) is consistent. To make it happen, click the mouse anywhere inside the editor and choose Source⇨Format.

✔ **Enclose a method body in a pair of curly braces.**

In Listing 5-1, the `main` method's body is enclosed in curly braces.

✔ **A Java statement ends with a semicolon.**

For example, in Listing 5-1, the call to the showMessageDialog method ends with a semicolon.

✔ **A declaration ends with a semicolon.**

Again in Listing 5-1, the first line of code (containing the package declaration) ends with a semicolon.

✔ **In spite of the previous two rules, don't place a semicolon immediately after a closing curly brace (}).**

Listing 5-1 ends with two closing curly braces, and neither of these braces is followed by a semicolon.

✔ **Use parentheses to enclose a method's parameters, and use commas to separate the parameters.**

In Listing 5-1 (where else?) the call to the showMessageDialog method has two parameters: null and "Hello". The declaration of the main method has only one parameter: args.

In the main method's parameter list, the String[] thing isn't a separate parameter. Instead, String[] is the args parameter's *type*. For more information about types, see Chapters 6, 9 and 12.

✔ **Use double quotation marks ("") to denote strings of characters.**

In Listing 5-1, the "Hello" parameter tells the showMessageDialog method to display the characters *Hello* on the face of the dialog box.

✔ **Use dots to separate the parts of a qualified name.**

In the Java API, the javax.swing package contains the JOptionPane class, which in turn contains the showMessageDialog method. So javax.swing.JOptionPane.showMessageDialog is the method's fully qualified name.

✔ **Use dots within a package name.**

The dots in a package name are a bit misleading. A package name hints at uses for the code inside the package. But a package name doesn't classify packages into subpackages and sub-subpackages.

For example, the Java API has the packages javax.swing, javax.security.auth, javax.security.auth.login, and many others. The word javax alone means nothing, and the javax.security.auth.login package isn't inside of the javax.security.auth package.

The most blatant consequence of a package name's dots is to determine a file's location on the hard drive. For example, because of its package name, the code in Listing 5-1 must be in a folder named myfirst project, which must be in a folder named allyourcode, which in turn must be in a folder named org, as shown in Figure 5-8.

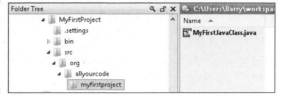

Comments are your friends

Listing 5-2 has an enhanced version of the code in Listing 5-1. In addition
to all the keywords, identifiers, and punctuation, Listing 5-2 has text that's
meant for human beings (like you and me) to read.

Listing 5-2:   Three Kinds of Comments

```
/*
 * Listing 5-2 in
 *    "Java For Android Developers For Dummies"
 *
 * Copyright 2013 Wiley Publishing, Inc.
 * All rights reserved.
] */

package org.allyourcode.myfirstproject;

/**
 * MyFirstJavaClass displays a dialog box
 * on the computer screen.
 *
 * @author   Barry Burd
 * @version 1.0 02/02/13
 * @see      java.swing.JOptionPane
 */
public class MyFirstJavaClass {

  /**
   * The starting point of execution.
   *
   * @param args
   *          (Not used.)
   */
  public static void main(String[] args) {
    javax.swing.JOptionPane.showMessageDialog
                             (null, "Hello"); //null?
  }

}
```

A *comment* is a special section of text inside a program whose purpose is to help people understand the program. A comment is part of a good program's documentation.

The Java programming language has three kinds of comments:

✔ **Traditional comments:** The first seven lines in Listing 3-6 (over in Chapter 3) form one *traditional* comment. The comment begins with /* and ends with */. Everything between the opening /* and the closing */ is for human eyes only. No information about `"Java For Android Developers For Dummies"` or `Wiley Publishing, Inc.` is translated by the compiler.

To read about compilers, see Chapter 1.

Lines 2–6 in Listing 5-2 have extra asterisks (*). I call them *extra* because these asterisks aren't required when you create a comment. They only make the comment look pretty. I include them in the listing because, for some reason that I don't entirely understand, most Java programmers insist on adding these extra asterisks.

✔ **End-of-line comments:** The text `//null?` in Listing 5-2 is an *end-of-line* comment — it starts with two slashes and goes to the end of a line of type. Once again, the compiler doesn't translate the text inside an end-of-line comment.

✔ **Javadoc comments:** A *javadoc* comment begins with a slash and two asterisks (/**). Listing 5-2 has two javadoc comments — one with the text `MyFirstJavaClass displays a dialog box . . .` and another with the text `The starting point. . . .`

A *javadoc* comment is a special kind of traditional comment: It's meant to be read by people who never even look at the Java code.

Wait — that doesn't make sense. How can you see the javadoc comments in Listing 5-2 if you never look at the listing?

Well, with a few points and clicks, you can find all the javadoc comments in Listing 5-2 and turn them into a nice-looking web page, as shown in Figure 5-9.

To make documentation pages for your own code, follow these steps:

1. **Put Javadoc comments in your code.**

2. **From the main menu in Eclipse, choose Project⇨Generate Javadoc.**

   As a result, the Javadoc Generation dialog box appears.

3. **In the Javadoc Generation dialog box, select the Eclipse project whose code you want to document.**

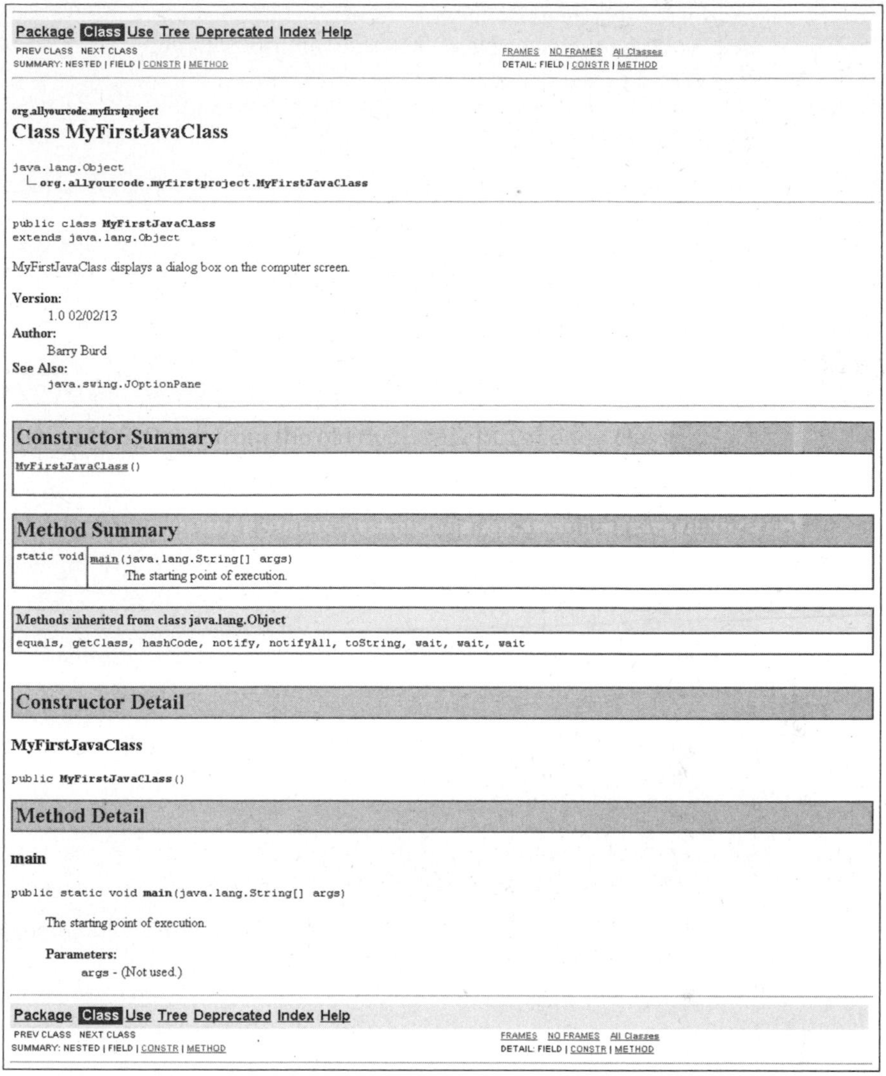

```
Package Class Use Tree Deprecated Index Help
PREV CLASS  NEXT CLASS                                          FRAMES  NO FRAMES  All Classes
SUMMARY: NESTED | FIELD | CONSTR | METHOD                      DETAIL: FIELD | CONSTR | METHOD

org.allyourcode.myfirstproject
Class MyFirstJavaClass

java.lang.Object
  └ org.allyourcode.myfirstproject.MyFirstJavaClass

public class MyFirstJavaClass
extends java.lang.Object

MyFirstJavaClass displays a dialog box on the computer screen.

Version:
    1.0 02/02/13
Author:
    Barry Burd
See Also:
    java.swing.JOptionPane

Constructor Summary

MyFirstJavaClass()

Method Summary

static void   main(java.lang.String[] args)
                  The starting point of execution.

Methods inherited from class java.lang.Object

equals, getClass, hashCode, notify, notifyAll, toString, wait, wait, wait

Constructor Detail

MyFirstJavaClass

public MyFirstJavaClass()

Method Detail

main

public static void main(java.lang.String[] args)

    The starting point of execution.

    Parameters:
        args - (Not used.)

Package Class Use Tree Deprecated Index Help
PREV CLASS  NEXT CLASS                                          FRAMES  NO FRAMES  All Classes
SUMMARY: NESTED | FIELD | CONSTR | METHOD                      DETAIL: FIELD | CONSTR | METHOD
```

Figure 5-9:
Javadoc
comments,
generated
from the
code in
Listing 5-2.

4. **Still in the Javadoc Generation dialog box, notice the name of the folder in the Destination field.**

   The computer puts the newly created documentation pages in that folder. If you prefer a different folder, you can change the folder name in this Destination field.

5. **Click Finish.**

   As a result, the computer creates the documentation pages.

If you visit the Destination folder and double-click the new `index.html` file's icon, you see your beautiful (and informative) documentation pages.

You can find the documentation pages for Java's built-in API classes by visiting `www.oracle.com/technetwork/java/javase/documentation`. Java's API contains thousands of classes, so don't memorize the names of the classes and their methods. Instead, you simply visit these online documentation pages.

What's Barry's excuse?

For years, I've been telling my students to put all kinds of comments in their code, and for years, I've been creating sample code (such as the code in Listing 5-1) containing few comments. Why?

Three little words: "Know your audience." When you write complicated, real-life code, your audience consists of other programmers, information technology managers, and people who need help deciphering what you've done. But when I write simple samples of code for this book, my audience is you — the novice Java programmer. Rather than read my comments, your best strategy is to stare at my Java statements — the statements that Java's compiler deciphers. That's why I put so few comments in this book's listings.

Besides, I'm a little lazy.

Another One-Line Method

Listing 5-3 contains another Hello World program. In fact, the code in Listing 5-3 is a bit simpler than the program in Listing 5-1.

Listing 5-3: A Console-Based Hello World Program

```
package com.allmycode.hello;

public class HelloText {

  public static void main(String[] args) {
    System.out.println("Hello");
  }

}
```

In Listing 5-3, the method call `System.out.println("Hello")` sends text to the Console view in Eclipse, as shown in Figure 5-10. Sending text to the Console is dull, dull, dull. But when you're writing code, a new program often doesn't do what you think it should do. And adding a quick `System.out.println` call to the program helps you understand how the program behaves behind the scenes.

Figure 5-10:
The Console
view in
Eclipse.

For concrete examples in which I use `System.out.println` to diagnose a program's behavior, see Chapter 13.

More Java Methods

To move beyond the rock-bottom simplicity of Listings 5-1 and 5-3, the code in Listing 5-4 mixes a few method declarations and a few method calls.

Listing 5-4:   A Goodbye World Program

```
package com.allmycode.games;

import javax.swing.JOptionPane;

public class CountLives {

  public static void main(String[] args) {
    countdown();
  }

  static void countdown() {
    JOptionPane.showMessageDialog(null,
        "You have 2 more lives.", "The Game",
        JOptionPane.INFORMATION_MESSAGE);
    JOptionPane.showMessageDialog(null,
        „You have 1 more life.", „The Game",
        JOptionPane.WARNING_MESSAGE);
    JOptionPane.showMessageDialog(null,
        „You have no more lives.", „The Game",
        JOptionPane.ERROR_MESSAGE);
  }

}
```

Figures 5-11, 5-12, and 5-13 show a complete run of the code shown in Listing 5-4.]

Figure 5-11:
The
INFORMATION
_MESSAGE
from the
first show
Message
Dialog call.

Figure 5-12:
The
WARNING_
MESSAGE
from the
second
show
Message
Dialog call.

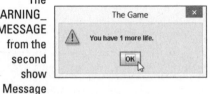

Figure 5-13:
The ERROR_
MESSAGE
from the
third show
Message
Dialog call.

Figure 5-14 gives a more schematic overview of what happens when the computer runs the code shown in Listing 5-4. The main method calls the countdown method, which in turn calls Java's showMessageDialog method three times.

Using an import declaration

Compare the `showMessageDialog` calls in Listings 5-1 and 5-4. In Listing 5-1, you use the fully qualified name `javax.swing.JOptionPane.showMessage Dialog`, but in Listing 5-4, you use the simpler name `JOptionPane. showMessageDialog`. What's this all about?

The answer is near the top of Listing 5-4. In that listing, you see the line

```
import javax.swing.JOptionPane;
```

This line, which announces that you intend to use the short name `JOptionPane` later in the listing's code, clarifies what you mean by `JOptionPane`. (You mean `javax.swing.JOptionPane`.) After having announced your intention in this *import declaration*, you can use the short name `JOptionPane` in the rest of the `CountLives` class code.

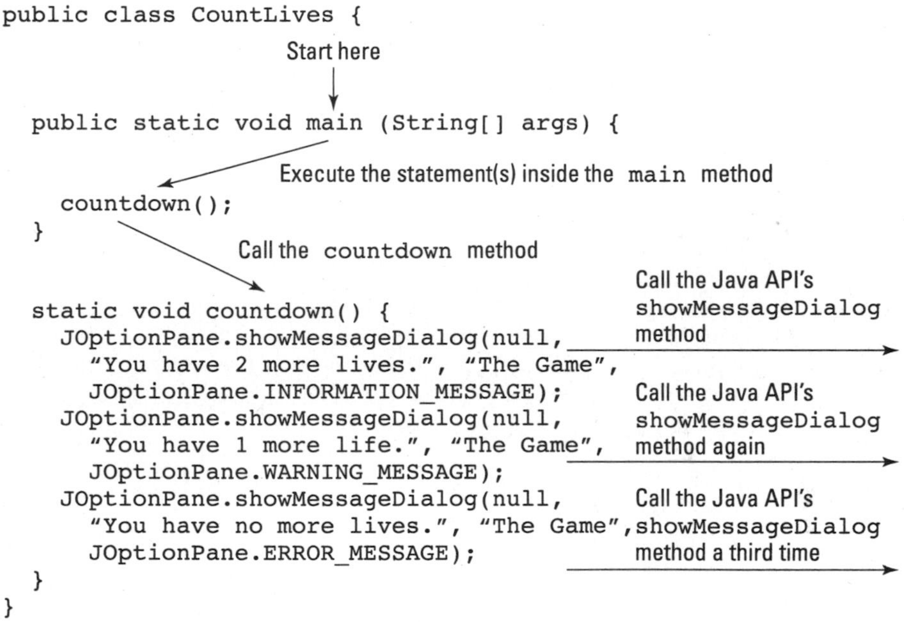

```
public class CountLives {
                              Start here
                                  ↓
  public static void main (String[] args) {
                          Execute the statement(s) inside the  main  method
      countdown();
  }
                    Call the  countdown  method
                                                    Call the Java API's
                                                    showMessageDialog
  static void countdown() {                         method
    JOptionPane.showMessageDialog(null,_____→
       "You have 2 more lives.", "The Game",
       JOptionPane.INFORMATION_MESSAGE);        Call the Java API's
    JOptionPane.showMessageDialog(null,         showMessageDialog
       "You have 1 more life.", "The Game",     method again
       JOptionPane.WARNING_MESSAGE);_____→
    JOptionPane.showMessageDialog(null,         Call the Java API's
       "You have no more lives.",  "The Game", showMessageDialog
       JOptionPane.ERROR_MESSAGE);              method a third time
                                                _____→
  }
}
```

Figure 5-14: Going with the flow.

If you don't insert an import declaration at the top of the Java code file, you have to repeat the full `javax.swing.JOptionPane` name wherever you use the name `JOptionPane` in your code. (Refer to Listing 5-1.)

The details of this import business can be nasty, but (fortunately) many IDEs have features to help you write import declarations. For example, in Eclipse, you can avoid typing import declarations. You can quickly compose code using the shorter `JOptionPane.showMessageDialog` name. Then from the main menu in Eclipse, choose Source⇨Organize Imports. When you do this, Eclipse adds the missing import declarations on your behalf.

More method parameters

Compare the `showMessageDialog` calls in Listings 5-1 and 5-4. The call in Listing 5-1 has two parameters, but each call in Listing 5-4 has four parameters. This is okay because the Java API contains at least two different `showMessageDialog` declarations — one with two parameters:

```
public static void showMessageDialog
        (Component parentComponent, Object message) {
// . . . etc.
```

And another with four parameters:

```
public static void showMessageDialog
        (Component parentComponent, Object message,
                    String title, int messageType) {
// . . . etc.
```

This example demonstrates *method overloading*. The Java API overloads the method name `showMessageDialog` by creating two (or more) ways to call `showMessageDialog`. A call with two parameters refers to one method declaration, and a call with four parameters refers to another declaration, as shown in Figure 5-15. The computer decides which method declaration to invoke by counting the parameters in the method call (and by checking other elements, as described in Chapter 7).

Here's what happens in the four-parameter version of `showMessageDialog`:

- ✔ **If the first parameter is `null`, the dialog box doesn't initially appear inside any other window.**

  This parameter serves the same purpose as the first parameter in the two-parameter `showMessageDialog` method.

- ✔ **The second parameter tells the `showMessageDialog` method which characters to display on the face of the dialog box.**

  This parameter serves the same purpose as the second parameter in the two-parameter `showMessageDialog` method.

Two parameters:

```
javax.swing.JOptionPane.showMessageDialog
                                (null, "Hello");
                                 ①        ②

public static void showMessageDialog
        (Component parentComponent, Object message) {
etc.                              ①                ②
```

Four parameters:

Figure 5-15:
Parameters
in the call
match up
with param-
eters in the
declaration.

```
                                    ①
JOptionPane.showMessageDialog (null,
  ② "You have 2 more lives.", "The Game", ③
    JOptionPane.INFORMATION_MESSAGE);
                                    ④

public static void showMes①geDialog            ②
        (Component parentComponent, Object message,
                            String title, int messageType) {
etc.                              ③              ④
```

✔ **The third parameter tells the** showMessageDialog **method which characters to display on the title bar of the dialog box.**

In Listing 5-4 (and back in Figures 5-11, 5-12, and 5-13), the title bar in every dialog box contains the words *The Game*.

✔ **The fourth parameter tells the** showMessageDialog **which icon to display on the face of the dialog box.**

Figures 5-11, 5-12, and 5-13 show three of the five icons that may appear with a call to showMessageDialog. The remaining two possibilities are the question-mark icon (with the JOptionPane.QUESTION_MESSAGE parameter) and no icon (with the JOptionPane.PLAIN_MESSAGE parameter).

The showMessageDialog method calls in Listing 5-4 illustrate a point from the "R.java and the legend of the two vaudevillians" sidebar in Chapter 4, where the words View.VISIBLE, View.INVISIBLE, and View.GONE stand for the numbers 0, 4, and 8, respectively. Android uses these three numbers to represent different levels of screen visibility. In the same way, the names JOptionPane.ERROR_MESSAGE, JOptionPane.INFORMATION_MESSAGE, and JOptionPane.WARNING_MESSAGE stand for the numbers 0, 1, and 2. The statements inside the declaration of the showOptionPane message respond to each of these numbers by displaying a different icon.

Fewer method parameters

Another story about method parameters in Listing 5-4 begs to be told. In Listing 5-4 I call a method named `countdown`, and in the same class I declare my new `countdown` method.

When you call a method that's declared in the same class, you can use the method's simple name. It's the same way in real life. No one in my family calls me Barry Burd at home (unless they're really angry with me).

You may remember how the computer counts a method call's parameters and matches this with the number of parameters in the method's declaration. In Listing 5-4, the `countdown` call has no parameters (only an empty pair of parentheses) and the `countdown` method's declaration has the same number of parameters; namely, none. So the call and the declaration are compatible, and the computer executes the declaration's instructions.

To declare (or to call) a method with no parameters, use an empty pair of parentheses.

Hello, Android

An Android project's `src` directory contains your project's Java source code. Files in this directory have names such as `MainActivity.java`, `MyService.java`, `DatabaseHelper.java`, and `MoreStuff.java`.

You can cram hundreds of Java files into an Android project's `src` directory. But when you create a new project, Eclipse typically creates just one file for you. By default, Android creates a file named `MainActivity.java`. Listing 5-5 shows you the code in the `MainActivity.java` file.

Listing 5-5: Android Creates This Skeletal Activity Class

```
package com.allmycode.myfirstandroidapp;

import android.os.Bundle;
import android.app.Activity;
import android.view.Menu;

public class MainActivity extends Activity {

  @Override
  protected void onCreate(Bundle savedInstanceState) {
    super.onCreate(savedInstanceState);
    setContentView(R.layout.activity_main);
  }
```

```
@Override
public boolean onCreateOptionsMenu(Menu menu) {
  // Inflate the menu; this adds items to the
  // action bar if it is present.
  getMenuInflater().inflate(R.menu.activity_main, menu);
  return true;
}

}
```

Where's the main method?

To start the run of a standard Java program, the computer looks for a method named `main`. But the code in Listing 5-5 has no `main` method. Okay, I give up — how does a smartphone find the starting point of execution in an Android app?

The answer involves an app's XML code. You can build a standard Java program with Java code alone, but an Android app needs additional code. For one thing, every Android app needs its own `AndroidManifest.xml` file.

Chapter 4 describes an `AndroidManifest.xml` file.

Listing 5-6 contains a snippet of code from an `AndroidManifest.xml` file. (The code that I set in boldface is the most interesting code. The code that's not set in boldface isn't uninteresting. It's simply less interesting.)

Listing 5-6:   The activity Element in an AndroidManifest.xml File

```
<activity
  android:name=
    "com.allmycode.myfirstandroidapp.MainActivity"
  android:label="@string/app_name" >
  <intent-filter>
    <action android:name=
      "android.intent.action.MAIN" />

    <category android:name=
      "android.intent.category.LAUNCHER" />
  </intent-filter>
</activity>
```

And here's what the code in Listing 5-6 "says" to your Android device:

✔ **The code's** `action` **element indicates that the program that's set forth in Listing 5-5 (the** `com.allmycode.myfirstandroidapp.MainActivity` **class) is** MAIN.

That is, the program in Listing 5-5 is the starting point of an app's execution. In response to this, your Android device reaches back inside the listing and executes the listing's onCreate method, onCreate OptionsMenu method, and several other methods that don't appear there.

✔ **The code's** category **element adds an icon to the device's Application Launcher screen.**

On most Android devices, the user sees the Home screen. Then, by touching one element or another on the Home screen, the user gets to see the Launcher screen, which contains several apps' icons. By scrolling this screen, the user can find an appropriate app's icon. When the user taps the icon, the app starts running.

In Listing 5-6, the category element's LAUNCHER value makes an icon for running com.allmycode.myfirstandroidapp.MainActivity (the Java program in Listing 5-5) available on the device's Launcher screen.

So there you have it. With the proper secret sauce (namely, the action and category elements in the AndroidManifest.xml file), an Android program's onCreate and onCreateOptionsMenu methods become the program's starting points of execution.

Extending a class

In Listing 5-5, the words extends and @Override tell an important story — a story that applies to all Java programs, not only to Android apps. The words extends and @Override tell the story of a class in the Android API. The API's android.app.Activity class forms the basis of all Android applications.

In Android developer lingo, an *activity* is one "screenful" of components. Each Android application can contain many activities. For example, an app's initial activity might list the films playing in your neighborhood. When you click a film's title, Android covers the entire list activity with another activity (perhaps an activity displaying a relevant film review).

When you *extend* the android.app.Activity class, you create a new kind of Android activity. In Listing 5-5, the words extends Activity tells the computer that a MainActivity is, in fact, an example of an Android Activity. That's good because the folks at Google have already written more than 5,000 lines of Java code to describe what an Android Activity can do. Being an example of an Activity in Android means that you can take advantage of all its prewritten code.

When you extend an existing Java class (such as the Activity class), you create a new class with the existing class's functionality. For details of this important concept, see Chapter 10.

Overriding methods

In Listing 5-5, a MainActivity is a kind of Android Activity. So a MainActivity is automatically a screenful of components with lots and lots of handy, prewritten code.

Of course, in some apps, you might not want all that prewritten code. After all, being a Republican or a Democrat doesn't mean believing everything in your party's platform. You can start by borrowing most of the platform's principles but then pick and choose among the remaining principles. In the same way, the code in Listing 5-5 declares itself to be an Android Activity, but then *overrides* two of the Activity class's existing methods.

In Listing 5-5, the word @Override indicates that the listing doesn't use the API's prewritten onCreate and onCreateOptionsMenu methods. Instead, the new MainActivity contains declarations for its own onCreate and onCreateOptionsMenu methods, as shown in Figure 5-16.

Activity
onCreate(Bundle : savedInstanceState) onStart() onResume() onPause() onStop() onDestroy() onCreateOptionsMenu(Menu : menu)

MainActivity
~~onCreate(Bundle: savedInstanceState)~~   onCreate(Bundle : savedinstancestate) onStart() onResume() onPause() onStop() onDestroy() ~~onCreateOptionsMenu(Menu : menu)~~   onCreateOptionsMenu(Menu : menu)

Figure 5-16: I don't like the prewritten onCreate and OnCreate Options Menu methods.

In particular, Listing 5-5's onCreate method calls setContentView(R.layout.activity_main), which displays the material described in the res/layout/activity_main.xml file (the buttons and the text fields, for example) on the screen.

For an introduction to the res/layout/activity_main.xml file, see Chapter 4.

The other method in Listing 5-5 (the `onCreateOptionsMenu` method) does a similar trick with the `res/menu/activity_main.xml` file to display items on the app's Action bar.

An activity's workhorse methods

Every Android activity has a *lifecycle* — a set of stages that the activity undergoes from birth to death to rebirth, and so on. In particular, when your phone launches an activity, the phone calls the activity's `onCreate` method. The phone also calls the activity's `onStart` and `onResume` methods.

In Listing 5-5, I choose to declare my own `onCreate` method, but I don't bother declaring my own `onStart` and `onResume` methods. Rather than override the `onStart` and `onResume` methods, I silently use the `Activity` class's prewritten `onStart` and `onResume` methods.

To find out why you'd choose to override `onResume`, see Chapter 14.

When your phone ends an activity's run, the phone calls three additional methods: the activity's `onPause`, `onStop`, and `onDestroy` methods. So one complete sweep of your activity, from birth to death, involves the run of at least six methods — `onCreate`, then `onStart`, and then `onResume`, and later `onPause`, and then `onStop`, and, finally, `onDestroy`. As it is with all life forms, "ashes to ashes, dust to dust."

Don't despair. For an Android activity, reincarnation is a common phenomenon. For example, if you're running several apps at a time, the phone might run low on memory. In this case, Android can kill some running activities. As the phone's user, you have no idea that any activities have been destroyed. When you navigate back to a killed activity, Android re-creates the activity for you and you're none the wiser.

Here's another surprising fact. When you turn a phone from Portrait mode to Landscape mode, the phone destroys the *current* activity (the activity that's in Portrait mode) and re-creates that activity in Landscape mode. The phone calls all six of the activity's lifecycle methods (`onPause`, `onStop`, and so on) in order to turn the activity's display sideways. It's similar to starting on the transporter deck of the *Enterprise* and being a different person after being beamed down to the planet (except that you act like yourself and think like yourself, so no one knows that you're a completely different person).

Indeed, methods like `onCreate` and `onCreateOptionsMenu` in Listing 5-5 are the workhorses of Android development.

Chapter 6

Java's Building Blocks

1've driven cars in many cities, and I'm ready to present my candid reviews:

✔ Driving in New York City is a one-sided endeavor. A New York City driver avoids hitting another car but doesn't avoid being hit by another car. In the same way, New York pedestrians do nothing to avoid being hit. Racing into the path of an oncoming vehicle is commonplace. Anyone who doesn't behave this way is either a New Jersey driver or a tourist from the Midwest. In New York City, safety depends entirely on the car that's moving toward a potential target.

✔ A driver in certain parts of California will stop on a dime for a pedestrian who's about to jaywalk. Some drivers stop even before the pedestrian is aware of any intention to jaywalk.

✔ Boston's streets are curvy and irregular, and accurate street signs are rare. Road maps are outdated because of construction and other contingencies. So driving in Boston is highly problematic. You can't find your way around Boston unless you already know your way around Boston, and you don't know your way around Boston unless you've already driven around Boston. Needless to say, I can't drive in Boston.

✔ London is quite crowded, but the drivers are polite (to foreigners, at least). Several years ago, I caused three car accidents in one week on the streets of London. And after each accident, the driver of the other car apologized to me!

I was particularly touched when a London cabby expressed regret that an accident (admittedly, my fault) might stain his driving record. Apparently, the rules for London cabbies are quite strict.

This brings me to the subject of the level of training required to drive a taxicab in London. The cabbies start their careers by memorizing the London street map. The map has over 25,000 streets, and the layout has no built-in clues. Rectangular grids aren't the norm, and numbered streets are quite uncommon. Learning all the street names takes several years, and the cabbies must pass a test in order to become certified drivers.

This incredibly circuitous discussion about drivers, streets, and my tendency to cause accidents leads me to the major point of this section: Java's built-in types are easy to learn. In contrast to London's 25,000 streets, and the periodic table's 100-some elements, Java has only eight built-in types. They're Java's *primitive types*, and this chapter describes them all.

Info Is as Info Does

"Reality! To Sancho, an inn; to Don Quixote, a castle; to someone else, whatever!"

—Miguel de Cervantes, as updated for "Man of La Mancha"

When you think a computer is storing the letter J, the computer is, in reality, storing 01001010. For the letter K, the computer stores 01001011. Everything inside the computer is a sequence of 0s and 1s. As every computer geek knows, a 0 or 1 is a *bit*.

As it turns out, the sequence 01001010, which stands for the letter J, can also stand for the number 74. The same sequence can also stand for $1.0369608636003646 \times 10^{-43}$. In fact, if the bits are interpreted as screen pixels, the same sequence can be used to represent the dots shown in Figure 6-1. The meaning of 01001010 depends on the way the software interprets this sequence of 0s and 1s.

Figure 6-1:
An extreme close-up of eight black-and-white screen pixels.

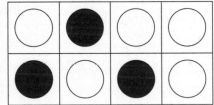

So how do you tell the computer what 01001010 stands for? The answer is in the concept of *type*.

The *type* of a variable is the range of values that the variable is permitted to store. Listing 6-1 illustrates this idea.

Listing 6-1: Goofing Around with Java Types

```
package com.allmycode.demos;

import javax.swing.JOptionPane;

public class TypeDemo1 {

  public static void main(String[] args) {
    int anInteger = 74;
    char aCharacter = 74;
    JOptionPane.showMessageDialog(null, anInteger,
        "An int variable", JOptionPane.PLAIN_MESSAGE);
    JOptionPane.showMessageDialog(null, aCharacter,
        "A char variable", JOptionPane.PLAIN_MESSAGE);
  }

}
```

A run of the code in Listing 6-1 looks like the displays in Figures 6-2 and 6-3.

Figure 6-2: Displaying 01001010 as an int value.

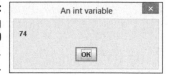

Figure 6-3: Displaying 01001010 as a char value.

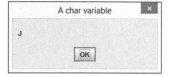

In Figure 6-2, the computer interprets 01001010 as a whole number. But in Figure 6-3, the computer interprets the same 01001010 bits as the representation of the character J. The difference stems from the two *type declarations* at the start of the main method in Listing 6-1:

```
int anInteger = 74;
char aCharacter = 74;
```

Each of these declarations consists of three parts: a variable name, a type name, and an initialization. The next few sections describe these parts.

Variable names

The identifiers anInteger and aCharacter in Listing 6-1 are variable names, or simply variables. A *variable name* is a nickname for a value (like the value 74).

I made up both variable names for the example in Listing 6-1, and I intentionally made up *informative* variable names. Instead of anInteger and aCharacter in Listing 6-1, I could have chosen flower and goose. But I use anInteger and aCharacter because informative names help other people read and understand my code. (In fact, informative names help me read and understand my own code!)

Like most of the names in a Java program, variable names can't have blank spaces. The only allowable punctuation symbol is the underscore character (_). Finally, you can't start a variable's name with a digit. For example, you can name your variable close2Call, but you can't name it 2Close2Call.

If you want to look like a seasoned Java programmer, start every variable name with a lowercase letter, and use uppercase letters to separate words within the name. For example, numberOfBunnies starts with a lowercase letter and separates words by using the uppercase letters O and B. This mixing of upper- and lowercase letters is called *camel case* because of its resemblance to a camel's humps.

Type names

In Listing 6-1, the words int and char are *type names*. The word int (in the first type declaration) tells the computer to interpret whatever value anInteger has as a "whole number" value (a value with no digits to the right of the decimal point). And the word char (in the second type declaration) tells the computer to interpret whatever value aCharacter has as a character value (a letter, a punctuation symbol, or maybe even a single digit). So in Listing 6-1, in the first call to `showMessageDialog`, when I display the value of `anInteger`, the computer displays the number 74. And in the second call to `showMessageDialog`, when I display the value of `aCharacter`, the computer displays the letter J.

In Listing 6-1, the words `int` and `char` tell the computer what types my variable names have. The names `anInteger` and `aCharacter` remind me, the programmer, what kinds of values these variables have, but the names `anInteger` and `aCharacter` provide no type information to the computer. The declarations `int rocky = 74` and `char bullwinkle = 74` would be fine, as long as I used the variable names `rocky` and `bullwinkle` consistently throughout Listing 6-1.

Assignments and initializations

Both type declarations in Listing 6-1 end with an initialization. As the name suggests, an *initialization* sets a variable to its initial value. In both declarations, I initialize the variable to the value 74.

You can create a type declaration without an initialization. For example, I can change the code in Listing 6-1 so that the first four lines inside the `main` method look like this:

```
int anInteger;
char aCharacter;
anInteger = 74;
aCharacter = 74;
```

A line like `anInteger = 74` is an *assignment*. An assignment changes a variable's value. An assignment isn't part of a type declaration. Instead, an assignment is separate from its type declaration (maybe many lines after the type declaration).

You can initialize a variable with one value and then, in an assignment statement, change the variable's value.

```
int year = 2008;
System.out.println(year);
System.out.println("Global financial crisis");
year = 2009;
System.out.println(year);
System.out.println("Obama elected US president");
year = 2010;
System.out.println(year);
System.out.println("Oil spill in the Gulf of Mexico");
```

Sometimes, you need a name for a value that doesn't change during the program's run. In such situations, the keyword `final` signals a variable whose value can't be reassigned.

```
final int NUMBER_OF_PLANETS = 9;
```

A `final` variable is a variable whose value doesn't vary. (As far as I know, no one's ever seriously suggested calling these things *invariables*.)

You can initialize a `final` variable's value, but after the initialization, you can't change the variable's value with an assignment statement. In other words, after you declare `final int NUMBER_OF_PLANETS = 9`, this assignment statement isn't legal:

```
NUMBER_OF_PLANETS = 8;
```

If Pluto is no longer a planet, you can't accommodate the change without changing the 9 in the `final int NUMBER_OF_PLANETS = 9` declaration.

In Java, the word `final` is one of Java's modifiers. A *modifier* is like an adjective in English. A modifier causes a slight change in the meaning of a declaration. For example, in this section, the word `final` modifies the `NUMBER_OF_PLANETS` declaration, making the value of `NUMBER_OF_PLANETS` unchangeable.

For more information about Java's modifiers, see Chapters 9 and 10.

As a rule, you use `final` variables to give friendly names to values that never (or rarely) change. For example, in a Java program, `6.626068e-34` stands for 6.626068×10^{-34}, which is the same as this:

```
0.000000000000000000000000000000006626068
```

In a quantum physics application, you probably don't want to retype the number `6.626068e-34` several times in your code. (You can type the number wrong even when you copy-and-paste.) To keep errors from creeping into your code, you declare

```
final double PLANCK_CONSTANT = 6.626068e-34;
```

From that point on, rather than typing 6.626068e-34 multiple times in your code, you can type only the name `PLANCK_CONSTANT` when needed.

You can use lowercase letters in any variable, including `final` variables. But Java programmers seldom write code this way. To keep from looking like a complete newbie, use only uppercase letters and digits in a `final` variable's name. Use underscores to separate words.

A loophole in the Java language specification allows you, under certain circumstances, to use an assignment statement to give a variable its initial value. For a variable, such as `amount`, declared inside of a method, you can write `final int amount;` on one line, and then `amount = 0;` on another line. Want my advice? Ignore this loophole. Don't even read this Technical Stuff icon!

Expressions and literals

In a computer program, an *expression* is a bunch of text that has a value. For example, in Listing 6-1, the number `74` and the words `anInteger` and `aCharacter` both have values. If I use the name `anInteger` in ten different places in my Java program, then I have ten expressions, and each expression has a value. If I decide to type `anInteger + 17` somewhere in my program, then `anInteger + 17` is an expression because `anInteger + 17` has a value. Listing 6-1 has a bunch of expressions other than the `74`, `anInteger` and `aCharacter` expressions, but I'll let you fish for all the expressions on your own.

A *literal* is a kind of expression whose value doesn't change from one Java program to another. For example, the expression `74` means "the numeric value 74" in every Java program. Likewise, the expression `'J'` means "the tenth uppercase letter in the Roman alphabet" in every Java program, and the word `true` means "the opposite of `false`" in every Java program. The expressions `true`, `74`, and `'J'` are literals. Similarly, the text `"An int variable"` in Listing 6-1 is a literal because, in any Java program, the text `"An int variable"` stands for the same three words.

In Java, single quotation marks stand for a character. You can change the second declaration in Listing 6-1 this way:

```
char aCharacter = 'J';
```

With this change, the program's run doesn't change. The dialog box shown in Figure 6-3 still contains the letter J.

In Java, a `char` value is a number in disguise. In Listing 6-1, you get the same result if the second type declaration is `char aCharacter = 'J'`. You can even do arithmetic with `char` values. For example, in Listing 6-1, if you change the second declaration to `char aCharacter = 'J' + 2`, you get the letter L.

The 01000001 01000010 01000011s

What does 01001010 have to do with the number 74 or with the letter J?

The answer for 74 involves the binary number representation. The familiar base-10 (decimal) system has a 1s column, a 10s column, a 100s column, a 1000s column, and so on. But the base-2 (binary) system has a 1s column, a 2s column, a 4s column, an 8s column, and so on. The figure shows how you get 74 from 01001010 using the binary column values.

The connection between 01001010 and the letter J might seem more arbitrary. In the early 1960s, a group of professionals devised the American Standard Code for Information Interchange (ASCII). In the ASCII representation, each character takes up 8 bits. You can see the representations for some of the characters in the sidebar table. For example, our friend 01001010 (which, as a binary number, stands for 74) is also the way the computer stores the letter J. The decision to make A be 01000001 and to make J be 01001010 has roots in the 20th century's typographic hardware. (The site www.wps.com/J/codes has some nice tidbits about all this.)

In the late 1980s, as modern communications led to increasing globalization, a group of experts began work on an enhanced code with up to 32 bits for each character. The lower eight Unicode bits have the same meanings as in the ASCII code, but with so many more bits, the Unicode standard has room for languages other than English. A Java char value is a 16-bit Unicode number, which means that, depending on the way you interpret it, a char is either a number between 0 and 65535 or a character in one of the many Unicode languages.

In fact, you can use non-English characters for identifiers in a Java program. In the figure, I use Eclipse to run a program with identifiers and output in Yiddish. The words in a few of the statements are out of order because I mix left-to-right and right-to-left languages. But otherwise, the stuff in the figure is a plain-old Java program!

```
UnicodeTest.java

    package com.allmycode.unicode;

    public class UnicodeTest {

        public static void main(String[] ארגס) {
            int אײן = 1;
            int צװײ = 2;
            int דרײַ = אײן + צװײ;
            System.out.println("ענטפער : ");
            System.out.println(דרײַ);
        }

    }

 Problems  Javadoc  Declaration  Search  Console  LogC
<terminated> UnicodeTest (1) [Java Application] C:\Program Files\Java\jdk1.6.0_32\bin\
ענטפער :
3
```

Bits	When Interpreted As an int	When Interpreted As a char	Bits	When Interpreted As an int	When Interpreted As a char
00100000	32	space	00111111	63	?
00100001	33	!	01000000	64	@
00100010	34	"	01000001	65	A
00100011	35	#	01000010	66	B
00100100	36	$	01000011	67	C
00100101	37	%	.	.	.
00100110	38	&	.	.	.
00100111	39	'	*etc.*	*etc.*	*etc.*
00101000	40	(	01011000	88	X
00101001	41	)	01011001	89	Y
00101010	42	*	01011010	90	Z
00101011	43	+	01011011	91	[
00101100	44	,	01011100	92	\
00101101	45	-	01011101	93	]
00101110	46	.	01011110	94	^
00101111	47	/	01011111	95	_
00110000	48	0	01100000	96	`
00110001	49	1	01100001	97	a
00110010	50	2	01100010	98	b
00110011	51	3	01100011	99	c
00110100	52	4	.	.	.
00110101	53	5	.	.	.
00110110	54	6	*etc.*	*etc.*	*etc.*
00110111	55	7	01111000	120	x
00111000	56	8	01111001	121	y
00111001	57	9	01111010	122	z
00111010	58	:	01111011	123	{
00111011	59	;	01111100	124	|
00111100	60	<	01111101	125	}
00111101	61	=	01111110	126	~
00111110	62	>	01111111	127	delete

How to string characters together

In Java, a single character isn't the same as a string of characters. Compare the character `'J'` with the string `"An int variable"` in Listing 6-1. A *character* literal has single quotation marks; a *string* literal has double quotation marks.

In Java, a string of characters may contain more than one character, but a string of characters doesn't necessarily contain more than one character. (Surprise!) You can write

```
char aCharacter = 'J';
```

because a character literal has single quotation marks. And because `String` is one of Java's types, you can also write

```
String myFirstName = "Barry";
```

initializing the `String` variable `myFirstName` with the `String` literal `"Barry"`. Even though `"A"` contains only one letter, you can write

```
String myMiddleInitial = "A";
```

because `"A"`, with its double quotation marks, is a `String` literal.

But in Java, a single character isn't the same as a one-character string, so you can't write

```
//Don't do this:
char theLastLetter = "Z";
```

Even though it contains only one character, the expression `"Z"` is a `String` value, so you can't initialize a `char` variable with the expression `"Z"`.

Java's primitive types

Java has two kinds of types: primitive and reference. Primitive types are the atoms — the basic building blocks. In contrast, reference types are the things you create by combining primitive types (and by combining other reference types).

This chapter covers (almost exclusively) Java's primitive types. Chapter 9 introduces Java's reference types.

Throughout this chapter, I give some attention to Java's `String` type. The `String` type in reality belongs in Chapter 9 because Java's `String` type is a reference type, not a primitive type. But I can't wait until Chapter 9 to use strings of characters in my examples. So consider this chapter's `String` material to be an informal (but useful) preview of Java's `String` type.

Table 6-1 describes all eight primitive Java types.

Table 6-1	Java's Primitive Types	
Type Name	**What a Literal Looks Like**	**Range of Values**
Integral types		
`byte`	`(byte)42`	−128 to 127
`short`	`(short)42`	−32768 to 32767
`int`	`42`	−2147483648 to 2147483647
`long`	`42L`	−9223372036854775808 to 9223372036854775807
Character type (which is, technically, an Integral type)		
`char`	`'A'`	Thousands of characters, glyphs, and symbols
Floating-point types		
`float`	`42.0F`	-3.4×10^{38} to 3.4×10^{38}
`double`	`42.0` or `0.314159e1`	-1.8×10^{308} to 1.8×10^{308}
Logical type		
`boolean`	`true`	true, false

You can divide Java's primitive types into three categories:

✔ **Integral**

The *integral* types represent whole numbers — numbers with no digits to the right of the decimal point. For example, the number `42` in a Java program represents the `int` value 42, as in 42 cents or 42 clowns or 42 eggs. A family can't possibly have 2.5 children, so an `int` variable is a good place to store the number of kids in a particular family.

The thing that distinguishes one integral type from another is the range of values you can represent with each type. For example, a variable of type `int` represents a number from −2147483648 to +2147483647.

When you need a number with no digits to the right of the decimal point, you can almost always use the int type. Java's byte, short, and long types are reserved for special range needs (and for finicky programmers).

✔ **Floating-point**

The *floating-point* types represent numbers with digits to the right of the decimal point, even if those digits are all zeros. For example, an old wooden measuring stick might be 1.001 meters long, and a very precise measuring stick might be 1.000 meters long.

The thing that distinguishes the two floating-point types (double and float) from one another is the range of values you can represent with the types. The double type has a much larger range and is much more accurate.

In spite of their names, Java programmers almost always use double rather than float, and when you write an ordinary literal (such as 42.0), that literal is a double value. (On the off chance that you want to create a float value, write 42.0F.)

✔ **Logical**

A boolean variable has one of two values: true or false. You can assign 74 to an int variable, and you can assign true (for example) to a boolean variable:

```
int numberOfPopsicles;
boolean areLemonFlavored;
numberOfPopsicles = 22;
areLemonFlavored = true;
```

You can do arithmetic with numeric values, and you can do a kind of "arithmetic" with boolean values. For more information, see the next section.

Things You Can Do with Types

You can do arithmetic with Java's *operators*. The most commonly used arithmetic operators are + (addition), – (subtraction), * (multiplication), / (division), and % (remainder upon division).

✔ **When you use an arithmetic operator to combine two int values, the result is another int value.**

For example, the value of 4 + 15 is 19. The value of 14 / 5 is 2 (because 5 "goes into" 14 two times, and even though the remainder is bigger than ½, the remainder is omitted). The value of 14 % 5 is 4 (because 14 divided by 5 leaves a remainder of 4).

The same kinds of rules apply to the other integral types. For example, when you add a `long` value to a `long` value, you get another `long` value.

✔ **When you use an arithmetic operator to combine two `double` values, the result is another `double` value.**

For example, the value of `4.0 + 15.0` is 19.0. The value of `14.0 / 5.0` is 2.8.

The same kind of rule applies to `float` values. For example, a `float` value plus a `float` value is another `float` value.

✔ **When you use an arithmetic operator to combine an `int` value with a `double` value, the result is another `double` value.**

Java *widens* the `int` value in order to combine it with the `double` value. For example, `4 + 15.0` is the same as `4.0 + 15.0`, which is 19.0. And `14 / 5.0` is the same as `14.0 / 5.0`, which is 2.8.

This widening also happens when you combine two different kinds of integral values or two different kinds of floating-point values. For example, the number 9000000000000000000 is too large to be an `int` value, so

```
9000000000000000000L + 1
```

is the same as

```
9000000000000000000L + 1L
```

which is

```
9000000000000000001L
```

Two other popular operators are increment `++` and decrement `--`. The most common use of the increment and decrement operators looks like this:

```
x++;
y--;
```

But you can also place the operators before the variables:

```
++x;
--y;
```

Placing the operator after the variable is called *postincrementing* (or *postdecrementing*). Placing the operator before the variable is called *preincrementing* (or *predecrementing*).

Both forms (before and after the variable) have the same effect on the variable's value; namely, the increment `++` operator always adds 1 to the value, and the decrement `--` operator always subtracts 1 from the value. The only difference is what happens if you dare to display (or otherwise examine) the value of something like `x++`. Figure 6-4 illustrates this unsettling idea.

```
package come.allmycode.demos;

import javax.swing.JOptionPane;

public class IncrementTest {

  public static void main (String[] args) {
    int x = 10;
    JOptionPane.showMessageDialog (null, ++x);


    JOptionPane.showMessageDialog (null, x);


    JOptionPane.showMessageDialog (null, x++);


    JOptionPane.showMessageDialog (null, x);
  }
}
```

> Displays 11 because the value of ++x is the same as the value of x+1

> Displays 11 because ++x (in the previous statement) added to 1 to x

> Displays 11 (SURPRISE!) because the value of x++ is the same as the value of x

> Displays12 (SURPRISE!) because x++ (in the previous statement) added 1 to x

Figure 6-4:
Preincrement and post-increment.

In practice, if you remember only that x++ adds 1 to the value of x, you're usually okay.

The curious behavior shown in Figure 6-4 was inspired by assembly languages of the 1970s. These languages have instructions that perform increment and decrement operations on a processor's internal registers.

Add letters to numbers (Huh?)

You can add strings and char values to other elements and to each other. Listing 6-2 has some examples.

Listing 6-2:   Java's Versatile Plus Sign

```
package com.allmycode.demos;

public class PlusSignTest {

  public static void main(String[] args) {
    int x = 74;
    System.out.println("Hello, " + "world!");
    System.out.println
      ("The value of x is " + x + ".");
    System.out.println
```

```
                ("The second letter of the alphabet is " +
                                        'B' + ".");
        System.out.println
          ("The fifth prime number is " + 11 + '.');
        System.out.println
          ("The sum of 18 and 21 is " + 18 + 21 +
                          ". Oops! That's wrong.");
        System.out.println
          ("The sum of 18 and 21 is " + (18 + 21) +
                                    ". That's better.");

    }

}
```

The `String` type more appropriately belongs in Chapter 9 because Java's `String` type isn't a primitive type. Even so, I start covering the `String` type in this chapter.

When you run the code in Listing 6-2, you see the output shown in Figure 6-5.

Figure 6-5:
A run of
the code in
Listing 6-2.

```
Hello, world!
The value of x is 74.
The second letter of the alphabet is B.
The fifth prime number is 11.
The sum of 18 and 21 is 1821. Oops! That's wrong.
The sum of 18 and 21 is 39. That's better.
```

Here's what's happening in Figure 6-5:

✔ **When you use the plus sign to combine two strings, it stands for string concatenation.**

   String concatenation is a fancy name for what happens when you display one string immediately after another. In Listing 6-2, the act of concatenating `"Hello, "` and `"world!"` yields the string

   `"Hello, world!"`

✔ **When you add a string to a number, Java turns the number into a string and concatenates the strings.**

   In Listing 6-2, the x variable is initialized to 74. The code displays `"The value of x is "` + x (a string plus an int variable). When adding the string `"The value of x is "` to the number 74, Java turns the int 74 into the string `"74"`. So `"The value of x is "` + x becomes `"The value of x is "` + `"74"`, which (after string concatenation) becomes `"The value of x is 74"`.

This automatic conversion of a number into a string is handy whenever you want to display a brief explanation along with a numeric value.

The computer's internal representation of the number 74 is 0000000000 00000000000001001010 (with 1 in the 64s place, 1 in the 8s place, and 1 in the 2s place). In contrast, the computer's internal representation of the string "74" is 00000000001101110000000000110100. (For some clues to help you understand why these bits represent the "74" string, see the table accompanying this chapter's earlier sidebar "The 01000001 01000010 01000011s.") The bottom line, as far as Java is concerned, is that the number 74 and the string "74" aren't the same.

✔ **When you add a string to any other kind of value, Java turns the other value into a string and concatenates the strings.**

The third System.out.println call in Listing 6-2 adds the char value 'B' to a string. The result, as you can see in Figure 6-5, is a string containing the letter B.

✔ **The order in which the computer performs operations can affect the outcome.**

The last two System.out.println calls in Listing 6-2 illustrate this point. In the next-to-last call, the computer works from left to right. The computer starts by combining "The sum of 18 and 21 is " with 18, getting "The sum of 18 and 21 is 18". Then, working its way rightward, the computer combines "The sum of 18 and 21 is 18" with 21 getting the screwy string "The sum of 18 and 21 is 1821".

In the last System.out.println call, I fix these problems by grouping 18 and 21 in parentheses. As a result, the computer starts by adding 18 and 21 to get 39. Then the computer combines "The sum of 18 and 21 is " with 39, getting the more sensible string "The sum of 18 and 21 is 39".

Java's exotic assignment operators

In a Java program, you can add 2 to a variable with a statement like this:

```
numberOfCows = numberOfCows + 2;
```

But to a seasoned Java developer, a statement of this kind is horribly *gauche*. You might as well wear white after Labor Day or talk seriously about a "nucular" reactor. Why?

Because Java has a fancy *compound assignment operator* that performs the same task in a more concise way. The statement

```
numberOfCows += 2;
```

adds 2 to `numberOfCows` and lets you easily recognize the programmer's intention. For a silly example, imagine having several similarly named variables in the same program:

```
int numberOfCows;
int numberOfCrows;
int numberOfCries;
int numberOfCrays;
int numberOfGrays;
```

Then the statement

```
numberOfCrows += 2;
```

doesn't force you to check both sides of an assignment. Instead, the `+=` operator makes the statement's intent crystal-clear.

Java's other compound assignment operators include `-=`, `*=`, `/=`, `%=`, and others. For example, to multiply `numberOfCows` by `numberOfDays`, you can write

```
numberOfCows *= numberOfDays;
```

A compound assignment, like `numberOfCrows += 2`, might take a tiny bit less time to execute than the cruder `numberOfCows = numberOfCows + 2`. But the main reason for using a compound assignment statement is to make the program easier for other developers to read and understand. The savings in computing time, if any, is usually minimal.

True bit

A `boolean` value is either `true` or `false`. Those are only two possible values, compared with the thousands of values an `int` variable can have. But these two values are quite powerful. (When someone says "You've won the lottery" or "Your shoe is untied," you probably care whether these statements are true or false. Don't you?)

When you compare things with one another, the result is a `boolean` value. For example, the statement

```
System.out.println(3 > 2);
```

puts the word `true` in Eclipse's Console view. In addition to Java's > (greater than) operator, you can compare values with < (less than), >= (greater than or equal), and <= (less than or equal).

You can also use a double-equal sign (==) to find out whether two values are equal to one another. The statement

```
System.out.println(15 == 9 + 9);
```

puts the word `false` in the Console view. You can also test for inequality. For example, the statement

```
System.out.println(15 != 9 + 9);
```

```
System.out.println(15 != 9 + 9);
```

puts the word `true` in the Console view. (A computer keyboard has no ≠ sign. To help you remember the != operator, think of the exclamation point as a work-around for making a slash through the equal sign.)

An expression whose value is either `true` or `false` is a *condition*. In this section, expressions such as 3 > 2 and 15 != 9 + 9 are examples of conditions.

The symbol to compare for equality isn't the same as the symbol that's used in an assignment or an initialization. Assignment or initialization uses a single equal sign (=), and comparison for equality uses a double equal sign (==). Everybody mistakenly uses the single equal sign to compare for equality several times in their programming careers. The trick is not to avoid making the mistake; the trick is to catch the mistake whenever you make it.

It's nice to display the word `true` or `false` in Eclipse's Console view, but `boolean` values aren't just for pretty displays. To find out how `boolean` values can control the sequence of steps in your program, see Chapter 8.

Java isn't like a game of horseshoes

Even when you correctly use the double equal sign, you have to be careful. Figure 6-6 shows you what happens in a paper-and-pencil calculation to convert 21 degrees Celsius to Fahrenheit. You get exactly 69.8.

Figure 6-6:
An exact
Celsius-to-
Fahrenheit
conversion.

```
         37.8 ←
①    21  ② 5)189.0  ③    37.8
   × 9        15        + 32
    189       39         69.8
              35
              40
              40    ── Exact answers
                    └─ No remainder
```

But when you add the following statement to a Java program, you see `false`, not `true`:

```
System.out.println(9.0 / 5.0 * 21 + 32.0 == 69.8);
```

Why isn't `9.0 / 5.0 * 21 + 32.0` the same as `69.8`? The answer is that Java's arithmetic operators don't use the decimal system — they use the *binary* system. And in binary arithmetic, things don't go as well as they do in Figure 6-6.

Figure 6-7 shows you how the computer divides 189.0 by 5. You might not understand (and you might not want to understand) how the computer computes the value 100101.110011001100110011 . . ., but when you stop after 64 bits or so, this answer isn't exactly 37.8. It's more like 37.800000000000004, which is slightly inaccurate. In a Java program, when you ask whether `9.0 / 5.0 * 21 + 32.0` is exactly equal to `69.8`, the computer says "No, that's false."

Avoid comparing `double` values or `float` values for equality (using ==) or for inequality (using !=). Comparing strings for equality (as in the expression `"passw0rd" == "passw0rd"`) is also unadvisable.

For details about comparing strings, see Chapter 8.

```
        100101.110011001100110011 ... etc.
101)10111101.000000000
    101
    0111
    0101
     1001
     0101
      100 0
      010 1
       1 10
       1 01
        1000
        0101
         110
         101
         1000
```

Figure 6-7:
A division
problem that
never ends.

Use Java's logical operators

Real-life situations might involve long chains of conditions. Here's an example I found in a letter from the U.S. Department of Education federal student loans department:

> Interest starts to accrue daily prior to repayment on all unsubsidized loans beginning on the first disbursement date and on all unsubsidized loans first disbursed on or after July 1, 2012 and before July 1, 2014 at the beginning of the grace period*. . . .
>
> *Grace Period — A 6-month period before the first payment on a subsidized or unsubsidized Stafford Loan is due. The grace period begins the day after the student graduates, leaves school, or drops below half-time status and ends the day before the repayment period begins.

Whew! I'm glad I didn't miss any of the fine print!

The good news is that an app's conditions can be expressed using Java's `&&`, `||` and `!` operators. The story begins in Listing 6-3. Here, the listing's code computes the price for a movie theater ticket.

Listing 6-3:   Pay the Regular Ticket Price?

```java
package com.allmycode.tickets;

import javax.swing.JOptionPane;

public class Regular {

  public static void main(String[] args) {
    String ageString;
    int age;
    boolean chargeRegularPrice;

    ageString = JOptionPane.showInputDialog("Age?");
    age = Integer.parseInt(ageString);
    chargeRegularPrice = 18 <= age && age < 65;
    JOptionPane.showMessageDialog(null,
        chargeRegularPrice, "Regular price?",
        JOptionPane.INFORMATION_MESSAGE);
  }

}
```

Figure 6-8 shows a run of the code in Listing 6-3 with the value of age set to 17; Figure 6-9 shows a run with age set to 18.

Figure 6-8:
A youngster
goes to the
movies.

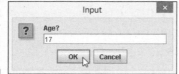 

Figure 6-9:
If you
can drink
alcohol in
Moldova,
you can pay
full price at
our theater!

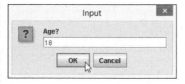 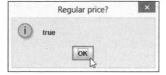

Figures 6-8 and 6-9 might look peculiar because I've chosen to display the words `true` and `false` instead of more user-friendly messages (such as `Charge this bum the regular price!`). I do better when I cover Java's `if` statements in Chapter 8.

In Listing 6-3, the value of `chargeRegularPrice` is `true` or `false` depending on the outcome of the `18 <= age && age < 65` condition test. The `&&` operator stands for a logical *and* combination, so `18 <= age && age < 65` is `true` as long as `age` is greater than or equal to 18 *and* `age` is less than 65.

To create a condition like `18 <= age && age < 65`, you have to use the `age` variable twice. You can't write `18 <= age < 65`. Other people might understand what `18 <= age < 65` means, but Java doesn't understand it.

In the earlier section "Java isn't like a game of horseshoes," I warn against using the `==` operator to compare two `double` values with one another. If you absolutely must compare `double` values with one another, give yourself a little leeway. Rather than writing `fahrTemp == 69.8`, write something like this:

```
(69.7779 < fahrTemp) && (fahrTemp < 69.8001)
```

Listing 6-3 has two other interesting new features. One feature is the use of `JOptionPane.showInputDialog`. This method displays a dialog box like the first box shown earlier, in Figure 6-8 (and the first box shown in Figure 6-9). The box has its own text field for the user's input. Normally, the user types something in the text field and then presses OK. Whatever the user types in the text field becomes the value of the call to JOptionPane.showInput-Dialog, as shown in Figure 6-10.

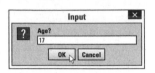

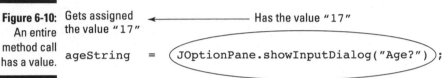

Figure 6-10:
An entire
method call
has a value.

In Figure 6-10, notice that the entire method call JOptionPane.showInputDialog("Age?") becomes synonymous with the string "17" (or with whatever the user types in the text field in the dialog box). So the statement

```
ageString = JOptionPane.showInputDialog("Age?");
```

effectively becomes the following statement:

```
ageString = "17";
```

The showInputDialog method always returns a string of characters, so in Listing 6-3, it's important that I declare appString to be of type String. The problem is that a string of characters isn't the same as a number. You can't use the < operator to compare "17" with "18". Java doesn't do arithmetic on strings of characters, even when those strings happen to look like numbers.

Before comparing the user's input with the numbers 18 and 65, you have to turn the user's input into a number. (You have to turn a string like "17" into an int value like 17.) To do that, you call Java's Integer.parseInt method:

✔ The Integer.parseInt method's parameter is a String value.

✔ The value of a call to the Integer.parseInt is an int value.

So, in Listing 6-3, the statement

```
age = Integer.parseInt(ageString);
```

assigns an int value to the variable age. That's good because, in the listing, age is declared to be of type int.

Listing 6-4 illustrates Java's || operator. (In case you're not sure, you type the || operator by pressing the | key twice.) The || operator stands for a logical *or* combination, so age < 18 || 65 <= age is true as long as age is less than 18 *or* age is greater than or equal to 65.

Listing 6-4: Pay the Discounted Ticket Price?

```java
package com.allmycode.tickets;

import javax.swing.JOptionPane;

public class Discount {

  public static void main(String[] args) {
    String ageString;
    int age;
    boolean chargeDiscountPrice;

    ageString = JOptionPane.showInputDialog("Age?");
    age = Integer.parseInt(ageString);
    chargeDiscountPrice = age < 18 || 65 <= age;
    JOptionPane.showMessageDialog(null,
        chargeDiscountPrice, "Discount price?",
        JOptionPane.INFORMATION_MESSAGE);
  }

}
```

Runs of the code from Listing 6-4 are shown in Figures 6-11 and 6-12.

Figure 6-11: Ah, to be young again!

 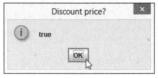

Figure 6-12: Ah, to be old at last!

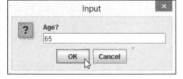 

Listing 6-5 adds Java's ! operator to the logical stew. If you're unfamiliar with languages like Java, you have to stop thinking that the exclamation point means, "Yes, definitely." Instead, Java's ! operator means *not*. In Listing 6-5, with isSpecialShowing being true or false, the expression

!isSpecialShowing stands for the opposite of isSpecialShowing. That is, when isSpecialShowing is true, !isSpecialShowing is false. And when isSpecialShowing is false, !isSpecialShowing is true.

Listing 6-5:   What about Special Showings?

```
package com.allmycode.tickets;

import javax.swing.JOptionPane;

public class Discount2 {

  public static void main(String[] args) {
    String ageString;
    int age;
    boolean chargeDiscountPrice;
    String specialShowingString;
    boolean isSpecialShowing;

    ageString = JOptionPane.showInputDialog("Age?");
    age = Integer.parseInt(ageString);

    specialShowingString = JOptionPane.showInputDialog
        ("Special showing (true/false)?");
    isSpecialShowing =
        Boolean.parseBoolean(specialShowingString);
    chargeDiscountPrice =
        (age < 18 || 65 <= age) && !isSpecialShowing;

    JOptionPane.showMessageDialog(null,
        chargeDiscountPrice, "Discount price?",
        JOptionPane.INFORMATION_MESSAGE);
  }

}
```

Runs of the code from Listing 6-5 are shown in Figures 6-13 and 6-14.

The primary condition in Listing 6-5 grants the discount price to kids and to seniors as long as the current feature isn't a "special showing" — one that the management considers to be a hot item, such as the first week of the run of a highly anticipated movie. When there's a special showing, no one gets the discounted price.

In Figures 6-13 and 6-14, I artificially force the user to type the word true or the word false (without quotation marks) in an input text field. Figure 6-15 shows how the user's response becomes a string of characters that's deposited into my specialShowingString variable.

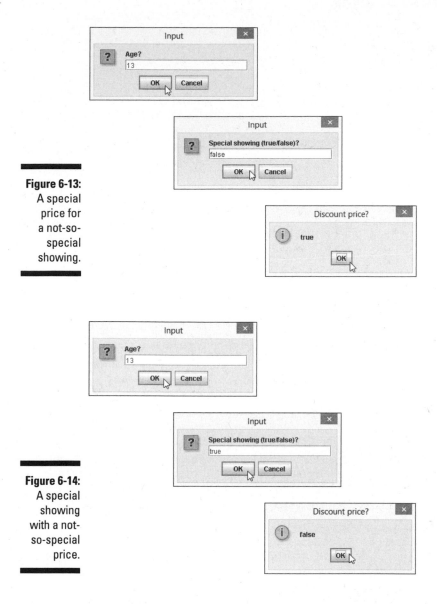

Figure 6-13:
A special price for a not-so-special showing.

Figure 6-14:
A special showing with a not-so-special price.

In the next statement in Listing 6-5, the method `Boolean.parseBoolean` does for `boolean` values what `Integer.parseInt` does for `int` values. The `Boolean.parseBoolean` method turns the value of `specialShowing` `String` (the string `"true"` or `"false"`) into an honest-to-goodness `boolean` value. To this `boolean` value, the computer can apply the `!` operator and, if needed, the `&&` and `||` operators.

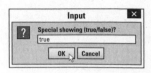

Figure 6-15:
Getting the
word *true*
from the
user's input.

Gets assigned
the value "true"

Has the value "true"

```
specialShowingString = JOptionPane.showInputDialog(...);
```

For any condition you want to express, you always have several ways to express it. For example, rather than test `numberOfCats != 3`, you can be more long-winded and test `!(numberOfCats == 3)`. Rather than test `myAge < yourAge`, you can get the same answer by testing `yourAge > myAge` or `!(myAge >= yourAge)`. Rather than type `a != b && c != d`, you can get the same result with `!(a == b || c == d)`. (A guy named Augustus DeMorgan told me about this last trick.)

Parenthetically speaking . . .

The big condition in Listing 6-5 (the condition `(age < 18 || 65 <= age) && !isSpecialShowing`) illustrates the need for (and the importance of) parentheses (but only when parentheses are needed (or when they help people understand your code)).

When you don't use parentheses, Java's *precedence rules* settle arguments about the meaning of the expression. They tell you whether the line

```
age < 18 || 65 <= age && !isSpecialShowing
```

stands for the expression

```
(age < 18 || 65 <= age) && !isSpecialShowing
```

or for this one:

```
age < 18 || (65 <= age && !isSpecialShowing)
```

According to the precedence rules, in the absence of parentheses, the computer evaluates `&&` before evaluating `||`. If you omit the parentheses, the computer first checks to find out whether `65 <= age && !isSpecial Showing`. Then the computer combines the result with a test of the `age < 18` condition. Imagine a 16-year-old kid buying a movie ticket on the day of a special showing. The condition `65 <= age && !isSpecialShowing` is `false`, but the condition `age < 18` is `true`. Because one of the two conditions on either side of the `||` operator is `true`, the whole nonparenthesized condition is `true` — and, to the theater management's dismay, the 16-year-old kid gets a discount ticket.

Sometimes, you can take advantage of Java's precedence rules and omit the parentheses in an expression. But I have a problem: I don't like memorizing precedence rules, and when I visit Java's online language specifications document (`docs.oracle.com/javase/specs/jls/se5.0/html/j3TOC.html`), I don't like figuring out how the rules apply to a particular condition.

When I create an expression like the one in Listing 6-5, I almost always use parentheses. In general, I use parentheses if I have any doubt about the way the computer behaves without them. I also add parentheses when doing so makes the code easier to read.

Sometimes, if I'm not sure about stuff and I'm in a curious frame of mind, I write a quick Java program to test the precedence rules. For example, I run Listing 6-5 with and without the condition's parentheses. I send a 16-year-old kid to the movie theater when there's a special showing and see whether the kid ever gets a discount ticket. This little experiment shows me that the parentheses aren't optional.

Chapter 7

Though These Be Methods, Yet There Is Madness in't

*I*n Chapter 5, I compare a method declaration to a recipe for scrambled eggs. In this chapter, I compute the tax and tip for a meal in a restaurant. And in Chapter 9 (spoiler alert!), I compare a Java class to the inventory in a cheese emporium. These comparisons aren't far-fetched. A method's declaration is a lot like a recipe, and a Java class bears some resemblance to a blank inventory sheet. But instead of thinking about methods, recipes, and Java classes, you might be reading between the lines. You might be wondering why this author uses so many food metaphors.

The truth is, my preoccupation with food is a recent development. Like most men my age, I've been told that I should shed my bad habits, lose a few pounds, exercise regularly, and find ways to reduce the stress in my life. (I've argued to my Wiley editors that submission deadlines are a source of stress, but so far the editors aren't buying a word of it. I guess I don't blame them.)

Above all, I've been told to adopt a healthy diet: Skip the chocolate, the cheeseburgers, the pizza, the fatty foods, the fried foods, the sugary snacks, and everything else that I normally eat. Instead, eat small portions of vegetables, carbs, and protein, and eat these things only at regularly scheduled meals. Sounds sensible, doesn't it?

I'm making a sincere effort. I've been eating right for about two weeks. My feelings of health and well-being are steadily improving. I'm only slightly hungry. (Actually, by "slightly hungry," I mean "extremely hungry." Yesterday I suffered a brief hallucination, believing that my computer keyboard was a giant Hershey's bar. And this morning I felt like gnawing on my office furniture. If I start trying to peeling my mouse, I'll stop writing and go out for a snack.)

One way or another, the gustatory arena provides many fine metaphors for object-oriented programming. A method's declaration is like a recipe. A declaration sits quietly, doing nothing, waiting to be executed. If you create a declaration but no one ever calls your declaration, then like a recipe for worm stew, your declaration goes unexecuted.

On the other hand, a *method call* is a call to action — a command to follow the declaration's recipe. When you call a method, the method's declaration wakes up and follows the instructions inside the body of the declaration.

In addition, a method call may contain parameters. You call

```
JOptionPane.showMessageDialog (null, ticketPrice)
```

with the parameters `null` and `ticketPrice`. The first parameter, `null`, tells the computer not to house the dialog box inside another window. The second parameter, `ticketPrice`, tells the computer what to display in the dialog box. In the world of food, you might call `meatLoaf(6)`, which means, "Follow the meat loaf recipe, and make enough to serve six people."

A method has two facets: the first is the method's declaration; the second consists of any statements making calls to the method.

Practice Safe Typing

"You can't fit a square peg into a round hole," or so the saying goes. In Java programming, the saying goes one step further: "Like all other developers, you sometimes make a mistake and try to fit a square peg into a round hole. Java's type system alerts you to the mistake and doesn't let you run the flawed code."

Here's an example illustrating pegs and holes: According to the U.S. census, the average number of children per family in the year 2000 was 0.9. But by mid-2000, the Duggar family (of *19 Kids & Counting* television fame) had 12 children. No matter when you take the census, the average number of children is a `double` value, and the number of children in a particular family is an `int` value.

In Figure 7-1, I try to calculate the Duggar family's divergence from the national average. I don't even show you a run of this program, because the program doesn't work. It's defective. It's damaged goods. As cousin Jeb would say, "This program is a dance party on a leaky raft in a muddy river."

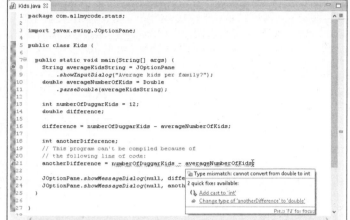

```
Kids.java ✕
  1  package com.allmycode.stats;
  2
  3  import javax.swing.JOptionPane;
  4
  5  public class Kids {
  6
  7⊖   public static void main(String[] args) {
  8      String averageKidsString = JOptionPane
  9          .showInputDialog("Average kids per family?");
 10      double averageNumberOfKids = Double
 11          .parseDouble(averageKidsString);
 12
 13      int numberOfDuggarKids = 12;
 14      double difference;
 15
 16      difference = numberOfDuggarKids - averageNumberOfKids;
 17
 18      int anotherDifference;
 19      // This program can't be compiled because of
 20      // the following line of code:
 21      anotherDifference = numberOfDuggarKids - averageNumberOfKids;
 22
 23      JOptionPane.showMessageDialog(null, diffe   Type mismatch: cannot convert from double to int
 24      JOptionPane.showMessageDialog(null, anoth  2 quick fixes available:
 25    }                                             ⬦ Add cast to 'int'
 26                                                   ⬦ Change type of 'anotherDifference' to 'double'
 27  }
                                                   Pre;; 'F2' for focus
```

Figure 7-1:
Trying to fit
a square
peg into a
round hole.

The code in Figure 7-1 deals with two types of values — double values (in the averageNumberOfKids variable) and int values (in the numberOfDuggarKids variable). You might plan to type 1 when the computer prompts you for Average kids per family. But the value stored in the averageNumberOfKids variable is of type double. An input like 1 or 1.0 doesn't scare the computer into storing anything but a double in the averageNumberOfKids variable.

The expression numberOfDuggarKids - averageNumberOfKids is an int minus a double, so (according to my sage advice in Chapter 6) the value of numberOfDuggarKids - averageNumberOfKids is of type double. Sure, if you type 1 when you're prompted for Average kids per family, then numberOfDuggarKids - averageNumberOfKids is 11.0, and 11.0 is sort of the same as the int value 11. But Java doesn't like things to be "sort of the same."

Java's *strong typing* rules say that you can't assign a double value (like 11.0) to an int variable (like anotherDifference). You don't lose any accuracy when you chop the *.0* off *11.0*. But with digits to the right of the decimal point (even with *0* to the right of the decimal point), Java doesn't trust you to stuff a double value into an int variable. After all, rather than type 1.0 when you're prompted for Average kids per family, you can type 0.9. Then you'd definitely lose accuracy, from stuffing *11.1* into an int variable.

You can try to assure Java that things are okay by using a plain, old assignment statement, like this:

```
double averageNumberOfKids;
averageNumberOfKids = 1;
```

When you do, the only way for `numberOfDuggarKids - averageNumberOfKids` to have any value other than 11.0 is for you to make more changes to the Java code. Even so, Java doesn't like assigning 11.0 to the `int` variable `anotherDifference`. This statement is still illegal:

```
anotherDifference =
            numberOfDuggarKids - averageNumberOfKids;
```

When you put numbers in your Java code (like 1 in the previous paragraph or like the number 12 in Figure 7-1) you *hardcode* the values. In this book, my liberal use of hardcoding keeps the examples simple and (more importantly) concrete. But in real applications, hardcoding is generally a bad idea. When you hardcode a value, you make it difficult to change. In fact, the only way to change a hardcoded value is to tinker with the Java code, and all code (written in Java or not) can be brittle. It's much safer to input values in a dialog box (or to read the value from a hard drive or an SD card) than to change a value in a piece of code.

Remember to do as I say and not as I do. Avoid hardcoding values in your programs.

Widening is good; narrowing is bad

Java prevents you from making any assignment that potentially *narrows* a value, as shown in Figure 7-2. For example, if with the declarations

```
int numberOfDuggarKids = 12;
long lotsAndLotsOfKids;
```

the following attempt to narrow from a `long` value to an `int` value is illegal:

```
numberOfDuggarKids = lotsAndLotsOfKids; //Don't do this!
```

An attempt to *widen* from an `int` value to a `long` value, however, is fine:

```
lotsAndLotsOfKids = numberOfDuggarKids;
```

In fact, back in Figure 7-1, I assign an `int` value to a `double` value with no trouble at all:

```
double difference;
difference = numberOfDuggarKids - averageNumberOfKids;
```

Assigning an `int` value to a `double` value is legal because it's an example of widening.

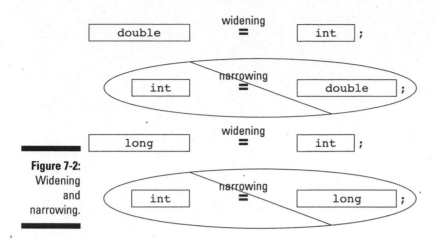

Figure 7-2:
Widening
and
narrowing.

Incompatible types

Aside from the technical terms *narrowing* and *widening*, there's another possibility — plain, old incompatibility — trying to fit one element into another when the two have nothing in common and have no hope of ever being mistaken for one another. You can't assign an `int` value to a `boolean` value or assign a `boolean` value to an `int` value:

```
int numberOfDuggarKids;
boolean isLarge;
numberOfDuggarKids = isLarge; //Don't do this!
isLarge = numberOfDuggarKids; //Don't do this!
```

You can't do either assignment because `boolean` values aren't numeric. In other words, neither of these assignments makes sense.

Java is a *strongly typed* computer programming language. It doesn't let you make assignments that might result in a loss of accuracy or in outright nonsense.

Using a hammer to bang a peg into a hole

In some cases, you can circumvent Java's prohibition against narrowing by *casting* a value. For example, you can create the `long` variable `lotsAndLotsOfKids` and make the assignment `numberOfDuggarKids = (int) lotsAndLotsOfKids`, as shown in Listing 7-1.

Listing 7-1:   Casting to the Rescue

```
package com.allmycode.stats;

import javax.swing.JOptionPane;

public class MoreKids {

   public static void main(String[] args) {
      long lotsAndLotsOfKids = 2147483647;
      int numberOfDuggarKids;

      numberOfDuggarKids = (int) lotsAndLotsOfKids;

      JOptionPane.showMessageDialog
                      (null, numberOfDuggarKids);
   }

}
```

The type name (int) in parentheses is a *cast operator*. It tells the computer that you're aware of the potential pitfalls of stuffing a long value into an int variable and that you're willing to take your chances.

When you run the code in Listing 7-1, the value of lotsAndLotsOfKids might be between –2147483648 and 2147483647. If so, the assignment numberOfDuggarKids = (int) lotsAndLotsOfKids is just fine. (*Remember:* An int value can be between –2147483648 and 2147483647. Refer to Table 6-1.)

But if the value of lotsAndLotsOfKids isn't between –2147483648 and 2147483647, the assignment statement in Listing 7-1 goes awry. When I run the code in Listing 7-1 with the different initialization

```
long lotsAndLotsOfKids = 2098797070970970956L;
```

the value of numberOfDuggarKids. becomes –287644852 (a negative number!).

When you use a casting operator, you're telling the computer, "I'm aware that I'm doing something risky but (trust me) I know what I'm doing." And if you don't know what you're doing, you get a wrong answer. That's life!

Calling a Method

After all the fuss I make in the previous section over type safety for assignment statements, I should give equal time to type safety for method calls. After all, a method call involves values going both ways — from the call to the running method and from the running method back to the call. Here are the details:

✔ **In a method call, each parameter has a value. The computer sends that value to one of the declaration's parameters.**

In a method call, each parameter has a type. The types of the parameters in the method's declaration must match the types of parameters in the method call.

✔ **A method declaration might contain a** `return` **statement, and the** `return` **statement might calculate a particular value. If so, the computer assigns that value back to the entire method call.**

A method's *return type* is the type of value calculated by the `return` statement. So the return type is the type of the method call's value.

To make this concept more concrete, consider the code in Listing 7-2.

Listing 7-2: Parameter Types and Return Types

```
package com.allmycode.money;

import java.text.NumberFormat;

import javax.swing.JOptionPane;

public class Mortgage {

  public static void main(String[] args) {
    double principal = 100000.00, ratePercent = 5.25;
    double payment;
    int years = 30;
    String paymentString;

    payment =
        monthlyPayment(principal, ratePercent, years);

    NumberFormat currency =
        NumberFormat.getCurrencyInstance();
    paymentString = currency.format(payment);
    JOptionPane.showMessageDialog(null,
        paymentString, "Monthly payment",
        JOptionPane.INFORMATION_MESSAGE);

  }

  static double monthlyPayment
    (double pPrincipal, double pRatePercent, int pYears) {

    double rate, effectiveAnnualRate;
    int paymentsPerYear = 12, numberOfPayments;
    rate = pRatePercent / 100.00;
    numberOfPayments = paymentsPerYear * pYears;
    effectiveAnnualRate = rate / paymentsPerYear;
```

(continued)

Listing 7-2 *(continued)*

```
    return pPrincipal * (effectiveAnnualRate /
            (1 - Math.pow(1 + effectiveAnnualRate,
                -numberOfPayments)));
    }

}
```

Again, to keep the example simple, I hardcode the values of the variables `principal`, `ratePercent`, and `years`, making Listing 7-2 useless for anything except one particular calculation. In a real app, you'd ask the user for the values of these variables.

Figure 7-3 shows the output of a run of the code in Listing 7-2.

Figure 7-3:
Pay it and
weep.

In Listing 7-2, I choose the parameter names `principal` and `pPrincipal`, `ratePercent` and `pRatePercent`, and `years` and `pYears`. I use the letter p to distinguish a declaration's parameter from a call's parameter. I do this to drive home the point that the names in the call aren't automatically the same as the names in the declaration. In fact, there are many variations on this call/declaration naming theme, and they're all correct. For example, you can use the same names in the call as in the declaration:

```
    payment =
        monthlyPayment(principal, ratePercent, years);


static double monthlyPayment
    (double principal, double ratePercent, int years) {
```

You can use expressions in the call that aren't single variable names:

```
    payment =
        monthlyPayment(amount + fees, rate * 100, 30);


static double monthlyPayment
    (double pPrincipal, double pRatePercent, int pYears) {
```

When you call a method from Java's API, you don't even know the names of parameters used in the method's declaration. And you don't care. The only things that matter are the positions of parameters in the list and the compatibility of the parameters:

✔ **The value of the call's leftmost parameter becomes the value of the declaration's leftmost parameter, no matter what name the declaration's leftmost parameter has.**

Of course, the types of the two leftmost parameters (the call's parameter and the declaration's parameter) must be compatible.

✔ **The value of the call's second parameter becomes the value of the declaration's second parameter, no matter what name the declaration's second parameter has.**

And so on.

Real Java developers start the names of variables and methods with lowercase letters. You can ignore this convention and create a method named `MonthlyPayment` or `MONTHLY_PAYMENT`, for example. But if you ignore the convention, some developers will wince when they read your code.

Method parameters and Java types

Listing 7-2 contains both the declaration and a call for the `monthlyPayment` method. Figure 7-4 illustrates the type matches between these two parts of the program.

```
double principal = 100000.00, ratePercent = 5.25;
double payment;
int years = 30;
```

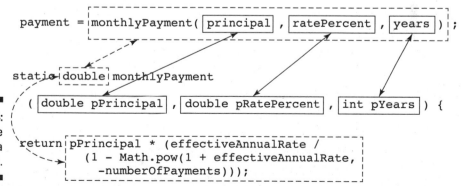

Figure 7-4: Each value fits like a glove.

```
payment = monthlyPayment( principal , ratePercent , years );

static double monthlyPayment

( double pPrincipal , double pRatePercent , int pYears ) {

return pPrincipal * (effectiveAnnualRate /
    (1 - Math.pow(1 + effectiveAnnualRate,
        -numberOfPayments)));
```

In Figure 7-4, the monthlyPayment method call has three parameters, and the monthlyPayment declaration's header has three parameters. The call's three parameters have the types double and then double and then int. And sure enough, the declaration's three parameters have the types double and then double and then int.

As in the earlier section "Practice Safe Typing," you don't need an exact match between a method call's parameter and the declaration's parameter. You can take advantage of widening. For example, in Listing 7-2, adding the following call would be okay:

```
payment = monthlyPayment(100000, 5, years);
```

You can pass an int value (like 100000) to the pPrincipal parameter, because the pPrincipal parameter is of type double. Java widens the values 100000 and 5 to the values 100000.0 and 5.0. But, once again, Java doesn't narrow your values. The following call causes a big red blotch in the Eclipse editor:

```
payment = monthlyPayment(principal, ratePercent, 30.0);
```

You can't stuff a double value (like 30.0) into the pYears parameter, because the pYears parameter is of type int.

In a method declaration, each parameter has the form

```
typeName variableName
```

For example, in the declaration that starts with static double monthlyPayment(double pPrincipal, the word double is a *typeName*, and the word pPrincipal is a *variableName*. But in a method call, each parameter is an expression with a certain value. In the main method in Listing 7-2, the call monthlyPayment(principal, ratePercent, years) contains three parameters: principal, ratePercent, and years. Each of these parameters has a value. So with the initializations in the main method, the call monthlyPayment(principal, ratePercent, years) is essentially the same as calling monthlyPayment(100000.00, 5.25, 30). In fact, a call like monthlyPayment(100000.00, 5.25, 30) or monthlyPayment(10 * 1000.00, 5 + 0.25, 30) is legal in Java. A method call's parameters can be expressions of any kind. The only requirement is that the expressions in the call have types that are compatible with the corresponding parameters in the method's declaration.

Return types

A method declaration's header normally looks like this:

```
someWords returnType methodName(parameters) {
```

For example, Listing 7-2 contains a method declaration with the following header:

```
static double monthlyPayment
  (double pPrincipal, double pRatePercent, int pYears)
```

In this header, the *returnType* is double, the *methodName* is monthly Payment, and the *parameters* are double pPrincipal, double pRatePercent, int pYears.

A method declaration's parameter list differs from the method call's parameter list. The declaration's parameter list contains the name of each parameter's type. In contrast, the call's parameter list contains no type names.

An entire method call can have a value, and the declaration's *returnType* tells the computer what type that value has. In Listing 7-2, the *returnType* is double, so the call

```
monthlyPayment(principal, ratePercent, years)
```

has a value of type double. (Refer to Figure 7-4.)

I hardcoded the values of principal, ratePercent, and years in Listing 7-2. So when you run Listing 7-2, the value of the monthlyPayment method call is always 552.20. The call's value is whatever comes after the word return when the method is executed. And in Listing 7-2, the expression

```
pPrincipal * (effectiveAnnualRate /
  (1 - Math.pow(1 + effectiveAnnualRate,
    -numberOfPayments)))
```

always comes out to be 552.20. Also, in keeping with the theme of type safety, the expression after the word return is of type double.

In summary, a call to the monthlyPayment method has the *return value* 552.20 and has the *return type* double.

Only book authors and bad programmers hardcode values like `principal`, `ratePercent`, and `years`. I hardcoded these values to keep the example as simple as possible. But, normally, values like these should be part of the program's input so that the values can change from one run to another.

The great void

A method to compute a monthly mortgage payment naturally returns a value. But a Java program's `main` method, or Java's own `showMessageDialog` method (with no user input), has little reason to return a value.

When a method doesn't return a value, the method's body has no `return` statement. And, in place of a return type, the header in the method's declaration contains the word `void`. A program's `main` method doesn't return a value, so when you create a main method, you type

```
public static void main(String args[]) {
```

To be painfully precise, you can put a `return` statement in a method that doesn't return a value. When you do, the `return` statement has no expression. It's just one word, `return`, followed by a semicolon. When the computer executes this `return` statement, the computer ends the run of the method and returns to the code that called the method. This rarely used form of the `return` statement works well in a situation in which you want to end the execution of a method before you reach the last statement in the method's declaration.

Displaying numbers

Here are a few lines that are scattered about in Listing 7-2:

```
import java.text.NumberFormat;

NumberFormat currency =
        NumberFormat.getCurrencyInstance();
paymentString = currency.format(payment);
```

Taken together, these statements give you easy formatting of numbers into local currency amounts. On my computer, when I call `getCurrencyInstance()` with no parameters, I get a number (like 552.2) formatted for United States currency. (Refer to Figure 7-3.) But if your computer is set to run in Germany, you see the message box shown in Figure 7-5.

Figure 7-5:
Displaying
the euro
symbol.

A country, its native language, or a variant of the native language is a *locale*. And by adding a parameter to the `getCurrencyInstance` call, you can format for locales other than your own. For example, by calling

```
NumberFormat.getCurrencyInstance(Locale.GERMANY)
```

anyone in any country can get the message box shown in Figure 7-5.

In the choice of available locales, standard Oracle Java is a bit better than Android Java. For example, the `Locale.GERMANY` trick works in standard Java and in Android Java. But some variants of the Thai language use their own, special digit symbols. (See Figure 7-6.) To form a number with Thai digits, you need

```
NumberFormat.getCurrencyInstance(
                    new Locale("th", "TH", "TH"))
```

And this locale works only in standard Java.

Figure 7-6:
Thai digit
symbols.

Method overload without software bloat

Chapter 5 introduces method overloading. But that chapter doesn't show you a complete example using method overloading. Listing 7-3 remedies this situation.

Listing 7-3: Filling but Not Fatty (Yes, I'm Still Hungry)

```java
package com.allmycode.money;

import java.text.NumberFormat;

import javax.swing.JOptionPane;

public class Mortgage {

  public static void main(String[] args) {
    double principal = 100000.00, ratePercent = 5.25;
    double payment;
    int years = 30;
    String paymentString;
    NumberFormat currency =
        NumberFormat.getCurrencyInstance();

    payment =
        monthlyPayment(principal, ratePercent, years);
    paymentString = currency.format(payment);
    JOptionPane.showMessageDialog(null,
        paymentString, "Monthly payment",
        JOptionPane.INFORMATION_MESSAGE);

    ratePercent = 3.0;
    payment = monthlyPayment(principal, ratePercent);
    paymentString = currency.format(payment);
    JOptionPane.showMessageDialog(null,
        paymentString, "Monthly payment",
        JOptionPane.INFORMATION_MESSAGE);

    payment = monthlyPayment();
    paymentString = currency.format(payment);
    JOptionPane.showMessageDialog(null,
        paymentString, "Monthly payment",
        JOptionPane.INFORMATION_MESSAGE);

  }

  static double monthlyPayment
    (double pPrincipal, double pRatePercent, int pYears) {

    double rate, effectiveAnnualRate;
    int paymentsPerYear = 12, numberOfPayments;
    rate = pRatePercent / 100.00;
    numberOfPayments = paymentsPerYear * pYears;
    effectiveAnnualRate = rate / paymentsPerYear;
    return pPrincipal * (effectiveAnnualRate /
            (1 - Math.pow(1 + effectiveAnnualRate,
              -numberOfPayments)));
```

```
   }

   static double monthlyPayment
    (double pPrincipal, double pRatePercent) {

     return monthlyPayment(pPrincipal, pRatePercent, 30);
   }

   static double monthlyPayment() {
     return 0.0;
   }
}
```

The three dialog boxes that you see when you run the code in Listing 7-3 are shown in Figure 7-7.

In Listing 7-3, the monthlyPayment method has three declarations, each with its own parameter list, and with each parameter list representing a different bunch of types. As a method name, the name monthlyPayment is *overloaded*.

✔ **The first monthlyPayment declaration is a copy of the declaration in Listing 7-2.**

When you call the first declaration, you supply values for three parameters — two double values and one int value:

```
monthlyPayment(principal, ratePercent, years)
```

Figure 7-7:
Running
the code in
Listing 7-3.

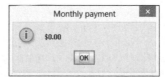

✔ **The second `monthlyPayment` declaration has only two parameters.**

When you call the second declaration, you supply values for only two `double` parameters:

```
monthlyPayment(principal, ratePercent)
```

When the computer encounters this `monthlyPayment` call with two `double` parameters, the computer executes the `monthlyPayment` declaration that has two `double` parameters. (See Listing 7-3.) This automatic choice of method declaration is what makes overloading work.

Notice the trick that I use in the body of the two-parameter `monthly Payment` declaration. To create the two-parameter declaration, I could get away with simply duplicating the code from the three-parameter `monthlyPayment` declaration:

```
// (Insert throat-clearing here.) This duplication
// of code isn't a very good idea.
static double monthlyPayment
  (double pPrincipal, double pRatePercent) {

  double rate, effectiveAnnualRate;
  int paymentsPerYear = 12, numberOfPayments;
  rate = pRatePercent / 100.00;
  numberOfPayments = paymentsPerYear * 30;
  effectiveAnnualRate = rate / paymentsPerYear;
  return pPrincipal * (effectiveAnnualRate /
          (1 - Math.pow(1 + effectiveAnnualRate,
            -numberOfPayments)));
}
```

But duplicating code is a bad idea. Copying and pasting code causes errors down the road. In Listing 7-3, I don't copy the three-parameter code. Instead, I call the three-parameter `monthlyPayment` method from the body of the two-parameter `monthlyPayment` method. I supply a default value of `30` for the third `pYears` parameter. In the program's documentation, I must state clearly that the two-parameter `monthly Payment` method assumes a 30-year mortgage term.

✔ **The third `monthlyPayment` declaration has no parameters.**

When you call the third declaration in Listing 7-3, you don't supply values for any parameters. Instead, you follow the method's name with an empty pair of parentheses:

```
monthlyPayment()
```

> The parameterless `monthlyPayment` method might be useful in those don't-know-what-else-to-do situations. You have to display something about a borrower who hasn't yet decided on the principal, rate, or number of years. With little or no information about a mortgage loan, you display `$0.00` as a temporary value for the borrower's monthly payment.

For method overloading to work, the parameter types in a call must match the parameter types in a declaration. In Listing 7-3, no two `monthlyPayment` declarations have the same number of parameters, so parameter matching isn't too challenging.

But there's more to matching than having the same number of parameters. For example, you can add another two-parameter declaration to the code in Listing 7-3:

```
static double monthlyPayment
    (double pPrincipal, int pYears) {
```

With this addition, you have more than one two-parameter `monthly Payment` declaration — an old declaration with two `double` parameters and a new declaration with a `double` parameter and an `int` parameter. If you call `monthlyPayment(principal, 15)`, the computer calls the newly added method. It calls the new method because the new method, with its `double` and `int` parameters, is a better match for your call than the old `monthlyPayment(`**`double`** `pPrincipal,` **`double`** `pRatePercent)` declaration in Listing 7-3.

Primitive Types and Pass-by Value

Java has two kinds of types: primitive and reference. The eight primitive types are the atoms — the basic building blocks. In contrast, the reference types are the things you create by combining primitive types (and by combining other reference types).

My coverage of Java's reference types begins in Chapter 9.

Here are two concepts you should remember when you think about primitive types and method parameters:

✓ **When you assign a value to a variable with a primitive type, you're identifying that variable name with the value.**

The same is true when you initialize a primitive type variable to a particular value.

✔ **When you call a method, you're *making copies* of each of the call's parameter values and initializing the declaration's parameters with those copied values.**

This scheme, in which you make copies of the call's values, is named *pass-by value*. Listing 7-4 shows you why you should care about any of this.

Listing 7-4:   Rack Up Those Points!

```
import javax.swing.JOptionPane;

public class Scorekeeper {

  public static void main(String[] args) {
    int score = 50000;
    int points = 1000;
    addPoints(score, points);
    JOptionPane.showMessageDialog(null, score,
        "New Score", JOptionPane.INFORMATION_MESSAGE);
  }

  static void addPoints(int score, int points) {
    score += points;
  }

}
```

In Listing 7-4, the addPoints method uses Java's compound assignment operator to add 1000 (the value of points) to the existing score (which is 50000). To make things as cozy as possible, I've used the same parameter names in the method call and the method declaration. (In both, I use the names score and points.)

So what happens when I run the code in Listing 7-4? I get the result shown in Figure 7-8.

Figure 7-8:
Getting
1000 more
points?

But wait! When you add 1000 to 50000, you don't normally get 50000. What's wrong?

With Java's pass-by value feature, you *make a copy* of each parameter value in a call. You initialize the declaration's parameters with the copied values. So immediately after making the call, you have two pairs of variables: the original `score` and `points` variables in the `main` method and the new `score` and `points` variables in the `addPoints` method. The new `score` and `points` variables have copies of values from the `main` method. (See Figure 7-9.)

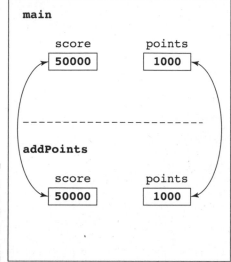

Figure 7-9: Java makes copies of the values of variables.

The statement in the body of the `addPoints` method adds 1000 to the value stored in its `score` variable. After adding 1000 points, the program's variables look like the stuff shown in Figure 7-10.

Notice how the value of the `main` method's `score` variable remains unchanged. After returning from the call to `addPoints`, the `addPoints` method's variables disappear. All that remains is the original `main` method and its variables. (See Figure 7-11.)

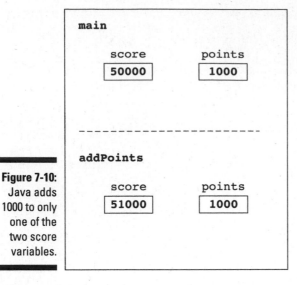

Figure 7-10:
Java adds
1000 to only
one of the
two score
variables.

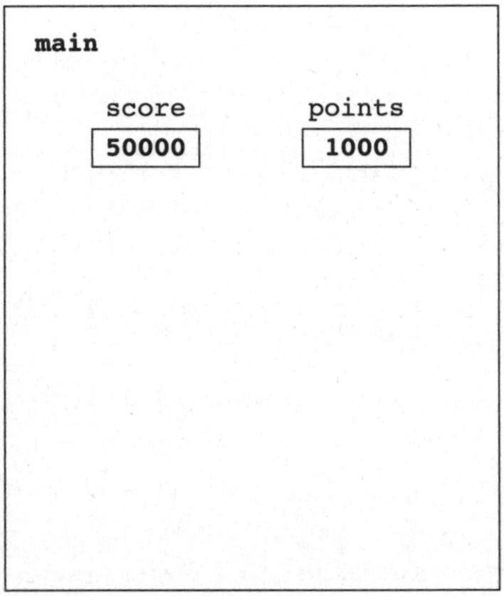

Figure 7-11:
The vari-
able with
value 51000
no longer
exists.

Finally, in Listing 7-4, the computer calls showMessageDialog to display the value of the main method's score variable. And (sadly, for the game player) the value of score is still 50000.

Perils and pitfalls of parameter passing

How would you like to change the value of 2 + 2? What would you like 2 + 2 to be? Six? Ten? Three hundred? In certain older versions of the FORTRAN programming language, you could make 2 + 2 be almost anything you wanted. For example, the following chunk of code (translated to look like Java code) would display 6 for the value of 2 + 2:

```
public void increment(int
    score) {
  score++;
}
...
increment(2);
JOptionPane.
  showMessageDialog(null, 2
  + 2);
```

When computer languages were first being developed, their creators didn't realize how complicated parameter passing can be. They weren't as careful about specifying the rules for copying parameters' values or for doing whatever else they wanted to do with parameters. As a result, some versions of FORTRAN indiscriminately passed memory addresses rather than values. Though address-passing alone isn't a terrible idea, things

become ugly if the language designer isn't careful.

In some early FORTRAN implementations, the computer automatically (and without warning) turned the literal 2 into a variable named two. (In fact, the newly created variable probably wasn't named two. But in this story, the actual name of the variable doesn't matter.) FORTRAN would substitute the variable name two in any place where the programmer typed the literal value 2. But then, while running this sidebar's code, the computer would send the address of the two variable to the increment method. The method would happily add 1 to whatever was stored in the two variable and then continue its work. Now the two variable stored the number 3. By the time you reached the showMessageDialog call, the computer would add to itself whatever was in two, getting 3 + 3, which is 6.

If you think parameter passing is a no-brainer, think again. Different languages use all different kinds of parameter passing. And in many situations, the minute details of the way parameters are passed makes a big difference.

What's a developer to do?

The program in Listing 7-4 has a big, fat bug. The program doesn't add 1000 to a player's score. That's bad.

You can squash the bug in Listing 7-4 in several different ways. For example, you can avoid calling the addPoints method by inserting score += points in the main method. But that's not a satisfactory solution. Methods such as addPoints are useful for dividing work into neat, understandable chunks. And avoiding problems by skirting around them is no fun at all.

A better way to get rid of the bug is to make the `addPoints` method return a value. Listing 7-5 has the code.

Listing 7-5:   A New-and-Improved Scorekeeper Program

```
import javax.swing.JOptionPane;

public class Scorekeeper {

  public static void main(String[] args) {
    int score = 50000;
    int points = 1000;
    score = addPoints(score, points);
    JOptionPane.showMessageDialog(null, score,
        "New Score", JOptionPane.INFORMATION_MESSAGE);
  }

  static int addPoints(int score, int points) {
    return score + points;
  }

}
```

In Listing 7-5, the new-and-improved `addPoints` method returns an `int` value; namely, the value of `score + points`. So the value of the `addPoints(score, points)` call is 51000. Finally, I change the value of `score` by assigning the method call's value, 51000, to the `score` variable.

Java's nitpicky rules insure that the juggling of the `score` variable's values is reliable and predictable. In the statement `score = addPoints(score, points)`, there's no conflict between the old value of `score` (50000 in the `addPoints` parameter list) and the new value of `score` (51000 on the left side of the assignment statement).

A run of the code in Listing 7-5 is shown in Figure 7-12. You probably already know what the run looks like. (After all, 50000 + 1000 is 51000.) But I can't bear to finish this example without showing the correct answer.

Figure 7-12:
At last,
a higher
score!

Making `addPoints` return a value isn't the only way to correct the problem in Listing 7-4. At least two other ways (using fields and passing objects) are among the subjects of discussion in Chapter 9.

A final word

The program in Listing 7-6 displays the total cost of a $100 meal.

Listing 7-6: Yet Another Food Example

```java
package org.allyourcode.food;

import java.text.NumberFormat;

import javax.swing.JOptionPane;

public class CheckCalculator {

  public static void main(String[] args) {
    NumberFormat currency =
        NumberFormat.getCurrencyInstance();
    JOptionPane.showMessageDialog(null,
        currency.format(addAll(100.00, 0.05, 0.20)));
  }

  static double addAll
        (double bill, double taxRate, double tipRate) {
    bill *= 1 + taxRate;
    bill *= 1 + tipRate;
    return bill;
  }

}
```

A run of the program in Listing 7-6 is shown in Figure 7-13.

Figure 7-13: Support your local eating establishment.

Listing 7-6 is nice, but this code computes the tip after the tax has been added to the original bill. Some of my less generous friends believe that the tip should be based on only the amount of the original bill. (Guys, you know who you are!) They believe that the code should compute the tax but that it should remember and reuse the original $100.00 amount when calculating the tip. Here's my friends' version of the `addAll` method:

```
static double addAll
      (double bill, double taxRate, double tipRate) {
  double originalBill = bill;
  bill *= 1 + taxRate;
  bill += originalBill * tipRate;
  return bill;
}
```

The new (stingier) total is shown in Figure 7-14.

Figure 7-14:
A dollar
saved is
a dollar
earned.

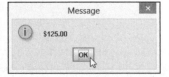

The revised `addAll` method is overly complicated. (In fact, in creating this example, I got this little method wrong two or three times before getting it right.) Wouldn't it be simpler to insist that the `bill` parameter's value never changes? Rather than mess with the `bill` amount, you make up new variables named `tax` and `tip` and total everything in the `return` statement:

```
static double addAll
      (double bill, double taxRate, double tipRate) {
  double tax = bill * taxRate;
  double tip = bill * tipRate;
  return bill + tax + tip;
}
```

When you have these new `tax` and `tip` variables, the `bill` parameter always stores its original value — the value of the untaxed, untipped meal.

After developing this improved code, you make a mental note that the `bill` variable's value shouldn't change. Months later, when your users are paying big bucks for your app and demanding many more features, you might turn the program into a complicated, all-purpose meal calculator with localized currencies and tipping etiquette from around the world. Whatever you do, you always want easy access to that original `bill` value.

After your app has gone viral, you're distracted by the need to count your earnings, pay your servants, and maintain the fresh smell of your private jet's leather seats. With all these pressing issues, you accidentally forget your old promise not to change the bill variable. You change the variable's value somewhere in the middle of your 1000-line program. Now you've messed everything up.

But wait! You can have Java remind you that the bill parameter's value doesn't change. To do this, you add the keyword final (one of Java's modifiers) to the method declaration's parameter list. And while you're at it, you can add final to the other parameters (taxRate and tipRate) in the addAll method's parameter list:

```
static double addAll (final double bill,
                      final double taxRate,
                      final double tipRate) {
  double tax = bill * taxRate;
  double tip = bill * tipRate;
  return bill + tax + tip;
}
```

With this use of the word final, you're telling the computer not to let you change a parameter's value. If you plug the newest version of addAll into the code in Listing 7-6, bill becomes 100.00 and bill stays 100.00 throughout the execution of the addAll method. If you accidentally add the statement

```
bill += valetParkingFee;
```

to your code, Eclipse flags that line as an error because a final parameter's value cannot be changed. Isn't it nice to know that, with servants to manage and your private jet to maintain, you can still rely on Java to help you write a good computer program?

Chapter 8

What Java Does (and When)

....

In This Chapter

▶ Making decisions with Java statements

▶ Repeating actions with Java statements

....

Human thought centers around nouns and verbs. Nouns are the "stuff," and verbs are the stuff's actions. Nouns are the pieces, and verbs are the glue. Nouns are, and verbs do. When you use nouns, you say "book," "room," or "stuff." When you use verbs, you say "do this," "do that," "tote that barge," or "lift that bale."

Java also has nouns and verbs. Java's nouns include `int`, `JOptionPane`, and `String`, along with Android-specific terms such as `Activity`, `Application`, and `Bundle`. Java's verbs involve assigning values, choosing among alternatives, repeating actions, and taking other courses of action.

This chapter covers some of Java's verbs. (In the next chapter, I bring in the nouns.)

Making Decisions

When you're writing computer programs, you're continually hitting forks in roads. Did the user type the correct password? If the answer is yes, let the user work; if it's no, kick the bum out. The Java programming language needs a way to make a program branch in one of two directions. Fortunately, the language has a way: It's the `if` statement. The use of the `if` statement is illustrated in Listing 8-1.

Listing 8-1:   Using an if Statement

```java
package com.allmycode.tickets;

import javax.swing.JOptionPane;

public class TicketPrice {

  public static void main(String[] args) {
    String ageString;
    int age;
    String specialShowingString;
    String price;

    ageString = JOptionPane.showInputDialog("Age?");
    age = Integer.parseInt(ageString);

    specialShowingString = JOptionPane.showInputDialog
        ("Special showing (y/n)?");

    if ((age < 18 || 65 <= age) &&
        specialShowingString.equals("n")) {
      price = "$7.00";
    } else {
      price = "$10.00";
    }

    JOptionPane.showMessageDialog(null,
        price, "Ticket price",
        JOptionPane.INFORMATION_MESSAGE);
  }

}
```

Listing 8-1 revives a question that I pose originally in Chapter 6: How much should a person pay for a movie ticket? Most people pay $10. But when the movie has no special showings, youngsters (under 18) and seniors (65 and older) pay only $7.

In Listing 8-1, a Java `if` statement determines a person's eligibility for the discounted ticket. If this condition is true:

```
(age < 18 || 65 <= age) && specialShowingString.
            equals("n")
```

the `price` becomes `"$7.00"`; otherwise, the `price` becomes `"$10.00"`. In either case, the code displays the `price` in a message box. (See Figure 8-1.)

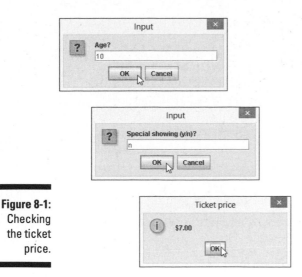

Figure 8-1:
Checking
the ticket
price.

Testing for equality

Java has several ways to test for equality: "Is this value the same as that
value?" None of these ways is the first one you'd consider. In particular,
to find out whether someone's age is 35, you *don't* write if (age = 35).
Instead, you use a double equal sign (==): if (age == 35). In Java, the
single equal sign (=) is reserved for *assignment*. So age = 35 means "Let
age stand for the value 35", and age == 35 means "True or false: Does age
stand for the value 35?"

Comparing two strings is a different story. When you compare two strings,
you don't use the double equal sign. Using it would ask a question that's
usually not what you want to ask: "Is this string stored in exactly the same
place in memory as that other string?" Instead, you usually ask, "Does this
string have the same characters in it as that other string?" To ask the second
question (the more appropriate one), use Java's equals method. To call
this equals method, follow one of the two strings with a dot and the word
equals, and then with a parameter list containing the other string:

```
if (specialShowingString.equals("n")) {
```

The equals method compares two strings to see whether they have the
same characters in them. In this paragraph's tiny example, the variable
specialShowingString refers to a string, and the text "n" refers to
a string. The condition specialShowingString.equals("n") is true
if specialShowingString refers to a string whose only character is the
letter n.

Java if statements

An `if` statement has this form:

```
if (condition) {
    statements to be executed when the condition is true
} else {
    statements to be executed when the condition is false
}
```

In Listing 8-1, the condition being tested is

```
(age < 18 || 65 <= age) &&
specialShowingString.equals("n")
```

The condition is either `true` or `false` — `true` for youngsters and seniors when there's no special showing and `false` otherwise.

Conditions in if statements

The condition in an `if` statement must be enclosed in parentheses. The condition must be a `boolean` expression — an expression whose value is either `true` or `false`. For example, the following condition is okay:

```
if (numberOfTries < 17) {
```

But the strange kind of condition that you can use in other (non-Java) languages — languages such as C++ — is not okay:

```
if (17) { //This is incorrect.
```

See Chapter 6 for information about Java's primitive types, including the `boolean` type.

Omitting braces

You can omit an `if` statement's curly braces when only one statement appears between the condition and the word `else`. You can also omit braces when only one statement appears after the word `else`. For example, the following chunk of code is right and proper:

```
if ((age < 18 || 65 <= age) &&
    specialShowingString.equals("n"))
  price = "$7.00";
else
  price = "$10.00";
```

The code is correct because only one statement (price = "$7.00") appears between the condition and the else, and only one statement (price = "$10.00") appears after the word else.

An if statement can also enjoy a full and happy life without an else part. The following example contains a complete if statement:

```
price = "$10.00";
if ((age < 18 || 65 <= age) &&
     specialShowingString.equals("n"))
  price = "$7.00";
```

Compound statements

An if statement is one of Java's *compound* statements because an if statement normally contains other Java statements. For example, the if statement in Listing 8-1 contains the assignment statement price = "$7.00" and the other assignment statement contains price = "$10.00".

A compound statement might even contain other compound statements. In this example:

```
price = "$10.00";
if (age < 18 || 65 <= age) {
  if (specialShowingString.equals("n")) {
    price = "$7.00";
  }
}
```

one if statement (with the condition age < 18 || 65 <= age) contains another if statement (with the condition specialShowingString.equals("n")).

A detour concerning Android screen densities

A device's *screen density* is the number of pixels squeezed into each inch of the screen. Older devices and less expensive devices have low screen densities, and newer, more expensive devices compete to have increasingly higher screen densities.

Android supports a wide range of screen densities. It also goes to the trouble of grouping the densities, as I show in Table 8-1.

Table 8-1	Android Screen Densities		
Name	**Acronym**	**Approximate* Number of Dots per Inch (dpi)**	**Fraction of the Default Density**
DENSITY_LOW	ldpi	120	¾
DENSITY_MEDIUM	mdpi	160	1
DENSITY_HIGH	hdpi	240	1⅛
DENSITY_XHIGH	xhdpi	320	2
DENSITY_XXHIGH	xxhdpi	480	3

* When the screen density of a device doesn't match a number in Column 3 of Table 8-1, Android does its best with the existing categories. For example, Android classifies density 265 dpi in the hdpi group.

Fun facts: DENSITY_XHIGH is the same as 1080p high-definition television in the United States. A seldom-used Android density, DENSITY_TV with 213 dpi, represents 720p television.

Screen densities can make a big difference. An image that looks good on a low-density screen might look choppy on a high-density screen. And an image designed for a high-density screen might be much too large for a low-density screen. That's why, when you create a new application, Android offers to create several different icons for your app. (See Figure 8-2. And I'm sorry, Paul — it's another cat picture!)

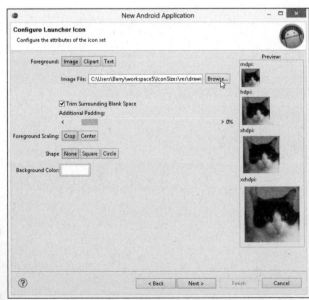

Figure 8-2:
One icon;
many sizes.

Choosing among many alternatives

A Java `if` statement creates a fork in the road: The computer chooses between two alternatives. But some problems lend themselves to forks with many prongs. What's the best way to decide among five or six alternative actions?

For me, multipronged forks are scary. In my daily life, I hate making decisions. (If a problem crops up, I would rather have it be someone else's fault.) So, writing the previous sections (on making decisions with Java's `if` statement) knocked the stuffing right out of me. That's why my mind boggles as I begin this section on choosing among many alternatives.

To prepare for this section's example, I created the four icons shown in Figure 8-2. The icons are for four of the densities depicted in Table 8-1. I have a medium-density icon, a high-density icon, an extra-high-density icon, and an extra-extra-high-density icon.

I named each icon `cat.png` and placed the four icons into four different folders. I added a fifth folder for the `ic_dialog_alert.png` icon, as shown in Figure 8-3.

Figure 8-3:
Folders
containing
images.

The folder structure matches the one you'd see in an Android app. To keep the example simple, I created a plain, old Java program to display the icons. The program is shown in Listing 8-2.

Listing 8-2:   Switching from One Icon to Another

```
package com.allmycode.icons;

import javax.swing.ImageIcon;
import javax.swing.JOptionPane;

public class ShowIcons {

  public static void main(String[] args) {
    String densityCodeString = JOptionPane
```

(continued)

Listing 8-2 *(continued)*

```
        .showInputDialog("Density?");

int densityCode =
    Integer.parseInt(densityCodeString);
String iconFileName = null, message = null;

switch (densityCode) {
case 160:
  iconFileName = "res/drawable-mdpi/cat.png";
  message = "mdpi";
  break;
case 240:
  iconFileName = "res/drawable-hdpi/cat.png";
  message = "hdpi";
  break;
case 320:
  iconFileName = "res/drawable-xhdpi/cat.png";
  message = "xhdpi";
  break;
case 480:
  iconFileName = "res/drawable-xxhdpi/cat.png";
  message = "xxhdpi";
  break;
default:
  iconFileName = "res/drawable/ic_dialog_alert.png";
  message =  "No suitable icon";
  break;
}

ImageIcon icon = new ImageIcon(iconFileName);
JOptionPane.showMessageDialog(null, message,
    "Icon", JOptionPane.INFORMATION_MESSAGE, icon);
  }
}
```

The code in Listing 8-2 is a standard Oracle Java program. The code illustrates some ideas about Android screen densities, but the program is *not* an Android application. This program can't run on an Android device. In Chapter 10, I begin building some examples that run on Android devices.

In Listing 8-2, the program asks the user to enter a screen-density value. If the user types 160, for example, the program responds by displaying my medium-density icon (the image in the cat.png file in my res/drawable-mdpi directory). Two runs of the program are shown in Figure 8-4.

Why the medium-density icon? The program enters the switch statement in Listing 8-2. The switch statement contains an expression (the value of densityCode). The switch statement also contains case clauses, followed (optionally) by a `default` clause. The program compares the value of `densityCode` with `160` (the number in the first of the `case` clauses). If the value of `densityCode` is equal to `160`, the program executes the statements after the words `case 160`.

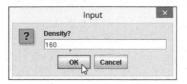
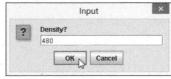

Figure 8-4:
Running
the code
shown in
Listing 8-2.

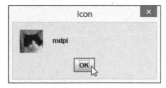

In Listing 8-2, the statements after `case 160` are

```
iconFileName = "res/drawable-mdpi/cat.png";
message = "mdpi";
break;
```

The first two statements set the values of `iconFileName` and `message` in preparation for the display of a message box. The third statement (the `break` statement) jumps out of the entire `switch` statement, skipping past all the other `case` clauses and past the `default` clause to get to the last part of the program.

After the `switch` statement, the statement

```
ImageIcon icon = new ImageIcon(iconFileName);
```

creates a new `icon` variable to refer to the image in the `iconFileName` file. (I have more to say about this kind of statement in Chapter 9.) Finally, the statement

```
JOptionPane.showMessageDialog(null, message,
    "Icon", JOptionPane.INFORMATION_MESSAGE, icon);
```

displays the `icon` image in a message box on the user's screen. (Refer to Figure 8-4.)

A simple slash?

Both the Windows and Macintosh operating systems have directories (also known as *folders*), and these directories may contain subdirectories, which in turn may contain their own subdirectories. At the bottom of the food chain is the humble file containing a document, an image, a sound, or whatever. On my Windows computer, one of my `cat.png` files lives in a directory named `drawable-hdpi`, which is inside a directory named `res`, which is inside an Eclipse project directory named `08-02`. The Eclipse project directory is inside my Eclipse `workspace` directory, which in turn is inside my `Barry` directory, which is inside my `Users` directory, as shown in the sidebar figure. It's a long chain of stuff leading eventually to a picture of a cat.

When you're visiting Times Square in New York City, you can say, "I'm walking to the McDonald's on 34th Street." You don't have to say "I'm walking to the McDonald's on 34th Street in New York City, USA." In a similar way, my code doesn't have to refer to the `cat.png` file by naming a whole bunch of directories and subdirectories. Instead, I can take advantage of the fact that Listing 08-02 is in my `08-02` directory. From the viewpoint of the `08-02` directory, I can refer directly to the `res` directory, which is contained immediately inside the `08-02` directory. In both the Windows and Macintosh operating system, I can use the forward slash character (`/`) to point from the `08-02` directory to my cat picture:

`res/drawable-hdpi/cat.png`

In Windows, the forward slash works in many directory-and-file situations. But the backslash (`\`) is used more commonly than the forward slash in Windows. So in Windows, I usually refer to my cat picture this way:

`res\drawable-hdpi\cat.png`

But there's a problem. In a Java string, a single backslash (`\`) has a special meaning. That special meaning depends on whatever character appears immediately after the backslash. For example, `\n` stands for "Go to a new line," `\t` stands for "Go to the next tab stop," and `\\` stands for "A single backslash." In Listing 8-2, a double-quoted string such as `"res\\drawable-mdpi\\cat.png"` stands for `res\drawable-mdpi\cat.png`. To the Windows operating system, this double-backslash business is another way to refer to the `cat.png` file that's in the `drawable-mdpi` subdirectory of the `res` directory.

Once again, if you're a Mac user, you use a forward slash (`/`) to separate directory names, and a forward slash has no special meaning inside a Java string. Mac users don't have to worry about doubling up on slashes.

Take a break

This news might surprise you: The end of a case clause (the beginning of another case clause) doesn't automatically make the program jump out of the switch statement. If you forget to add a break statement at the end of a case clause, the program finishes the statements in the case clause *and then continues executing the statements in the next* case *clause*. Imagine that I write the following code (and omit a break statement):

```
switch (densityCode) {
case 160:
  iconFileName = "res/drawable-mdpi/cat.png";
  message = "mdpi";
case 240:
  iconFileName = "res/drawable-hdpi/cat.png";
  message = "hdpi";
  break;
... Etc.
```

With this modified code (and with densityCode equal to 160), the program sets iconFileName to "res/drawable-mdpi/cat.png", sets message to "mdpi", sets iconFileName to "res/drawable-hdpi/cat.png", sets message to "hdpi", and, finally, breaks out of the switch statement (skipping past all other case clauses and the default clause). The result is that iconFileName has the value "res/drawable-hdpi/cat.png" (not "res/drawable-mdpi/cat.png") and that message has the value "hdpi" (not "mdpi").

This phenomenon of jumping from one case clause to another in the absence of a break statement) is called *fall-through,* and, occasionally, it's useful. Imagine a dice game in which 7 and 11 are instant wins; 2, 3, and 12 are instant losses; and any other number (from 4 to 10) tells you to continue playing. The code for such a game might look like this:

```
switch (roll) {
case 7:
case 11:
  message = "win";
  break;
case 2:
case 3:
case 12:
  message = "lose";
  break;
case 4:
case 5:
case 6:
case 8:
case 9:
```

```
case 10:
  message = "continue";
  break;
default:
  message = "not a valid dice roll";
  break;
}
```

If you roll a 7, you execute all the statements immediately after case 7 (of which there are none), and then you fall-through to case 11, executing the statement that assigns "win" to the variable message.

Every beginning Java programmer forgets to put a break statement at the end of a case clause. When you make this mistake, don't beat yourself up about it. Just remember what's causing your program's unexpected behavior, add break statements to your code, and move on. As you gain experience in writing Java programs, you'll make this mistake less and less frequently. (You'll still make the mistake occasionally, but not as often.)

The computer selects a case clause

When you run the code in Listing 8-2, the user doesn't have to enter the number 160. If the user enters 320, the program skips past the statements in the case 160 clause and then skips past the statements in the 240 clause. The program hits pay dirt when it reaches the case 320 clause, and executes that clause's statements, making iconFileName be "res/drawable-xhdpi/cat.png" and making message be xhdpi. The case clause's break statement makes the program skip the rest of the stuff in the switch statement.

The default clause

A switch statement's optional default clause is a catchall for values that don't match any of the case clauses' values. For example, if you run the program and the user enters the number 265, the program doesn't fix on any of the case clauses. (To select a switch statement's case clause, the value after the word switch has to be an exact match of the value after the word case.) So if densityCode is 265, the program skips past all the case clauses and executes the code in the default clause, making iconFileName be "res/drawable/ic_dialog_alert.png" and making message be "No suitable icon". In this way, the program in Listing 8-2 doesn't mirror Android's screen-resolution tricks. (Android uses an existing icon even if the screen's density doesn't exactly match one of the numbers 160, 240, 320, or 480.)

The last `break` statement in Listing 8-2 tells the computer to jump to the end of the `switch` statement, skipping any statements after the `default` clause. But look again. Nothing comes after the `default` clause in the `switch` statement! Which statements are being skipped? The answer is none. I put a `break` at the end of the `default` clause for good measure. This extra `break` statement doesn't do anything, but it doesn't do any harm, either.

Some formalities concerning Java switch statements

A `switch` statement has the following form:

```
switch (expression) {
case constant1:
    statements to be executed when the
    expression has value contstant1
case constant2:
    statements to be executed when the
    expression has value contstant2
case ...

default:
    statements to be executed when the
    expression has a value different from
    any of the constants
}
```

You can't put any old expression in a `switch` statement. The expression that's tested at the start of a `switch` statement must have one of these elements:

- A primitive type: `char`, `byte`, `short`, or `int`
- A reference type: `Character`, `Byte`, `Short`, or `Integer`
- An `enum` type

An `enum` type is a type whose values are limited to the few that you declare. For example, the line

```
enum TrafficSignal {GREEN, YELLOW, RED};
```

defines a type whose only values are GREEN, YELLOW, and RED. Elsewhere in your code, you can write

```
TrafficSignal signal;
signal = TrafficSignal.GREEN;
```

to make use of the `TrafficSignal` type.

Starting with Java 7, you can put a `String` type expression at the start of a `switch` statement. But the last time I checked, Java 5 or 6 is required for developing Android code. You can't use Java 7 or later to create an Android app. So with `densityCodeString` declared to be of type `String`, you can't create a `switch` statement whose first line is `switch (display CodeString)`, and you can't have a `case` clause that begins with `case "hdpi"`.

Repeating Instructions Over and Over Again

In 1966, the company that brings you Head & Shoulders shampoo made history. On the back of the bottle, the directions for using the shampoo read, "Lather, rinse, repeat." Never before had a complete set of directions (for doing anything, let alone shampooing hair) been summarized so succinctly. People in the direction-writing business hailed it as a monumental achievement. Directions like these stood in stark contrast to others of the time. (For instance, the first sentence on a can of bug spray read, "Turn this can so that it points away from your face." Duh!)

Aside from their brevity, the characteristic that made the Head & Shoulders directions so cool was that, with three simple words, they managed to capture a notion that's at the heart of all instruction-giving: repetition. That last word, *repeat,* turned an otherwise bland instructional drone into a sophisticated recipe for action.

The fundamental idea is that when you're following directions, you don't just follow one instruction after another. Instead, you make turns in the road. You make decisions ("If HAIR IS DRY, then USE CONDITIONER,") and you repeat steps ("LATHER-RINSE, and then LATHER-RINSE again."). In application development, you use decision-making and repetition all the time.

Check, and then repeat

The program in Listing 8-2 is nice (if I say so myself). But the program has its flaws. I expect the user to type a number and for things to go wrong if the user doesn't type a number, as shown in Figure 8-5. The program doesn't even like numbers with decimal points.

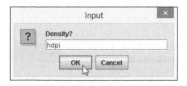

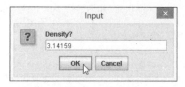

Figure 8-5:
My program
wants
integers!

You should anticipate all kinds of user input. To do that, you have several alternatives. One thing you can do is to dismiss bad input and ask the user for better input — so you might have to repeat your input request over and over again. Listing 8-3 shows you one way to do it.

Listing 8-3:   Look Before You Leap

```
package com.allmycode.icons;

import javax.swing.ImageIcon;
import javax.swing.JOptionPane;

public class ShowIconsWithWhile {

  public static void main(String[] args) {
    String densityCodeString =
        JOptionPane.showInputDialog("Density?");

    while ( !densityCodeString.equals("160") &&
            !densityCodeString.equals("240") &&
            !densityCodeString.equals("320") &&
            !densityCodeString.equals("480")      ) {

        densityCodeString = JOptionPane
          .showInputDialog("Invalid input. Try again:");

    }

    int densityCode =
        Integer.parseInt(densityCodeString);
    String iconFileName = null, message = null;

    switch (densityCode) {
    case 160:
      iconFileName = „res/drawable-mdpi/cat.png";
      message = „mdpi";
      break;
    case 240:
      iconFileName = „res/drawable-hdpi/cat.png";
      message = „hdpi";
      break;
    case 320:
      iconFileName = „res/drawable-xhdpi/cat.png";
      message = „xhdpi";
      break;
    case 480:
      iconFileName = „res/drawable-xxhdpi/cat.png";
      message = „xxhdpi";
      break;
    default:
      iconFileName = „res/drawable/ic_dialog_alert.png";
      message =  „No suitable icon";
      break;
    }

    ImageIcon icon = new ImageIcon(iconFileName);
    JOptionPane.showMessageDialog(null, message,
        „Icon", JOptionPane.INFORMATION_MESSAGE, icon);
  }
}
```

A run of the code in Listing 8-3 is shown in Figure 8-6.

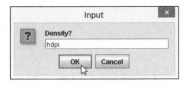

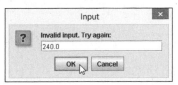

Figure 8-6:
Try, try, try
again.

The code in Listing 8-3 begins by displaying an input dialog box with the
"Density?" message. If the user responds with a value other than 160, 240,
320, or 480, the code dives into its while statement, displaying the message
"Invalid input. Try again:" in the input dialog box over and over
again. The code continues displaying this input dialog box until the user
responds with one of the four valid values — 160, 240, 320, or 480.

In plain language, the while statement in Listing 8-3 says:

```
while ( densityCodeString isn't 160 and
        densityCodeString isn't 240 and
        densityCodeString isn't 320 and
        densityCodeString isn't 480       ) {

  get a value for the densityCodeString

}
```

In even plainer language, the while statement says:

```
while ( densityCodeString isn't acceptable ) {

  get a value for the densityCodeString

}
```

The `while` statement is one of Java's compound statements. It's also one of Java's *looping* statements because, when executing a `while` statement, the computer can go into a loop, spinning around and around, executing a certain chunk of code over and over again.

In a looping statement, each go-around is an *iteration*.

If you stare at Listing 8-3, you might notice this peculiarity: The `while` statement at the top of the program ensures that the density is either 160, 240, 320, or 480. But toward the end of the program, the `switch` statement's `default` clause provides for the possibility that the density isn't one of those 160, 240, 320, or 480 values. What gives? The answer is that it never hurts to double-check. You may think that your `while` statement can spit out only 160, 240, 320, or 480, but you might have forgotten about an unusual scenario that causes the density to be another, strange number. And what happens if another developer (someone trying to improve on your code) messes with your `while` statement and lets bad density values trickle over to the `switch` statement? Adding a `default` clause to a `switch` statement is never costly, and the `default` clause always adds an extra layer of protection from errors.

Some formalities concerning Java while statements

A `while` statement has this form:

```
while (condition) {
    statements inside the loop
}
```

The computer repeats the *statements inside the loop* over and over again as long as the condition in parentheses is true:

```
Check to make sure that the condition is true;
Execute the statements inside the loop.

Check again to make sure that the condition is true;
Execute the statements inside the loop.

Check again to make sure that the condition is true;
Execute the statements inside the loop.

And so on.
```

At some point, the `while` statement's condition becomes false. (Generally, this happens because one of the statements in the loop changes one of the program's values.) When the condition becomes false, the computer stops repeating the statements in the loop. (That is, the computer stops *iterating*.) Instead, the computer executes whatever statements appear immediately after the end of the `while` statement:

```
Check again to make sure that the condition is true;
Execute the statements inside the loop.

Check again to make sure that the condition is true;
Execute the statements inside the loop.

Check again to make sure that the condition is true;
Oops! The condition is no longer true!
Execute the code immediately after the while statement.
```

In Listing 8-3, the code

```
int densityCode =
    Integer.parseInt(densityCodeString);
```

comes immediately after the end of the `while` statement.

Variations on a theme

Many of the `if` statement's tricks apply to `while` statements as well. A `while` statement is a compound statement, so it might contain other compound statements. And when a `while` statement contains only one statement, you can omit curly braces. So the following code is equivalent to the `while` statement in Listing 8-3:

```
while ( !densityCodeString.equals("160") &&
        !densityCodeString.equals("240") &&
        !densityCodeString.equals("320") &&
        !densityCodeString.equals("480")        )

  densityCodeString = JOptionPane
    .showInputDialog("Density?");
```

After all, the code

```
densityCodeString = JOptionPane
    .showInputDialog("Density?");
```

is only one (admittedly large) assignment statement.

A `while` statement's condition might become false in the middle of an iteration, before all the iteration's statements have been executed. When this happens, the computer doesn't stop the iteration dead in its tracks. Instead, the computer executes the rest of the loop's statements. After executing the rest of the loop's statements, the computer checks the condition (finding the condition to be false) and marches on to whatever code comes immediately after the `while` statement.

The previous icon should come with some fine print. To be painfully accurate, I should point out a few ways for you to stop abruptly in the middle of a loop iteration. You can execute a `break` statement to jump out of a `while` statement immediately. (It's the same `break` statement that you use in a `switch` statement.) Alternatively, you can execute a `continue` statement (the word `continue`, followed by a semicolon) to jump abruptly out of an iteration. When you jump out with a `continue` statement, the computer ends the current iteration immediately and then checks the `while` statement's condition. A true condition tells the computer to begin the next loop iteration. A false condition tells the computer to go to whatever code comes after the `while` statement.

Priming the pump

Java's `while` statement uses the policy "Look before you leap." The computer always checks a condition before executing the statements inside the loop. Among other things, this forces you to prime the loop. When you prime a loop, you create statements that affect the loop's condition before the beginning of the loop. (Think of an old-fashioned water pump and how you have to prime the pump before water comes out.) In Listing 8-3, the initialization in

```
String densityCodeString =
    JOptionPane.showInputDialog("Density?");
```

primes the loop. This initialization — the = part — gives `densityCodeString` its first value so that when you check the condition `!densityCodeString.equals("160") && ...` *Etc.* for the first time, the variable `density CodeString` has a value that's worth comparing.

Here's something you should consider when you create a `while` statement: The computer can execute a while statement without ever executing the statements inside the loop. For example, the code in Listing 8-3 prompts the user one time before the `while` statement. If the user enters a good density value, the `while` statement's condition is false. The computer skips past the statement inside the loop and goes immediately to the code after the `while` statement. The computer never displays the `Invalid input. Try again` prompt.

Repeat, and then check

The while statement (which I describe in the previous section) is the workhorse of repetition in Java. Using while statements, you can do any kind of looping that you need to do. But sometimes it's convenient to have other kinds of looping statements. For example, occasionally you want to structure the repetition so that the first iteration takes place without checking a condition. In that situation, you use Java's do statement. Listing 8-4 is almost the same as Listing 8-3. But in Listing 8-4, I replace a while statement with a do statement.

Listing 8-4:   Leap before You Look

```
package com.allmycode.icons;

import javax.swing.ImageIcon;
import javax.swing.JOptionPane;

public class ShowIconsWithDo {

  public static void main(String[] args) {
    String densityCodeString =
        JOptionPane.showInputDialog("Density?");

    do {

        densityCodeString = JOptionPane
          .showInputDialog("Density?");

    } while ( !densityCodeString.equals("160") &&
              !densityCodeString.equals("240") &&
              !densityCodeString.equals("320") &&
              !densityCodeString.equals("480")      );

    int densityCode =
        Integer.parseInt(densityCodeString);
    String iconFileName = null, message = null;

    switch (densityCode) {
    case 160:
      iconFileName = "res/drawable-mdpi/cat.png";
      message = "mdpi";
      break;
    case 240:
      iconFileName = "res/drawable-hdpi/cat.png";
      message = "hdpi";
      break;
    case 320:
```

(continued)

Listing 8-4 *(continued)*

```
        iconFileName = "res/drawable-xhdpi/cat.png";

        message = "xhdpi";
        break;
    case 480:
        iconFileName = "res/drawable-xxhdpi/cat.png";
        message = "xxhdpi";
        break;
    default:
        iconFileName = "res/drawable/ic_dialog_alert.png";
        message =  "No suitable icon";
        break;
    }

    ImageIcon icon = new ImageIcon(iconFileName);
    JOptionPane.showMessageDialog(null, message,
        "Icon", JOptionPane.INFORMATION_MESSAGE, icon);
  }
}
```

With a do statement, the computer jumps right in, takes action, and then
checks a condition to see whether the result of the action is what you want. If
it is, execution of the loop is done. If not, the computer goes back to the top
of the loop for another go-round.

Some formalities concerning Java do statements

A do statement has the following form:

```
do {
    statements inside the loop
} while (condition)
```

The computer executes the *statements inside the loop* and then checks to see
whether the condition in parentheses is true. If the condition in parentheses
is true, the computer executes the *statements inside the loop* again. And so on.

Java's do statement uses the policy "Leap before you look." The statement
checks a condition immediately *after* each iteration of the statements inside
the loop.

A do statement is good for situations in which you know for sure that you should perform the loop's statements at least once. Unlike a while statement, a do statement generally doesn't need to be primed. On the downside, a do statement doesn't lend itself to situations in which the first occurrence of an action is slightly different from subsequent occurrences. For example, with the properly primed while statement in Listing 8-3, the message in the first input dialog box is Density? and all subsequent messages say Invalid input. Try again. With the do statement in Listing 8-4, all input dialog boxes simply say Density?.

Count, count, count

This section's example is a kludge.

> *kludge (klooj) n. Anything that solves a problem in an awkward way, either to fix the problem quickly or (in Chapter 8 of Java Programming For Android Developers For Dummies) to illustrate a point.*

In fact, after examining this example, you might wonder whether anyone ever uses the Java feature that's illustrated in this section. Well, this section's feature (the for statement) appears quite frequently in Java programs. Life is filled with examples of counting loops, and app development mirrors life — or is it the other way around? When you tell a device what to do, you're often telling it to display three lines, process ten accounts, dial a million phone numbers, or whatever.

For example, to display the first thousand rows of an Android data table, you might use this Java for statement:

```
cursor.moveToFirst();

for (int i = 0; i < 999; i++) {
    String _id = cursor.getString(0);
    String name = cursor.getString(1);
    String amount = cursor.getString(2);
    textViewDisplay.append(i + ": " + _id + " " +
                            name + " " + amount + "\n");
    cursor.moveToNext();
}
```

Unfortunately, examples involving Android's data tables and phone numbers can be quite complicated. Start with a simple example — one that displays icons in three different sizes. Listing 8-5 has the code.

Listing 8-5:   A Loop That Counts

```java
package com.allmycode.icons;

import javax.swing.ImageIcon;
import javax.swing.JOptionPane;

public class ShowIconsWithFor {

  public static void main(String[] args) {

    int densityCode;
    String iconFileName = null, message = null;

    for (int i = 1; i <= 3; i++) {
      densityCode = i * 160;

      switch (densityCode) {
      case 160:
        iconFileName = "res/drawable-mdpi/cat.png";
        message = "mdpi";
        break;
      case 240:
        iconFileName = "res/drawable-hdpi/cat.png";
        message = "hdpi";
        break;
      case 320:
        iconFileName = "res/drawable-xhdpi/cat.png";
        message = "xhdpi";
        break;
      case 480:
        iconFileName = "res/drawable-xxhdpi/cat.png";
        message = "xxhdpi";
        break;
      default:
        iconFileName = "res/drawable/ic_dialog_alert.png";
        message = "No suitable icon";
        break;
      }

      ImageIcon icon = new ImageIcon(iconFileName);
      JOptionPane.showMessageDialog(null, message,
          "Icon", JOptionPane.INFORMATION_MESSAGE, icon);
    }
  }
}
```

Listing 8-5 declares an int variable named i. The starting value of i is 1. As long as the condition i <= 3 is true, the computer executes the statements inside the loop and then executes i++ (adding 1 to the value of i). After three iterations, the value of i gets to be 4, in which case the condition i <= 3 is no longer true. At that point, the program stops repeating the statements inside the loop and moves on to execute any statements that come after the for statement. (Ha-ha! Listing 8-5 has no statements after the for statement!)

In this example, the statements inside the loop include

```
densityCode = i * 160;
```

which makes densityCode be either 160, 320, or 480 (depending on the value of i). The loop's statements also include a big switch statement (which creates icon and message values from the densityCode) and a couple of statements to display the icon and the message. The result is the display, one after another, of the three icons for the three densities 160, 320, and 480. Listing 8-5 displays all three icons, one after another, without ever getting input from the user, as shown in Figure 8-7.

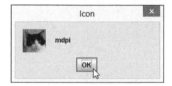

Figure 8-7:
One run of
the code in
Listing 8-5.

Some formalities concerning Java for statements

A `for` statement has the following form:

```
for (initialization ; condition ; update) {
    statements inside the loop
}
```

✔ An *initialization* (such as int i = 1 in Listing 8-5) defines the action to be taken before the first loop iteration.

✔ A *condition* (such as i <= 3 in Listing 8-5) defines the element to be checked before an iteration. If the condition is `true`, the computer executes the iteration. If the condition is `false`, the computer doesn't execute the iteration, and it moves on to execute whatever code comes after the `for` statement.

✔ An *update* (such as i++ in Listing 8-5) defines an action to be taken at the end of each loop iteration.

You can omit the curly braces when only one statement is inside the loop.

What's Next?

This chapter describes several ways to jump from one place in your code to another.

Java provides other ways to move from place to place in a program, including enhanced `for` statements and `try` statements. But descriptions of these elements don't belong in this chapter. To understand the power of enhanced `for` statements and `try` statements, you need a firm grasp of classes and objects, so Chapter 9 dives fearlessly into the classes-and-objects waters.

I'm your swimming instructor. Everyone into the pool!

Part III

Working with the Big Picture: Object-Oriented Programming

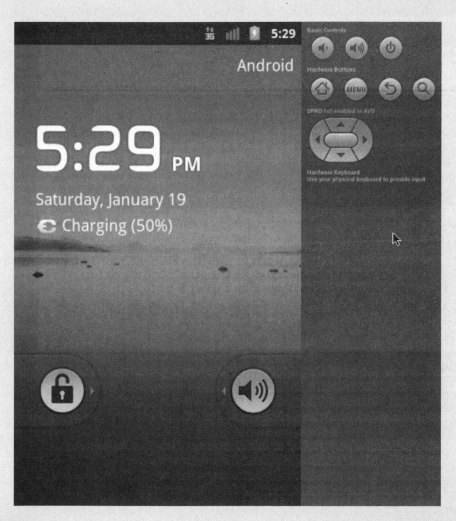

In this part . . .

✔ Understanding object-oriented programming (at last!)

✔ Reusing code

✔ Establishing lines of communication among the parts of your app

Chapter 9

Why Object-Oriented Programming Is Like Selling Cheese

· ·

In This Chapter

▶ The truth about object-oriented programming

▶ Why a class is actually a Java type

▶ An end to the mystery surrounding words like `static`

· ·

A ndy's Cheese and Java Emporium carries fine cheeses and freshly brewed java from around the world (especially from Java in Indonesia). The Emporium is in Cheesetown, Pennsylvania, a neighborhood along the Edenville–Cheesetown Road in Franklin County.

The emporium sells cheese by the bag, each containing a certain variety, such as Cheddar, Swiss, Munster, or Limburger. Bags are labeled by weight and by the number of days the cheese was aged (admittedly, an approximation). Bags also carry the label *Domestic* or *Imported,* depending on the cheese's country of origin.

Before starting up the emporium, Andy had lots of possessions — material and otherwise. He had a family, a cat, a house, an abandoned restaurant property, a bunch of restaurant equipment, a checkered past, and a mountain of debt. But for the purpose of this narrative, Andy had only one thing: a form. Yes, Andy had developed a form for keeping track of his emporium's inventory. The form is shown in Figure 9-1.

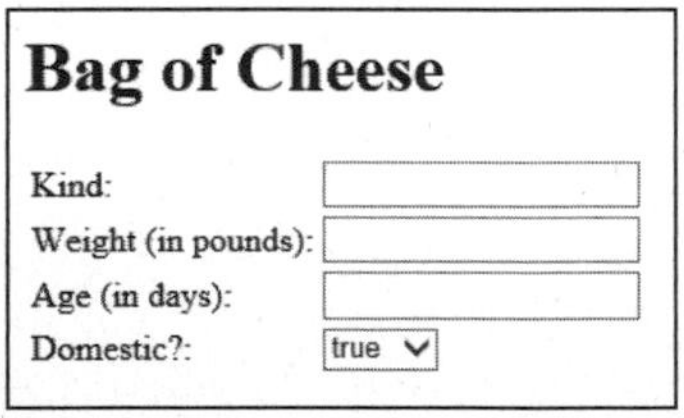

Figure 9-1:
An online
form.

Bag of Cheese

Kind:	
Weight (in pounds):	
Age (in days):	
Domestic?:	true ▾

Exactly one week before the emporium's grand opening, Andy's supplier delivered one bag of cheese. Andy entered the bag's information into the inventory form. The result is shown in Figure 9-2.

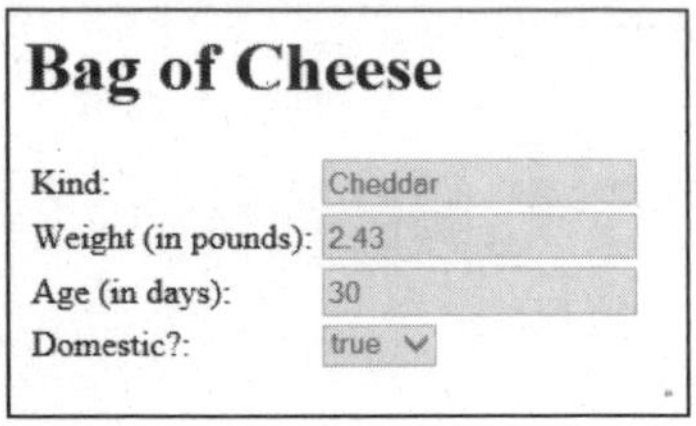

Figure 9-2:
A virtual bag of cheese.

Bag of Cheese

Kind: Cheddar
Weight (in pounds): 2.43
Age (in days): 30
Domestic?: true ∨

Andy had only a form and a bag of cheese (which isn't much to show for all his hard work), but the next day the supplier delivered five more bags of cheese. Andy's second entry looked like the one shown in Figure 9-3, and the next several entries looked similar.

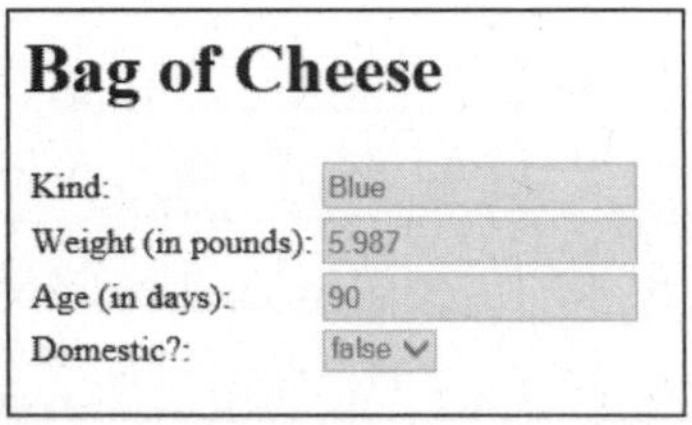

Figure 9-3:
Another virtual bag of cheese.

Bag of Cheese

Kind: Blue
Weight (in pounds): 5.987
Age (in days): 90
Domestic?: false ∨

At the end of the week, Andy was giddy: He had exactly one inventory form and six bags of cheese.

The story doesn't end here. As the grand opening approached, Andy's supplier brought many more bags so that, eventually, Andy had his inventory form and several hundred bags of cheese. The business even became an icon on Interstate Highway 81 in Cheesetown, Pennsylvania. But as far as you're concerned, the business had, has, and always will have only one form and any number of cheese bags.

That's the essence of object-oriented programming!

Classes and Objects

Java is an object-oriented programming language. A program that you create in Java consists of at least one class.

A class is like Andy's blank form, described in this chapter's introduction. That is, a class is a general description of some kind of thing. In the introduction to this chapter, the class (the form) describes the characteristics that any bag of cheese possesses. But imagine other classes. For example, Figure 9-4 illustrates a bank account class:

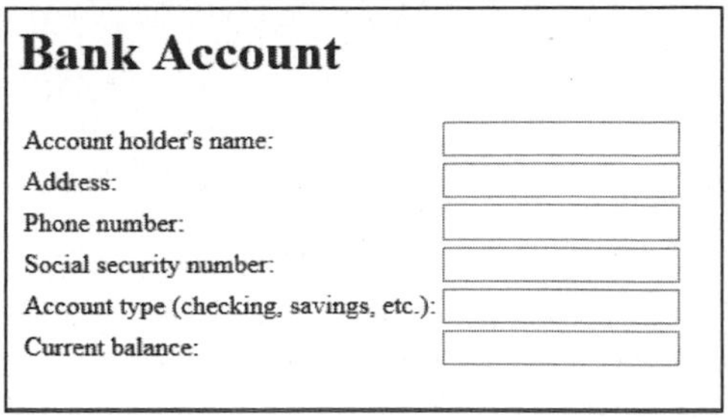

Bank Account

Account holder's name: _____

Address: _____

Phone number: _____

Social security number: _____

Account type (checking, savings, etc.): _____

Current balance: _____

Figure 9-4:
A bank
account
class.

Figure 9-5 illustrates a sprite class, which is a class for a character in a computer game:

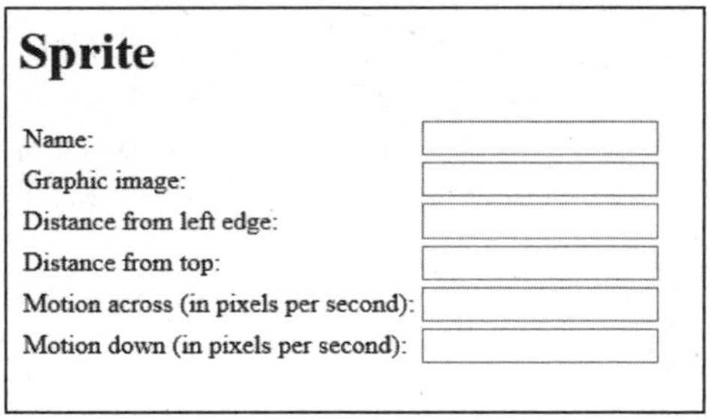

Sprite

Name: _____

Graphic image: _____

Distance from left edge: _____

Distance from top: _____

Motion across (in pixels per second): _____

Motion down (in pixels per second): _____

Figure 9-5:
A sprite
class.

What is a class, really?

In practice, a class doesn't look like any of the forms in Figures 9-1 through 9-5. In fact, a class doesn't look like anything. Instead, a Java class is a bunch of text describing the kinds of things that I refer to as "blanks to be filled in." Listing 9-1 contains a real Java class — the kind of class you write when you program in Java.

Listing 9-1:   A Class in the Java Programming Language

```
package com.allmycode.andy;

public class BagOfCheese {
   String kind;
   double weight;
   int daysAged;
   boolean isDomestic;
}
```

As a developer, your primary job is to create classes. You don't develop attractive online forms like the form in Figure 9-1. Instead, you write Java language code — code containing descriptions, like the one in Listing 9-1.

Compare Figure 9-1 with Listing 9-1. In what ways are they the same, and in what ways are they different? What does one have that the other doesn't have?

✔ **The form in Figure 9-1 appears on a user's screen. The code in Listing 9-1 does not.**

A Java class isn't necessarily tied to a particular display. Yes, you can display a bank account on a user's screen. But the bank account isn't a bunch of items on a computer screen — it's a bunch of information in the bank's computers.

In fact, some Java classes are difficult to visualize. Android's SQLite OpenHelper class assists developers in the creation of databases. An SQLiteOpenHelper doesn't look like anything in particular, and certainly not an online form or a bag of cheese.

✔ **Online forms appear in some contexts but not in others. In contrast, classes affect every part of every Java program's code.**

Forms show up on web pages, in dialog boxes, and in other situations. But when you use a word processing program to type a document, you deal primarily with free-form input. I didn't write this paragraph by filling in some blanks. (Heaven knows! I wish I could!)

The paragraphs I've written started out as part of a document in an Android word processing application. In the document, every paragraph has its own alignment, borders, indents, line spacing, styles, and many other characteristics. As a Java class, a list of paragraph characteristics might look something like this:

```
class Paragraph {
   int alignment;
   int borders;
   double leftIndent;
   double lineSpacing;
   int style;
}
```

When I create a paragraph, I don't fill in a form. Instead, I type words, and the underlying word processing app deals silently with its `Paragraph` class.

✔ **The form shown in Figure 9-1 contains several fields, and so does the code in Listing 9-1.**

In an online form, a field is a blank space — a place that's eventually filled with specific information. In Java, a *field* is any characteristic that you (the developer) attribute to a class. The `BagOfCheese` class in Listing 9-1 has four fields, and each of the four fields has a name: `kind`, `weight`, `daysAged`, or `isDomestic`.

Like an online form, a Java class describes items by listing the characteristics that each of the items has. Both the form in Figure 9-1 and the code in Listing 9-1 say essentially the same thing: Each bag of cheese has a certain kind of cheese, a certain weight, a number of days that the cheese was aged, and a domestic-or-imported characteristic.

✔ **The code in Listing 9-1 describes exactly the kind of information that belongs in each blank space. The form in Figure 9-1 is much more permissive.**

Nothing in Figure 9-1 indicates what kinds of input are permitted in the Weight field. The weight in pounds can be a whole number (0, 1, 2, and so on) or a decimal number (such as 3.14159, the weight of a big piece of "pie"). What happens if the user types the words *three pounds* into the form in Figure 9-1? Does the form accept this input, or does the computer freeze up? A developer can add extra code to test for valid input in a form, but, on its own, a form cares little about the kind of input that the user enters.

In contrast, the code in Listing 9-1 contains this line:

```
double weight;
```

This line tells Java that every bag of cheese has a characteristic named `weight` and that a bag's weight must be of type `double`. Similarly, each bag's `daysAged` value is an `int`, each bag's `isDomestic` value is `boolean`, and each bag's `kind` value has the type `String`.

The unfortunate pun in the previous paragraph makes life more difficult for me, the author! A Java `String` has nothing to do with the kind of cheese that peels into strips. A Java `String` is a sequence of characters, like the sequence `"Cheddar"` or the sequence `"qwoiehasljsal"` or the sequence `"Go2theMoon!"`. So the `String kind` line in Listing 9-1 indicates that a bag of cheese might contain `"Cheddar"`, but it might also contain `"qwoiehasljsal"` cheese or `"Go2theMoon!"` cheese. Well, that's what happens when Andy starts a business from scratch.

What is an object?

At the start of this chapter's detailed Cheese Emporium exposé, Andy had nothing to his name except an online form — the form in Figure 9-1. Life was simple for Andy and his dog Fido. But eventually the suppliers delivered bags of cheese. Suddenly, Andy had more than just an online form —he had things whose characteristics matched the fields in the form. One bag had the characteristics shown in Figure 9-2; another bag had the characteristics shown in Figure 9-3.

In the terminology of object-oriented programming, each bag of cheese is an *object*, and each bag of cheese is an *instance* of the class in Listing 9-1.

You can also think of classes and objects as part of a hierarchy. The `BagOfCheese` class is at the top of the hierarchy, and each instance of the class is attached to the class itself. See Figures 9-6 and 9-7.

BagOfCheese
kind: String weight: double daysAged: int isDomestic: boolean

Figure 9-6:
First, Andy
has a class.

The diagrams in Figures 9-6 and 9-7 are part of the standardized Unified Modeling Language (UML). For more info about UML, visit www.omg.org/spec/UML/.

BagOfCheese

kind: String
weight: double
daysAged: int
isDomestic: boolean

Figure 9-7:
Later, Andy
has a class
and two
objects.

:BagOfCheese

kind = "Cheddar"
weight = 2.43
daysAged = 30
isDomestic = true

:BagOfCheese

kind = "Blue"
weight = 5.987
daysAged = 90
isDomestic = false

An object is a particular thing. (For Andy, an object is a particular bag of cheese.) A class is a description with blanks to be filled in. (For Andy, a class is a form with four blank fields: a field for the kind of cheese, another field for the cheese's weight, a third field for the number of days aged, and a fourth field for the Domestic-or-Imported designation.)

And don't forget: Your primary job is to create classes. You don't develop attractive online forms like the form in Figure 9-1. Instead, you write Java language code — code containing descriptions, like the one in Listing 9-1.

Creating objects

Listing 9-2 contains real-life Java code to create two objects — two instances of the class in Listing 9-1.

Listing 9-2:   Creating Two Objects

```
package com.allmycode.andy;

import javax.swing.JOptionPane;

public class CreateBags {
  public static void main(String[] args) {
    BagOfCheese bag1 = new BagOfCheese();
    bag1.kind = "Cheddar";
    bag1.weight = 2.43;
    bag1.daysAged = 30;
```

(continued)

Listing 9-2 *(continued)*

```
    bag1.isDomestic = true;

    BagOfCheese bag2 = new BagOfCheese();
    bag2.kind = "Blue";
    bag2.weight = 5.987;
    bag2.daysAged = 90;
    bag2.isDomestic = false;

    JOptionPane.showMessageDialog(null,
        bag1.kind + ", " +
        bag1.weight + ", " +
        bag1.daysAged + ", " +
        bag1.isDomestic);

    JOptionPane.showMessageDialog(null,
        bag2.kind + ", " +
        bag2.weight + ", " +
        bag2.daysAged + ", " +
        bag2.isDomestic);
    }
}
```

A run of the code in Listing 9-2 is shown in Figure 9-8.

Figure 9-8:
Running the
code from
Listing 9-2.

To vary the terminology, I might say that the code in Listing 9-2 creates "two BagOfCheese objects" or "two BagOfCheese instances," or I might say that the new BagOfChecse() statements in Listing 9-2 *instantiate* the BagOfCheese class. One way or another, Listing 9-1 declares the existence of one class, and Listing 9-2 declares the existence of two objects.

In Listing 9-2, each use of the words new BagOfCheese() is a *constructor call.* For details, see the "Calling a constructor" section later in this chapter.

To run the code in Listing 9-2, you put two Java files (BagOfCheese.java from Listing 9-1 and CreateBags.java from Listing 9-2) in the same Eclipse project.

In Listing 9-2, I use ten statements to create two bags of cheese. The first statement (BagOfCheese bag1 = new BagOfCheese()) does three things:

- With the words

  ```
  BagOfCheese bag1
  ```

  the first statement declares that the variable bag1 refers to a bag of cheese.
- With the words

  ```
  new BagOfCheese()
  ```

  the first statement creates a bag with no particular cheese in it. (If it helps, you can think of it as an empty bag reserved for eventually storing cheese.)
- Finally, with the equal sign, the first statement makes the bag1 variable refer to the newly created bag.

The next four statements in Listing 9-2 assign values to the fields of bag1:

```
bag1.kind = "Cheddar";
bag1.weight = 2.43;
bag1.daysAged = 30;
bag1.isDomestic = true;
```

To refer to one of an object's fields, follow a reference to the object with a dot and then the field's name. (For example, follow bag1 with a dot, and then the field name kind.)

The next five statements in Listing 9-2 do the same for a second variable, bag2, and a second bag of cheese.

Reusing names

In Listing 9-2, I declare two variables — bag1 and bag2 — to refer to two different BagOfCheese objects. That's fine. But sometimes having only one variable and reusing it for the second object works just as well, as shown in Listing 9-3.

Listing 9-3: Reusing the bag Variable

```
package com.allmycode.andy;

import javax.swing.JOptionPane;

public class CreateBags {
  public static void main(String[] args) {
    BagOfCheese bag = new BagOfCheese();
    bag.kind = "Cheddar";
    bag.weight = 2.43;
    bag.daysAged = 30;
    bag.isDomestic = true;

    JOptionPane.showMessageDialog(null,
        bag.kind + ", " +
        bag.weight + ", " +
        bag.daysAged + ", " +
        bag.isDomestic);

    bag = new BagOfCheese();
    bag.kind = "Blue";
    bag.weight = 5.987;
    bag.daysAged = 90;
    bag.isDomestic = false;

    JOptionPane.showMessageDialog(null,
        bag.kind + ", " +
        bag.weight + ", " +
        bag.daysAged + ", " +
        bag.isDomestic);
  }
}
```

In Listing 9-3, when the computer executes the second bag = new BagOfCheese() statement, the old object (the bag containing cheddar) has disappeared. Without bag (or any other variable) referring to that cheddar object, there's no way your code can do anything with the cheddar object. Fortunately, by the time you reach the second bag = new BagOfCheese() statement, you're finished doing everything you want to do with the original cheddar bag. In this case, reusing the bag variable is acceptable.

When you reuse a variable (like the one and only bag variable in Listing 9-3), you do so by using an assignment statement, not an initialization. In other words, you don't write BagOfCheese bag a second time in your code. If you do, you see error messages in the Eclipse editor.

To be painfully precise, you can, in fact, write `BagOfCheese bag` more than once in the same piece of code. For an example, see the use of shadowing later in this chapter, in the "Constructors with parameters" section.

In Listing 9-1, none of the `BagOfCheese` class's fields is `final`. In other words, the class's code lets you reassign values to the fields inside a `BagOfCheese` object. With this information in mind, you can shorten the code in Listing 9-3 even more, as shown in Listing 9-4.

Listing 9-4: Reusing a bag Object's Fields

```
package com.allmycode.andy;

import javax.swing.JOptionPane;

public class CreateBags {
  public static void main(String[] args) {
    BagOfCheese bag = new BagOfCheese();
    bag.kind = "Cheddar";
    bag.weight = 2.43;
    bag.daysAged = 30;
    bag.isDomestic = true;

    JOptionPane.showMessageDialog(null,
        bag.kind + ", " +
        bag.weight + ", " +
        bag.daysAged + ", " +
        bag.isDomestic);

    // bag = new BagOfCheese();
    bag.kind = "Blue";
    bag.weight = 5.987;
    bag.daysAged = 90;
    bag.isDomestic = false;

    JOptionPane.showMessageDialog(null,
        bag.kind + ", " +
        bag.weight + ", " +
        bag.daysAged + ", " +
        bag.isDomestic);
  }
}
```

With the second constructor call in Listing 9-4 commented out, you don't make the `bag` variable refer to a new object. Instead, you economize by assigning new values to the existing object's fields.

In some situations, reusing an object's fields can be more efficient (quicker to execute) than creating a new object. But whenever I have a choice, I prefer to write code that mirrors real data. If an actual bag's content doesn't change from cheddar cheese to blue cheese, I prefer not to change a BagOfCheese object's kind field from "Cheddar" to "Blue".

Calling a constructor

In Listing 9-2, the words new BagOfCheese() look like method calls, but they aren't — they're constructor calls. A *constructor call* creates a new object from an existing class. You can spot a constructor call by noticing that

✔ **A constructor call starts with Java's new keyword:**

```
new BagOfCheese()
```

and

✔ **A constructor call's name is the name of a Java class:**

```
new BagOfCheese()
```

When the computer encounters a method call, the computer executes the statements inside a method's declaration. Similarly, when the computer encounters a constructor call, the computer executes the statements inside the constructor's declaration. When you create a new class (as I did in Listing 9-1), Java can create a constructor declaration automatically. If you want, you can type the declaration's code manually. Listing 9-5 shows you what the declaration's code would look like:

Listing 9-5: The Parameterless Constructor

```
package com.allmycode.andy;

public class BagOfCheese {
   String kind;
   double weight;
   int daysAged;
   boolean isDomestic;

   BagOfCheese() {
   }
}
```

In Listing 9-5, the boldface code

```
BagOfCheese() {
}
```

is a very simple constructor declaration. This declaration (unlike most constructor declarations) has no statements inside its body. This declaration is simply a *header* (`BagOfCheese()`) and an empty body (`{}`).

You can type Listing 9-5 exactly as it is. Alternatively, you can omit the code in boldface type, and Java creates that constructor for you automatically. (You don't see the constructor declaration in the Eclipse editor, but Java behaves as if the constructor declaration exists.) To find out when Java creates a constructor declaration automatically and when it doesn't, see the "Constructors with parameters" section, later in this chapter.

A constructor's declaration looks much like a method declaration. But a constructor's declaration differs from a method declaration in two ways:

- **A constructor's name is the same as the name of the class whose objects the constructor constructs.**

    In Listing 9-5, the class name is `BagOfCheese`, and the constructor's header starts with the name `BagOfCheese`.

- **Before the constructor's name, the constructor's header has no type.**

    Unlike a method header, the constructor's header doesn't say `int BagOfCheese()` or even `void BagOfCheese()`. The header simply says `BagOfCheese()`.

The constructor declaration in Listing 9-5 contains no statements. That isn't typical of a constructor, but it's what you get in the constructor that Java creates automatically. With or without statements, calling the constructor in Listing 9-5 creates a brand-new `BagOfCheese` object.

More About Classes and Objects (Adding Methods to the Mix)

In Chapters 5 and 7, I introduce parameter passing. In those chapters, I unobtrusively avoid details about passing objects to methods. (At least, I hope it's unobtrusive.) In this chapter, I shed my coy demeanor and face the topic (passing objects to methods) head-on.

I start with an improvement on an earlier example. The code in Listing 9-2 contains two nasty-looking `showMessageDialog` calls. You can streamline the code there by moving the calls to a method. Here's how:

1. **View the code from Listing 9-2 in the Eclipse editor.**

The `CreateBags.java` file is in the 09-01 project that you import in Chapter 2.

2. **Use the mouse to select the entire statement containing the first call to** `JOptionPane.showMessagedialog`.

   Be sure to highlight all words in the statement, starting with the word `JOptionPane` and ending with the semicolon four lines later.

3. **On the Eclipse main menu, choose Refactor➪Extract Method.**

   The Extract Method dialog box in Eclipse appears, as shown in Figure 9-9.

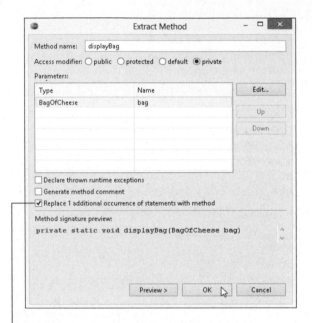

Figure 9-9:
The Extract
Method dia-
log box.

Check this check box.

4. **In the Method Name field in the Extract Method dialog box, type** displayBag.

5. **(Optional) In the Name column in the Extract Method dialog box, change** bag1 **to** bag.

6. **Make sure that a check mark appears in the box labeled Replace 1 Additional Occurrence of Statements with Method.**

   This check mark indicates that Eclipse will replace both `show MessageDialog` calls with a call to the new `displayBag` method.

7. Click OK.

Eclipse dismisses the Extract Method dialog box and replaces your Java code with the new code in Listing 9-6.

Listing 9-6:   A Method Displays a Bag of Cheese

```
package com.allmycode.andy;

import javax.swing.JOptionPane;

public class CreateBags {
  public static void main(String[] args) {
    BagOfCheese bag1 = new BagOfCheese();
    bag1.kind = "Cheddar";
    bag1.weight = 2.43;
    bag1.daysAged = 30;
    bag1.isDomestic = true;

    BagOfCheese bag2 = new BagOfCheese();
    bag2.kind = "Blue";
    bag2.weight = 5.987;
    bag2.daysAged = 90;
    bag2.isDomestic = false;

    displayBag(bag1);

    displayBag(bag2);
  }

  private static void displayBag(BagOfCheese bag) {
    JOptionPane.showMessageDialog(null,
        bag.kind + ", " +
        bag.weight + ", " +
        bag.daysAged + ", " +
        bag.isDomestic);
  }
}
```

According to the `displayBag` declaration (Listing 9-6), the `displayBag` method takes one parameter. That parameter must be a `BagOfCheese` instance. Inside the body of the method declaration, you refer to that instance with the parameter name `bag`. (You refer to `bag.kind`, `bag.weight`, `bag.daysAged`, and `bag.isDomestic`.)

In the `main` method, you create two `BagOfCheese` instances: `bag1` and `bag2`. You call `displayBag` once with the first instance (`displayBag(bag1)`), and call it a second time with the second instance (`displayBag(bag2)`).

Constructors with parameters

Listing 9-7 contains a variation on the theme from Listing 9-2.

Listing 9-7:   Another Way to Create Two Objects

```
package com.allmycode.andy;

import javax.swing.JOptionPane;

public class CreateBags {
  public static void main(String[] args) {
    BagOfCheese bag1 =
        new BagOfCheese("Cheddar", 2.43, 30, true);
    BagOfCheese bag2 =
        new BagOfCheese("Blue", 5.987, 90, false);

    displayBag(bag1);

    displayBag(bag2);
  }

  private static void displayBag(BagOfCheese bag) {
    JOptionPane.showMessageDialog(null,
        bag.kind + ", " +
        bag.weight + ", " +
        bag.daysAged + ", " +
        bag.isDomestic);
  }
}
```

Listing 9-7 calls a BagOfCheese constructor with four parameters, so the code has to have a four-parameter constructor. In Listing 9-8, I show you how to declare that constructor.

Listing 9-8:   A Constructor with Parameters

```
package com.allmycode.andy;

public class BagOfCheese {
  String kind;
  double weight;
  int daysAged;
  boolean isDomestic;

  BagOfCheese() {
  }

  BagOfCheese(String pKind, double pWeight,
```

```
              int pDaysAged, boolean pIsDomestic) {
    kind = pKind;
    weight = pWeight;
    daysAged = pDaysAged;
    isDomestic = pIsDomestic;
  }
}
```

Listing 9-8 borrows some tricks from Chapters 5 and 7. In those chapters, I introduce the concept of *overloading* — reusing a name by providing different parameter lists. Listing 9-8 has two different BagOfCheese constructors — one with no parameters and another with four parameters. When you call a BagOfCheese constructor (as in Listing 9-7), Java knows which declaration to execute by matching the parameters in the constructor call. The call in Listing 9-7 has parameters of type String, double, int, and boolean, and the second constructor in Listing 9-8 has the same types of parameters in the same order, so Java calls the second constructor in Listing 9-8.

You might also notice another trick from Chapter 7. In Listing 9-8, in the second constructor declaration, I use different names for the parameters and the class's fields. For example, I use the parameter name pKind and the field name kind. So what happens if you use the same names for the parameters and the fields, as in this example:

```
// DON'T DO THIS
BagOfCheese(String kind, double weight,
            int daysAged, boolean isDomestic) {
  kind = kind;
  weight = weight;
  daysAged = daysAged;
  isDomestic = isDomestic;
}
```

Figure 9-10 shows you exactly what happens. (***Hint:*** Nothing good happens!)

Aside from all the yellow warning markers in the Eclipse editor, the code with duplicate parameter and field names gives you the useless results from Figure 9-10. The code in Listing 9-8 makes the mistake of containing two kind variables — one inside the constructor and another outside of the constructor, as shown in Figure 9-11.

When you have a field and a parameter with the same name, kind, the parameter name *shadows* the field name inside the method or the constructor. So, outside the constructor declaration, the word kind refers to the field name. Inside the constructor declaration, however, the word kind refers only to the parameter name. So, in the horrible code with duplicate names, the statement

```
kind = kind;
```

does nothing to the `kind` field. Instead, this statement tells the computer to make the `kind` parameter refer to the same string that the `kind` parameter already refers to.

If this explanation sounds like nonsense to you, it is.

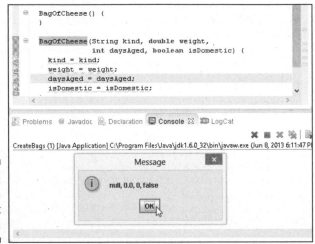

Figure 9-10: Some unpleasant results.

```
public class BagOfCheese {
    String kind;           ◄──── Outside of the constructor
    double weight;              One of the class's fields
    int daysAged;
    boolean isDomestic;

    BagOfCheese (String kind, double weight,
                 int daysAged, boolean isDomestic) {
        ... = kind;     ◄──── Inside the constructor
        ... = weight;         One of the constructor's local
        ... = daysAged;       variables (A different variable
        ... = isDomestic;     which happens to have the
    }                         same name as one of the
}                             class's fields)
```

Figure 9-11: Two `kind` variables.

The `kind` variable in the constructor declaration's parameter list is *local* to the constructor. Any use of the word `kind` outside the constructor cannot refer to the constructor's local `kind` variable.

Fields are different. You can refer to a field anywhere in the class's code. For example, in Listing 9-8, the second constructor declaration has no local `kind` variable of its own. Inside that constructor's body, the word `kind` refers to the class's field.

One way or another, the second constructor in Listing 9-8 is cumbersome. Do you always have to make up peculiar names like `pKind` for a constructor's parameters? No, you don't. To find out why, see the "This is it!" section.

The default constructor

In Listing 9-1, I don't explicitly type a parameterless constructor into my program's code, and Java creates a parameterless constructor for me. (I don't see a parameterless constructor in Listing 9-1, but I can still call `new BagOfCheese()` in Listing 9-2.) But in Listing 9-8, if I didn't explicitly type the parameterless constructor in my code, Java wouldn't have created a parameterless constructor for me. A call to `new BagOfCheese()` would have been illegal. (The Eclipse editor would tell me that *The BagOfCheese() constructor is undefined.*)

Here's how it works: When you define a class, Java creates a parameterless constructor (known formally as a *default constructor*) if, and only if, you haven't explicitly defined any constructors in your class's code. When Java encounters Listing 9-1, Java automatically adds a parameterless constructor to your `BagOfCheese` class. But when Java encounters Listing 9-8, you have to type the lines

```
BagOfCheese() {
}
```

into your code. If you don't, calls to `new BagOfCheese()` (with no parameters) will be illegal.

This is it!

The naming problem that crops up earlier in this chapter, in the "Constructors with parameters" section, has an elegant solution. Listing 9-9 illustrates the idea.

Listing 9-9: Using Java's `this` Keyword

```
package com.allmycode.andy;

public class BagOfCheese {
  String kind;
  double weight;
  int daysAged;
  boolean isDomestic;

  BagOfCheese() {
  }

  public BagOfCheese(String kind, double weight,
                     int daysAged, boolean isDomestic) {
    super();
    this.kind = kind;
    this.weight = weight;
    this.daysAged = daysAged;
    this.isDomestic = isDomestic;
  }
}
```

To use the class in Listing 9-9, you can run the `CreateBags` code in Listing 9-7. When you do, you see the run shown earlier, in Figure 9-8.

You can persuade Eclipse to create the oversized constructor that you see in Listing 9-9. Here's how:

1. **Start with the code from Listing 9-1 (or Listing 9-3) in the Eclipse editor.**

2. **Click the mouse cursor anywhere inside the editor.**

3. **On the Eclipse main menu, select Source⟹ Generate Constructor Using Fields.**

   The Generate Constructor Using Fields dialog box in Eclipse appears, as shown in Figure 9-12.

4. **In the Select Fields to Initialize pane in the dialog box, make sure that all four of the** `BagOfCheese` **fields are selected.**

   Doing so ensures that the new constructor will have a parameter for each of the class's fields.

5. **Click OK.**

   That does it! Eclipse dismisses the dialog box and adds a freshly brewed constructor to the editor's code.

Figure 9-12:
The
Generate
Constructor
Using Fields
dialog box.

Java's `this` keyword refers to "the object that contains the current line of code." So in Listing 9-9, the word `this` refers to an instance of `BagOfCheese` (that is, to the object that's being constructed). That object has a `kind` field, so `this.kind` refers to the first of the object's four fields (and not to the constructor's `kind` parameter). That object also has `weight`, `daysAged`, and `isDomestic` fields, so `this.weight`, `this.daysAged`, and `this.isDomestic` refer to that object's fields, as shown in Figure 9-13. And the assignment statements inside the constructor give values to the new object's fields.

Listing 9-9 contains the call `super()`. To find out what `super()` means, see Chapter 10.

Giving an object more responsibility

You have a printer and you try to install it on your computer. It's a capable printer, but it didn't come with your computer, so your computer needs a program to *drive* the printer: a printer *driver*. Without a driver, your new printer is nothing but a giant paperweight.

But, sometimes, finding a device driver can be a pain in the neck. Maybe you can't find the disk that came with the printer. (That's always my problem.)

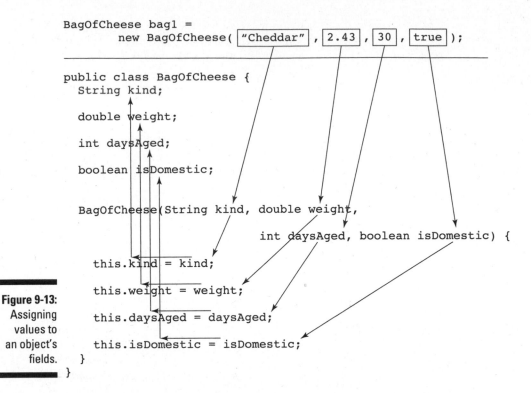

Figure 9-13:
Assigning
values to
an object's
fields.

I have one off-brand printer whose driver is built into its permanent memory. When I plug the printer into a USB port, the computer displays a new storage location. (The location looks, to ordinary users, like another of the computer's disks.) The drivers for the printer are stored directly on the printer's internal memory. It's as though the printer knows how to drive itself!

Now consider the code in Listings 9-7 and 9-8. You're the CreateBags class (refer to Listing 9-7), and you have a new gadget to play with — the Bag OfCheese class in Listing 9-8. You want to display the properties of a particular bag, and you don't enjoy reinventing the wheel. That is, you don't like declaring your own displayBag method (the way you do in Listing 9-7). You'd rather have the BagOfCheese class come with its own displayBag method.

Here's the plan: Move the displayBag method from the CreateBags class to the BagOfCheese class. That is, make each BagOfCheese object be responsible for displaying itself. With the Andy's Cheese Emporium metaphor that starts this chapter, each bag's form has its own Display button, as shown in Figure 9-14.

The interesting characteristic of a Display button is that when you press it, the message you see depends on the bag of cheese you're examining. More precisely, the message you see depends on the values in that particular form's fields.

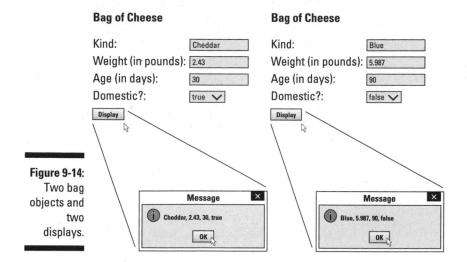

Figure 9-14:
Two bag objects and two displays.

The same thing happens in Listing 9-11 when you call `bag1.displayBag()`. Java runs the `displayBag` method shown in Listing 9-10. The values used in that method call — `kind`, `weight`, `daysAged`, and `isDomestic` — are the values in the `bag1` object's fields. Similarly, the values used when you call `bag2.displayBag()` are the values in the `bag2` object's fields.

Listing 9-10:   A Self-Displaying Class

```
package com.allmycode.andy;

import javax.swing.JOptionPane;

class BagOfCheese {
  String kind;
  double weight;
  int daysAged;
  boolean isDomestic;

  BagOfCheese() {
  }

  public BagOfCheese(String kind, double weight,
```

(continued)

Listing 9-10 *(continued)*

```
                      int daysAged, boolean isDomestic) {
    super();
    this.kind = kind;
    this.weight = weight;
    this.daysAged = daysAged;
    this.isDomestic = isDomestic;
  }

  public void displayBag() {
    JOptionPane.showMessageDialog(null,
        kind + ", " +
        weight + ", " +
        daysAged + ", " +
        isDomestic);
  }
}
```

Listing 9-11:   Having a Bag Display Itself

```
package com.allmycode.andy;

public class CreateBags {
  public static void main(String[] args) {
    BagOfCheese bag1 =
        new BagOfCheese("Cheddar", 2.43, 30, true);
    BagOfCheese bag2 =
        new BagOfCheese("Blue", 5.987, 90, false);

    bag1.displayBag();

    bag2.displayBag();
  }
}
```

In Listing 9-10, the BagOfCheese object has its own, parameterless display
Bag method. And in Listing 9-11, the following two lines make two calls to the
displayBag method — one call for bag1 and another call for bag2:

```
    bag1.displayBag();

    bag2.displayBag();
```

A call to displayBag behaves differently depending on the particular bag
that's being displayed. When you call bag1.displayBag(), you see the
field values for bag1, and when you call bag2.displayBag(), you see the
field values for bag2.

To call one of an object's methods, follow a reference to the object with a dot and then the method's name.

Members of a class

Notice the similarity between fields and methods:

- As I say earlier in this chapter, in the "Creating objects" section:

  To refer to one of an object's fields, follow a reference to the object with a dot and then the field's name.

- As I say earlier in this chapter, in the "Giving an object more responsibility" section:

  To call one of an object's methods, follow a reference to the object with a dot and then the method's name.

The similarity between fields and methods stretches far and wide in object-oriented programming. The similarity is so strong that special terminology is necessary to describe it. In addition to each BagOfCheese object having its own values for the four fields, you can think of each object as having its own copy of the displayBag method. So the BagOfCheese class in Listing 9-10 has five *members*. Four of the members are the fields kind, weight, daysAged, and isDomestic, and the remaining member is the displayBag method.

Reference types

Here's a near-quotation from the earlier section "Creating objects:"

> *In Listing 9-2, the initialization of bag1 makes the bag1 variable refer to the newly created bag.*

In the quotation, I choose my words carefully. "The initialization makes the bag1 variable *refer to* the newly created bag." Notice how I italicize the words *refer to*. A variable of type int *stores* an int value, but the bag1 variable in Listing 9-2 *refers to* an object.

What's the difference? The difference is similar to holding an object in your hand versus pointing to it in the room. Figure 9-15 shows you what I mean.

```
int daysAged;
```

```
  30
```

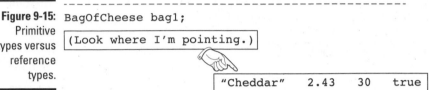

Figure 9-15:
Primitive
types versus
reference
types.

```
BagOfCheese bag1;
```
```
(Look where I'm pointing.)
```
```
  "Cheddar"   2.43    30    true
```

Java has two kinds of types: primitive types and reference types.

- ✔ I cover primitive types in Chapter 6. Java's eight primitive types are `int`, `double`, `boolean`, `char`, `byte`, `short`, `long`, and `float`.

- ✔ A *reference type* is the name of a class or (as you see in Chapter 10) an interface.

In Figure 9-15, the variable `daysAged` contains the value `30` (indicating that the cheese in a particular bag has been aged for 30 days). I imagine the value `30` being right inside the `daysAged` box because the `daysAged` variable has type `int` — a primitive type.

But the variable `bag1` has type `BagOfCheese`, and `BagOfCheese` isn't a primitive type. (I know of no computer programming language in which a bag of cheese is a built-in, primitive type!) So the `bag1` variable doesn't contain `"Cheddar" 2.43 30 true`. Instead, the variable `bag1` contains the information required to locate the `"Cheddar" 2.43 30 true` object. The variable `bag1` stores information that *refers to* the `"Cheddar" 2.43 30 true` object.

The types `int`, `double`, `boolean`, `char`, `byte`, `short`, `long`, and `float` are primitive types. A primitive type variable (`int daysAged`, `double weight`, `boolean`, and `isDomestic`, for example) stores a value. In contrast, a class is a reference type, such as `String`, which is defined in Java's API, and `BagOfCheese`, which you or I declare ourselves. A reference type variable (`BagOfCheese bag` and `String kind`, for example) *refers* to an object.

Figure 9-15 would be slightly more accurate (but a bit more complicated) if the bottommost box contained a picture of a hand followed by the values 2.43 30 true. The hand would point outside of the box to the string "Cheddar".

In this section, I say that the `bag1` variable *refers to* the `"Cheddar"` `2.43` `30` `true` object. It's also common to say that the `bag1` variable *points to* the `"Cheddar"` `2.43` `30` `true` object. Alternatively, you can say that the `bag1` variable stores the number of the memory address where the `"Cheddar"` `2.43` `30` `true` object's values begin. Neither the pointing language nor the memory language expresses the truth of the matter, but if the rough terminology helps you understand what's going on, there's no harm in using it.

Pass by reference

In the previous section, I emphasize that classes are reference types. A variable whose type is a class contains something that refers to blah, blah, blah. You might ask, "Why should I care?"

Look at Listing 7-4, over in Chapter 7, and notice the result of passing a primitive type to a method:

> *When the method's body changes the parameter's value, the change has no effect on the value of the variable in the method call.*

This principle holds true for reference types as well. But in the case of a reference type, the value that's passed is the information about where to find an object, not the object itself. When you pass a reference type in a method's parameter list, you can change values in the object's fields.

See, for example, the code in Listing 9-12.

Listing 9-12: Another Day Goes By

```
package com.allmycode.andy;

public class CreateBags {
  public static void main(String[] args) {
    BagOfCheese bag1 =
        new BagOfCheese("Cheddar", 2.43, 30, true);

    addOneDay(bag1);

    bag1.displayBag();
  }

  static void addOneDay(BagOfCheese bag) {
    bag.daysAged++;
  }
}
```

A run of the code in Listing 9-12 is shown in Figure 9-16. In that run, the constructor creates a bag that is aged 30 days, but the addOneDay method successfully adds a day. In the end, the display in Figure 9-16 shows 31 days aged.

Figure 9-16:
Thirty-one
days old.

Unlike the story with int values, you can change a bag of cheese's daysAged value by passing the bag as a method parameter. Why does it work this way?

When you call a method, you make a copy of each parameter's value in the call. You initialize the declaration's parameters with the copied values. Immediately after making the addOneDay call in Listing 9-12, you have two variables: the original bag1 variable in the main method and the new bag variable in the addOneDay method. The new bag variable has a copy of the value from the main method, as shown in Figure 9-17. That "value" from the main method is a reference to a BagOfCheese object. In other words, the bag1 and bag variables refer to the same object.

The statement in the body of the addOneDay method adds 1 to the value stored in the object's daysAged field. After one day is added, the program's variables look like the information in Figure 9-18.

Notice how both the bag1 and bag variables refer to an object whose daysAged value is 31. After returning from the call to addOneDay, the bag variable goes away. All that remains is the original main method and its bag1 variable, as shown in Figure 9-19. But bag1 still refers to an object whose daysAged value has been changed to 31.

In Chapter 7, I show you how to pass primitive values to method parameters. Passing a primitive value to a method parameter is called *pass-by value*. In this section, I show you how to pass both primitive values and objects to method parameters. Passing an object (such as bag1) to a method parameter is called *pass-by reference*.

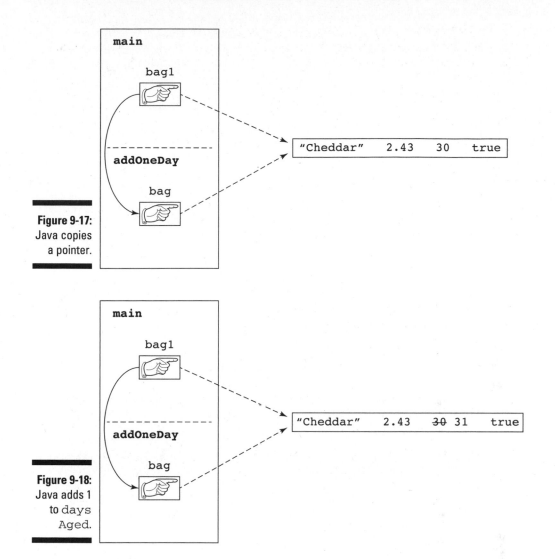

Figure 9-17:
Java copies
a pointer.

Figure 9-18:
Java adds 1
to days
Aged.

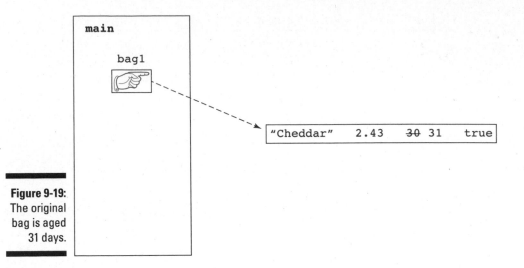

Java's Modifiers

Throughout this book, you see words like static and public peppered throughout the code listings. You might wonder what these words mean. (Actually, if you're reading from front to back, you might have grown accustomed to seeing them and started thinking of them as background noise.) In the next few sections, I tackle some of these *modifier* keywords.

Public classes and default-access classes

Most of the classes in this chapter's listings begin with the word public. When a class is public, any program in any package can use the code (or at least some of the code) inside that class. If a class isn't public, then for a program to use the code inside that class, the program must be inside the same package as the class. Listings 9-13, 9-14, and 9-15 illustrate these ideas.

Listing 9-13:   What Is a Paragraph?

```
package org.allyourcode.wordprocessor;

class Paragraph {
    int alignment;
    int borders;
    double leftIndent;
    double lineSpacing;
    int style;
}
```

Listing 9-14:   Making a Paragraph with Code in the Same Package

```
package org.allyourcode.wordprocessor;

class MakeParagraph {

  public static void main(String[] args) {
    Paragraph paragraph = new Paragraph();
    paragraph.leftIndent = 1.5;
  }

}
```

Listing 9-15:   Making a Paragraph with Code in Another Package

```
package com.allyourcode.editor;

import org.allyourcode.wordprocessor.Paragraph;

public class MakeAnotherParagraph {

  public static void main(String[] args) {
    Paragraph paragraph = new Paragraph();
    paragraph.leftIndent = 1.5;
  }

}
```

The Paragraph class in Listing 9-13 has *default access* — that is, the Paragraph class isn't public. The code in Listing 9-14 is in the same package as the Paragraph class (the org.allyourcode.wordprocessor package). So In Listing 9-14, you can declare an object to be of type Paragraph, and you can refer to that object's leftIndent field.

The code in Listing 9-15 isn't in the same org.allyourcode.wordprocessor package. For that reason, the use of names like Paragraph and leftIndent (from Listing 9-13) aren't legal in Listing 9-15, even if Listings 9-13 and 9-15 are in the same Eclipse project. When you type Listings 9-13, 9-14, and 9-15 into the Eclipse editor, you see a red, blotchy mess for Listing 9-15, as shown in Figure 9-20.

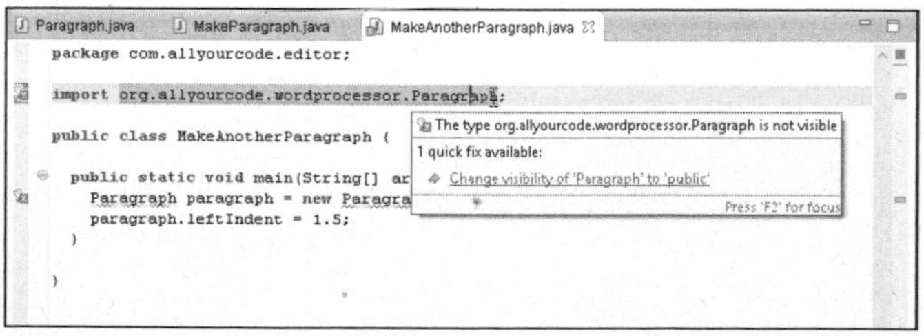

Figure 9-20:
Errors in
Listing 9-15.

An Android activity can invoke the code from another package (that is, another Android app). To do this, you don't use names from the other package in your activity's code. For details, see the discussion of `start Activity` in Chapter 12.

The `.java` file containing a public class must have the same name as the public class, so the file containing the code in Listing 9-1 must be named `BagOfCheese.java`.

Even the capitalization of the filename must be the same as the public class's name. You see an error message if you put the code in Listing 9-1 inside a file named `bagofcheese.java`. In the file's name, you have to capitalize the letters B, O, and C.

Because of the file-naming rule, you can't declare more than one public class in a `.java` file. If you put the public classes from Listings 9-1 and 9-2 into the same file, would you name the file `BagOfCheese.java` or `CreateBags.java`? Neither name would satisfy the file-naming rule. For that matter, *no* name would satisfy it.

It's customary to declare a class containing a `main` method to be public. I sometimes ignore this convention, but when I do, the code looks strange to me later. Once, I faced a situation in which a Java class had to be public simply because that class contained a `main` method. I promised myself that I'd use this example in my writing later, but since then I haven't been able to remember the situation. Oh, well!

Access for fields and methods

A class can have either public access or nonpublic (default) access. But a member of a class has four possibilities: public, private, default, and protected.

A class's fields and methods are the class's *members*. For example, the class in Listing 9-10 has five members: the fields `kind`, `weight`, `daysAged`, and `isDomestic` and the method `displayBag`.

Here's how member access works:

- ✔ A default member of a class (a member whose declaration doesn't contain the words `public`, `private`, or `protected`) can be used by any code inside the same package as that class.
- ✔ A private member of a class cannot be used in any code outside the class.

✔ A public member of a class can be used wherever the class itself can be used; that is:

- Any program in any package can refer to a public member of a public class.

- For a program to reference a public member of a default access class, the program must be inside the same package as the class.

To see these rules in action, check out the public class in Listing 9-16.

Listing 9-16:   A Class with Public Access

```
package org.allyourcode.bank;

public class Account {
    public String customerName;
    private int internalIdNumber;
    String address;
    String phone;
    public int socialSecurityNumber;
    int accountType;
    double balance;

    public static int findById(int internalIdNumber) {
        Account foundAccount = new Account();
        // Code to find the account goes here.
        return foundAccount.internalIdNumber;
    }
}
```

The code in Figures 9-21 and 9-22 uses the Account class and its fields.

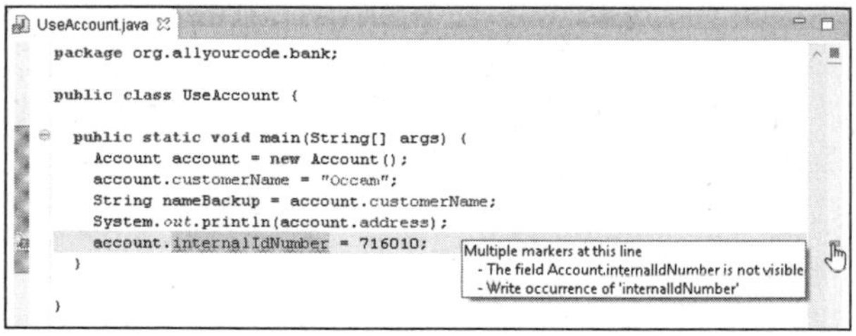

Figure 9-21: Referring to a public class in the same package.

```
UseAccount.java
    package org.allyourcode.bank;

    public class UseAccount {

        public static void main(String[] args) {
            Account account = new Account();
            account.customerName = "Occam";
            String nameBackup = account.customerName;
            System.out.println(account.address);
            account.internalIdNumber = 716010;
        }
    }
```

Multiple markers at this line
- The field Account.internalIdNumber is not visible
- Write occurrence of 'internalIdNumber'

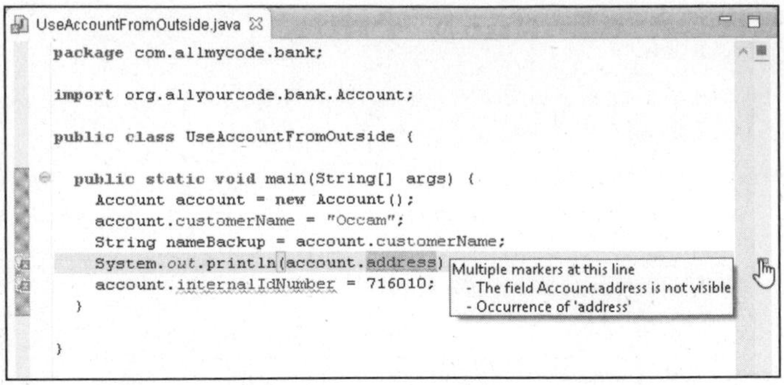

Figure 9-22:
Referring
to a public
class in a
different
package.

In Figures 9-21 and 9-22, notice that

✔ The UseAccount class is in the same package as the Account class.

✔ The UseAccount class can create a variable of type Account.

✔ The UseAccount class's code can refer to the public customerName field of the Account class and to the default address field of the Account class.

✔ The UseAccount class cannot refer to the private internalIdNumber field of the Account class, even though UseAccount and Account are in the same package.

✔ The UseAccountFromOutside class is not in the same package as the Account class.

✔ The UseAccountFromOutside class can create a variable of type Account. (An import declaration keeps me from having to repeat the fully qualified org.allyourcode.bank.Account name everywhere in the code.)

✔ The UseAccountFromOutside class's code can refer to the public customerName field of the Account class.

✔ The UseAccountFromOutside class's code cannot refer to the default address field of the Account class or to the private internalIdNumber field of the Account class.

Now examine the nonpublic class in Listing 9-17.

Listing 9-17:   A Class with Default Access

```
package org.allyourcode.game;

class Sprite {
  public String name;
```

```
String image;
double distanceFromLeftEdge, distanceFromTop;
double motionAcross, motionDown;
private int renderingMethod;

void render() {
  if (renderingMethod == 2) {
    // Do stuff here
  }
 }
}
```

The code in Figures 9-23 and 9-24 uses the `Sprite` class and its fields.

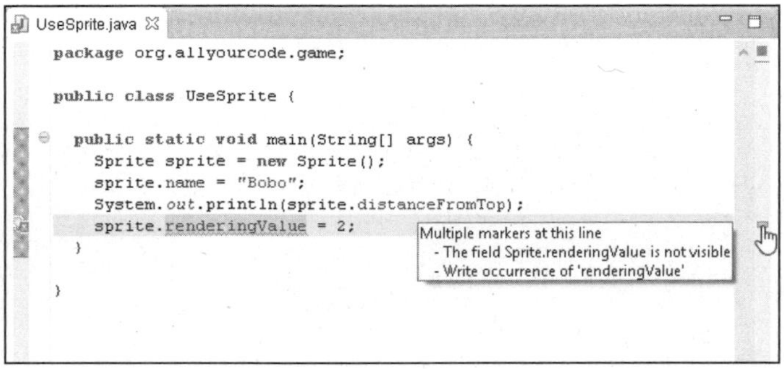

Figure 9-23:
Referring to a default access class in the same package.

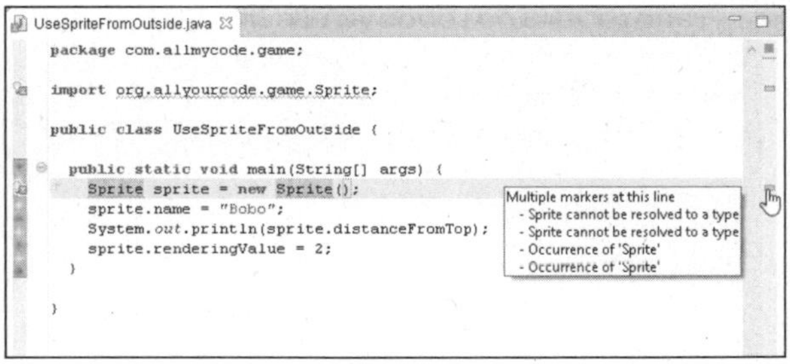

```
UseSprite.java

package org.allyourcode.game;

public class UseSprite {

  public static void main(String[] args) {
    Sprite sprite = new Sprite();
    sprite.name = "Bobo";
    System.out.println(sprite.distanceFromTop);
    sprite.renderingValue = 2;
  }

}
```
Multiple markers at this line
- The field Sprite.renderingValue is not visible
- Write occurrence of 'renderingValue'

Figure 9-24:
Referring to a default access class in a different package.

```
UseSpriteFromOutside.java

package com.allmycode.game;

import org.allyourcode.game.Sprite;

public class UseSpriteFromOutside {

  public static void main(String[] args) {
    Sprite sprite = new Sprite();
    sprite.name = "Bobo";
    System.out.println(sprite.distanceFromTop);
    sprite.renderingValue = 2;
  }

}
```
Multiple markers at this line
- Sprite cannot be resolved to a type
- Sprite cannot be resolved to a type
- Occurrence of 'Sprite'
- Occurrence of 'Sprite'

In Figures 9-23 and 9-24, notice that

✔ The `UseSprite` class is in the same package as the `Sprite` class.

✔ The `UseSprite` class can create a variable of type `Sprite`.

✔ The `UseSprite` class's code can refer to the public `name` field of the `Sprite` class and to the default `distanceFromTop` field of the `Sprite` class.

✔ The UseSprite class cannot refer to the private renderingValue field of the Sprite class, even though UseSprite and Sprite are in the same package.

✔ The UseSpriteFromOutside class isn't in the same package as the Sprite class.

✔ The UseSpriteFromOutside class cannot create a variable of type Sprite. (Not even an import declaration can save you from an error message here.)

✔ Inside the UseAccountFromOutside class, references to sprite.name, sprite.distanceFromTop, and sprite.renderingValue are all meaningless because the sprite variable doesn't have a type.

Using getters and setters

In Figures 9-21 and 9-22, the UseAccount and UseAccountFromOutside classes can set an account's customerName and get the account's existing customerName:

```
account.customerName = "Occam";
String nameBackup = account.customerName;
```

But neither the UseAccount class nor the UseAccountFromOutside class can tinker with an account's internalIdNumber field.

What if you want a class like UseAccount to be able to get an existing account's internalIdNumber but not to change an account's internalIdNumber? (In many situations, getting information is necessary, but changing existing information is dangerous.) You can do all this with a *getter* method, as shown in Listing 9-18.

Listing 9-18: Creating a Read-Only Field

```
package org.allyourcode.bank;

public class Account {
  public String customerName;
  private int internalIdNumber;
  String address;
  String phone;
  public int socialSecurityNumber;
  int accountType;
  double balance;

  public static int findById(int internalIdNumber) {
```

```
    Account foundAccount = new Account();
    // Code to find the account goes here.
    return foundAccount.internalIdNumber;
  }

  public int getInternalIdNumber() {
    return internalIdNumber;
  }
}
```

With the `Account` class in Listing 9-18, another class's code can call

```
System.out.println(account.getInternalIdNumber());
```

or

```
int backupIdNumber = account.getInternalIdNumber();
```

The `Account` class's `internalIdNumber` field is still private, so another class's code has no way to assign a value to an account's `internalId Number` field. To enable other classes to change an account's private `internalIdNumber` value, you can add a setter method to the code in Listing 9-18, like this:

```
public void setInternalIdNumber(int internalIdNumber) {
  this.internalIdNumber = internalIdNumber;
}
```

Getter and setter methods aren't built-in features in Java — they're simply ordinary Java methods. But this pattern (having a method whose purpose is to access an otherwise inaccessible field's value) is used so often that programmers use the terms *getter* and *setter* to describe it.

Getter and setter methods are *accessor* methods. Java programmers almost always follow the convention of starting an accessor method name with `get` or `set` and then capitalizing the name of the field being accessed. For example, the field `internalIdNumber` has accessors named `getInternal IdNumber` and `setInternalIdNumber`. The field `renderingValue` has accessors named `getRenderingValue` and `setRenderingValue`.

You can have Eclipse create getters and setters for you. Here's how:

1. **Start with the code from Listing 9-16 in the Eclipse editor.**

2. **Click the mouse cursor anywhere inside the editor.**

3. **On the Eclipse main menu, select Source⇨Generate Getters and Setters.**

The Generate Getters and Setters dialog box in Eclipse appears, as shown in Figure 9-25.

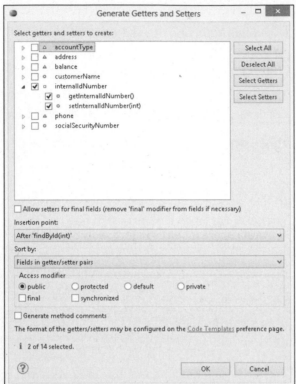

Figure 9-25: The Generate Getters and Setters dialog box.

4. **In the Select Getters and Setters to Create pane in the dialog box, expand the** `internalIdNumber` **branch.**

5. **Within the** `internalIdNumber` **branch, select either or both of the getInternalIdNumber() or setInternalIdNumber(int) check boxes.**

   Eclipse creates only the getters and setters whose check boxes you select.

6. **Click OK.**

   Eclipse dismisses the dialog box and adds freshly brewed getter and setter methods to the editor's code.

I cover protected access in Chapter 10.

What does static mean?

This chapter begins with a discussion of cheese and its effects on Andy's business practices. Andy has a blank form that represents a class. He also has a bunch of filled-in forms, each of which represents an individual bag-of-cheese object.

One day, Andy decides to take inventory of his cheese by counting all the bags of cheese (see Figure 9-26).

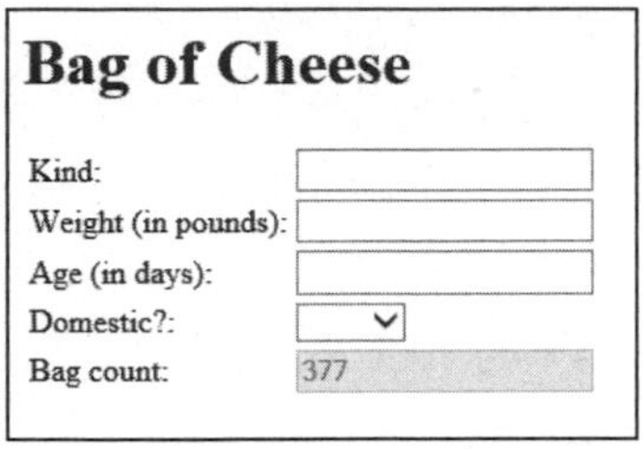

Figure 9-26: Counting bags of cheese.

Bag of Cheese

Kind:	
Weight (in pounds):	
Age (in days):	
Domestic?:	⌄
Bag count:	377

Compare the various fields shown in Figure 9-27. From the object-oriented point of view, how is the `daysAged` field so different from the `count` field?

The answer is that a single bag can keep track of how many days it has been aged, but it shouldn't count *all* the bags. As far back as Listing 9-1, a `BagOfCheese` object has its own `daysAged` field. That makes sense. (Well, it makes sense to an object-oriented programmer.)

But giving a particular object the responsibility of counting all objects in its class doesn't seem fair. To have each `BagOfCheese` object speak on behalf of all the others violates a prime directive of computer programming: The structure of the program should imitate the structure of the real-life data. For example, I can post a picture of myself on Facebook, but I can't promise to count everyone else's pictures on Facebook. ("All you other Facebook users, count your own @#!% pictures!")

A field to count all bags of cheese belongs in one central place. That's why, in Figure 9-27, I have one, and only one, `count` field. Each object has its own `daysAged` value, but only the class itself has a `count` value.

A field or method that belongs to an entire class rather than to each individual object is a *static* member of the class. To declare a static member of a class, you use Java's `static` keyword (what a surprise!), as shown in Listing 9-19.

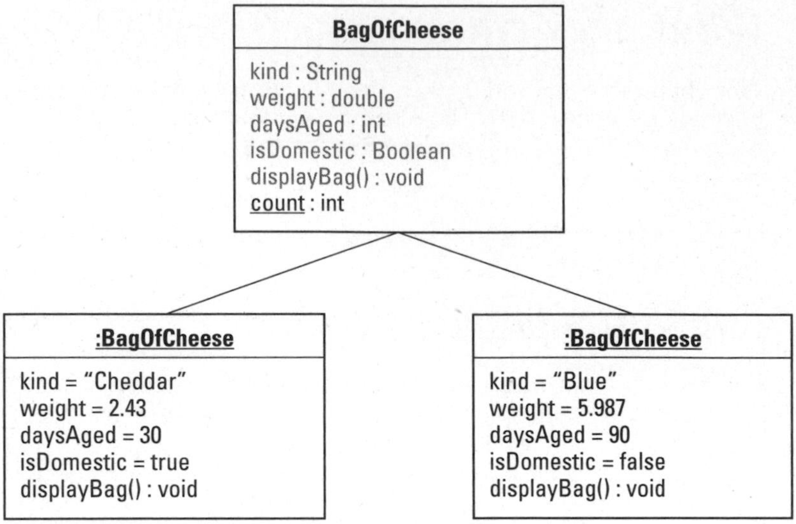

Figure 9-27:
The UML
diagram
has only
one count
variable.

Listing 9-19:   Creating a Static Field

```
package com.allmycode.andy;

class BagOfCheese {
   String kind;
   double weight;
   int daysAged;
   boolean isDomestic;

   static int count = 0;

   public BagOfCheese() {
      count++;
   }
}
```

To refer to a class's static member, you preface the member's name with the
name of the class, as shown in Listing 9-20.

Listing 9-20:   Referring to a Static Field

```
package com.allmycode.andy;

import javax.swing.JOptionPane;

public class CreateBags {

   public static void main(String[] args) {
```

```
      new BagOfCheese();
      new BagOfCheese();
      new BagOfCheese();
      JOptionPane.showMessageDialog
              (null, BagOfCheese.count);
   }

}
```

Knowing when to create a static member

In many situations, you declare an element to be static in order to mirror the structure of real-life data — but sometimes you declare it to be static for technical reasons. For example, a program's main method has to be static in order to provide the Java virtual machine with easy access to the method.

Listing 9-21 is a copy of an example from Chapter 7. In the listing, the main method has to be static. I've learned to live with that fact.

Listing 9-21:   Declaring and Calling a Static Method

```
import javax.swing.JOptionPane;

public class Scorekeeper {

  public static void main(String[] args) {
    int score = 50000;
    int points = 1000;
    score = addPoints(score, points);
    JOptionPane.showMessageDialog(null, score,
        "New Score", JOptionPane.INFORMATION_MESSAGE);
  }

  static int addPoints(int score, int points) {
    return score + points;
  }

}
```

But what about the addPoints method in Listing 9-21? Why is the addPoints method static? If you remove the word static from the addPoints method's declaration, you get this ferocious-looking error: Cannot make a static reference to non-static method. What gives?

To understand what's going on, consider the three ways to refer to a member (a field or a method):

✔ **You can preface the member name with a name that refers to an object.**

For example, in Listing 9-11, I preface calls to displayBag with the names bag1 and bag2, each of which refers to an object:

```
bag1.displayBag();
bag2.displayBag();
```

When you do this, you're referring to something that belongs to each individual object. (You're referring to the object's nonstatic field, or calling the object's nonstatic method.)

✔ **You can preface the member name with a name that refers to a class.**

For example, in Listing 9-20, I prefaced the field name count with the class name BagOfCheese.

When you do this, you're referring to something that belongs to the entire class. (You're referring to the class's static field, or calling the class's static method.)

✔ **You can preface the member name with nothing.**

For example, in Listing 9-10, inside the displayBag method, I use the names kind, weight, daysAged, and isDomestic with no dots in front of them:

```
public void displayBag() {
  JOptionPane.showMessageDialog(null,
      kind + ", " +
      weight + ", " +
      daysAged + ", " +
      isDomestic);
}
```

In Listing 9-21, I preface the static method name addPoints with no dots in front of the name:

```
score = addPoints(score, points);
```

When you do this, you're referring to either a nonstatic member belonging to a particular object or to a static member belonging to a particular class. It all depends on the location of the code containing the member name, as described in this list:

• If the code is inside a nonstatic method, the name refers to an element belonging to an object. That is, the name refers to an object's nonstatic field or method.

For example, in Listing 9-10, the following code snippet is in the non-static displayBag method:

```
kind + ", " +
weight + ", " +
daysAged + ", " +
isDomestic);
```

In this context, the names `kind`, `weight`, `daysAged`, and `is
Domestic` refer to a particular object's properties.

- If the code is inside a static method, the name refers to something
belonging to an entire class. That is, the name refers to a class's
static field or method.

In Listing 9-21, the line

```
score = addPoints(score, points);
```

is inside the static `main` method, so the name `addPoints` refers to
the `Scorekeeper` class's static `addPoints` method.

Java provides a loophole in which you break one of the three rules I just
described. You can preface a member name with a name that refers to an
object. If the member is static, it's the same as prefacing the member name
with the name of a class (whatever class you used when you declared that
name).

Consider the code in Listing 9-21. If the `addPoints` method isn't static, each
instance of the `Scorekeeper` class has its own `addPoints` method, and
each `addPoints` method belongs to an instance of the `Scorekeeper` class.
The trouble is that the code in Listing 9-21 doesn't construct any instances of
the `Scorekeeper` class. (The listing declares the `Scorekeeper` class itself,
but doesn't create any instances.) The listing has no copies of `addPoints` to
call. (See Figure 9-28.)Without `addPoints` being static, the statement `score
= addPoints(score, points)` is illegal.

Sure, you can call the `Scorekeeper` constructor to create a `Scorekeeper`
instance:

```
Scorekeeper keeper = new Scorekeeper();
```

But that doesn't solve the problem. The call to `addPoints` is inside the
`main` method, and the `main` method is static. So the `addPoints` call doesn't
come from the new `keeper` object, and the call doesn't refer to the `keeper`
object's `addPoints` method.

You can fix the problem (of `addPoints` not being static) by using a two-
step approach: Create a `Scorekeeper` instance, *and* call the new instance's
`addPoints` method, as shown here and in Figure 9-29:

```
Scorekeeper keeper = new Scorekeeper();
keeper.addPoints(score, points);
```

But this approach complicates the example from Chapter 7.

In Listing 9-21, the one and only static `addPoints` method belongs to the
entire `Scorekeeper` class, as shown in Figure 9-30. Also, the static `main`

method and the call to `addPoints` belong to the entire `Scorekeeper` class, so the `addPoints` call in Listing 9-21 has a natural target, as shown in Figure 9-29.

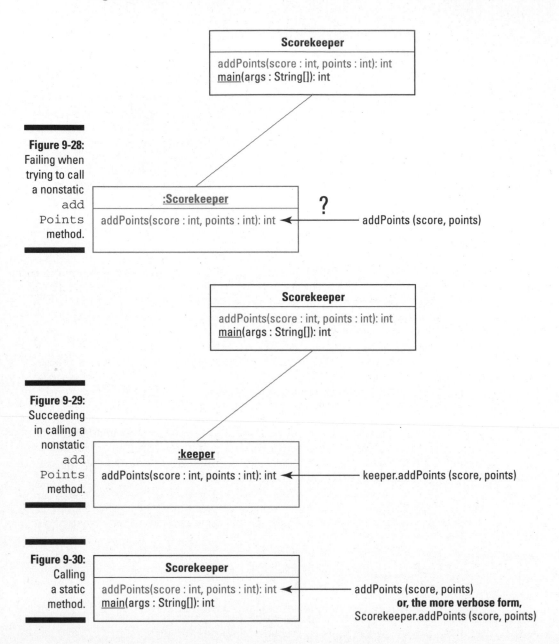

Figure 9-28:
Failing when trying to call a nonstatic add Points method.

Figure 9-29:
Succeeding in calling a nonstatic add Points method.

Figure 9-30:
Calling a static method.

What's Next?

This chapter talks about individual classes. Most classes don't exist in isolation from other classes. Most classes belong to hierarchies of classes, subclasses, and sub-subclasses, so the next chapter covers the relationships among classes.

Chapter 10

Saving Time and Money: Reusing Existing Code

. . . .

In This Chapter

▶ Tweaking your code

▶ Adding new life to old code

▶ Making changes without spending a fortune

. . . .

*W*ouldn't it be nice if every piece of software did just what you wanted it to do? In an ideal world, you could simply buy a program, make it work right away, plug it seamlessly into new situations, and update it easily whenever your needs changed. Unfortunately, software of this kind doesn't exist. (*Nothing* of this kind exists.) The truth is that no matter what you want to do, you can find software that does some of it, but not all of it.

This is one reason that object-oriented programming has been successful. For years, companies were buying prewritten code only to discover that the code didn't do what they wanted it to do. So the companies began messing with the code. Their programmers dug deep into the program files, changed variable names, moved subprograms around, reworked formulas, and generally made the code worse. The reality was that if a program didn't already do what you wanted (even if it did something ever so close to it), you could never improve the situation by mucking around inside the code. The best option was to chuck the whole program (expensive as that was) and start over. What a sad state of affairs!

Object-oriented programming has brought about a big change. An object-oriented program is, at its heart, designed to be modified. Using correctly written software, you can take advantage of features that are already built in, add new features of your own, and override features that don't suit your needs. The best aspect of this situation is that the changes you make are clean — no clawing and digging into other people's brittle program code. Instead, you make nice, orderly additions and modifications without touching the existing code's internal logic. It's the ideal solution.

The Last Word on Employees — Or Is It?

When you write an object-oriented program, you start by considering the data. You're writing about accounts. So what's an account? You're writing code to handle button clicks. So what's a button? You're writing a program to send payroll checks to employees. What's an employee?

In this chapter's first example, an employee is someone with a name and a job title — sure, employees have other characteristics, but for now I stick to the basics:

```
class Employee {
  String name;
  String jobTitle;
}
```

Of course, any company has different kinds of employees. For example, your company may have full-time and part-time employees. Each full-time employee has a yearly salary:

```
class FullTimeEmployee extends Employee {
  double salary;
}
```

In this example, the words `extends Employee` tell Java that the new class (the `FullTimeEmployee` class) has all the properties that any `Employee` has and, possibly, more. In other words, every `FullTimeEmployee` object is an `Employee` object (an employee of a certain kind, perhaps). Like any `Employee`, a `FullTimeEmployee` has a `name` and a `jobTitle`. But a `FullTimeEmployee` also has a salary. That's what the words `extends Employee` do for you.

A part-time employee has no fixed yearly salary. Instead, every part-time employee has an hourly pay rate and a certain number of hours worked in a week:

```
class PartTimeEmployee extends Employee {
  double hourlyPay;
  int hoursWorked;
}
```

So far, a `PartTimeEmployee` has four characteristics: `name`, `jobTitle`, `hourlyPay`, and number of `hoursWorked`.

Then you have to consider the big shots — the executives. Every executive is a full-time employee. But in addition to earning a salary, every executive receives a bonus (even if the company goes belly-up and needs to be bailed out):

```
class Executive extends FullTimeEmployee {
    double bonus;
}
```

Java's `extends` keyword is cool because, by extending a class, you inherit all the complicated code that's already in the other class. The class you extend can be a class that you have (or another developer has) already written. One way or another, you're able to reuse existing code and to add ingredients to the existing code.

Here's another example: The creators of Android wrote the `Activity` class, with its 5,000 lines of code. You get to use all those lines of code for free by simply typing `extends Activity`:

```
public class MainActivity extends Activity {
```

With the two words `extends Activity`, your new `MainActivity` class can do all the things that a typical Android activity can do — start running, find items in the app's `res` directory, show a dialog box, respond to a low-memory condition, start another activity, return an answer to an activity, finish running, and much more.

Extending a class

So useful is Java's `extends` keyword that developers have several different names to describe this language feature:

- **Superclass/subclass:** The `Employee` class (see the earlier section "The Last Word on Employees — Or Is It?") is the *superclass* of the `FullTimeEmployee` class. The `FullTimeEmployee` class is a *subclass* of the `Employee` class.

- **Parent/child:** The `Employee` class is the *parent* of the `FullTimeEmployee` class. The `FullTimeEmployee` class is a *child* of the `Employee` class.

  In fact, the `Executive` class extends the `FullTimeEmployee` class, which in turn extends the `Employee` class. So `Executive` is a *descendent* of `Employee`, and `Employee` is an *ancestor* of `Executive`. The Unified Modeling Language (UML) diagram in Figure 10-1 illustrates this point.

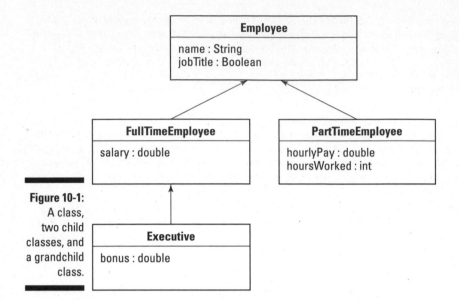

Figure 10-1:
A class,
two child
classes, and
a grandchild
class.

✔ **Inheritance:** The `FullTimeEmployee` class *inherits* the `Employee` class's members. (If any of the `Employee` class's members were declared to be `private`, the `FullTimeEmployee` class wouldn't inherit those members.)

The `Employee` class has a `name` field, so the `FullTimeEmployee` class has a `name` field, and the `Executive` class has a `name` field. In other words, with the declarations of `Employee`, `FullTimeEmployee`, and `Executive` at the start of this section, the code in Listing 10-1 is legal.

All descendants of the `Employee` class have `name` fields, even though a `name` field is explicitly declared only in the `Employee` class itself.

Listing 10-1:   Using the `Employee` Class and Its Subclasses

```
public class Main {

  public static void main(String[] args) {
    Employee employee = new Employee();
    employee.name = "Sam";

    FullTimeEmployee ftEmployee = new FullTimeEmployee();
    ftEmployee.name = "Jennie";

    Executive executive = new Executive();
    executive.name = "Harriet";
  }
}
```

Almost every Java class extends another Java class. I write *almost* because one (and only one) class doesn't extend any other class. Java's built-in `Object` class doesn't extend anything. The `Object` class is at the top of Java's class hierarchy. Any class whose header has no `extends` clause automatically extends Java's `Object` class. So every other Java class is, directly or indirectly, a descendent of the `Object` class, as shown in Figure 10-2.

The notion of extending a class is one pillar of object-oriented programming. In the 1970s, computer scientists were noticing that programmers tended to reinvent the wheel. If you needed code to balance an account, for example, you started writing code from scratch to balance an account. Never mind that other people had written their own account-balancing code. Integrating other peoples' code with yours, and adapting other peoples' code to your own needs, was a big headache. All things considered, it was easier to start from scratch.

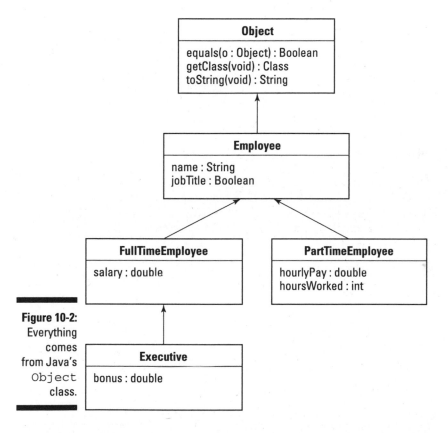

Figure 10-2:
Everything
comes
from Java's
`Object`
class.

Then, in the 1980s, object-oriented programming became popular. The notion of classes and subclasses provided a clean way to connect existing code (such as Android's `Activity` class code) with new code (such as your new `MainActivity` class code). By extending an existing class, you hook into the class's functionality, and you reuse features that have already been programmed.

By reusing code, you avoid the work of reinventing the wheel. But you also make life easier for the end user. When you extend Android's `Activity` class, your new activity behaves like other peoples' activities because both your activity and the other peoples' activities inherit the same behavior from Android's `Activity` class. With so many apps behaving the same way, the user learns familiar patterns. It's a win-win situation.

Overriding methods

In this section, I expand on all the employee code snippets from the start of this chapter. From these snippets, I can present a fully baked program example. The example, as laid out in Listings 10-2 through 10-6, illustrates some important ideas about classes and subclasses.

Listing 10-2:   What Is an Employee?

```
package org.allyourcode.company;

import javax.swing.JOptionPane;

public class Employee {
  String name;
  String jobTitle;

  public Employee() {
  }

  public Employee(String name, String jobTitle) {
    this.name = name;
    this.jobTitle = jobTitle;
  }

  public void showPay() {
    JOptionPane.showMessageDialog(null, name +
        ", Pay not known");
  }
}
```

Listing 10-3: Full-Time Employees Have Salaries

```
package org.allyourcode.company;

import java.text.NumberFormat;
import java.util.Locale;

import javax.swing.JOptionPane;

public class FullTimeEmployee extends Employee {
  double salary;

  static NumberFormat currency =
      NumberFormat.getCurrencyInstance(Locale.US);

  public FullTimeEmployee() {
  }

  public FullTimeEmployee(String name,
                          String jobTitle,
                          double salary) {
    this.name = name;
    this.jobTitle = jobTitle;
    this.salary = salary;
  }

  public double pay() {
    return salary;
  }

  @Override
  public void showPay() {
    JOptionPane.showMessageDialog(null, name + ", " +
        currency.format(pay()));
  }
}
```

Listing 10-4: Executives Get Bonuses

```
package org.allyourcode.company;

public class Executive extends FullTimeEmployee {
  double bonus;

  public Executive() {
  }

  public Executive(String name, String jobTitle,
                   double salary, double bonus) {
    this.name = name;
```

(continued)

Listing 10-4 *(continued)*

```java
    this.jobTitle = jobTitle;
    this.salary = salary;
    this.bonus = bonus;
  }

  @Override
  public double pay() {
    return salary + bonus;
  }
}
```

Listing 10-5: Part-Time Employees Are Paid by the Hour

```java
package org.allyourcode.company;

import java.text.NumberFormat;
import java.util.Locale;

import javax.swing.JOptionPane;

public class PartTimeEmployee extends Employee {
  double hourlyPay;
  int hoursWorked;

  static NumberFormat currency =
      NumberFormat.getCurrencyInstance(Locale.US);

  public PartTimeEmployee() {
  }

  public PartTimeEmployee(String name,
                          String jobTitle,
                          double hourlyPay,
                          int hoursWorked) {
    this.name = name;
    this.jobTitle = jobTitle;
    this.hourlyPay = hourlyPay;
    this.hoursWorked = hoursWorked;
  }

  public double pay() {
    return hourlyPay * hoursWorked;
  }

  @Override
  public void showPay() {
    JOptionPane.showMessageDialog(null, name + ", " +
        currency.format(pay()));
  }
}
```

Listing 10-6:   Putting Your Employee Classes to the Test

```
package org.allyourcode.company;

public class Main {

  public static void main(String[] args) {
    Employee employee =
        new Employee("Barry", "Author");

    FullTimeEmployee ftEmployee =
        new FullTimeEmployee("Ed", "Manager", 10000.00);

    PartTimeEmployee ptEmployee =
        new PartTimeEmployee("Joe", "Intern", 8.00, 20);

    Executive executive =
        new Executive("Jane", "CEO", 20000.00, 5000.00);

    employee.showPay();
    ftEmployee.showPay();
    ptEmployee.showPay();
    executive.showPay();
  }

}
```

Figure 10-3 shows a run of the code in Listings 10-2 through 10-6, and Figure 10-4 contains a UML diagram for the classes in these listings. (In Figure 10-4, I ignore the Main class from Listing 10-6. The Main class isn't interesting, because it's not part of the Employee class hierarchy. The Main class is simply a subclass of Java's Object class.)

In Figure 10-4, I use strikethrough text and simulated handwriting to represent overridden methods. These typographical tricks are my own inventions. Neither the strikethrough nor the simulated handwriting is part of the UML standard. In fact, the UML standard has all kinds of rules that I ignore in this book. My main purpose in showing you the rough UML diagrams is to help you visualize the hierarchies of classes and their subclasses.

Consider the role of the showPay method in Figure 10-4 and in Listings 10-2 through 10-6. In the figure, showPay appears in all except the Executive class; in the listings, I define showPay in all except the Executive class.

The showPay method appears for the first time in the Employee class (refer to Listing 10-2), where it serves as a placeholder for not knowing the employee's pay. The FullTimeEmployee class (refer to Listing 10-3) would inherit this vacuous showPay class except that the FullTimeEmployee class declares its own version of showPay. In the terminology from Chapter 5, the showPay method in FullTimeEmployee *overrides* the showPay method in Employee.

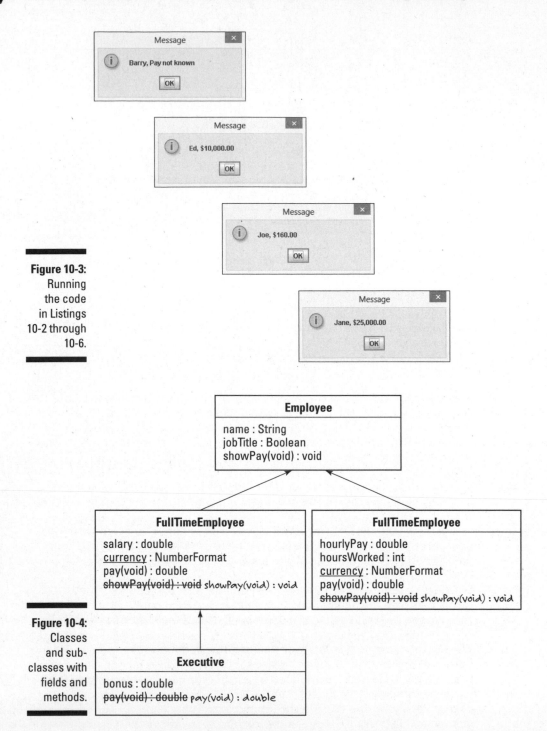

Figure 10-3:
Running
the code
in Listings
10-2 through
10-6.

Figure 10-4:
Classes
and sub-
classes with
fields and
methods.

Listing 10-6 contains a call to a full-time employee's `showPay` method:

```
FullTimeEmployee ftEmployee = ... Etc.
ftEmployee.showPay();
```

And in Figure 10-3, the call to `ftEmployee.showPay()` gives you the `FullTimeEmployee` class's version of `showPay`, not the `Employee` class's clueless version of `showPay`. (If `ftEmployee.showPay()` called the `Employee` class's version of `showPay`, you'd see `Ed, Pay not known` in Figure 10-3.) Overriding a method declaration means taking precedence over that existing version of the method.

Of course, overriding a method isn't the same as obliterating a method. In Listing 10-6, the snippet

```
Employee employee = ... Etc.
employee.showPay();
```

conjures up the `Employee` class's noncommittal version of `showPay`. It happens because an object declared with the `Employee` constructor has no `salary` field, no `hourlyPay` field, and no `showPay` method other than the method declared in the `Employee` class. The `Employee` class, and any objects declared using the `Employee` constructor, could do their work even if the other classes (`FullTimeEmployee`, `PartTimeEmployee`, and so on) didn't exist.

The only way to override a method is to declare a method with the same name and the same parameters inside a subclass. By *same parameters,* I mean the same number of parameters, each with the same type. For example, `calculate(int count, double amount)` overrides `calculate(int x, double y)` because both declarations have two parameters: The first parameter in each declaration is of type `int`, and the second parameter in each declaration is of type `double`. But `calculate(int count, String amount)` doesn't override `calculate(int count, double amount)`. In one declaration, the second parameter has type `double`, and in the other declaration, the second parameter has type `String`. If you call `calculate(42, 2.71828)`, you get the `calculate(int x, double y)` method, and if you call `calculate(42, "Euler")` you get the `calculate(int count, String amount)` method.

Listings 10-2 through 10-5 have other examples of overriding methods. For example, the `Executive` class in Listing 10-4 overrides its parent class's `pay` method, but not the parent class's `showPay` method. Calculating an executive's pay is different from calculating an ordinary full-time employee's pay. But after you know the two peoples' pay amounts, showing an executive's pay is no different from showing an ordinary full-time employee's pay.

When I created this section's examples, I considered giving the Employee class a pay method (returning 0 on each call). This strategy would make it unnecessary for me to create identical showPay methods for the FullTimeEmployee and PartTimeEmployee classes. For various reasons, (none of them interesting), I decided against doing it that way.

Overriding works well in situations in which you want to tweak an existing class's features. Imagine having a news ticker that does everything you want except scroll sideways. (I'm staring at one on my computer right now! As one news item disappears toward the top, the next news item scrolls in from below. The program's options don't allow me to change this setting.) After studying the code's documentation, you can subclass the program's Ticker class and override the Ticker class's scroll method. In your new scroll method, the user has the option to move text upward, downward, sideways, or inside out (whatever that means).

Java annotations

In Java, elements that start with an at-sign (@) are *annotations*. Java didn't have annotations until Java 5.0, so if you try to use the @Override annotation with Java 1.4.2, for example, you'll see some nasty-looking error messages. That's okay because Android requires Java 5.0 or Java 6. You can't use earlier versions of Java to create Android apps.

In Listings 10-3, 10-4, and 10-5, each @Override annotation reminds Java that the method immediately below the annotation has the same name and the same parameter types as a method in the parent class. The use of the @Override annotation is optional. If you remove all @Override lines from Listings 10-3, 10-4, and 10-5, the code works the same way.

So why use the @Override annotation? Imagine leaving it off and mistakenly putting the following method in Listing 10-4:

```
public void showPay(double salary) {
  JOptionPane.showMessageDialog(null, name + ", " +
      currency.format(salary));
}
```

You might think that you've overridden the parent class's showPay method, but you haven't! The Employee class's showPay method has no parameters, and your new FullTimeEmployee class's showPay method has a parameter. Eclipse looks at this stuff in the editor and says, "Okay, I guess the developer is inheriting the Employee class's showPay method and declaring an additional version of showPay. Both showPay methods are available in the

`FullTimeEmployee` class." (By the way, when Eclipse speaks, you can't see my lips moving.)

Everything goes fine until you run the code and see the message `Pay not known` when you call `ftEmployee.showPay()`. The Java virtual machine is calling the parameterless version of `showPay`, which the `FullTimeEmployee` class inherits from its parent.

The problem in this hypothetical example isn't so much that you commit a coding error — everybody makes mistakes like this one. (Yes, even I do. I make lots of them.) The problem is that, without an `@Override` annotation, you don't catch the error until you're running the program. That is, you don't see the error message as soon as you compose the code in the Eclipse editor. Waiting until runtime can be as painless as saying, "Aha! I know why this program didn't run correctly." But waiting until runtime can also be quite painful — as painful as saying, "My app was rated 1 on a scale of 5 because of this error that I didn't see until a user called my bad `showPay` method."

Ideally, Eclipse is aware of your intention to override an existing method, and it can complain to you while you're staring at the editor. If you use the `@Override` annotation in conjunction with the bad `showPay` method, you see the blotches shown in Figure 10-5. That's good because you can fix the problem long before the problem shows up in a run of your code.

Figure 10-5:
The `show-Pay` method doesn't override the parent class's `showPay` method.

```
  @Override
  public void showPay(double salary) {
      JOptionPane.showMessageDialog(null, name + ", " +
              currency format(salary);
  }                                                                      |
  The method showPay(double) of type FullTimeEmployee must override or implement a supertype method
}
```

More about Java's Modifiers

I start the conversation about Java's modifiers in Chapters 6 and 9. Chapter 6 describes the keyword `final` as it applies to variables, and Chapter 9 deals with the keywords `public` and `private`. In this section, I add a few more fun facts about Java modifiers.

The word `final` has many uses in Java programs. In addition to having final variables, you can have these elements:

- **Final class:** If you declare a class to be `final`, no one (not even you) can extend it.
- **Final method:** If you declare a method to be `final`, no one (not even you) can override it.

Figures 10-6 and 10-7 put these rules into perspective. In Figure 10-6, I can't extend the `Stuff` class, because the `Stuff` class is `final`. And in Figure 10-7, I can't override the `Stuff` class's `increment` method because that `increment` method is `final`.

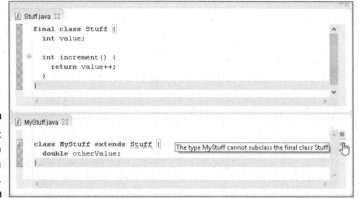

Figure 10-6: Trying to extend a final class.

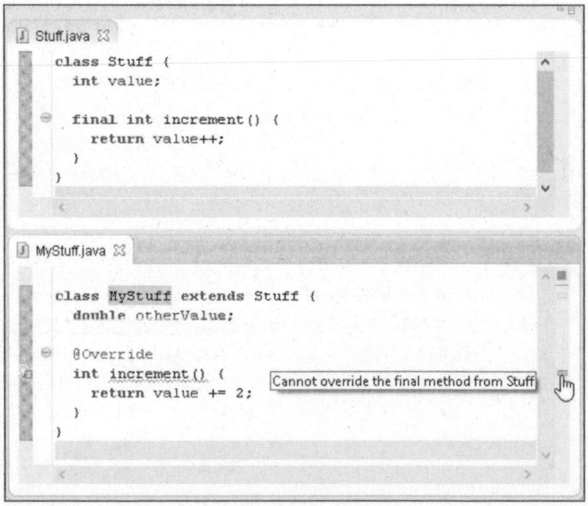

Figure 10-7: Trying to override a final method.

You can apply Java's `protected` keyword to a class's members. This `protected` keyword has always seemed a bit strange to me. In common English usage, when my possessions are "protected," my possessions aren't as available as they'd normally be. But in Java, when you preface a field or a method with the `protected` keyword, you make that field or method a bit more available than it would be by default, as shown in Figure 10-8.

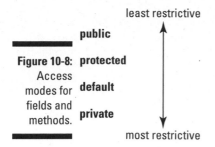

least restrictive

public

Figure 10-8: protected
Access
modes for default
fields and
methods. private

most restrictive

Here's what I say in Chapter 9 about members with default access:

> *A default member of a class (a member whose declaration doesn't contain the words* `public`, `private`, *or* `protected`*) can be used by any code inside the same package as that class.*

The same thing is true about a `protected` class member. But in addition, a `protected` member is inherited outside the class's package by any subclass of the class containing that protected member.

Huh? What does that last sentence mean, about `protected` members? To make things concrete, Figure 10-9 shows you the carefree existence in which two classes are in the same package. With both `Stuff` and `MyStuff` in the same package, the `MyStuff` class inherits the `Stuff` class's default `value` variable and the `Stuff` class's default `increment` method.

If you move the `Stuff` class to a different package, `MyStuff` no longer inherits the `Stuff` class's default `value` variable or the `Stuff` class's default `increment` method, as shown in Figure 10-10.

But if you turn `value` into a `protected` variable and you turn `increment` into a `protected` method, the `MyStuff` class again inherits its parent class's `value` variable and `increment` method, as shown in Figure 10-11.

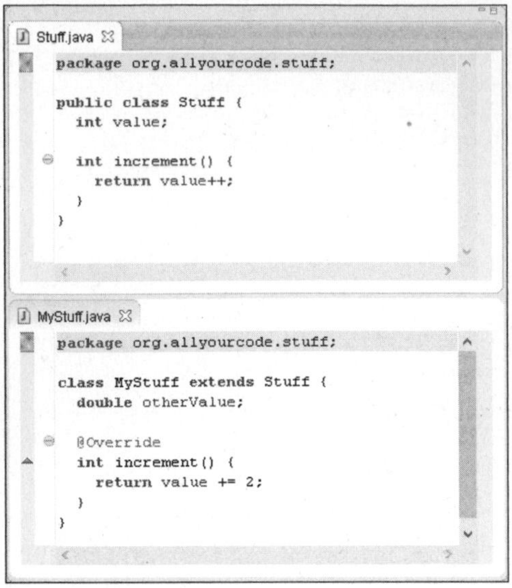

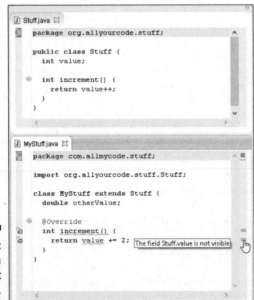

Figure 10-9:
Two classes
in the same
package.

Figure 10-10:
Classes in
different
packages.

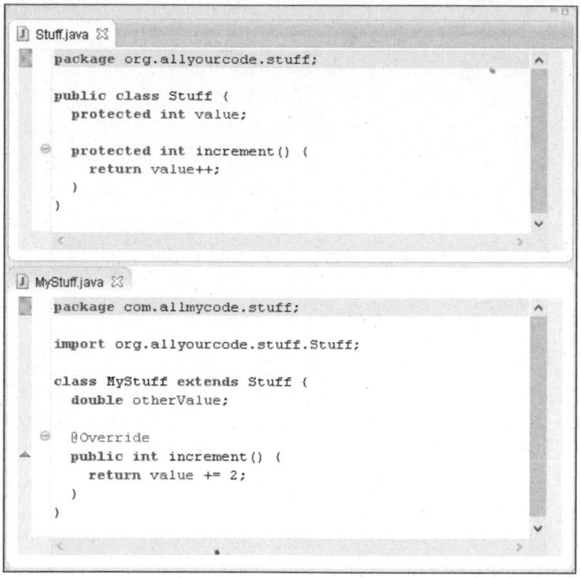

Figure 10-11:
Using the
protected
modifier.

Notice one more detail in Figure 10-11. I change the `MyStuff` class's `increment` method from default to `public`. I do this to avoid seeing an interesting little error message. You can't override a method with another method whose access is more restrictive than the original method. In other words, you can't override a public method with a private method. You can't even override a public method with a default method.

Java's default access is more restrictive than protected access (see Figure 10-8). So you can't override a protected method with a default method. In Figure 10-11, I avoid the whole issue by making public the `MyStuff` class's `increment` method. That way, I override the `increment` method with the least restrictive kind of access.

Keeping Things Simple

Most computer programs operate entirely in the virtual realm. They have no bricks, nails, or girders. So you can type a fairly complicated computer program in minutes. Even with no muscle and no heavy equipment, you can create a structure whose complexity rivals that of many complicated physical structures. You, the developer, have the power to build intricate, virtual bridges.

One goal of computer programming is to manage complexity. A good app isn't simply useful or visually appealing — a good app's code is nicely organized, easy to understand, and easy to modify.

Certain programming languages, like C++, support *multiple inheritance,* in which a class can have more than one parent class. For example, in C++ you can create a `Book` class, a `TeachingMaterial` class, and a `Textbook` class. You can make `Textbook` extend both `Book` and `TeachingMaterial`. This feature makes class hierarchies quite flexible, but it also makes those same hierarchies extremely complicated. You need tricky rules to decide how to inherit the `move` methods of both the computer's `Mouse` class and the rodent's `Mouse` class.

To avoid all this complexity, Java doesn't support multiple inheritance. In Java, each class has one (and only one) superclass. A class can have any number of subclasses. You can (and will) create many subclasses of Android's `Activity` class. And other developers create their own subclasses of Android's `Activity` class. But classes don't have multiple personalities. A Java class can have only one parent. The `Executive` class (refer to Listing 10-4) cannot extend both the `FullTimeEmployee` class and the `PartTimeEmployee` class.

Using an interface

The relationship between a class and its subclass is one of inheritance. In many real-life families, a child inherits assets from a parent. That's the way it works.

But consider the relationship between an editor and an author. The editor says, "By signing this contract, you agree to submit a completed manuscript by the fifteenth of July." Despite any excuses that the author gives before the deadline date (and, believe me, authors make plenty of excuses), the relationship between the editor and the author is one of obligation. The author agrees to take on certain responsibilities; and, in order to continue being an author, the author must fulfill those responsibilities. (By the way, there's no subtext in this paragraph — none at all.)

Now consider Barry Burd. Who? Barry Burd — that guy who writes *Java Programming For Android Developers For Dummies and certain other For Dummies* books (all from Wiley Publishing). He's a parent, and he's also an author. You want to mirror this situation in a Java program, but Java doesn't support multiple inheritance. You can't make Barry extend both a `Father` class and an `Author` class at the same time.

Fortunately for Barry, Java has interfaces. A class can extend only one parent class, but a class can implement many interfaces. A parent class is a bunch of stuff that a class inherits. On the other hand, as with the relationship between an editor and an author, an *interface* is a bunch of stuff that a class is obliged to provide.

Here's another example. Listings 10-2 through 10-5 describe what it means to be an employee of various kinds. Though a company might hire consultants, consultants who work for the company aren't employees. Consultants are normally self-employed. They show up temporarily to help companies solve problems and then leave the companies to work elsewhere. In the United States, differentiating between an employee and a consultant is important: So serious are the U.S. tax withholding laws that labeling a consultant an "employee" of any kind would subject the company to considerable legal risk.

To include consultants with employees in your code, you need a `Consultant` class that's separate from your existing `Employee` class hierarchy. On the other hand, consultants have a lot in common with a company's regular employees. For example, every consultant has a `showPay` method. You want to represent this commonality in your code, so you create an interface. The interface obligates a class to give meaning to the method name `showPay`, as shown in Listing 10-7.

Listing 10-7: Behold! An Interface!

```
package org.allyourcode.company;

public interface Payable {

  public void showPay();

}
```

The element in Listing 10-7 isn't a class — it's a Java interface. Here's a description of the listing's code:

> As an interface, I have a header, but no body, for the `showPay` method. In this interface, the `showPay` method takes no arguments and returns `void`. A class that claims to implement me (the `Payable` interface) must provide (either directly or indirectly) a body for the `showPay` method. That is, a class that claims to implement `Payable` must, in one way or another, implement the `showPay` method.

To find out about the difference between a method declaration's header and its body, see Chapter 5.

Listings 10-8 and 10-9 implement the `Payable` interface and provide bodies for the `showPay` method.

Listing 10-8:   Implementing an Interface

```
package org.allyourcode.company;

import java.text.NumberFormat;
import java.util.Locale;

import javax.swing.JOptionPane;

public class Consultant implements Payable {

  String name;
  double hourlyFee;
  int hoursWorked;

  static NumberFormat currency =
      NumberFormat.getCurrencyInstance(Locale.US);

  public Consultant() {
  }

  public Consultant(String name, String jobTitle,
                    double hourlyFee, int hoursWorked) {
    this.name = name;
    this.hourlyFee = hourlyFee;
    this.hoursWorked = hoursWorked;
  }

  public double pay() {
    return hourlyFee * hoursWorked;
  }

  @Override
  public void showPay() {
    JOptionPane.showMessageDialog(null, name + ", " +
        currency.format(pay()));
  }
}
```

Listing 10-9:   Another Class Implements the Interface

```
package org.allyourcode.company;

import javax.swing.JOptionPane;

public class Employee implements Payable {
```

```
String name;
String jobTitle;

public Employee() {
}

public Employee(String name, String jobTitle) {
  this.name = name;
  this.jobTitle = jobTitle;
}

@Override
public void showPay() {
  JOptionPane.showMessageDialog(null, name +
      ", Pay not known");
}
}
```

In Listings 10-8 and 10-9, both the `Consultant` and `Employee` classes implement the `Payable` interface — the interface that summarizes what it means to be paid by the company. Implementing this interface guarantees that these classes have bodies for the showPay method. This guarantee allows any other code to safely call `employee.showPay()` or `consultant.showPay()`.

In this section's example, two otherwise unrelated classes (`Employee` and `Consultant`) both implement the `Payable` interface. When I picture a Java interface, it's an element that cuts across levels of Java's class/subclass hierarchy, as shown in Figure 10-12.

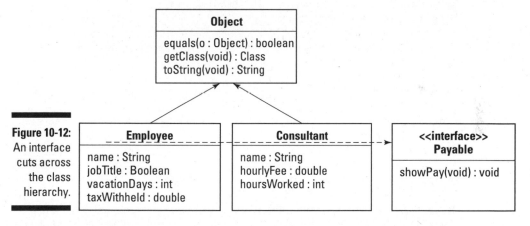

Figure 10-12: An interface cuts across the class hierarchy.

The dotted line in Figure 10-12 isn't part of standard UML. The folks who manage the standard have much better ways to represent interfaces than I use in this chapter's figures.

Creating a callback

In this chapter's (just discussed) "Using an interface" section, I reveal how an interface helps me realize the commonalities among various pay-receiving classes. The interface gives me an elegant way to mirror the connections in the real-world's data. But aside from its elegance, the interface in the "Using an interface" section doesn't make any problems easier to solve. The code with and without the interface is basically the same.

So in this section, I describe another problem that I solve using an interface. (In fact, the use of an interface plays a key role in the problem's solution.) This section's code is a bit more complicated than the code in the "Using an interface" section, but this section's code illustrates a widely used programming technique.

Many scenarios in application development involve *callbacks*. Imagine a stopwatch program. The program tells you when ten seconds have gone by. It has two statements: one to start a countdown and another to notify the user that the time is up. You can write the code this way:

```
try {
  Thread.sleep(10000);
} catch (InterruptedException e) {
  e.printStackTrace();
}
JOptionPane.showMessageDialog(null, "Time's up!");
```

Java's built-in `Thread` class has a `sleep` method that makes your app's action pause for any number of milliseconds you want. Ten thousand milliseconds is the same as ten seconds.

The `try`/`catch` business surrounding the `sleep` method call is part of the Java exception-handling feature. I cover it in Chapter 13.

Your code looks sensible, but it's seriously flawed. While your program puts itself to sleep for ten seconds, the user doesn't get a response from it — its buttons are frozen. Your program is sleeping, so the user can't use any other feature that your program offers. The user touches your program's widgets and presses your program's Cancel button, but the program doesn't respond. Yes, this is a great way to guarantee a 1-of-5 rating at Google Play (its app store).

To fix the problem, you take advantage of somebody's `TimerCommon` class, a general-purpose class that sleeps for a certain period on behalf of your program. While the `TimerCommon` object sleeps, your program can remain awake, responding to the user's clicks, taps, inputs, swipes, or whatever.

(By the way, the `TimerCommon` class isn't part of the Java API. Somebody posted the `TimerCommon` class on the web along with a note permitting any developer to use the code.)

When the `TimerCommon` object wakes up, the object calls one of your program's methods. (In this section's example, your method is named `alert`.) Until the `TimerCommon` object calls your `alert` method, the method sits quietly in your program, doing nothing. Rather than execute the `alert` method, your program responds to the user's requests. Slick!

Now review the general flow of execution in the stopwatch code: First you set the `TimerCommon` object in motion. The `TimerCommon` object takes a brief nap. Finally, when the `TimerCommon` object wakes up, the `TimerCommon` object calls you back. In other words, the `TimerCommon` object issues a *callback,* as shown in Figure 10-13.

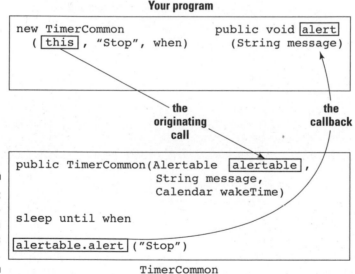

Figure 10-13: The Timer-Common object calls you back.

Listings 10-10 through 10-13 have the basic code to illustrate the callback technique.

Listing 10-10:   Implementing the Alertable Interface

```java
package org.allyourcode.stopwatch;

import java.util.Calendar;

import javax.swing.JOptionPane;

import com.example.timers.Alertable;
import com.example.timers.TimerCommon;

public class StopWatch implements Alertable {

  public StopWatch(int seconds) {
    Calendar wakeTime = Calendar.getInstance();
    wakeTime.add(Calendar.SECOND, seconds);
    new TimerCommon(this, "Stop", wakeTime);
  }

  @Override
  public void alert(String message) {
    JOptionPane.showMessageDialog(null, message);
  }
}
```

Listing 10-11:   The Alertable Interface

```java
package com.example.timers;

public interface Alertable {

  public void alert(String message);
}
```

Listing 10-12:   Receiving an Alertable Parameter Value

```java
package com.example.timers;

import java.util.Calendar;

public class TimerCommon {

  public TimerCommon(Alertable alertable,
                     String message,
                     Calendar wakeTime) {

    long whenMillis = wakeTime.getTimeInMillis();
```

```
   long currentMillis = System.currentTimeMillis();

   try {
     Thread.sleep(whenMillis - currentMillis);
   } catch (InterruptedException e) {
     e.printStackTrace();
   }

   alertable.alert(message);
 }
}
```

Listing 10-13:   Everything Has to Start Somewhere!

```
package org.allyourcode.stopwatch;

public class Main {

  public static void main(String[] args) {
    new StopWatch(10);
  }
}
```

When you run the code in Listings 10-10 through 10-13, you experience a ten-second delay. Then you see the dialog box shown in Figure 10-14.

Figure 10-14:
Running
the code
in Listings
10-10
through
10-13.

At the start of this section, I complain that without `TimerCommon`, your stopwatch code isn't responsive to new user input. Well, I must confess that the code in Listings 10-10 through 10-13 doesn't solve the responsiveness problem. To make the program more responsive, you use the interface tricks in Listings 10-10 through 10-13, and, in addition, you put `TimerCommon` in a thread of its own. The trouble is that the separate thread business doesn't help you understand how interfaces work, so I don't bother creating an extra thread in this section's example. For a more honest multi-threading example, see Chapter 13.

One program; two Eclipse projects

To emphasize my point about the `StopWatch` and `TimerCommon` classes being developed independently, I've spread Listings 10-10 through 10-13 over two different Eclipse projects. The `StopWatch` and `Main` classes star in the 10-10 project, and `Alertable` and `TimerCommon` star in the 10-11 project. To make this multiproject code work, you have to tell Eclipse about one project's dependency on the other. Here's how:

1. **Right-click (in Windows) or Control-click (on a Mac) the 10-10 project's branch in the Package Explorer in Eclipse.**

   You do this because, in this section's example, the code in the 10-10 project makes use of the code in the 10-11 project. (The `StopWatch` class creates a new `TimerCommon` instance.)

2. **From the contextual menu that appears, choose Properties.**

   The dialog box labeled Properties for 10-10 opens. On the left side, you see a list of categories.

3. **In the list of categories, click to select the Project References item.**

4. **In the main body of the dialog box, select the check box labeled 10-11, as shown in the first sidebar figure.**

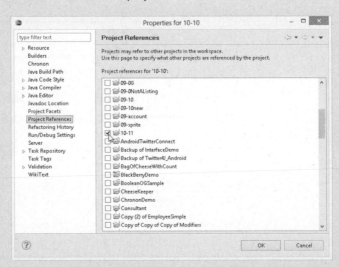

5. **In the list of categories, select the Java Build Path item.**

   Remember that the 10-10 project uses the constructor that's declared in the 10-11 project.

6. **In the main body of the Properties for 10-10 dialog box, select the Projects tab, as shown in the second sidebar figure.**

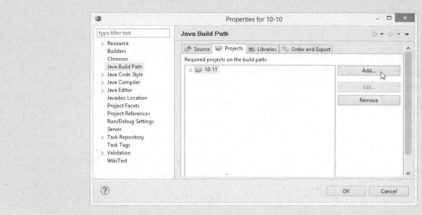

7. **On the right side of the Projects tab, click the Add button.**

   The Required Project Selection dialog box opens.

8. **In the Required Project Selection dialog box, select the 10-11 option to place a check mark next to it.**

   Remember (again) that the 10-10 project uses the constructor that's declared in the 10-11 project.

9. **Click OK to dismiss the Required Project Selection dialog box.**

   As a result, the Properties for 10-10 dialog box looks like the one shown in the second sidebar figure.

10. **Click OK to save your changes and to dismiss the Properties for 10-10 dialog box.**

    Now Eclipse knows that Project 10-10 depends on some code from 10-11.

A brief explanation of this section's code

In Listing 10-10, your code calls `new TimerCommon(this, "Stop", when)`. Here's the equivalent command, translated into English:

> Create a new `TimerCommon` object; tell it to call `this` code back at the moment that I've named `when`. Have the new `TimerCommon` object deliver a `"Stop"` message back to `this` code.

A detailed explanation of this section's code

The constructor call in Listing 10-13 creates a `StopWatch` instance. To understand how Listings 10-10 through 10-12 work, you have to trace the progress of that `StopWatch` instance throughout the run of the program (you can follow along in Figure 10-13):

✔ **In Listing 10-10, Java's** `this` **keyword represents the** `StopWatch` **instance.**

The word `this` appears inside a `TimerCommon` constructor. So the next bunch of code to be executed is the code inside the `TimerCommon` constructor's body.

✔ **In the** `TimerCommon` **constructor's body (refer to Listing 10-12), the** `alertable` **parameter becomes synonymous with the original** `StopWatch` **instance.**

The `TimerCommon` instance "sleeps" for a while.

✔ **Finally, with** `alertable` **referring to the** `StopWatch` **instance, Listing 10-12 calls** `alertable.alert(message)`.

In other words, Listing 10-12 calls back the original `StopWatch` instance. Listing 10-12 knows how to call the original `StopWatch` instance, because the `StopWatch` instance passed itself (the keyword `this`) in the `TimerCommon` construction call.

How do interfaces help with all this? Remember that the `TimerCommon` class isn't your own code. Someone else wrote the `TimerCommon` class and placed it in a separate `com.example.timers` package. Whoever wrote the `TimerCommon` class knew nothing about you or your `StopWatch` class (the code in Listing 10-10). In particular, the `TimerCommon` class doesn't contain the following code:

```
public TimerCommon(StopWatch yourStopWatch,
                   String message,
                   Calendar wakeTime) {

yourStopWatch.alert(message);
```

Instead, the `TimerCommon` class is written for a more general audience. The `TimerCommon` class contains the following lines:

```
public TimerCommon(Alertable alertable,
                   String message,
                   Calendar wakeTime) {

alertable.alert(message);
```

The class's constructor expects its first argument to implement the `Alertable` interface. And sure enough, the first argument in `new TimerCommon(this, "Stop", when)` in Listing 10-10 is `this`, which is your `StopWatch` instance, which (Oh, joy!) implements `Alertable`. Here's the best part: As long as your class implements the `Alertable` interface, your class is guaranteed to have an `alert` method with one `String` argument (refer to Listing 10-11). So the `TimerCommon` class can safely call your code's `alert` method.

Time doesn't pass

Java's `Calendar` class has a misleading name: An instance of the `Calendar` class is a moment in time, not an entire month or year full of times. In Listing 10-10, the line

```
wakeTime = Calendar.
    getInstance()
```

makes `wakeTime` refer to a particular moment. In fact, when you call the parameter-less `Calendar.getInstance()`, you get the current moment (the precise millisecond in which the method call is executed). You can check that moment's fields (the `YEAR`, `MONTH`, `DAY_OF_MONTH`, `HOUR`, `MINUTE`, `SECOND` and `MILLISECOND` fields). But you can also see the moment as a number of milliseconds since midnight on January 1, 1970.

A `Calendar` object's `getTimeIn Millis` method finds the exact number of milliseconds since January 1, 1970 for that object. (Nowadays, it's a huge number.) The call `add(Calendar.SECOND, seconds)` adds a certain number of seconds to a particular `Calendar` moment. And the `System` class's static `currentTimeMillis` method provides a one-step way to find out how many milliseconds have passed since that landmark date in 1970.

How versatile is this interface?

The previous section shows what an interface can do. There, an interface bridges the gap between two otherwise unrelated pieces of code. To belabor this point even further (if that's possible), consider a new app of mine — a reminder app.

Here I sit, halfway around the world from where you created your stopwatch program. I know all about the `TimerCommon` class, but I know nothing about your stopwatch app. (Okay, maybe in real life, you live 20 miles from me in New Jersey, and I know about your stopwatch app because I wrote it for this chapter and the app isn't really yours. Who cares?) Here I am, halfway around the world, knowing nothing about your stopwatch app, using the `TimerCommon` class to create a completely different program — a reminder program. The code is in Listings 10-14 through 10-16.

Listing 10-14:   What Is an Appointment?

```
package com.allmycode.reminder;

import java.util.Calendar;

public class Appointment {
  String name;
```

(continued)

Listing 10-14 *(continued)*

```
  Calendar when;

  public Appointment(String name, Calendar when) {
    this.name = name;
    this.when = when;
  }
}
```

Listing 10-15: A Reminder Is an Appointment That's Alertable

```
package com.allmycode.reminder;

import java.awt.Toolkit;
import java.util.Calendar;

import javax.swing.JOptionPane;

import com.example.timers.Alertable;
import com.example.timers.TimerCommon;

public class Reminder extends Appointment
                      implements Alertable {

  public Reminder(String name, Calendar when) {
    super(name, when);
    new TimerCommon(this, name, when);
  }

  @Override
  public void alert(String message) {
    Toolkit.getDefaultToolkit().beep();
    JOptionPane.showMessageDialog(null, message,
        "Reminder!", JOptionPane.WARNING_MESSAGE);
  }
}
```

Listing 10-16: Creating a Reminder

```
package com.allmycode.reminder;

import java.util.Calendar;

public class Main {

  public static void main(String[] args) {
    Calendar when = Calendar.getInstance();
    when.add(Calendar.SECOND, 5);
    new Reminder("Take a break!", when);
  }
}
```

The call to `beep()` in Listing 10-15 makes some sort of noise (no big surprise). But you might want to know a bit about the details. Java has a `Toolkit` class with a static `getDefaultToolkit` method. A call to `Toolkit.getDefault Toolkit()` returns a connection to the user's operating system. This connection (an instance of the `Toolkit` class) has its own `beep` method. There! Now you know.

As in your case, my class implements the `Alertable` interface and has an `alert(String message)` method. In Listing 10-15, my `Reminder` object passes itself (`this`) to a new `TimerCommon` object. Because the `TimerObject` class's code expects the first constructor parameter to be `Alertable`, everything is okay. The `TimerCommon` object sleeps until it's time to remind the user. At the appropriate time, the `TimerCommon` object calls my object's `alert` method — again, the use of an interface adds versatility to the code by cutting across class/subclass lines, as shown in Figure 10-15.

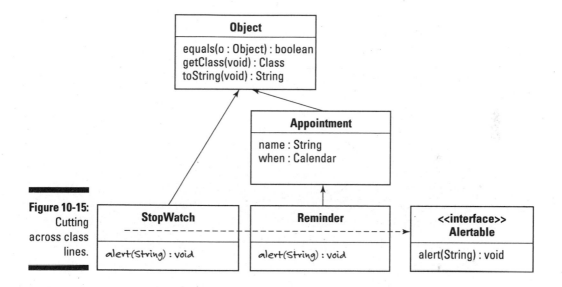

Figure 10-15: Cutting across class lines.

Java's super keyword

Here's an excerpt from Listing 10-15:

```
public class Reminder extends Appointment
                      implements Alertable {

  public Reminder(String name, Calendar when) {
    super(name, when);
    new TimerCommon(this, name, when);
  }
```

In Listing 10-15, the word super stands for *the superclass's constructor*. In particular, the call super(name, when) tells Java to find the superclass of the current class, to call that superclass's constructor, and to feed the parameter values name and when to the superclass constructor.

My Reminder class extends the Appointment class (refer to Listing 10-14). So in Listing 10-15, the call super(name, when) invokes one of the Appointment class's constructors.

Of course, the Appointment class had better have a constructor whose types match the super call's parameter types (String for name and Calendar for when). Otherwise, the Eclipse editor displays lots of red marks. Fortunately, the Appointment class in Listing 10-14 has the appropriate two-parameter constructor.

```
public Appointment(String name, Calendar when) {
   this.name = name;
   this.when = when;
}
```

What Does This Have to Do with Android?

Employees and consultants make good examples of classes and subclasses. But at this point in the book, you might be interested in a more practical programming example. How about an Android app? The first example is ruefully simple, but it's one that an Android programmer sees every day. It's an Android *Activity*.

A typical Android app displays one screen at a time, as shown in Figure 10-16. A screenful of material might present the user with a list of options and a Start button. The next screenful (after the user clicks Start, for example) shows some helpful information, such as a map, a video, or a list of items for sale. When the user touches on this information screen, the app's display changes to reveal a third screen, showing detailed information about whatever option the user selected. Eventually, the user dismisses the detail screen by clicking the Back button.

In Android terminology, each screenful of material is an *activity*. As the user progresses through the sequence of screens displayed in Figure 10-16, Android displays three activities. (It displays the middle activity twice — once after the user clicks Start and a second time after the user dismisses the detailed-info activity.)

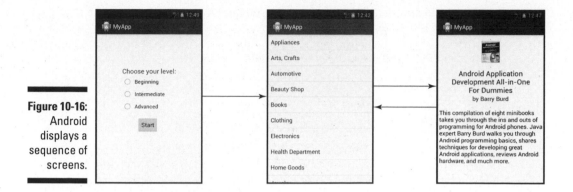

Figure 10-16:
Android
displays a
sequence of
screens.

Android developers deal with activities all the time, so the creators of Android have created an `Activity` class. The `Activity` class is part of Android's Application Programming Interface (API), the enormous library of classes that's available to every Android developer. You download the Android API when you follow the instructions in Chapter 2.

In Chapter 4, you create a brand-new Android app. Eclipse creates some skeletal code (enough to run a simple "Hello" program). I've copied this skeletal code in Listing 10-17.

Listing 10-17:   Eclipse Creates a Main Activity

```
package com.allmycode.myfirstandroidapp;

import android.os.Bundle;
import android.app.Activity;
import android.view.Menu;

public class MainActivity extends Activity {

  @Override
  protected void onCreate(Bundle savedInstanceState) {
    super.onCreate(savedInstanceState);
    setContentView(R.layout.activity_main);
  }

  @Override
  public boolean onCreateOptionsMenu(Menu menu) {
    getMenuInflater().inflate(R.menu.main, menu);
    return true;
  }

}
```

The following list can help you relate elements from Listing 10-17 to this chapter's discussion of classes, subclasses, and interfaces:

- ✔ **Every Android app is in a package of its own.**

  The app in Listing 10-17 belongs to the package named `com.allmy code.myfirstandroidapp`.

- ✔ **If the first part of a package name is** `android`, **that package probably belongs to Google's Android operating system code.**

  For example, Android's `Activity` class lives in the `android.app` package. When I import `android.app.Activity`, I can refer to the `Activity` class in the rest of Listing 10-17 without repeating the class's fully qualified name.

  Java has no rule to enforce package naming conventions. You can create your own package and name it `android.app`, and you can use that package in code that has nothing to do with Google Android. But a good developer never looks for trouble. If convention dictates that the word `android` signals a package in the official Android API, don't use the word `android` in your own package names.

- ✔ **The** `MainActivity` **class extends the** `android.app.Activity` **class.**

  A `MainActivity` *is an* `Activity`. Therefore, the `MainActivity` in Listing 10-17 has all the rights and responsibilities that any `Activity` instance has. For example, the `MainActivity` has `onCreate` and `onCreateOptionsMenu` methods, which it overrides in Listing 10-17.

  In fact, the `MainActivity` class inherits about 5,000 lines of Java code from Android's `Activity` class. The inherited methods include ones such as `getCallingActivity`, `getCallingPackage`, `getParent`, `getTitle`, `getTitleColor`, `getWindow`, `onBackPressed`, `onKey Down`, `onKeyLongPress`, `onLowMemory`, `onMenuItemSelected`, `setTitle`, `setTitleColor`, `startActivity`, `finish`, and many, many others. You inherit all this functionality by typing two simple words: `extends Activity`.

  The Android `Activity` class extends another class: Android's own `ContextThemeWrapper`. Without knowing what a `ContextTheme Wrapper` is (and without caring), your app's own `MainActivity` class (refer to Listing 10-17) extends Android's `Activity` class, which in turn extends Android's `ContextThemeWrapper` class. So in the terminology of familial relationships, your `MainActivity` class is a descendant of Android's `ContextThemeWrapper`. Your `MainActivity` class is a kind of `ContextThemeWrapper`.

✔ **On creating an activity, you find out what was going on when the activity was last destroyed.**

The parameter `savedInstanceState` stores information about what was going on when the activity was last destroyed. If the `savedInstance State` contains any meaningful information, it's because the activity was destroyed in the middle of a run. Maybe the user tilted the device sideways, causing the activity to be destroyed and then re-created in Landscape mode. (See Chapter 5.)

In Listing 10-17, you feed the information in the `savedInstanceState` parameter to the code's superclass, which is Android's `Activity` class. In turn, the `Activity` class's constructor does all kinds of useful things with `savedInstanceState`. Among other things, the `Activity` class's constructor restores much of your activity to the state it was in when your activity was last destroyed.

✔ **The** `MainActivity` **class inherits a** `setContentView` **method from the** `Activity` **class.**

A call to the `setContentView` method's parameter is a code number (as described in a sidebar in Chapter 4). The `setContentView` method looks up that code number and finds an XML file in your project's `res\layout` directory. (In this example, the filename is `activity_main.xml`.) The method then *inflates* the XML file: That is, the method interprets the XML file's text as the description of a nice-looking arrangement of items on the user's screen. This arrangement becomes the overall look of your activity's screen.

✔ **The** `MainActivity` **class overrides the** `Activity` **class's** `onCreate OptionsMenu` **method.**

At some point during the display of `MainActivity` on the screen, Android creates the activity's Options menu. (Normally, the user opens the Options menu by touching an icon containing a few dots or dashes.) In Listing 10-17, the call to `inflate` once again turns the text from an XML file (`res\menu\main.xml`) into a bunch of menu items and menu actions.

The `onCreateOptionsMenu` method returns `true`, which means, "Yes, I've done all that I have to do in setting up the activity's Options menu." (A `false` value would indicate that other code must do the follow-up work to help set up the Options menu.)

So much for Eclipse's autogenerated app. In the next few chapters, I introduce more Java features, and I show you how to build more functionality on top of the autogenerated Android app.

Part IV

Powering Android with Java Code

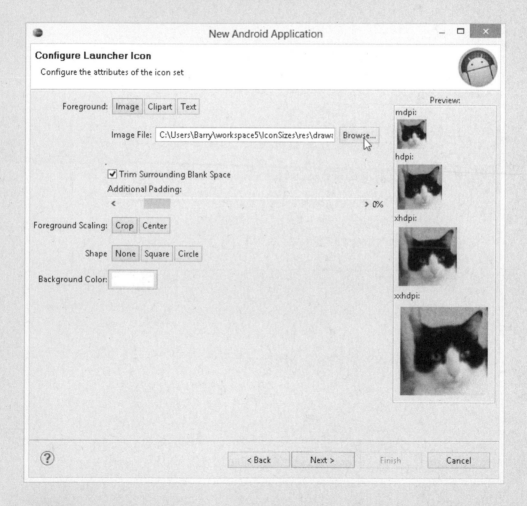

In this part . . .

- ✔ Responding to touches, clicks, and pops
- ✔ Becoming a collector (in the Java sense)
- ✔ Creating an app that uses social media
- ✔ Creating an Android game

Chapter 11

A Simple Android Example: Responding to a Button Click

*I*n common English usage, an *insider* is someone with information that's not available to most people. An insider gets special information because of her position within an organization.

American culture has many references to insiders. Author John Gunther became famous for writing *Inside Europe* and *Inside Africa* and other books in his *Inside* series. On TV crime shows, an inside job is a theft or a murder committed by someone who works in the victim's own company. So significant is the power of inside information that in most countries, insider stock trading is illegal.

In the same way, a Java class can live inside another Java class. When this happens, the inner class has useful insider information. This chapter explains why.

The First Button-Click Example

Ever heard that wonderful old joke about a circus acrobat jumping over mice? Unfortunately, I'd get sued for copyright infringement if I included it in this book. Anyway, the joke is about starting small and working your way up to bigger things. That's what you do when you read *Java Programming For Android Developers For Dummies*. Most of the programs in this book aren't

Android apps. Instead, the programs are standard Oracle Java apps — apps that run on a desktop or a laptop computer, not on an Android device. In fact, the `JOptionPane.showMessageDialog` method that I use in many of this book's examples runs only on a desktop or laptop, not on Android.

Why does a book with the word *Android* featured prominently in its title contain many examples that don't run on phones or tablet devices? The answer is that you must always start practicing by jumping over small mice. Compare the sets of instructions in Chapters 3 and 4, and notice how much more work is involved in running a Hello World Android app. When you practice creating several Android apps, you become accustomed to the eccentricities of Android's emulator. But when you're learning Java, you don't want an emulator's quirks to get in the way. Java is Java, whether it's a standard Java app to display the words *Hello World* or an Android app to send a spaceship to another world.

Anyway, by the time you reach Chapter 11, you're ready to see some Java features running on a phone or on a phone emulator. So this chapter's example, simple though it might be, is specific to Android.

Creating the Android app

You can import this chapter's code from my website (`http://allmycode.com/Java4Android`) by following the instructions in Chapter 2. But if you want to create the example on your own, follow the next several steps:

1. **Follow the instructions in Chapter 4 to create a skeletal Android application.**

2. **Expand your new project's branch in Eclipse's Package Explorer tree, on the left.**

3. **In the project's branch, navigate to the** `res/layout` **directory.**

4. **In the** `res/layout` **directory, double-click the** `activity_main.xml` **item.**

   A graphical layout of your app shows up in Eclipse's editor, as shown in Figure 11-1.

   You can resize this Graphical Layout view of the app by clicking the little magnifying glass icons near the upper-right corner of the editor.

   The `activity_main.xml` file contains a bunch of XML code describing the look (the layout) of your Android activity. To switch between the picture displayed in Figure 11-1 and the actual XML code, select either the Graphical Layout tab or the `activity_main.xml` tab at the bottom of Eclipse's editor.

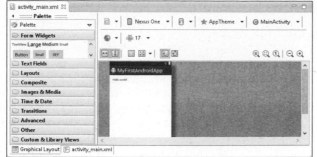

Figure 11-1:
A blank
layout.

5. **In the palette on the left side of the graphical layout, expand the Form Widgets category.**

   In this Form Widgets category, you find `TextView` elements, buttons, check boxes, and other doodads, as shown in Figure 11-2.

Palette

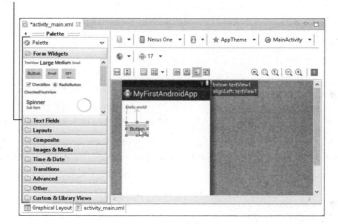

Figure 11-2:
Dragging a
button onto
your app's
layout.

6. **Drag a button from the Form Widgets category onto your app's layout (refer to Figure 11-2).**

7. **Notice the names of the items in Eclipse's Outline view.**

   Most likely, the names you see are `RelativeLayout`, `textView1`, and `button1`, as shown in Figure 11-3.

8. **On Eclipse's main menu, select File⇨Save.**

   Doing so saves your changes to the `activity_main.xml` file.

Figure 11-3:
Eclipse's
Outline
view.

9. **In the Package Explorer tree, navigate to your project's** src **directory.**

10. **Inside the** src **directory, expand the branch for the package containing the project.**

    The package name will resemble the name com.example.myfirst androidapp.

11. **Within the package's branch, double-click the** MainActivity.java **file.**

    The activity's Java file appears in Eclipse's editor. Eclipse created all this code for you.

12. **In the editor, add the following fields to the** MainActivity **class's code:**

    ```
    Button button;
    TextView textView;
    ```

    Listing 11-1 shows you exactly where to place the new section of code. (Note that you still have to add some more code; that comes up in Step 13.)

    Android's Button class is in the android.widget package. To use the short name Button, your code needs an import declaration. You can type an import declaration yourself. Alternatively, Eclipse can add the import declaration for you. After adding the Button button1 field and seeing the nasty red squiggle underneath the name TextView, press Ctrl+Shift+O. (That's the letter *O,* not the digit 0.) This shortcut adds the import declaration automatically. If you don't like memorizing shortcut keys, you can achieve the same effect by selecting Source⇨Organize Imports from Eclipse's main menu.

13. **In Eclipse's editor, add the following statements immediately after the call to** setContentView**:**

    ```
    button = (Button) findViewById(R.id.button1);
    button.setOnClickListener
                        (new MyOnClickListener(this));
    textView = (TextView) findViewById(R.id.textView1);
    ```

    Listing 11-1 has the proper placement of this new code.

The editor displays a red squiggle under the name `MyOnClick Listener` because you haven't yet declared the `MyOnClickListener` class. You do that in the next few steps.

In this step, I assume that the item names you see in Step 7 are `text View1` and `button1`. If you see different names (such as `textView01` and `button01`), use those alternative names after each occurrence of `R.id` in Listing 11-1. For example, rather than use `R.id.button1`, use `R.id.button01`. (No matter what names you see in Step 7, you don't have to change the names `button` and `textView` that you create in Step 12. You can make up any variable names as long as you use these variable names consistently throughout the class's code.)

14. **In Eclipse's main menu, select File⇨Save.**

    Doing so saves your changes to the `MainActivity.java` file.

15. **In the Package Explorer, right-click (on a Mac, Control-click) the branch displaying your app's package name.**

    The package name will resemble `com.example.myfirstandroidapp`.

16. **From the resulting contextual menu that appears, select New⇨Class.**

    The New Java Class dialog box appears.

17. **In the Name field of the New Java Class dialog box, type `MyOnClick Listener` (the same name you typed in the code in Step 13).**

18. **Click Finish to dismiss the New Java Class dialog box.**

    The New Java Class dialog box goes away, and a minimal `MyOnClickListener` class appears in Eclipse's editor. This class contains (more or less) the following code:

```
package com.example.myfirstandroidapp;

public class MyOnClickListener {

}
```

19. **Add code to the (newly created) `MyOnClickListener` class, as shown in Listing 11-2.**

20. **In Eclipse's main menu, select File⇨Save.**

    Doing so saves your changes to the new `MyOnClickListener.java` file.

21. **Run your new Android app.**

When you run the new app, you start with the display shown in Figure 11-4. After clicking the button, you see the display shown in Figure 11-5.

Listing 11-1: **Your Main Activity**

```java
package com.example.myfirstandroidapp;

import android.app.Activity;
import android.os.Bundle;
import android.view.Menu;
import android.widget.Button;
import android.widget.TextView;

public class MainActivity extends Activity {
  Button button;
  TextView textView;

  @Override
  protected void onCreate(Bundle savedInstanceState) {
    super.onCreate(savedInstanceState);
    setContentView(R.layout.activity_main);
    button = (Button) findViewById(R.id.button1);
    button.setOnClickListener
                              (new MyOnClickListener(this));
    textView = (TextView) findViewById(R.id.textView1);
  }

  @Override
  public boolean onCreateOptionsMenu(Menu menu) {
    getMenuInflater().inflate(R.menu.main, menu);
    return true;
  }

}
```

Listing 11-2: **A Class Listens for Button Clicks**

```java
package com.example.myfirstandroidapp;

import android.view.View;
import android.view.View.OnClickListener;

public class MyOnClickListener
                      implements OnClickListener {
  MainActivity caller;

  public MyOnClickListener(MainActivity activity) {
    this.caller = activity;
  }

  public void onClick(View view) {
    caller.textView.setText("You clicked the button!");
  }
}
```

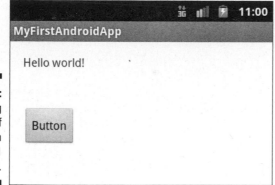

Figure 11-4:
Beginning
a run of
the code in
Listings 11-1
and 11-2.

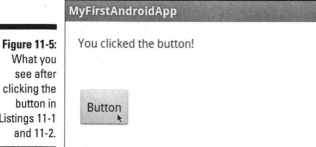

Figure 11-5:
What you
see after
clicking the
button in
Listings 11-1
and 11-2.

The code in Listings 11-1 and 11-2 performs a callback, much the same as the callback I describe in Chapter 10. In this chapter's callback, the `MyOnClickListener` class calls back to the activity's `textView` object. As in Chapter 10, the callback is possible for two reasons:

✔ **Android's built-in** `setOnClickListener` **method expects its parameter to implement Android's** `OnClickListener` **interface.**

Here's how it works in Listings 11-1 and 11-2:

- In Listing 11-1, the call to `setOnClickListener` has, as its parameter, a new `MyOnClickListener` object.
- As Listing 11-2 shows, the `MyOnClickListener` class implements Android's `OnClickListener` interface.

If I don't make the `MyWhatever` class implement the `OnClickListener` interface, this call is illegal:

```
button.setOnClickListener(new MyWhatever(this));
```

✔ **The** MyOnClickListener **object knows how to call back the activity that constructed it.**

Again, in Listing 11-1, the MyOnClickListener constructor call passes this to its new MyOnClickListener object. ("Call *me* back," says your activity's code in Listing 11-1.) See Figure 11-6.

Then, in Listing 11-2, the MyOnClickListener constructor makes a mental note of who gets called back, by storing a reference to your activity in its own caller field. So, when push comes to shove, the code in Listing 11-2 calls back caller.textView.setText, which changes the words displayed in the original activity's textView.

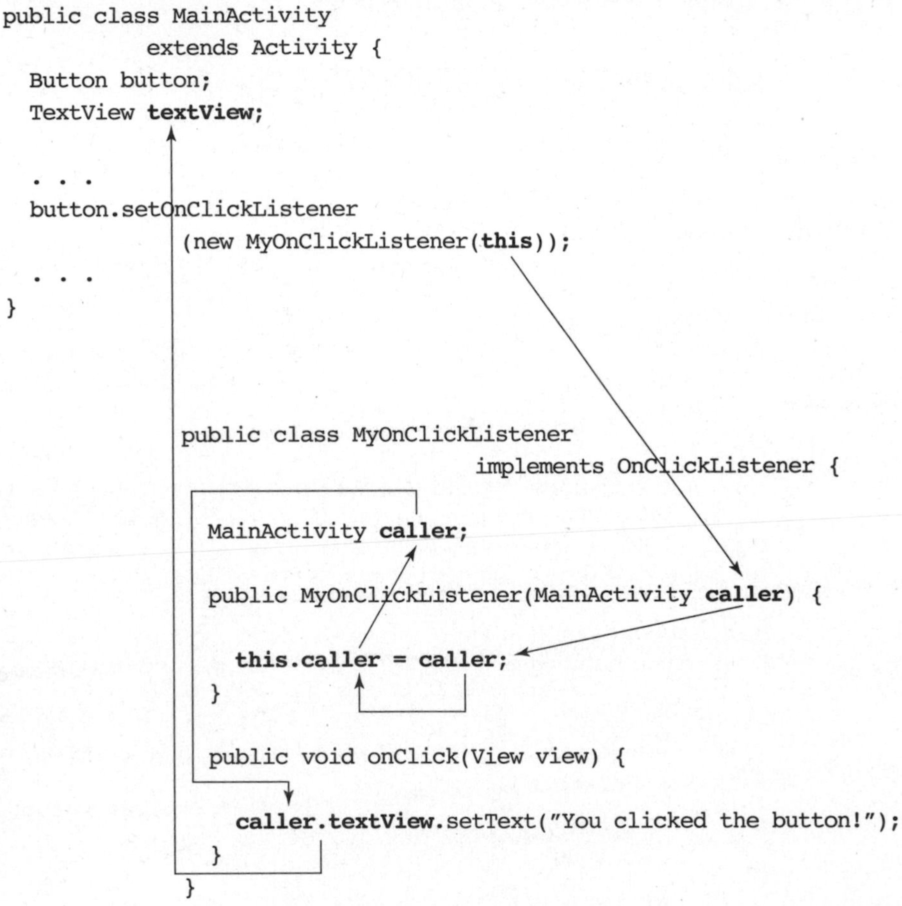

```
public class MainActivity
          extends Activity {
  Button button;
  TextView textView;

  . . .
  button.setOnClickListener
          (new MyOnClickListener(this));
  . . .
}




          public class MyOnClickListener
                            implements OnClickListener {

            MainActivity caller;

            public MyOnClickListener(MainActivity caller) {

              this.caller = caller;
            }

            public void onClick(View view) {

              caller.textView.setText("You clicked the button!");
            }
          }
```

Figure 11-6:
The journey
of your
applica-
tion's main
activity.

Making a view available to your Java code

In Listing 11-2, you execute the statement

```
caller.textView.setText("You clicked the button!");
```

For this statement to work correctly, the textView variable must refer to a particular widget on the activity's screen. In particular, the textView variable must refer to the widget that displays the words *Hello world!* in Figure 11-4. Presumably, this "widget" that displays those words is an instance of Android's TextView class. But who knows? Maybe the code has a mistake in it. (I don't presume to know much about the textView variable until later in this section.)

Anyway, there's a problem. That Hello World widget isn't declared anywhere inside Listings 11-1 or 11-2. Instead, it appears because of some stuff in the application's activity_main.xml file. You need a way to connect the stuff in the XML file with the textView variable in your Java code.

How can you do that? In Chapter 4, I describe the way code numbers stand for strings in Android apps. You put a line such as

```
<string name="hello_world">Hello world!</string>
```

in one of your project's XML files. As a result, Android automatically puts the following lines (and many more lines like them) inside an R.java file:

```
public final class R {

  public static final class string {
    public static final int hello_world=0x7f040001;
  }

}
```

Because of this code number mechanism, you can refer to Hello world! in your code with the value R.string.hello_world. Under the hood, the name R.string.hello_world stands for the hexadecimal number 0x7f040001, though you care only about the name R.string.hello_world.

One way or another, this whole code-number mechanism with its R.java file allows you to connect values in your XML files with names in your Java code.

All hexadecimal numbers in `R.java` files are arbitrary values. The number to represent the `hello_world` string (the number 0x7f040001 in my example) might be different in someone else's `R.java` file or even in the `R.java` file that Eclipse generates for you tomorrow. You can use the name `R.string.hello_world` in your code, but never use the number 0x7f040001.

Sometimes, I can't resist seeing my code's sordid underbelly. If mysterious hex numbers bother you, find a website that converts hexadecimal numbers to and from decimal numbers. You can type 0x7f040001, for example, into a field on the web page and learn that it has the same value as the ordinary decimal number 2130968577. You can't do much with this information, but it's nice to know that hexadecimal numbers don't involve any special magic.

An Android app has several XML files, one of which describes the layout of the app's main activity. Listing 11-3 contains the `activity_main.xml` file for this section's example.

Listing 11-3: A Layout File

```xml
<RelativeLayout xmlns:android=
        "http://schemas.android.com/apk/res/android"
    xmlns:tools="http://schemas.android.com/tools"
    android:layout_width="match_parent"
    android:layout_height="match_parent"
    android:paddingBottom=
        "@dimen/activity_vertical_margin"
    android:paddingLeft=
        "@dimen/activity_horizontal_margin"
    android:paddingRight=
        "@dimen/activity_horizontal_margin"
    android:paddingTop=
        "@dimen/activity_vertical_margin"
    tools:context=".MainActivity" >

    <TextView
        android:id="@+id/textView1"
        android:layout_width="wrap_content"
        android:layout_height="wrap_content"
        android:text="@string/hello_world" />

    <Button
        android:id="@+id/button1"
        android:layout_width="wrap_content"
        android:layout_height="wrap_content"
        android:layout_alignLeft="@+id/textView1"
        android:layout_below="@+id/textView1"
        android:layout_marginTop="46dp"
        android:text="Button" />

</RelativeLayout>
```

The code that you see in your own project's `activity_main.xml` file might not be exactly the same as the code in Listing 11-3. For example, when you drag a button onto your layout in Step 6, you might drop the button in a slightly different place inside your activity's screen. This is no big deal.

Fortunately, you don't have to type the code in Listing 11-3. Eclipse's tools do the typing for you when you create your new Android project and you drop a button into the app's graphical layout.

In Listing 11-3, the lines

```
<TextView
    android:id="@+id/textView1"
    . . .
<Button
    android:id="@+id/button1"
```

tell Android to display a text view and a button on your activity's screen. These lines also tell Eclipse to create code numbers for the new text view and the new button. Finally, these particular lines tell Eclipse to add some code to your project's `R.java` file, as shown in Listing 11-4.

Listing 11-4:   A Few Lines from Your Project's R.java File

```
public final class R {
  ...

  public static final class id {
    public static final int button1=0x7f080001;
    public static final int textView1=0x7f080000;
  }

  ...
}
```

The lines in this listing associate the names `R.id.button1` and `R.id.textView1` with the numbers `0x7f080001` and `0x7f080000`. So, indirectly, the lines in Listing 11-4 associate the names `R.id.button1` and `R.id.textView1` with the button and the text view on your main activity's screen.

In your application's main activity (refer to Listing 11-1), Android's `findViewById` method completes the chain of associations. The `findViewById` method takes a number as its parameter (a number such as 0x7f080000 — the value of `R.id.textView1`). The `findViewById` method looks up that number and finds the widget associated with it (a widget from Listing 11-3).

Figure 11-7 illustrates the chain of associations in concrete terms. Using the code snippet in Listing 11-4, the call

```
findViewById(R.id.textView1)
```

sends Android hunting for a view that's connected with the number 0x7f080000. And because of the clever way that Eclipse generates the R.java file, the number 0x7f080000 is associated with the appropriate text view widget on the activity's screen. Armed with the intermediate name R.id. textView1, your Java code manages to find the appropriate widget in the activity's screen layout.

In activity_main.xml:
```
<TextView
        android:id="@+id/textView1"  ←──────────────── 1. Adds a text view to
    . . .                                               your activity's screen
<Button
        android:id="@+id/button1"
```

In R.java:
```
public final class R {

  public static final class id {
     public static final int button1=0x7f080001;
     public static final int textView1=0x7f080000; ←──┐
  }                                                    │
}                                                   2. Associates the Java
                                                    name R.id.textView1
                                                    with the new text view
```

Figure 11-7: How the *textView* variable becomes synonymous with a widget on the screen.

In Listing 11-1:
```
textView = (TextView) findViewById(R.id.textView1); ←──┐
                                                        │
                                                   3. Makes the textView
                                                   field refer to the widget on
                                                   your activity's screen
```

Casting, again

When you call findViewById, Java doesn't know what kind of view it will find. The findViewById method always returns a View instance, but lots of Android's classes extend the View class. For example, the classes Button, TextView, ImageView, CheckBox, Chronometer, and RatingBar all extend Android's View class. If you type the following code:

```
// DON'T DO THIS!!

TextView textView;

textView = findViewById(R.id.textView1);
```

Java lets out a resounding, resentful roar: "How dare you assume that the object returned by a call to findViewById refers to an instance of the TextView class!" (Actually, Java quietly and mechanically displays an error message in Eclipse's editor. But I like to personify Java as though it's a stern taskmaster.)

In Listing 11-1, you appease the Java gods by adding a casting operator to the code. You tell Java to convert whatever pops out of the findViewById method call into a TextView object.

```
textView = (TextView) findViewById(R.id.textView1);
```

While you're typing the code, Java humors you and says, "Your casting operator shows me that you're aware of the difference between a TextView and any old View. I'll do my best to interpret the View object that I find at runtime as a TextView object." (Actually, while you're typing the code, Java says nothing. The fact that Java doesn't display any error messages when you use this casting trick is a good sign. Java's casting feature saves the day!)

Casting prevents you from seeing an error message while you develop your code. In that way, casting is quite a useful feature of Java. But casting can't save you if your code contains runtime errors. In Step 7, you verify that the name textView1 represents a TextView widget. When the app runs, Java grabs the R.id.textView1 widget from the activity_main.xml file, and everything works just fine. But you may sometimes forget to check your R.java names against the widgets in the XML file. A call to findViewById spits out an ImageView widget when your casting tells Java to expect a TextView widget. When this happens, Java chokes on the casting operator and your app crashes during its run. Back to the drawing board!

For a more complete discussion of casting, see Chapter 7.

Introducing Inner Classes

Does the diagram in Figure 11-6 seem unnecessarily complicated? Look at all those arrows! You might expect to see a few somersaults as the `caller` object bounces from place to place! The `MyOnClickListener` class (refer to Listing 11-2) devotes much of its code to obsessively keeping track of this `caller` object. Is there a simpler way to handle a simple button click?

There is. You can define a class inside another class. When you do, you're creating an *inner class*. It's a lot like any other class. But within an inner class's code, you can refer to the enclosing class's fields with none of the froufrou in Listing 11-2. That's why, at the beginning of this chapter, I sing the praises of insider knowledge.

One big class with its own inner class can replace both Listings 11-1 and 11-2. And the new inner class requires none of the exotic gyrations that you see in the old `MyOnClickListener` class. Listing 11-5 contains this wonderfully improved code.

Listing 11-5:   A Class within a Class

```java
package com.allmycode.myfirstandroidapp;

import android.app.Activity;
import android.os.Bundle;
import android.view.Menu;
import android.view.View;
import android.view.View.OnClickListener;
import android.widget.Button;
import android.widget.TextView;

public class MainActivity extends Activity {
  Button button;
  TextView textView;

  @Override
  protected void onCreate(Bundle savedInstanceState) {
    super.onCreate(savedInstanceState);
    setContentView(R.layout.activity_main);
    button = (Button) findViewById(R.id.button1);
    button.setOnClickListener(new MyOnClickListener());
    textView = (TextView) findViewById(R.id.textView1);
  }

  @Override
  public boolean onCreateOptionsMenu(Menu menu) {
    getMenuInflater().inflate(R.menu.main, menu);
    return true;
```

```
    }

  class MyOnClickListener implements OnClickListener {

    public void onClick(View view) {
      textView.setText("You clicked the button!");
    }
  }
}
```

When you run the code in Listing 11-5, you see the results shown earlier, in Figures 11-4 and 11-5.

Notice the relative simplicity of the new MyOnClickListener class in Listing 11-5. Going from the old MyOnClickListener class (refer to Listing 11-2) to the new MyOnClickListener inner class (refer to Listing 11-5), you reduce the code's size by a factor of three. But aside from the shrinkage, all the complexity of Figure 11-6 is absent from Listing 11-5. The use of this, caller, and textView in Listings 11-1 and 11-2 feels like a tangled rope. But in Listing 11-5, when you pull both ends of the rope, you find that the rope *isn't* knotted.

An inner class needs no fancy bookkeeping in order to keep track of its enclosing class's fields. Near the end of Listing 11-5, the line

```
textView.setText("You clicked the button!");
```

refers to the MainActivity class's textView field, which is exactly what you want. It's that straightforward.

No Publicity, Please!

Notice that the code in Listing 11-5 uses the MyOnClickListener class only once. (The only use is in a call to button.setOnClickListener.) So I ask, do you really need a name for something that's used only once? No, you don't. (If there's only one cat in the house, it's safe to say "Hey, cat!")

When you give a name to your disposable class, you have to type the name twice: once when you call the class's constructor:

```
button.setOnClickListener(new MyOnClickListener());
```

and a second time when you declare the class:

```
class MyOnClickListener implements OnClickListener {
```

To eliminate this redundancy, you can substitute the entire definition of the class in the place where you'd ordinarily call the constructor. When you do this, you have an *anonymous inner class*. Listing 11-6 shows you how it works.

Listing 11-6:   A Class with No Name (Inside a Class with a Name)

```
package com.allmycode.myfirstandroidapp;

import android.app.Activity;
import android.os.Bundle;
import android.view.Menu;
import android.view.View;
import android.view.View.OnClickListener;
import android.widget.Button;
import android.widget.TextView;

public class MainActivity extends Activity {
  Button button;
  TextView textView;

  @Override
  protected void onCreate(Bundle savedInstanceState) {
    super.onCreate(savedInstanceState);
    setContentView(R.layout.activity_main);
    button = (Button) findViewById(R.id.button1);
    button.setOnClickListener(new OnClickListener() {
      public void onClick(View view) {
        textView.setText("You clicked the button!");
      }
    });
    textView = (TextView) findViewById(R.id.textView1);
  }

  @Override
  public boolean onCreateOptionsMenu(Menu menu) {
    getMenuInflater().inflate(R.menu.main, menu);
    return true;
  }

}
```

A run of the code from Listing 11-6 is shown in Figures 11-4 and 11-5. In other words, the listing does exactly the same thing as its wordier counterparts in this chapter. The big difference is that, unlike this chapter's previous examples, the listing uses an anonymous inner class.

An anonymous inner class is a lot like an ordinary inner class. The big difference is that an anonymous inner class has no name. Nowhere in Listing 11-6 do you see a name like `MyOnClickListener`. Instead, you see what looks like an entire class declaration inside a call to `button.setOnClick` `Listener`. It's as though the `setOnClickListener` call says, "The following listener class, which no one else refers to, responds to the button clicks."

As far as I'm concerned, the most difficult aspect of using an anonymous inner class is keeping track of the code's parentheses, curly braces, and other non-alphabetic characters. Notice, for example, the string of closing punctuation characters — `!");}});` — that straddles a few lines in Listing 11-6. The indentation in that listing helps a little bit when you try to read a big *mush* of anonymous inner class code, but it doesn't help a lot. Fortunately, there's a nice correspondence between the code in Listing 11-5 and the anonymized code in Listing 11-6. Figure 11-8 illustrates this correspondence.

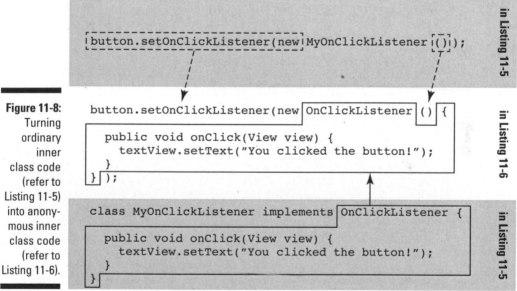

Figure 11-8:
Turning
ordinary
inner
class code
(refer to
Listing 11-5)
into anony-
mous inner
class code
(refer to
Listing 11-6).

I feel obliged to include a written explanation of the material in Figure 11-8. Here goes:

> To go from a named inner class to an anonymous inner class, you replace the named class's constructor call with the entire class declaration. In place of the class name, you put the name of the interface that the inner class implements (or, possibly, the name of the class that the inner class extends).

If you find my explanation helpful, I'm pleased. But if you don't find it helpful, I'm neither offended nor surprised. When I create a brand-new inner class, I find my gut feeling and Figure 11-8 to be more useful than Java's formal grammar rules.

My humble advice: Start by writing code with no inner classes, such as the code in Listing 11-5. Later, when you become bored with ordinary Java classes, experiment by changing some of your ordinary classes into anonymous inner classes.

Doing It the Easy Way

With all the fuss about callbacks and inner classes in this chapter, I'm tempted to end the chapter right here. So this is the last paragraph in Chapter 11. Don't read any further in this chapter. Really, there's nothing more to see here. Move on, everybody!

I warned you to skip the rest of this chapter

Starting with Android 1.6 (code-named Donut, API Level 4), developers can add click-handling code to a button, or to any other Android widget, without creating a separate class. You don't need the extra Java file in Listing 11-2 or the inner class in Listing 11-5 or the anonymous inner class in Listing 11-6.

The onClick attribute described in this section (which you shouldn't be reading) lets you handle clicks and other occurrences without coding any additional classes. The onClick feature is quite convenient. But the onClick feature's existence doesn't mean that you, the Android developer, don't have to understand callbacks and inner classes. Interfaces, callbacks, and inner classes are used implicitly and explicitly in almost every Android application. And, among all the introductory inner class examples, button clicking is one of the easiest to understand. The use of an inner class to handle a button click is an old standby among Java programming examples, so I use this example in Chapter 11, even though Android provides this section's fast, convenient onClick attribute work-around.

The "no-hassle" way to click a button

In this section's example, your app's activity class handles the button click on its own. You don't create an additional class to handle the click.

You can follow the instructions in Chapter 2 to import this section's example from my website (`http://allmycode.com/Java4Android`). But if you want to create the example on your own, follow these steps:

1. **Follow Steps 1 through 7 earlier in this chapter, in the section "The First Button-Click Example."**

2. **Right-click (in Windows) or Control-click (on the Mac) the picture of the button in the graphical layout.**

3. **From the contextual menu that appears, select Other Properties⇨Inherited from View⇨OnClick.**

   A dialog box with a field labeled New onClick Value appears, as shown in Figure 11-9.

```
android.widget.Button                                    ×

New onClick Value:

whenButtonClicked


                    Clear        OK        Cancel
```

4. **In the New onClick Value field, type the name of a method.**

   In Figure 11-9, I typed the name `whenButtonClicked`. In the next several steps, I assume that you type the same name, `whenButtonClicked`.

5. **Click OK to dismiss the dialog box.**

6. **In Eclipse's main menu, select File⇨Save.**

   Doing so saves your changes to the `activity_main.xml` file.

   Your actions in Steps 2 through 6 tell Android to look for a method with the following header when the user clicks the button:

   ```
   public void whenButtonClicked(View view)
   ```

   In the remaining steps, you add that `whenButtonClicked` method to your app's Java code.

7. **In the Package Explorer, navigate to your project's `src` directory.**

8. **Inside the `src` directory, expand the branch for the package containing the project.**

   The package name is probably similar to `com.example.myfirst androidapp`.

9. **Within the package's branch, double-click the** `MainActivity.java` **file.**

   The activity's Java file appears in Eclipse's editor. Eclipse created all this Java code for you.

10. **In the editor, add the following field to your** `MainActivity` **class's code:**

    ```
    TextView textView;
    ```

    See Listing 11-7.

After typing the `TextView` declaration, select Source⇨Organize Imports from Eclipse's main menu. When you do, Eclipse automatically adds the `TextView` class's import declaration to your code.

11. **In Eclipse's editor, add the following statement immediately after the call to** `setContentView`:

    ```
    textView = (TextView) findViewById(R.id.textView1);
    ```

    Refer to Listing 11-7.

12. **Type the** `whenButtonClicked` **method in your code.**

    You can find the method in Listing 11-7.

13. **From Eclipse's main menu, select File⇨Save.**

    Doing so saves your changes to the `activity_main.xml` file.

14. **Run your project.**

    The project runs exactly as it did in this chapter's examples. Under the hood, Android creates all the necessary callbacks to have your `whenButtonClicked` method respond to the user's actions.

Listing 11-7:   Adding the whenButtonClicked Method to Your Code

```
package com.example.myfirstandroidappnew;

import android.app.Activity;
import android.os.Bundle;
import android.view.Menu;
import android.view.View;
import android.widget.TextView;

public class MainActivity extends Activity {
    TextView textView;

    @Override
    protected void onCreate(Bundle savedInstanceState) {
```

```
      super.onCreate(savedInstanceState);
      setContentView(R.layout.activity_main);
      textView = (TextView) findViewById(R.id.textView1);
    }

    public void whenButtonClicked(View view) {
      textView.setText("You clicked the button!");
    }

    @Override
    public boolean onCreateOptionsMenu(Menu menu) {
      getMenuInflater().inflate(R.menu.main, menu);
      return true;
    }

}
```

Chapter 12

Dealing with a Bunch of Things at a Time

All the world's a class,

And all the data, merely objects.

—Jimmy Shakespeare, 11-year-old computer geek

A class is a blueprint for things, and an *object* is a thing made from the blueprint. By *thing,* I mean a particular employee, a customer, an Android activity, or a more ethereal element, such as an SQLiteOpenHelper. Here's another quotation, this one from a more reliable source:

In fact, some Java classes are difficult to visualize. Android's SQLiteOpenHelper class assists developers in the creation of databases. An SQLiteOpenHelper doesn't look like anything in particular, and certainly not an online form or a bag of cheese.

—Barry Burd, Java Programming for Android Developers For Dummies, *Chapter 9*

This chapter covers a concept that you might not normally consider a class or an object — namely, a bunch of things. I use the word *bunch,* by the way, to avoid the formal terminology. (There's nothing wrong with the formal terminology, but I want to save it for this chapter's official grand opening, in the first section.)

Creating a Collection Class

A *collection class* is a class whose job is to store a bunch of objects at a time — a bunch of `String` objects, a bunch of `BagOfCheese` objects, a bunch of tweets, or whatever. You can create a collection class with the code in Listing 12-1.

Listing 12-1:   Your First Collection Class

```
package com.allmycode.collections;

import java.util.ArrayList;

public class SimpleCollectionsDemo {

  public static void main(String[] args) {
    ArrayList arrayList = new ArrayList();
    arrayList.add("Hello");
    arrayList.add(", ");
    arrayList.add("readers");
    arrayList.add("!");

    for (int i = 0; i < 4; i++) {
      System.out.print(arrayList.get(i));
    }
  }

}
```

When you run the code in Listing 12-1, you see the output shown in Figure 12-1.

Figure 12-1:
Running
the code in
Listing 12-1.

The code in Listing 12-1 constructs a new `ArrayList` instance and makes the `arrayList` variable refer to that new instance. The `ArrayList` class is one of many kinds of collection classes.

The statement `ArrayList arrayList = new ArrayList()` creates an empty list of things and makes the `arrayList` variable refer to that empty list. What does a list look like when it's empty? I don't know. I guess it looks like a blank sheet of paper. Anyway, the difference between having an empty list and having *no* list is important. Before executing `ArrayList arrayList = new ArrayList()`, you have no list. After executing `ArrayList arrayList = new ArrayList()`, you have a list that happens to be empty.

The code in Listing 12-1 calls `arrayList.add` four times in order to put these four objects (all strings) into the list:

- ✔ `"Hello"`
- ✔ `", "`
- ✔ `"readers"`
- ✔ `"!"`

After calling `arrayList.add`, the list is no longer empty.

To display the objects in Eclipse's Console view, the code calls `System.out.print` four times, each time with a different object from the `arrayList` collection.

If you don't see Eclipse's Console view, click Window➪Show View➪Console.

There's a difference between `System.out.println` and `System.out.print` (without the `ln` ending): The `System.out.println` method goes to a new line after displaying its text; the `System.out.print` method does *not* go to a new line after displaying its text. In Listing 12-1, for example, with four calls to `System.out.print`, all four chunks of text appear on the same line in Eclipse's Console view.

The `for` statement in Listing 12-1 marches through the values in the `arrayList`. Every value in the list has an *index*, each ranging from 0 to 3.

In a Java collection, the initial index is always 0, not 1.

Java generics

If you look at Listing 12-1 in Eclipse's editor, you see lots of yellow warning markers, as shown in Figure 12-2. The warning text looks something like this: "ArrayList is a raw type. References to generic type ArrayList<E> should be parameterized." What does that mean?

Starting with Java 5, the collection classes use generic types. You can recognize a generic type because of the angle brackets around its type name. For example, the following declaration uses `String` for a generic type:

```
ArrayList<String> arrayList = new ArrayList<String>();
```

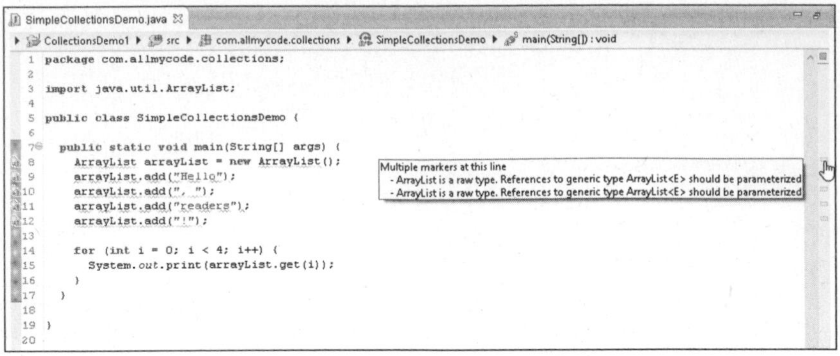

Figure 12-2:
What are all
these warn-
ings about?

This improved declaration tells Java that the `arrayList` variable refers to a bunch of objects, each of which is an instance of `String`. When you substitute this new declaration in place of the nongeneric declaration from Listing 12-1, the yellow warning markers disappear, as you can see in Figure 12-3.

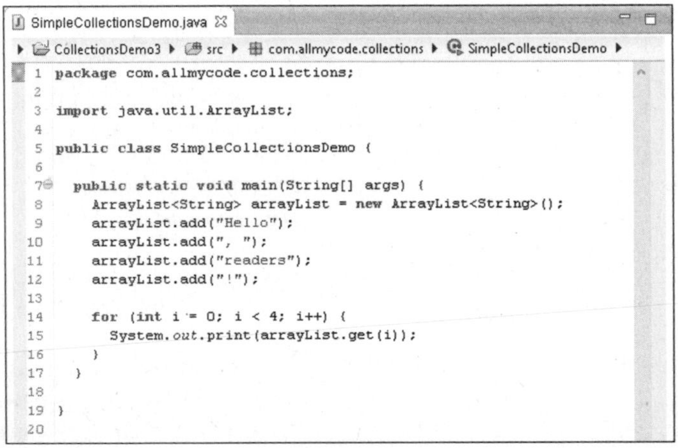

Figure 12-3:
Using
generics.

The yellow markers show warnings, not errors (refer to Figure 12-2), so you can get away with using the nongeneric declaration in Listing 12-1. But creating a nongeneric collection has some disadvantages. When you don't use generics (as in Listing 12-1), you create a collection that might contain objects of any kind. In that case, Java can't take advantage of any special properties of the items in the collection.

Here's an example. Chapter 9 starts with a description of the `BagOfCheese` class (which I've copied in Listing 12-2).

Listing 12-2:   A Class in the Java Programming Language

```
package com.allmycode.andy;

public class BagOfCheese {
   String kind;
   double weight;
   int daysAged;
   boolean isDomestic;
}
```

You can put a few `BagOfCheese` objects into a nongeneric collection. But when you examine the objects in the collection, Java remembers only that the items in the collection are objects. Java doesn't remember that they're `BagOfCheese` objects, as shown in Figure 12-4.

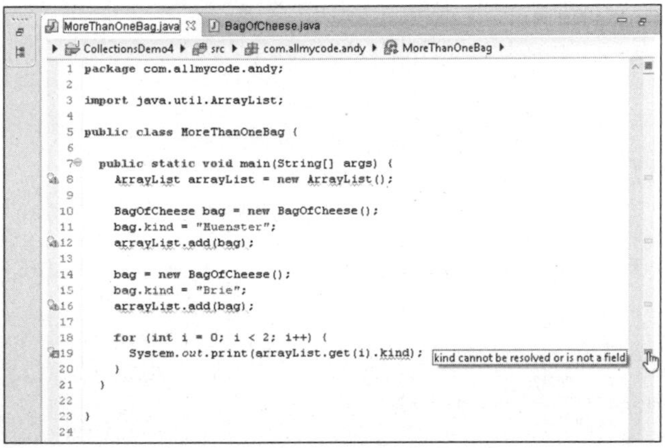

Figure 12-4:
Your code
without
casting.

```
package com.allmycode.andy;

import java.util.ArrayList;

public class MoreThanOneBag {

    public static void main(String[] args) {
      ArrayList arrayList = new ArrayList();

      BagOfCheese bag = new BagOfCheese();
      bag.kind = "Muenster";
      arrayList.add(bag);

      bag = new BagOfCheese();
      bag.kind = "Brie";
      arrayList.add(bag);

      for (int i = 0; i < 2; i++) {
         System.out.print(arrayList.get(i).kind);   [kind cannot be resolved or is not a field]
      }
    }
}
```

In Figure 12-4, Java doesn't remember that what you get from `arrayList` is always a `BagOfCheese` instance. So Java refuses to reference the object's `kind` field. (The last marker in Figure 12-4 is an error marker. Java can't run the code in that figure.)

Using casting, you can remind Java that the item you're getting from `array-List` is a `BagOfCheese` instance.

```
System.out.print(((BagOfCheese) arrayList.get(i)).kind);
```

When you cast `arrayList.get(i)` to a `BagOfCheese` instance, you don't see the error message in Figure 12-4. You can run the code, warnings and all. Life is good, but the code is ugly! Look at all the parentheses you need in order to make the casting work correctly. It's a mess.

If you tweak the code to make `arrayList` generic, Java knows that what you get from `arrayList` is always a `BagOfCheese` instance, and every `BagOfCheese` instance has a `kind` field, as shown in Figure 12-5. No casting is required.

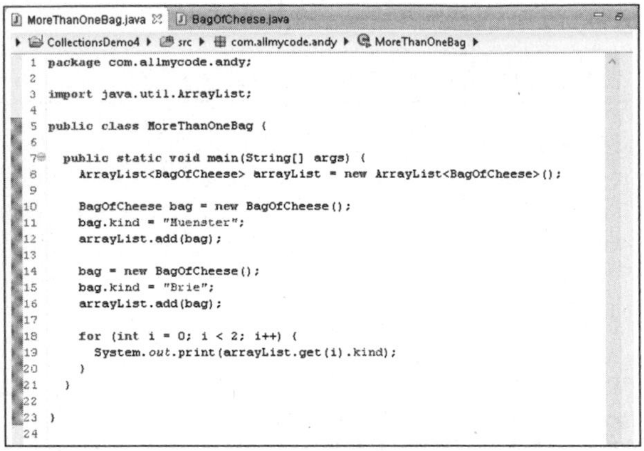
MoreThanOneBag.java
BagOfCheese.java
CollectionsDemo4 ▸ src ▸ com.allmycode.andy ▸ MoreThanOneBag ▸
package com.allmycode.andy;
import java.util.ArrayList;
public class MoreThanOneBag {
public static void main(String[] args) {
ArrayList<BagOfCheese> arrayList = new ArrayList<BagOfCheese>();
BagOfCheese bag = new BagOfCheese();
bag.kind = "Muenster";
arrayList.add(bag);
bag = new BagOfCheese();
bag.kind = "Brie";
arrayList.add(bag);
for (int i = 0; i < 2; i++) {
System.out.print(arrayList.get(i).kind);
}
}
}

Figure 12-5: Java generics save the day.

You can use generics to create your own collection class. When you do, the generic type serves as a placeholder for an otherwise unknown type. Listing 12-3 contains a home-grown declaration of an `OrderedPair` class.

Listing 12-3: A Custom-Made Collection Class

```
package com.allmycode.collections;

public class OrderedPair<T> {
  private T x;
  private T y;

  public T getX() {
    return x;
  }
  public void setX(T x) {
    this.x = x;
  }
  public T getY() {
    return y;
  }
  public void setY(T y) {
    this.y = y;
  }
}
```

An OrderedPair object has two components: an x component and a y component. If you remember your high school math, you can probably plot ordered pairs of numbers on a two-dimensional grid. But who says that every ordered pair must contain numbers? The newly declared OrderedPair class stores objects of type T, and T can stand for any Java class. In Listing 12-4, I show you how to create an ordered pair of BagOfCheese objects.

Listing 12-4:   Using the Custom-Made Collection Class

```
package com.allmycode.collections;

public class PairOfBags {

  public static void main(String[] args) {
    OrderedPair<BagOfCheese> pair =
        new OrderedPair<BagOfCheese>();

    BagOfCheese bag = new BagOfCheese();
    bag.kind = "Muenster";
    pair.setX(bag);

    bag = new BagOfCheese();
    bag.kind = "Brie";
    pair.setY(bag);

    System.out.println(pair.getX().kind);
    System.out.println(pair.getY().kind);
  }

}
```

Java's wrapper classes

Chapters 6 and 9 describe the difference between primitive types and reference types:

> ✔ **Each primitive type is baked into the language.**
>
> Java has eight primitive types.
>
> ✔ **Each reference type is a class or an interface.**
>
> You can define your own reference type. So the number of reference types in Java is potentially endless.

The difference between primitive types and reference types is one of Java's most controversial features, and developers often complain about the differences between primitive values and reference values.

Here's one of the primitive-versus-reference-type "gotchas:" You can't store a primitive value in an `ArrayList`. You can write

```
// THIS IS OKAY:
ArrayList<String> arrayList = new ArrayList<String>();
```

because String is a reference type. But you can't write

```
// DON'T DO THIS:
ArrayList<int> arrayList = new ArrayList<int>();
```

because `int` is a primitive type. Fortunately, each of Java's primitive types has a *wrapper* type, which is a reference type whose purpose is to contain another type's value. For example, an object of Java's `Integer` type contains a single `int` value. An object of Java's `Double` type contains a single `double` value. An object of Java's `Character` type contains a single `char` value. You can't create an `ArrayList` of int values, but you can create an `ArrayList` of `Integer` values.

```
// THIS IS OKAY:
ArrayList<Integer> arrayList = new ArrayList<Integer>();
```

Every primitive type's name begins with a lowercase letter. Every wrapper type's name begins with an uppercase letter.

In addition to containing primitive values, wrapper classes provide useful methods for working with primitive values. For example, the `Integer` wrapper class contains `parseInt` and other useful methods for working with `int` values:

```
String string = "17";
int number = Integer.parseInt(string);
```

On the downside, working with wrapper types can be clumsy. For example, you can't use arithmetic operators with Java's numeric wrapper types. Here's the way I usually create two `Integer` values and add them together:

```
Integer myInteger = new Integer(3);
Integer myOtherInteger = new Integer(15);

Integer sum =
  myInteger.intValue() + myOtherInteger.intValue();
```

Stepping through a collection

The program in Listing 12-1 uses a `for` loop with indexes to step through a collection. The code does what it's supposed to do, but it's a bit awkward. When you're piling objects into a collection, you shouldn't have to worry about which object is first in the collection, which is second, and which is third, for example.

Java has two features that make it easier to step through a collection of objects. One feature is the *iterator*. Listing 12-5 shows you how an iterator works.

Listing 12-5:   Iterating through a Collection

```java
package com.allmycode.collections;

import java.util.ArrayList;
import java.util.Iterator;

public class SimpleCollectionsDemo {

  public static void main(String[] args) {
    ArrayList<String> arrayList = new ArrayList<String>();
    arrayList.add("Hello");
    arrayList.add(", ");
    arrayList.add("readers");
    arrayList.add("!");

    Iterator<String> iterator = arrayList.iterator();
    while (iterator.hasNext()) {
      System.out.print(iterator.next());
    }
  }
}
```

The output from running Listing 12-5 is shown earlier, in Figure 12-1.

When you have a collection (such as an `ArrayList`), you can create an iterator to go along with that collection. In Listing 12-5, I show you how to create an iterator to go along with the `arrayList` collection, by calling

```java
Iterator<String> iterator = arrayList.iterator();
```

After you've made this call, the variable iterator refers to something that can step through all values in the `arrayList` collection. Then, to step from one value to the next, you call `iterator.next()` repeatedly. And, to find out whether another `iterator.next()` call will yield results, you call `iterator.hasNext()`. The call to `iterator.hasNext()` returns a `boolean` value: `true` when there are more values in the collection and `false` when you've already stepped through all the values in the collection.

An even nicer way to step through a collection is with Java's *enhanced* `for` *statement*. Listing 12-6 shows you how to use it.

Listing 12-6:   Using the Enhanced for Statement

```
package com.allmycode.collections;

import java.util.ArrayList;

public class SimpleCollectionsDemo {

  public static void main(String[] args) {
    ArrayList<String> arrayList = new ArrayList<String>();
    arrayList.add("Hello");
    arrayList.add(", ");
    arrayList.add("readers");
    arrayList.add("!");

    for (String string : arrayList) {
      System.out.print(string);
    }
  }
}
```

An enhanced `for` statement doesn't have a counter. Instead, the statement has the format shown in Figure 12-6.

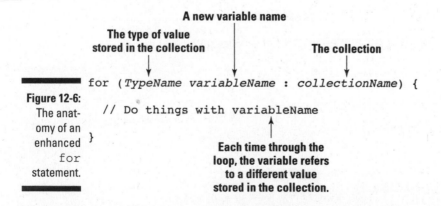

A new variable name

The type of value stored in the collection

The collection

```
for (TypeName variableName : collectionName) {

    // Do things with variableName

}
```

Figure 12-6: The anatomy of an enhanced `for` statement.

Each time through the loop, the variable refers to a different value stored in the collection.

The enhanced `for` statement in Listing 12-6 achieves the same effect as the iterator in Listing 12-5 and the ordinary `for` statement in Listing 12-1. That is, the enhanced `for` statement steps through the values stored in the `array List` collection.

The enhanced `for` statement was introduced in Java 5.0. It's "enhanced" because, for stepping through a collection, it's easier to use than a pre-Java 5.0 `for` statement.

A cautionary tale

In an enhanced `for` statement, the variable that repeatedly stands for different values in the collection never refers directly to any of those values. Instead, this variable always contains a copy of the value in the collection. So, if you assign a value to that variable, you don't change any values inside the collection.

Here's a quiz. (Don't be scared. The quiz isn't graded.) What's the output of the following code?

```java
package com.allmycode.collections;

import java.util.ArrayList;

public class SimpleCollectionsDemo {

  public static void main(String[] args) {
    ArrayList<String> arrayList = new ArrayList<String>();
    arrayList.add("Hello");
    arrayList.add(", ");
    arrayList.add("readers");
    arrayList.add("!");

    // THIS IS PRETTY BAD CODE
    for (String string : arrayList) {
      string = "Oops!";
      System.out.print(string);
    }

    System.out.println();

    for (String string : arrayList) {
      System.out.print(string);
    }
  }
}
```

The output is shown in Figure 12-7.

Figure 12-7:
Running this
section's
bad code.

In the first `for` statement, the variable `string` is reassigned to refer to the word `"Oops!"` each time through the loop. The call to `System.out.print` displays that word `"Oops!"`. So far, so good.

But in the second `for` statement, the variable `string` isn't reassigned. Instead, the `string` variable retains whatever value it copies from the `arrayList` collection. So the second `for` statement displays the words `Hello, readers!`.

Java's many collection classes

The `ArrayList` class that I use in many of this chapter's examples is only the tip of the Java collections iceberg. The Java library contains many collections classes, each with its own advantages. Table 12-1 contains an abbreviated list.

Table 12-1	Some Collection Classes
Class Name	**Characteristic**
`ArrayList`	A resizable array.
`LinkedList`	A list of values, each having a field that points to the next one in the list.
`Stack`	A structure (which grows from bottom to top) that's optimized for access to the topmost value. You can easily add a value to the top or remove it from the top.
`Queue`	A structure (which grows at one end) that's optimized for adding values to one end (the rear) and removing values from the other end (the front).
`PriorityQueue`	A structure, like a queue, that lets certain (higher-priority) values move toward the front.
`HashSet`	A collection containing no duplicate values.
`HashMap`	A collection of key/value pairs.

Each collection class has its own set of methods (in addition to the methods that it inherits from `AbstractCollection`, the ancestor of all collection classes).

To find out which collection classes best meet your needs, visit the Android API documentation pages at `http://developer.android.com/reference`.

Arrays

In the "Stepping through a collection" section, earlier in this chapter, I cast aspersions on the use of an index in Listing 12-1. "You shouldn't have to worry about which object is first in the collection, which is second, and which is third," I write. Well, that's my story and I'm sticking to it, except in the case of an array. An array is a particular kind of collection that's optimized for indexing. That is, you can easily and efficiently find the 100th value stored in an array, the 1,000th value stored in an array, or the 1,000,000th value stored in an array.

The array is a venerable, tried-and-true feature of many programming languages, including newer languages such as Java and older languages such as FORTRAN. In fact, the array's history goes back so far that most languages (including Java) have special notation for dealing with arrays. Listing 12-7 illustrates the notation for arrays in a simple Java program.

Listing 12-7:   Creating and Using an Array

```
package com.allmycode.collections;

public class SimpleCollectionsDemo {

  public static void main(String[] args) {
    String[] myArray = new String[4];
    myArray[0] = "Hello";
    myArray[1] = ", ";
    myArray[2] = "readers";
    myArray[3] = "!";

    for(int i = 0; i < 4; i++) {
      System.out.print(myArray[i]);
    }

    System.out.println();

    for (String string : myArray) {
      System.out.print(string);
    }
  }

}
```

Figure 12-8 shows the output of a run of the code in Listing 12-7. Both the ordinary `for` loop and the enhanced `for` loop display the same output.

Figure 12-8:
Running
the code in
Listing 12-7.

```
Problems  Javadoc  Declaration  Search  Console

<terminated> SimpleCollectionsDemo (3) [Java Application] C:\Program Files\
Hello, readers!
Hello, readers!
```

In Listing 12-7, the ordinary `for` loop uses indexes, with each index marked by square brackets. As it is with all Java collections, the initial value's index is 0, not 1. Notice also the number 4 in the array's declaration — it indicates that "you can store 4 values in the array." The number 4 *doesn't* indicate that "you can assign a value to `myArray[4]`." In fact, if you add a statement such as `myArray[4] = "Oops!"` to the code in Listing 12-7, you get a nasty error message (`ArrayIndexOutOfBoundsException`) when you run the program.

The statement `String[] myArray = new String[4]` creates an empty array and makes the `myArray` variable refer to that empty array. The array can potentially store as many as four values. But, initially, that variable refers to an array that contains no values. It's not until Java executes the first assignment statement (`myArray[0] = "Hello"`) that the array contains any values.

You can easily and efficiently find the 100th value stored in an array or the 1,000,000th value stored in an array. Not bad for a day's work. So, what's the downside of using an array? The biggest disadvantage of an array is that each array has a fixed limit on the number of values it can hold. When you create the array in Listing 12-7, Java reserves space for as many as four `String` values. If, later in the program, you decide that you want to store a fifth element in the array, you need some clumsy, inefficient code to make yourself a larger array. You can also overestimate the size you need for an array, as shown in this example:

```
String[] myArray = new String[20000000];
```

When you overestimate, you probably waste a lot of memory space.

Another unpleasant feature of an array is the difficulty you can have in inserting new values. Imagine having a wooden box for each year in your collection of *Emperor Constantine Comics*. The series dates back to the year 307 A.D., when Constantine became head of the Roman Empire. You have only 1,700 boxes because you're missing about six years (mostly from the years 1150 to 1155). The boxes aren't numbered, but they're stacked one next to another in a line that's 200 meters long. (The line is as long as the 55th floor of a sky-scraper is tall.)

At a garage sale in Istanbul, you find a rare edition of *Emperor Constantine Comics* from March 1152. After rejoicing over your first comic from the year 1152, you realize that you have to insert a new box into the pile between the years 1151 and 1153, which involves moving the year 2013 box about ten centimeters to the left, and then moving the 2012 box in place of the 2013 box, and then moving the 2011 box in place of the 2012 box. And so on. Life for the avid *Emperor Constantine Comics* collector is about to become tiresome! Inserting a value into the middle of a large array is equally annoying.

Java's varargs

In an app of some kind, you need a method that displays a bunch of words as a full sentence. How do you create such a method? You can pass a bunch of words to the sentence. In the method's body, you display each word, followed by a blank space, as shown here:

```
for (String word : words) {
  System.out.print(word);
  System.out.print(" ");
}
```

To pass words to the method, you create an array of `String` values:

```
String[] stringsE = { "Goodbye,", "kids." };
displayAsSentence(stringsE);
```

Notice the use of the curly braces in the initialization of `stringsE`. In Java, you can initialize any array by writing the array's values, separating the values from one another by commas, and surrounding the entire bunch of values with curly braces. When you do this, you create an *array initializer*.

Listing 12-8 contains an entire program to combine words into sentences.

Listing 12-8:   A Program without Varargs

```
package com.allmycode.arrays;

public class UseArrays {

  public static void main(String[] args) {
    String[] stringsA = { "Hello,", "I", "must", "be",
                                        "going." };
    String[] stringsB = { "     ", "-Groucho" };
    String[] stringsC = { "Say", "Goodnight,",
                                          "Gracie." };
```

(continued)

Listing 12-8 *(continued)*

```java
    String[] stringsD = { "        ", "-Nathan Birnbaum" };
    String[] stringsE = { "Goodbye,", "kids." };
    String[] stringsF = { "        ", "-Clarabell" };

    displayAsSentence(stringsA);
    displayAsSentence(stringsB);
    displayAsSentence(stringsC);
    displayAsSentence(stringsD);
    displayAsSentence(stringsE);
    displayAsSentence(stringsF);
  }

  static void displayAsSentence(String[] words) {
    for (String word : words) {
      System.out.print(word);
      System.out.print(" ");
    }
    System.out.println();
  }
}
```

When you run the code in Listing 12-8, you see the output shown in Figure 12-9.

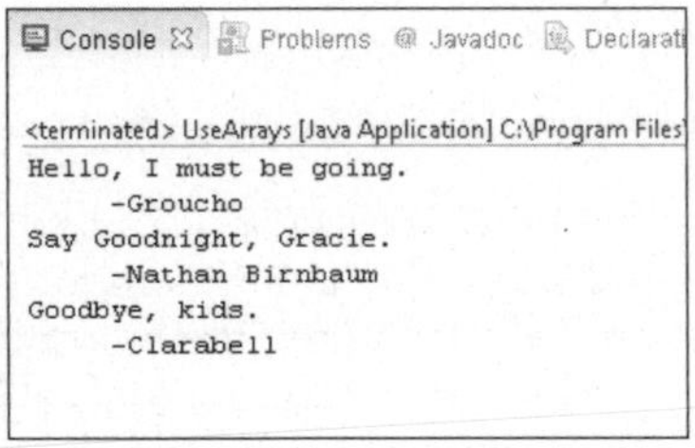

Figure 12-9:
Running
the code in
Listing 12-8.

```
Console ⊠  Problems  @ Javadoc  Declarati
<terminated> UseArrays [Java Application] C:\Program Files
Hello, I must be going.
     -Groucho
Say Goodnight, Gracie.
     -Nathan Birnbaum
Goodbye, kids.
     -Clarabell
```

The code in Listing 12-8 is awkward because you have to declare six different arrays of `String` values. You can't combine the variable declarations and the method call. A statement such as

```java
displayAsSentence("Say", "Goodnight,", "Gracie.");
```

is illegal because the call's parameter list has three values, and because the `displayAsSentence` method (in Listing 12-8) has only one parameter (one array). You can try fixing the problem by declaring `displayAsSentence` with three parameters:

```java
static void displayAsSentence
    (String word0, String word1, String word2) {
```

But then you're in trouble when you want to pass five words to the method.

To escape from this mess, Java 5.0 introduces varargs. A parameter list with *varargs* has a type name followed by three dots. The dots represent any number of parameters, all of the same type. Listing 12-9 shows you how it works.

Listing 12-9: **A Program with Varargs**

```
package com.allmycode.varargs;

public class UseVarargs {

  public static void main(String[] args) {
    displayAsSentence("Hello,", "I", "must", "be",
                                        "going.");
    displayAsSentence("      ", "-Groucho");
    displayAsSentence("Say", "Goodnight,", "Gracie.");
    displayAsSentence("      ", "-Nathan Birnbaum");
    displayAsSentence("Goodbye,", "kids.");
    displayAsSentence("      ", "-Clarabell");
  }

  static void displayAsSentence(String... words) {
    for (String word : words) {
      System.out.print(word);
      System.out.print(" ");
    }
    System.out.println();
  }
}
```

In Listing 12-9, the parameter list (`String... words`) stands for any number of `String` values — one `String` value, one hundred `String` values, or even no `String` values. So in Listing 12-9, I can call the `displayAsSentence` method with two parameters (`"Goodbye,"`, `"kids."`), with three parameters (`"Say"`, `"Goodnight,"`, `"Gracie."`), and with five parameters (`"Hello,"`, `"I"`, `"must"`, `"be"`, `"going."`).

In the body of the `displayAsSentence` method, I treat the collection of parameters as an array. I can step through the parameters with an enhanced `for` statement, or I can refer to each parameter with an array index. For example, in Listing 12-9, during the first call to the `displayAsSentence` method, the expression `words[0]` stands for `"Hello"`. During the second call to the `displayAsSentence` method, the expression `words[2]` stands for `"Goodnight"`. And so on.

Using Collections in an Android App

I conclude this chapter with an Android app that's all about collections. This example will never become Google Play's featured app of the day, but the app demonstrates some of Java's collection features, and it shows you how to do a few interesting Android tricks.

The app begins by displaying five check boxes, as shown in Figure 12-10.

The user selects a few of the check boxes and then clicks the Show the List button. After the button is clicked, the app switches to a new activity (an Android `ListActivity`) that displays the numbers of the check boxes the user clicked, as shown in Figure 12-11.

In the app's code, I use an array to store the check boxes, I use an `ArrayList` for the items in the `ListActivity`, and I use an Android `ArrayAdapter` to determine which numbers the `ListActivity` displays.

Figure 12-10: The app's main activity.

Figure 12-11: The app's other activity.

The main activity's initial layout

In an Android app, you use *layouts* to describe the arrangement of widgets on the device's screen. The Android API has several kinds of layouts, including these:

- **LinearLayout:** Arranges widgets in a line across the screen, or in a column down the screen.

- **GridLayout:** Arranges widgets in a rectangular grid (that is, in the cells of a table whose borders are invisible).

- **RelativeLayout:** Arranges widgets by describing their positions relative to one another. For example, you can make the top of button2 be 50 pixels below the bottom of button1.

In a LinearLayout, items appear one to the right of the other, or one beneath the other, depending on the layout's orientation. According to the code in Listing 12-10, the app's main activity has a LinearLayout with vertical orientation. So when you add items to the layout, new items appear beneath existing items on the activity's screen.

Listing 12-10:   The Main Activity's Layout

```xml
<?xml version="1.0" encoding="utf-8"?>
<LinearLayout xmlns:android=
        "http://schemas.android.com/apk/res/android"
    android:id="@+id/linearLayout"
    android:layout_width="fill_parent"
    android:layout_height="fill_parent"
    android:orientation="vertical" >

    <TextView
        android:id="@+id/textView1"
        android:layout_width="wrap_content"
        android:layout_height="wrap_content"
        android:text="@string/main_activity" >
    </TextView>

    <Button
        android:id="@+id/button1"
        android:layout_width="wrap_content"
        android:layout_height="wrap_content"
        android:onClick="onShowListClick"
        android:text="@string/show_list" >
    </Button>

</LinearLayout>
```

As always, you can download this chapter's Android app from the book's website (www.allmycode.com/Java4Android). But if you create the app from scratch, you can create most of Listing 12-10 by dragging and dropping items into Eclipse's graphical layout.

By default, Eclipse doesn't create an android:id attribute when you drag a LinearLayout or a RelativeLayout onto the Graphical Layout pane. But, as you can see in the next section, you need a way to refer back to the overall layout in this app's main activity. To create the code in Listing 12-10, you add your own android:id attribute to the code's LinearLayout element, either by right-clicking (in Windows) or Control-clicking (on the Mac) the layout on the Graphical Layout tab or typing the words android:id="@+id/linearLayout" on the activity_main.xml tab.

In this app example, the layout's TextView element is mere eye candy. The only interesting widget in Listing 12-10 is the button. When the user clicks the button, Android calls your main activity's onShowListClick method.

Both standard Oracle Java and Android Java have layouts. But the kinds of layouts that come with standard Java are different from the kinds that come with Android Java. For example, Android's LinearLayout is similar to (but not identical to) standard Java's FlowLayout. Android's FrameLayout is something like two of standard Java's layouts: CardLayout and OverlayLayout. Standard Java's BorderLayout has no direct counterpart in Android. But, in Android, you can achieve the same effect as a BorderLayout by combining some of Android's existing layouts or by creating your own custom layout.

The app's main activity

In Chapter 5, I introduce the lifecycle of an Android activity. Unlike a standard Java program, an Android activity has no main method. Instead, the Android operating system calls the activity's onCreate, onStart, and onResume methods.

Listing 12-11 contains the code for the app's main activity (refer to Figure 12-10). The MainActivity class in Listing 12-11 has all three lifecycle methods — onCreate, onStart and onResume, although you see only onCreate in Listing 12-11. The other two lifecycle methods (onStart and onResume) come quietly as a result of extending Android's Activity class.

Listing 12-11:   The Main Activity's Java Code

```java
package com.allmycode.lists;

import android.app.Activity;
import android.content.Intent;
import android.os.Bundle;
import android.view.View;
import android.widget.CheckBox;
import android.widget.LinearLayout;

public class MainActivity extends Activity {
  static CheckBox[] checkBoxes = new CheckBox[5];

  @Override
  public void onCreate(Bundle savedInstanceState) {
    super.onCreate(savedInstanceState);
    setContentView(R.layout.activity_main);
    LinearLayout layout =
        (LinearLayout) findViewById(R.id.linearLayout);

    for (int i = 0; i < 5; i++) {
      checkBoxes[i] = new CheckBox(this);
      layout.addView(checkBoxes[i]);
    }
  }

  public void onShowListClick(View view) {
    Intent intent =
        new Intent(this, MyListActivity.class);
    startActivity(intent);
  }
}
```

The onCreate method in Listing 12-11 calls findViewById to locate the layout on the activity's screen. After assigning the result to the layout variable, the onCreate method's for loop adds five check boxes to layout. In the CheckBox constructor call . . .

> Hey, wait a minute! Don't I have to declare the five check boxes in the activity_main.xml file of Listing 12-10? Can I really add a widget to a layout using Java code? Yes, I can. To place a widget (a TextView, a Button, a CheckBox, or whatever) on the screen, I can either declare the widget in my activity_main.xml file or (as I do in Listing 12-11) call the layout's addView method in my Java code.

> Most Android developers agree that the activity_main.xml route is often the better way to go. After all, the widgets on a screen are just

"there" all at once. They don't usually appear one by one, as though someone commands them into existence. But creating check boxes with Java code is particularly good for this chapter's sample app, especially because I want to consider the check boxes as numbered from 0 to 4.

Anyway, in the `CheckBox` constructor call, the parameter `this` represents the app's main activity. When you create a widget in an Android app, you do so within a *context*, which is a pile of information about the environment in which a widget lives. A context includes facts such as an activity's package name, the values in the activity's `strings.xml` file, and a list of files associated with the activity.

Now here's the strange part: Android's `Activity` class is a subclass of Android's `Context` class. In other words. every activity *is* a context. In the `CheckBox` constructor in Listing 12-11, passing `this` to the constructor means that I'm passing a context to the constructor. For all the Android code that I've written, I've never gotten used to thinking of an activity as a kind of context. But the `android.app.Activity` class is a subclass of a subclass of a subclass of the `android.context.Context` class. So it's true. I can pass my main activity to the `CheckBox` constructor in Listing 12-11.

The `onShowListClick` method in Listing 12-11 responds to the click of the Show the List button in Figure 12-10. In that method's body, the call to `startActivity(intent)` makes a second activity replace the main activity. The main activity becomes *stopped* (that is, hidden) and another activity (an instance of the `MyListActivity` class) takes over the device's screen.

Android uses `Intent` objects to transition from one activity to another. The `Intent` object in Listing 12-11 is called an *explicit intent* because the name of the new activity's class (`MyListActivity`) is in the intent's constructor.

The alternative to an explicit intent is an *implicit intent*. With an implicit intent, you don't provide the new activity's class name. Instead, you provide information about the kinds of things you want the new activity to be able to do. When you call `startActivity` with an implicit intent, Android goes searching around the user's device for any activity (in your app or in other people's apps) that can do the kinds of things you want done. For example, with the intent `new Intent(Intent.ACTION_VIEW, "http://www.allmycode. com")`, Android searches for a web browser activity — an activity that can view this book's website. Anyway, don't get me started on Android's implicit intents. They can be extremely complicated. (Okay, if you insist, I describe implicit intents in great detail in my book *Android Application Development All-in-One For Dummies,* published by John Wiley & Sons, Inc.)

The app's List Activity

When the code in Listing 12-11 calls `startActivity(intent)`, an instance of the `MyListActivity` takes over the user's screen. The code for the `MyListActivity` class is in Listing 12-12, and the activity's screen is pictured earlier, in Figure 12-11.

Listing 12-12:   The App's List Activity

```
package com.allmycode.lists;

import java.util.ArrayList;

import android.app.ListActivity;
import android.os.Bundle;
import android.widget.ArrayAdapter;

public class MyListActivity extends ListActivity {

  public void onCreate(Bundle savedInstanceState) {
    super.onCreate(savedInstanceState);

    ArrayList<Integer> listItems =
        new ArrayList<Integer>();
    for (int i = 0; i < 5; i++) {
      if (MainActivity.checkBoxes[i].isChecked()) {
        listItems.add(i);
      }
    }

    setListAdapter(new ArrayAdapter<Integer>(this,
        R.layout.my_list_layout, listItems));
  }
}
```

Android's `ListActivity` class is a subclass of the `Activity` class. So the class described in Listing 12-12 is a kind of activity. In particular, a `ListActivity` displays one thing after another, each in its own slot. The screen shown in Figure 12-11 displays three slots.

In a `ListActivity`, each slot can consist of one row or two rows or as many rows as the developer sees fit. The number of rows is determined by the layout of things in yet another XML file. On the screen shown in Figure 12-11, each slot has only one row.

When you declare a `ListActivity`, you call Android's `setListAdapter` method. In the call to `setListAdapter` in Listing 12-12, you have three parameters:

✔ **You provide a context.**

In Listing 12-12, I provide the familiar `this` context.

✔ **You point to an XML file in your application's `res/layout` directory.**

In Listing 12-12 I point to the `my_list_layout.xml` file.

✔ **You provide a collection of items, each to be displayed in its own slot.**

In Listing 12-12, I provide `listItems`, which I declare to be an `ArrayList` of `Integer` values.

With respect to the layout file, Android treats a `ListActivity` a bit differently from the way it treats an ordinary `Activity`. To display a `ListActivity` (like the activity in Listing 12-12), Android reuses a layout XML file over and over again. Android reuses the layout file once for each of the items being displayed. In other words, the layout file for a `ListActivity` doesn't describe the entire screen. Instead, the layout file for a `ListActivity` describes only one of the many slots on the user's screen.

The `my_list_layout.xml` file for this chapter's app is shown in Listing 12-13. That XML file contains a single text view. So in Figure 12-11, each item in the list (each number beneath the "Using Collections" title) is in a single text view. Each slot in the list has a single text view. That's the way a `ListActivity` works.

Listing 12-13:   The R.layout.my_list_layout.xml File

```xml
<?xml version="1.0" encoding="utf-8"?>
<TextView xmlns:android=
        "http://schemas.android.com/apk/res/android"
    android:id="@+id/identView"
    android:layout_width="wrap_content"
    android:layout_height="wrap_content">
</TextView>
```

The items displayed in Figure 12-11 correspond to the selected check boxes in Figure 12-10. (**Remember:** When Java numbers the items in a collection, Java starts with 0.) To get the right numbers in `MyListActivity`, I fill the `listItems` collection in Listing 12-12. A `for` statement marches through the main activity's `checkBoxes` collection. The `for` statement adds the number i to `listItems` whenever the call to `checkBoxes[i].isChecked()` returns `true`.

For any check box that isn't selected, the call to `checkBoxes[i].is Checked()` returns `false`. So that `i` value doesn't get into the `listItems` collection. But for any check box that's selected, the call to `checkBoxes[i].isChecked()` returns `true`. That `i` value gets into the `listItems` collection and is displayed on the user's screen.

The app's AndroidManifest.xml file

When Eclipse creates a new Android project, Eclipse also offers to create a main activity. If you accept the offer to create a main activity, Eclipse puts an `activity` element in the project's `AndroidManifest.xml` file. This happens behind the scenes. So, when you add a second activity to an app (such as the activity in Listing 12-12) you can easily forget to manually add an `activity` element.

Listing 12-14 contains the `AndroidManifest.xml` file for this chapter's Android app:

Listing 12-14:   The AndroidManifest.xml file

```xml
<?xml version="1.0" encoding="utf-8"?>
<manifest xmlns:android=
    "http://schemas.android.com/apk/res/android"
  package="com.allmycode.lists"
  android:versionCode="1"
  android:versionName="1.0" >

  <uses-sdk
    android:minSdkVersion="8"
    android:targetSdkVersion="15" />

  <application
    android:icon="@drawable/icon"
    android:label="@string/app_name" >

    <activity
      android:name=".MainActivity"
      android:label="@string/app_name" >
      <intent-filter>
        <action android:name=
            "android.intent.action.MAIN" />
        <category android:name=
            "android.intent.category.LAUNCHER" />
      </intent-filter>
```

(continued)

Listing 12-14 *(continued)*

```
    </activity>

    <activity android:name=".MyListActivity" />

  </application>

</manifest>
```

Notice that the code in Listing 12-14 contains two `activity` elements.

- ✔ The first `activity` element's `android:name` attribute has value `.MainActivity`.

  Eclipse creates this first element when you create the Android project, As the `android:name` attribute indicates, this element applies to the app's `MainActivity` class. Inside the `activity` element, the `intent-filter` element indicates that this activity's code can be the starting point of the app's execution, and this activity's icon can appear on the device's Apps screen.

- ✔ The second activity element's `android:name` attribute has value `.MyListActivity`.

  If you create this chapter's Android app on your own, you must edit the app's `AndroidManifest.xml` file and type this code by hand. As the `android:name` attribute indicates, this element applies to the app's `MyListActivity` class (refer to Listing 12-12).

  The `MyListActivity` class isn't the starting point of the app's execution, and the user shouldn't be able to launch this activity from the device's Apps screen. So the second `activity` element doesn't have the MAIN and LAUNCHER information that's in the listing's first `activity` element.

  In fact, I've rigged this app so that `MyListActivity` requires no `intent-filter` information, and no information at all between the `activity` element's start and end tags. So, in Listing 12-14, the second `activity` element has no start and end tags. Instead, this `activity` element has one empty element tag.

For more information about start tags, end tags, and empty element tags, see Chapter 4.

If you add an activity's Java code to an Android application, you must also add an `activity` element to the application's `AndroidManifest.xml` file.

Chapter 13

An Android Social Media App

In This Chapter

▶ Posting on Twitter with Android code

▶ Tweeting with your app on a user's behalf

▶ Using Java exceptions to get out of a jam

reader from Vancouver (in British Columbia, Canada) writes:

> "Hello, Barry. I just thought I would ask that you include the area that seems to get attention from app developers: programs connecting with social sites. I look forward to reading the new book! Best regards, David."

Well, David, you've inspired me to create a Twitter app. This chapter's example does two things: Post a new tweet, and get a twitter user's timeline. The app can perform many more Twitter tasks — for example, search for tweets, look for users, view trends, check friends and followers, gather suggestions, and do lots of other things that Twitter users want done. For simplicity, though, I have the app perform only two tasks: tweet and display a timeline.

I can summarize the essence of this chapter's Twitter code in two short statements. To post a tweet, the app executes

```
twitter.updateStatus("This is my tweet.");
```

And, to display a user's timeline, the app executes

```
List<twitter4j.Status> statuses =
    twitter.getUserTimeline("allmycode");
```

Of course, these two statements only serve as a summary, and a summary is never the same as the material it summarizes. Imagine standing on the street in Times Square and shouting the statement "Twitter dot update status: 'This is my tweet.'" Nothing good happens because you're issuing the correct command in the wrong context. In the same way, the context surrounding a call to twitter.updateStatus in an app matters an awful lot.

This chapter covers all the context surrounding your calls to `twitter.updateStatus` and `twitter.getUserTimeline`. In the process, you can read about Java's exceptions — a vital feature that's available to all Java programmers.

The Twitter App's Files

You can import this chapter's code from my website (http://allmycode.com/Java4Android) by following the instructions in Chapter 2. As is true for any Android app, this chapter's Eclipse project contains about 40 files in about 30 different folders. In this chapter, I concentrate on the project's `MainActivity.java` file. But a few other files require some attention.

The Twitter4J API jar file

Android has no built-in support for communicating with Twitter. Yes, the raw materials are contained in Android's libraries, but to deal with all of Twitter's requirements, someone has to paste together those raw materials in a useful way. Fortunately, several developers have done all the pasting and made their libraries available for use by others. The library that I use in this chapter is Twitter4J. Its website is `http://twitter4j.org`.

Chapter 4 describes the role of `.jar` files in Java program development. For this chapter's example to work, your project must include a `.jar` file containing the Twitter4J libraries. If you've successfully imported this book's code into Eclipse, the 13-01 project contains the necessary `.jar` file.

If you're creating this chapter's example on your own, or if you're having trouble with the project's existing `.jar` files, you can add the Twitter4J libraries by following these steps:

1. **Visit** `http://twitter4j.org`.

2. **Find the link to download the latest stable version of Twitter4J.**

   To run this chapter's example, I use Twitter4J version 3.0.3. If you download a later version, it'll probably work. But I make no promises about the backward compatibility, forward compatibility, or sideward compatibility of the various Twitter4J versions. If my example doesn't run properly for you, you can search the Twitter4J site for a download link to version 3.0.3.

3. **Click the link to download the Twitter4J software.**

   The file that I downloaded is `twitter4j-3.0.3.zip`.

4. **Look for a** `twitter4j-core.jar` **file inside the downloaded** `.zip` **file.**

   In the `.zip` file that I downloaded, I found a file named `twitter4j-core-3.0.3.jar`.

5. **Extract the** `twitter4j-core.jar` **file to a place on your computer's hard drive.**

   Any location on your hard drive is okay, as long as you remember where you put the `twitter4j-core.jar` file.

6. **In Eclipse's Package Explorer, right-click (or Control-click on a Mac) this chapter's project.**

7. **In the resulting context menu, select Properties.**

   Eclipse's Properties dialog box appears.

8. **On the left side of the Properties dialog box, select Java Build Path.**

9. **In the middle of the Properties dialog box, select the Libraries tab.**

10. **On the right side of the Properties dialog box, click the Add External JARs button.**

    Eclipse displays the JAR Selection dialog box.

11. **In the JAR Selection dialog box, navigate to the directory containing your** `twitter4j-core.jar` **file.**

    What I refer to as your `twitter4j-core.jar` file is probably named `twitter4j-core-3.0.3.jar` or similar.

12. **Select the** `twitter4j-core.jar` **file and close the JAR Selection dialog box.**

    Doing so adds your `twitter4j-core.jar` file to the list of items on the Libraries tab.

13. **In the middle of the Properties dialog box, switch from the Libraries tab to the Order and Export tab.**

    The Order and Export tab contains a list of items, one of which is your `twitter4j-core.jar` file.

14. **Make sure that the check box next to your** `twitter4j-core.jar` **file is selected.**

    Doing so ensures that this `.jar` file is uploaded to whatever device you use to test the application. Without the check mark indicating the selection, Eclipse compiles the code using the `.jar` file but doesn't bother sending the `.jar` file to an emulator or to your phone. It's quite frustrating.

15. Select your `twitter4j-core.jar` **item on the Order and Export tab. Then, on the right side of the Properties dialog box, click the Up button a few times.**

Keep clicking the Up button until your `twitter4j-core.jar` file is at the top of the Order and Export tab's list.

16. Click OK to dismiss the Properties dialog box.

If you look at Eclipse's Package Explorer, your project now has a Referenced Libraries branch. When you expand the Referenced Libraries branch, you see a branch for your `twitter4j-core.jar` file.

The manifest file

Every Android app has an `AndroidManifest.xml` file. Listing 13-1 contains the `AndroidManifest.xml` file for this chapter's Twitter app.

Listing 13-1:   The AndroidManifest.xml File

```
<?xml version="1.0" encoding="utf-8"?>
<manifest xmlns:android=
    "http://schemas.android.com/apk/res/android"
  package="com.allmycode.twitter"
  android:versionCode="1"
  android:versionName="1.0" >

  <uses-sdk
    android:minSdkVersion="8"
    android:targetSdkVersion="17" />
  <uses-permission android:name=
    „android.permission.INTERNET"/>

  <application
    android:allowBackup="true"
    android:icon="@drawable/ic_launcher"
    android:label="@string/app_name"
    android:theme="@style/AppTheme" >
    <activity
      android:name="com.allmycode.twitter.MainActivity"
      android:label="@string/app_name"
      android:windowSoftInputMode="adjustPan" >
      <intent-filter>
        <action android:name=
            "android.intent.action.MAIN" />
        <category android:name=
            "android.intent.category.LAUNCHER" />
      </intent-filter>
```

```
        </activity>
    </application>

</manifest>
```

When you use Eclipse to create a new Android application project, Eclipse writes most of the code in Listing 13-1 automatically. For this chapter's project, I have to add two additional snippets of code:

- ✔ **The** `windowSoftInputMode` **attribute tells Android what to do when the user activates the onscreen keyboard.**

  The `adjustPan` value tells Android not to squash together all my screen's widgets. (Take my word for it: The app looks ugly without this `adjustPan` value.)

- ✔ **The** `uses-permission` **element warns Android that my app requires Internet connectivity.**

  When a user installs an app that uses the `android.permission.INTERNET` permission, Android warns the user that the app requires full network access. Yes, a large percentage of users ignore this kind of warning. But the app can't access Twitter without the permission. If you forget to add this `uses-permission` element (as I often do), the app doesn't obey any of your Twitter commands. And when your app fails to contact the Twitter servers, Android often displays only cryptic, unhelpful error messages.

The error messages from an unsuccessful run of your Android app range from extremely helpful to extremely unhelpful. One way or another, it never hurts to read these messages. You can find most of the messages in Eclipse's Console view or in Eclipse's LogCat view.

For more information about `AndroidManifest.xml` files, see Chapter 4.

The main activity's layout file

Chapter 4 introduces the use of a layout file to describe the look of an activity on the screen. The layout file for this chapter's example has no extraordinary qualities. I include it in Listing 13-2 for completeness. As usual, you can import this chapter's code from my website (`http://allmycode.com/Java4Android`). But if you're living large and creating the app on your own from scratch, you can copy the contents of Listing 13-2 to the project's `res/layout/activity_main.xml` file. Alternatively, you can use Eclipse's toolset to drag and drop, point and click, or type and tap your way to the graphical layout shown in Figure 13-1.

Listing 13-2:   The Layout File

```xml
<RelativeLayout xmlns:android=
    "http://schemas.android.com/apk/res/android"
  xmlns:tools="http://schemas.android.com/tools"
  android:layout_width="match_parent"
  android:layout_height="match_parent"
  android:paddingBottom="@dimen/activity_vertical_margin"
  android:paddingLeft="@dimen/activity_horizontal_margin"
  android:paddingRight=
      "@dimen/activity_horizontal_margin"
  android:paddingTop="@dimen/activity_vertical_margin"
  tools:context=".MainActivity" >

  <TextView
    android:id="@+id/textView2"
    android:layout_width="wrap_content"
    android:layout_height="wrap_content"
    android:layout_alignBaseline="@+id/editTextUsername"
    android:layout_alignBottom="@+id/editTextUsername"
    android:layout_alignLeft="@+id/editTextTweet"
    android:text="@string/at_sign"
    android:textAppearance=
        "?android:attr/textAppearanceLarge" />

  <EditText
    android:id="@+id/editTextUsername"
    android:layout_width="wrap_content"
    android:layout_height="wrap_content"
    android:layout_above="@+id/timelineButton"
    android:layout_toRightOf="@+id/textView2"
    android:ems="10"
    android:hint="@string/type_username_here" />

  <TextView
    android:id="@+id/textViewTimeline"
    android:layout_width="wrap_content"
    android:layout_height="wrap_content"
    android:layout_alignLeft="@+id/timelineButton"
    android:layout_below="@+id/timelineButton"
    android:maxLines="100"
    android:scrollbars="vertical"
    android:text="@string/timeline_here" />

  <Button
    android:id="@+id/timelineButton"
    android:layout_width="wrap_content"
    android:layout_height="wrap_content"
    android:layout_alignLeft="@+id/textView2"
    android:layout_centerVertical="true"
    android:onClick="onTimelineButtonClick"
    android:text="@string/timeline" />
```

```
<Button
   android:id="@+id/tweetButton"
   android:layout_width="wrap_content"
   android:layout_height="wrap_content"
   android:layout_above="@+id/editTextUsername"
   android:layout_alignLeft="@+id/editTextTweet"
   android:layout_marginBottom="43dp"
   android:onClick="onTweetButtonClick"
   android:text="@string/tweet" />

<EditText
   android:id="@+id/editTextTweet"
   android:layout_width="wrap_content"
   android:layout_height="wrap_content"
   android:layout_above="@+id/tweetButton"
   android:layout_alignParentLeft="true"
   android:layout_marginLeft="14dp"
   android:ems="10"
   android:hint="@string/type_your_tweet_here" />

<TextView
   android:id="@+id/textViewCountChars"
   android:layout_width="wrap_content"
   android:layout_height="wrap_content"
   android:layout_alignBaseline="@+id/tweetButton"
   android:layout_alignBottom="@+id/tweetButton"
   android:layout_toRightOf="@+id/timelineButton"
   android:text="@string/zero" />

</RelativeLayout>
```

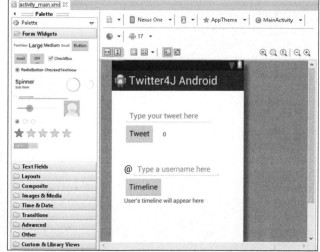

Figure 13-1:
The graphical layout of the main activity's screen.

The twitter4j.properties file

This chapter's example involves a file that you don't find in most other apps. It's a file of the kind you see in Listing 13-3.

Listing 13-3: A Fake twitter4j.properties File (Yes, It's Fake!)

```
oauth.consumerKey=01qid0qod5drmwVJIkU1dg
oauth.consumerSecret=TudvMiX1h37WsIvq173SNWnRIhI0ALnGfS1
oauth.accessToken=1385541-ueSEFeFgwQJ8vUpfy6LBv6FibSfm5aXF
oauth.accessTokenSecret=G2FXeXYLSHPI7XlVdMsS2eGfIaKU6nJc
```

The `twitter4j.properties` file lives directly inside your project's `src` directory, as shown in Figures 13-2 and 13-3. Each line of the file gives your app important information for communicating with Twitter.

Figure 13-2: The location of `twitter4j.properties` on a Windows computer.

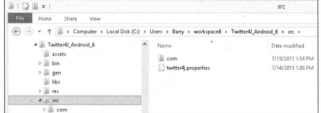

Figure 13-3: The location of `twitter4j.properties` on a Mac.

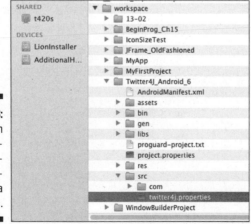

When you run this chapter's example, the code has to talk to Twitter on your behalf. And normally, to talk to Twitter, you supply a username and password. But should you be sharing your Twitter password with any app that comes your way? Probably not. Your password is similar to the key to your house. You don't want to give copies of your house key to strangers, and you don't want an Android app to remember your Twitter password.

So how can your app post a tweet without having your Twitter password? One answer is *OAuth,* a standardized way to have apps log on to host computers. If the gobbledygook in Listing 13-3 is copied correctly, the app acquires revocable permission to act on behalf of the Twitter user. And the app never gets hold of the user's password.

Now, here come the disclaimers:

- **A discussion of how OAuth works, and why it's safer than using ordinary Twitter passwords, is far beyond the scope of this book.**

    I don't pretend to explain OAuth and its mysteries in this chapter.

- **True app security requires more than a simple** `twitter4j.properties` **file.**

    The goal of this chapter is to show how an app can talk to a social media site. In the code, I use OAuth and Twitter4J commands to achieve that goal as quickly as I can, without necessarily showing you the "right" way to do it. For more comprehensive coverage of OAuth, visit `http://oauth.net`: the official website for OAuth developers.

- **The codes in Listing 13-3 don't work.**

    I'm not prepared to share my own OAuth codes with the general public, so to create Listing 13-3, I took the general outline of my real `twitter4j.properites` file and then ran my fingers over the keyboard to replace most of the characters.

    To run this chapter's app, you have to create your own set of OAuth keys and copy them to your `twitter4j.properties` file. The next section outlines the steps.

Getting OAuth codes

For your Android app to communicate with Twitter servers, you need your own OAuth codes. To get them, follow this section's steps.

The following instructions apply to the Twitter web pages for developers at the time of this book's publication. Twitter might change the design of its website at any time without notice. (At any rate, it won't notify me!)

1. **Sign in to your Twitter user account (or register for an account if you don't already have one).**

2. **Visit** `https://dev.twitter.com/apps/new`.

   If the stars are aligned harmoniously, you should see Twitter's Create an Application page.

3. **On the Create an Application page, fill in all required fields along with the (misleadingly optional) Callback URL field.**

   When I visit the page, I see the Name field, the Description field, the Website field, and the Callback URL field. All but the Callback URL field are listed as being required.

   Typing your name in the Name field is a no-brainer. But what do you use for the other fields? After all, you aren't creating an industrial-strength Android app. You're creating only a test app — an app to help you see how to use Twitter4J.

   The good news is that almost anything you type in the Description field is okay. The same is true for the Website and Callback URL fields, as long as you type things that look like real URLs.

   I've never tried typing a `twitter.com` URL in either the Website or Callback URL fields, but I suspect that typing a `twitter.com` URL doesn't work.

   To communicate with Twitter via an Android app, you need a callback URL. In other words, for this chapter's example, the callback URL isn't optional. Neither the Website field nor the Callback URL field has to point to a real web page. But you must fill in those two fields.

   The Callback URL field isn't marked as being required. Nevertheless, you must type a URL in the Callback URL field.

4. **After agreeing to the terms, and doing the other stuff to prove that you're a good person, click the Create Your Twitter Application button.**

   Doing so brings you to a page where you see some details about your new application — the Details tab, in other words. On this page, you see four important items: your app's access level, consumer key, and consumer secret and a button that offers to create your app's access token.

   In the OAuth world, an app whose code communicates with Twitter's servers is a *consumer*. To identify itself as a trustworthy consumer, an app must send passwords to Twitter's servers. In OAuth terminology, these passwords are called the *consumer key* and the *consumer secret*.

5. **On that same web page, select your application's Settings tab.**

6. **Among the settings, look for a choice of access types. Change your app's access from Read Only (the default) to Read, Write and Access Direct Messages.**

   For this toy application, you select Read, Write and Access Direct Messages — the most permissive access model that's available. This option prevents your app from hitting brick walls because of access problems. But when you develop a real-life application, you do the opposite — you select the least permissive option that suits your application's requirements.

   First change your app's access level, and then create the app's access token (as explained in Step 9). Don't create the access token before changing the access level. If you try to change the access level after you've created the access token, your app won't work. What's worse, the `dev.twitter.com` page won't warn you about the problem. Believe me — I've wasted hours of my life on this Twitter quirk.

7. **Click the button that offers to update your application's settings.**

   Doing so changes your app's access level to Read, Write and Access Direct Messages.

8. **Return to your application's Details tab.**

   I'm not thrilled with the way Twitter's developer site works. A title near the top of the Settings tab reads *Application Details*, and there's no title near the top of the Details tab. Anyway, find the Details tab and click on it.

9. **Click the button that offers to create your access token.**

   After doing so, your app's Details tab now displays your app's access token and the access token secret, in addition to your app's access level, consumer key, and consumer secret.

10. **Copy the four codes (Consumer Key, Consumer Secret, Access Token, and Access Token Secret) from your app's Details tab to the appropriate lines in your** `twitter4j.properties` **file.**

   Whew! You're done creating your `twitter4j.properites` file!

The Application's Main Activity

What's a *Java Programming For Android Developers For Dummies* book without some Java code? Listing 13-4 contains the Twitter app's Java code.

Listing 13-4:   The MainActivity.java file

```java
package com.allmycode.twitter;

import java.util.List;

import twitter4j.Twitter;
import twitter4j.TwitterException;
import twitter4j.TwitterFactory;
import android.app.Activity;
import android.os.AsyncTask;
import android.os.Bundle;
import android.text.Editable;
import android.text.TextWatcher;
import android.text.method.ScrollingMovementMethod;
import android.view.View;
import android.widget.EditText;
import android.widget.TextView;

public class MainActivity extends Activity {
  TextView textViewCountChars, textViewTimeline;
  EditText editTextTweet, editTextUsername;

  @Override
  protected void onCreate(Bundle savedInstanceState) {
    super.onCreate(savedInstanceState);
    setContentView(R.layout.activity_main);
    editTextTweet =
        (EditText) findViewById(R.id.editTextTweet);
    editTextTweet.addTextChangedListener
                                (new MyTextWatcher());
    textViewCountChars =
        (TextView) findViewById(R.id.textViewCountChars);
    editTextUsername =
        (EditText) findViewById(R.id.editTextUsername);
    textViewTimeline =
        (TextView) findViewById(R.id.textViewTimeline);
    textViewTimeline.setMovementMethod
                        (new ScrollingMovementMethod());
  }

  // Button click listeners

  public void onTweetButtonClick(View view) {
    new MyAsyncTaskTweet().execute
                  (editTextTweet.getText().toString());
  }

  public void onTimelineButtonClick(View view) {
    new MyAsyncTaskTimeline().execute
              (editTextUsername.getText().toString());
```

```
}

// Count characters in the Tweet field

class MyTextWatcher implements TextWatcher {

  @Override
  public void afterTextChanged(Editable s) {
    textViewCountChars.setText
              ("" + editTextTweet.getText().length());
  }

  @Override
  public void beforeTextChanged(CharSequence s,
                   int start, int count, int after) {
  }

  @Override
  public void onTextChanged(CharSequence s,
                   int start, int before, int count) {
  }

}

// The AsyncTask classes

public class MyAsyncTaskTweet
           extends AsyncTask<String, Void, String> {

  @Override
  protected String doInBackground(String... tweet) {
    String result = "";

    Twitter twitter = TwitterFactory.getSingleton();
    try {
      twitter.updateStatus(tweet[0]);
      result =
          getResources().getString(R.string.success);
    } catch (TwitterException twitterException) {
      result =
          getResources().getString(R.string.failure);
    }

    return result;
  }

  @Override
  protected void onPostExecute(String result) {
    editTextTweet.setHint(result);
    editTextTweet.setText("");
  }
```

(continued)

Listing 13-4 *(continued)*

```
    }

    public class MyAsyncTaskTimeline
                extends AsyncTask<String, Void, String> {

      @Override
      protected String doInBackground(String... username) {
        String result = new String("");
        List<twitter4j.Status> statuses = null;

        Twitter twitter = TwitterFactory.getSingleton();
        try {
          statuses = twitter.getUserTimeline(username[0]);

        } catch (TwitterException twitterException) {
          twitterException.printStackTrace();
        }

        for (twitter4j.Status status : statuses) {
          result += status.getText();
          result += "\n";
        }
        return result;
      }

      @Override
      protected void onPostExecute(String result) {
        editTextUsername.setText("");
        textViewTimeline.setText(result);
      }
    }
  }
```

Twitter's network protocols require that the device that runs this chapter's app is set to the correct time. I don't know how correct the "correct time" has to be, but I've had lots of trouble running the app on emulators. Either my emulator is set to get the time automatically from the network (and it gets the time incorrectly) or I set the time manually and the *seconds* part of the time isn't close enough. One way or another, the error message that comes back from Twitter (usually specifying a null authentication challenge) isn't helpful. So I avoid lots of hassle by avoiding emulators whenever I test this code. Rather than run an emulator, I set my phone or tablet to get the network time automatically. Then I run this chapter's app on that phone or tablet. I recommend that you do the same.

When you run the app, you see two areas. One area contains a Tweet button; the other area contains a Timeline button, as shown in Figure 13-4.

Figure 13-4:
The main
activity in
its pristine
state.

In Figure 13-4, the text in both text fields is light gray. This happens because I use `android:hint` attributes in Listing 13-2. A *hint* is a bunch of characters that appear only when a text field is otherwise empty. When the user clicks inside the text field, or types any text inside the text field, the hint disappears.

Type a tweet into the text field on top, and then press the Tweet button, as shown in Figure 13-5. If your attempt to tweet is successful, the message `Success!` replaces the tweet in the text field, as shown in Figure 13-6. If, for one reason or another, your tweet can't be posted, the message `Failed to tweet` replaces the tweet in the text field, as shown in Figure 13-7.

Figure 13-5:
The user
types a
tweet.

Twitter4J Android

Don't retweet this

Tweet   18

Figure 13-6:
The app
indicates a
successful
tweet.

Twitter4J Android

Success!

Tweet   0

Figure 13-7:
The app
brings bad
tidings to
the user.

Next, type a username in the lower text field, and then click Timeline. If all
goes well, a list of the user's most recent tweets appears below the Timeline
button, as shown in Figure 13-8. You can scroll the list to see more of the
user's tweets.

Figure 13-8:
A user's
timeline.

The onCreate method

The `onCreate` method in Listing 13-4 calls `findViewById` to locate some of
the widgets declared in Listing 13-2.

For insight into the workings of Android's `findViewById` method, see
Chapter 11.

The `onCreate` method also creates a `MyTextWatcher` instance to listen
for changes in the field where the user types a tweet. Android notifies the
`MyTextWatcher` instance whenever the user types characters in (or deletes
characters from) the app's `editTextTweet` field. Later in Listing 13-4, the
actual `TextChangedListener` class's `afterTextChanged` method counts

the number of characters in the `editTextTweet` field. The method displays the count in the tiny `textViewCountChars` field. (With the advent of Twitter, the number 140 has become quite important.)

This chapter's app doesn't do anything special if a user types more than 140 characters into the `editTextTweet` field. In a real-life app, I'd add code to handle 141 characters gracefully, but when I create sample apps, I like to keep the code as uncluttered as possible.

Android actually notifies the `MyTextWatcher` instance three times for each text change in the `editTextTweet` field — once before changing the text, once during the change of the text, and once after changing the text. In Listing 13-4, I don't make `MyTextWatcher` execute any statements before or during the changing of the text. In `MyTextWatcher`, the only method whose body contains statements is the `afterTextChanged` method. Even so, in order to implement Android's `TextWatcher` interface, the `MyTextWatcher` class must provide bodies for the `beforeTextChanged` and the `onTextChanged` methods.

Finally, in the `onCreate` method, the call to `setMovementMethod(new ScrollingMovementMethod())` permits scrolling on the list of items in a user's timeline.

The button listener methods

Listing 13-2 describes two buttons, each with its own `onClick` method. I declare the two methods in Listing 13-4 — the `onTweetButtonClick` method and the `onTimelineButtonClick` method. Each of the methods has a single statement in its body — a call to execute a newly constructed `AsyncTask` of some kind. Believe me, this is where the fun begins!

The trouble with threads

In Chapter 10, I describe the callback as the solution to all your activity's timing problems. Your activity wants to be alerted after a certain number of seconds passes. You can't stall the execution of your activity during those seconds. If you do, your activity is completely unresponsive to user input during those seconds. At best, users give your app a bad rating on Google Play; at worst, users pound on their screens, breaking the glass, blaming you, and sending you the repair bill.

Rather than put your activity to sleep for ten seconds, you create another class that sleeps on your activity's behalf. When the other class's nap is finished, that other class issues a callback to your original activity. Everything is hunky-dory except for what I say in Chapter 10, in a paragraph with the little Technical Stuff icon on it:

"Well, I must confess that the code in Listings 10-10 through 10-13 doesn't solve the responsiveness problem. To make the program more responsive, you use the interface tricks in Listings 10-10 through 10-13 and, in addition, you put TimerCommon in a thread of its own."

Chapter 10 is the wrong place to describe threads. So in Chapter 10, the discussion of activity timing ends with a disappointing thud. (Yes, I'm secure enough to admit it.) Creating a thread means executing several different pieces of code at the same time. For the Java developer, things become complicated in no time at all. Juggling several simultaneous pieces of code is like juggling several raw eggs: One way or another, you're sure to end up with egg on your face.

To help fix all this, the creators of Android developed a multi-threading framework. Within this framework, you bundle all your delicately timed code into a carefully defined box. This box contains all the ready-made structure for managing threads in a well-behaved way. Rather than worry about where to put your sleep method calls and how to change a field's text in a timely fashion, you simply plug certain statements into certain places in the box and let the box's ready-made structure take care of all the routine threading details.

This marvelous box, the miracle cure for all your activity-timing ills, belongs to Android's AsyncTask classes. To understand these classes, you need a bit of terminology explained:

- **Thread:** A bunch of statements to be executed in the order prescribed by the code

- **Multi-threaded code:** A bunch of statements in more than one thread

   Java executes each thread's statements in the prescribed order. But if your program contains two threads, Java might not execute all the statements in one thread before executing all the statements in the other thread. Instead, Java might intermingle execution of the statements in the two threads. For example, I ran the following code several times:

```
package com.allmycode.threads;

public class TwoThreads {

  public static void main(String[] args) {
    new OneThread().start();
    new AnotherThread().start();
  }
```

```
      }

class OneThread extends Thread {
  public void run() {
    System.out.print("1");
    System.out.print("2");
    System.out.print("3");
  }
}

class AnotherThread extends Thread {
  public void run() {
    System.out.print("A");
    System.out.print("B");
    System.out.print("C");
  }
}
```

The first time I ran the code, the output was 1AB23C. The second time, the output was 123ABC. The tenth time, the output was ABC123. The eleventh time, the output was 12AB3C. The output 1 always comes before the output 2 because the statements to output 1 and 2 are in the same thread. But you can't predict whether Java will display 1 or A first, because the statements to output 1 and A are in two different threads.

✔ **The UI thread:** The thread that displays widgets on the screen

In an Android program, your main activity runs primarily in the UI thread.

The "UI" in "UI Thread" stands for "user interface." Another name for the UI thread is the *main thread*. The use of this terminology predates the notion of a main activity in Android.

✔ **A background thread:** Any thread other than the UI thread

In an Android program, when you create an AsyncTask class, some of that class's code runs in a background thread.

In addition to all the terminology, you should know about two rules concerning threads:

✔ **Any time-consuming code should be in a background thread — not in the UI thread.**

If you put time-consuming code in the UI thread, the app responds sluggishly to the user's clicks and keystrokes. Needless to say, users don't like this. In Chapter 10, a call to sleep for ten seconds is time-consuming code. In this chapter, any access to data over the Internet (like posting a tweet or getting a Twitter user's timeline) is time-consuming code.

🖝 **Any code that modifies a property of the screen must be in the UI thread.**

If, in a background thread, you have code that modifies text on the screen, you're either gumming up the UI thread or creating code that doesn't compile. Either way, you don't want to do it.

Android's AsyncTask

A class that extends Android's `AsyncTask` looks like the outline in Listing 13-5.

Listing 13-5: The Outline of an AsyncTask Class

```
public class MyAsyncTaskName
    extends AsyncTask<Type1, Type2, Type3> {

    @Override
    protected void onPreExecute () {
        // Execute statements in the UI thread before the
        // starting background thread. For example, display
        // an empty progress bar.
    }

    @Override
    protected Type3 doInBackground(Type1... param1) {
        // Execute statements in the background thread.
        // For example, get info from Twitter.

        return resultValueOfType3;
    }

    @Override
    protected void onProgressUpdate(Type2... param) {
        // Update a progress bar (or some other kind of
        // progress indicator) during execution of the
        // background thread.
    }

    @Override
    protected void onPostExecute(Type3 resultValueOfType3) {
        // Execute statements in the UI thread after
        // finishing the statements in the background thread.
        // For example, display info from Twitter in the
        // activity's widgets.
    }
}
```

When you create an `AsyncTask` class, Android executes each method in its appropriate thread. In the `doInBackground` method (refer to Listing 13-5), you put code that's too time-consuming for the UI thread. So Android executes the `doInBackground` method in the background thread. (Big surprise!) In Listing 13-5's other three methods (`onPreExecute`, `onProgressUpdate`, and `onPostExecute`), you put code that updates the widgets on the device's screen. So Android executes these methods in the UI thread, as shown in Figure 13-9.

Android also makes your life easier by coordinating the execution of an `AsyncTask` class's methods. For example, `onPostExecute` doesn't change the value of a screen widget until after the execution of `doInBackground`. (Refer to Figure 13-9.) In this chapter's Twitter app, the `onPostExecute` method doesn't update the screen until after the `doInBackground` method has fetched a user's timeline from Twitter. The user doesn't see a timeline until the timeline is ready to be seen.

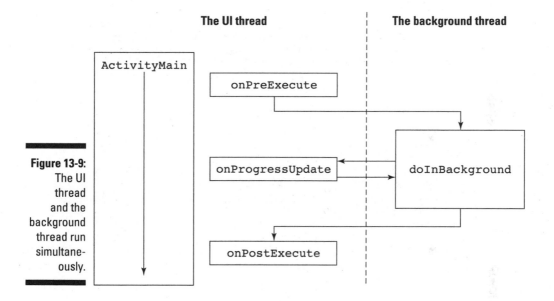

Figure 13-9: The UI thread and the background thread run simultaneously.

You'd think that with all this coordination of method calls, you lose any benefit from having more than one thread. But that's not the case. Because the `doInBackground` method runs outside the UI thread, your activity can respond to the user's clicks and drags while the `doInBackground` method waits for a response from the Twitter servers. It's all good.

My Twitter app's AsyncTask classes

Listing 13-5 contains four methods. But in Listing 13-4, I override only two of the methods — `doInBackground` and `onPostExecute`. The `MyAsyncTaskTweet` and `MyAsyncTaskTimeline` classes in Listing 13-4 inherit the other two methods from their superclass.

Notice (in Listings 13-4 and 13-5) the use of generic type names in an `AsyncTask` class. An `AsyncTask` is versatile enough to deal with all types of values. In Listing 13-4, the first generic parameter of `MyAsyncTaskTweet` has type `String` because a tweet is a string of as many as 140 characters. But someone else's `AsyncTask` might accept an image or a music file as its input. So when you create an `AsyncTask` class, you "fill in the blanks" by putting the following three type names inside the angle brackets:

- ✔ **The first type name (*Type1* in Listing 13-5) stands for a value (or values) that you pass to the** `doInBackground` **method.**

  The `doInBackground` method, with its `varargs` parameter, uses these values to decide what has to be done.

- ✔ **The second type name (*Type2* in Listing 13-5) stands for a value (or values) that mark the background thread's progress in completing its work.**

  This chapter's example has no progress bar, nor a progress indicator of any kind. So in Listing 13-4, the second type name is `Void`.

  In Java, the `Void` class is a wrapper class for the `void` value. Put that in your black hole of nothingness!

- ✔ **The third type name (*Type3* in Listing 13-5) stands for a value that the** `doInBackground` **method returns and that the** `onPostExecute` **method takes as a parameter.**

  In the `doInBackground` method of Listing 13-4, this third type name is `String`. It's `String` because the `doInBackground` method returns the word `"Success!"` or the words `"Failed to tweet"`, and the `onPostExecute` method displays these words in the screen's `editTextTweet` field.

Figure 13-10 summarizes the way generic type names influence the methods' types in Listing 13-4, and Figure 13-11 summarizes how values move from one place to another in the `MyAsyncTaskTweet` class of Listing 13-4.

An `AsyncTask` can be fairly complicated. But when you compare Android's `AsyncTask` to the do-it-yourself threading alternatives, the `AsyncTask` idea isn't bad at all. In fact, when you get a little practice and create a few of your own `AsyncTask` classes, you get used to thinking that way. The whole business starts to feel quite natural.

```
new MyAsyncTaskTweet().execute(editTextTweet.getText().toString())

    public class MyAsyncTaskTweet extends AsyncTask<String, Void, String> {

      @Override
      protected String doInBackground(String... tweet) {
        String result = "";

        Twitter twitter = TwitterFactory.getSingleton();
        try {
          twitter.updateStatus(tweet[0]).getText();
          result = getResources().getString(R.string.success);
        } catch (TwitterException twitterException) {
          result = getResources().getString(R.string.failure);
        }

        return result;
      }

      @Override
      protected void onPostExecute(String result) {
        editTextTweet.setHint(result);
        editTextTweet.setText("");
      }
    }
```

Figure 13-10:
The use of
types in an
Async
Task
class.

```
new MyAsyncTaskTweet().execute(editTextTweet.getText().toString())

    public class MyAsyncTaskTweet extends AsyncTask<String, Void, String> {

      @Override
      protected String doInBackground(String... tweet) {
        String result = "";

        Twitter twitter = TwitterFactory.getSingleton();
        try {
          twitter.updateStatus(tweet[0]).getText();
          result = getResources().getString(R.string.success);
        } catch (TwitterException twitterException) {
          result = getResources().getString(R.string.failure);
        }

        return result;
      }

      @Override
      protected void onPostExecute(String result) {
        editTextTweet.setHint(result);
        editTextTweet.setText("");
      }
    }
```

Figure 13-11:
The flow of
values in an
Async
Task
class.

Cutting to the chase, at last

At the beginning of this chapter, I promise that a statement like

```
twitter.updateStatus("This is my tweet.");
```

lies at the heart of the code to post a tweet. You can see this by looking at the first `doInBackground` method in Listing 13-4. Here's a quick excerpt from that method:

```
protected String doInBackground(String... tweet) {

  Twitter twitter = TwitterFactory.getSingleton();
  twitter.updateStatus(tweet[0]);
```

In the Twitter4J API,

- ✔ A `Twitter` **object is a gateway to the Twitter servers.**

- ✔ `TwitterFactory` **is a class that helps you create a new** `Twitter` **object.**

  In Java, a *factory* class is a class that can call a constructor on your behalf.

- ✔ **Calling the** `getSingleton` **method creates a new** `Twitter` **object.**

  A factory method, such as `getSingleton`, calls a constructor on your behalf.

- ✔ **A call to the** `Twitter` **class's** `updateStatus` **method posts a brand-new tweet.**

In Listing 13-4, the parameter to the `updateStatus` method is an array element. That's because, in the `doInBackground` method's header, `tweet` is a `varargs` parameter. You can pass as many values to `doInBackground` as you want. In the body of the method, you treat `tweet` as though it's an ordinary array. The first `tweet` value is `tweet[0]`. If there were a second `tweet` value, it would be `tweet[1]`. And so on.

For the lowdown on varargs parameters, see Chapter 12.

In Listing 13-4, the code to fetch a user's timeline looks something like this:

```
List<twitter4j.Status> statuses = null;

Twitter twitter = TwitterFactory.getSingleton();
statuses = twitter.getUserTimeline(username[0]);
```

A fellow named Yusuke Yamamoto developed Twitter4J (or at least, Yusuke Yamamoto was the Twitter4J project leader), and at some point Mr. Yamamoto decided that the `getUserTimeline` method returns a collection of twitter4J.Status objects. (Each twitter4J.Status instance contains one tweet.) So, to honor the contract set by calling the getUserTimeline method, the code in Listing 13-4 declares statuses to be a collection of twitter4J.Status objects.

A few lines later in the code, an enhanced for statement steps through the collection of statuses values and appends each value's text to a big result string. The loop adds "\n" (Java's go-to-the-next-line character) after each tweet for good measure. In the onPostExecute method, the code displays the big result string in the screen's textViewTimeline field.

In Listing 13-4, in the second doInBackground method, I use the fully quali-fied name twitter4j.Status. I do this to distinguish the twitter4J. Status class from Android's own AsyncTask.Status class (an inner class of the AsyncTask class).

For insight into Java's inner classes, refer to Chapter 11.

Java's Exceptions

Have I ever had something go wrong during the run of a program? (**Hint:** The answer is yes.) Have you ever tried to visit a website and been unable to pull up the page? (Indubitably, the answer is yes.) Is it possible that Java state-ments can fail when they try to access the Twitter server? (Absolutely!)

In Java, most of the things that go wrong during the execution of a program are *exceptions.* When something goes wrong, your code *throws* an exception. If your code provides a way to respond to an exception, your code *catches* the exception.

Like everything else in Java, an exception is an object. Every exception is an instance of Java's Exception class. When your code tries to divide by zero (which is always a "no-no"), your code throws an instance of the ArithmeticException class. When your code can't read from a stored file, your code throws an instance of the IOException class. When your code can't access a database, your code throws an instance of the SQLException class. And when your Twitter4J code can't access the Twitter servers, your code throws an instance of the TwitterException class.

The classes ArithmeticException, IOException, SQLException, TwitterException, and many, many others are subclasses of Java's Exception class. The classes Exception, ArithmeticException, IOException, and SQLException are each part the Java's standard API library. The class TwitterException is declared separately in the Twitter4J API.

Java has two kinds of exceptions: *unchecked exceptions* and *checked exceptions*. The easiest way to tell one kind of exception from the other is to watch Eclipse's response when you type and run your code.

✔ **When you execute a statement that can throw an unchecked exception, you don't have to add additional code.**

For example, an `ArithmeticException` is an unchecked exception. You can write and run the following (awful) Java program:

```
package com.allmycode.exceptions;

public class DoNotDoThis {

  public static void main(String[] args) {
    int i = 3 / 0;
  }

}
```

When you try to run this code, the program crashes. In Eclipse's Console view, you see the message shown in Figure 13-12.

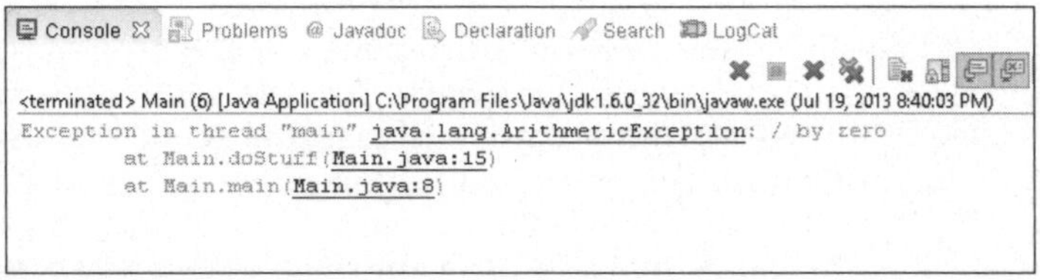

Figure 13-12:
Shame on
you! You
divided by
zero.

```
Console ⊠  Problems  @ Javadoc  Declaration  Search  LogCat
                                    ✖ ▬ ✖ ✖ | ▤ ▤ ▣ ▣
<terminated> Main (6) [Java Application] C:\Program Files\Java\jdk1.6.0_32\bin\javaw.exe (Jul 19, 2013 8:40:03 PM)
Exception in thread "main" java.lang.ArithmeticException: / by zero
        at Main.doStuff(Main.java:15)
        at Main.main(Main.java:8)
```

✔ **When you execute a statement that can throw a checked exception, you must add code.**

A `TwitterException` is an example of a checked exception, and a call to `getUserTimeline` can throw a `TwitterException`. To find out what happens when you call `getUserTimeline` without adding code, see a portion of Eclipse's editor in Figure 13-13.

In Figure 13-13, the error message indicates that by calling the `getUserTimeline` method, you run the risk of throwing a `TwitterException`. The word "Unhandled" means that `TwitterException` is one of Java's checked exceptions, and that you haven't provided any code to address the possibility of the exception's being thrown. That is, if the app can't communicate with the Twitter servers, and Java throws a `TwitterException`, your code has no "Plan B."

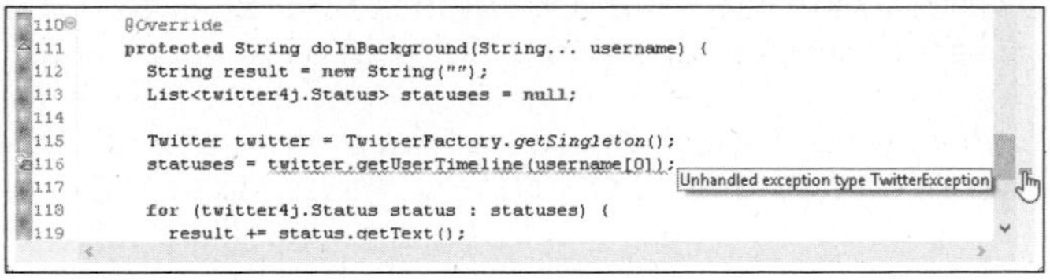

Figure 13-13:
Java insists
that you
add code
to acknowl-
edge an
exception.

```
110⊖      @Override
111    protected String doInBackground(String... username) {
112        String result = new String("");
113        List<twitter4j.Status> statuses = null;
114
115        Twitter twitter = TwitterFactory.getSingleton();
116        statuses = twitter.getUserTimeline(username[0]);
                                              Unhandled exception type TwitterException
117
118        for (twitter4j.Status status : statuses) {
119            result += status.getText();
```

So in Listing 13-4, I add Java's `try`/`catch` statement to my `getUserTime-`
`line` call. Here's the translation of the `try`/`catch` statement:

```
try to execute this statement (or statements): {
   statuses = twitter.getUserTimeline(username[0]);

} If you throw a TwitterException while you're trying, {
   display a stack trace in Eclipse's LogCat view.
}
```

A *stack trace* is the kind of output (refer to Figure 13-12) that tells you which
sequence of method calls caused the throwing of the exception. A stack trace
can help you diagnose your code's ills.

Catch clauses

A `try`/`catch` statement has only one `try` clause. But a `try`/`catch` statement can have many `catch` clauses, as shown in this example:

```
try {
   count = numberOfTweets / averagePerDay;
   statuses = twitter.getUserTimeline(username[0]);
} catch (TwitterException e) {
   System.out.println("Difficulty with Twitter");
} catch (ArithmeticException a) {
   a.printStackTrace();
} catch (Exception e) {
   System.out.println("Something went wrong.");
}

System.out.println("No longer contacting Twitter");
```

When an exception is thrown inside a `try` clause, Java examines the accompanying list of `catch` clauses. Every `catch` clause has a parameter list, and
every parameter list contains a type of exception.

Java starts at whatever `catch` clause appears immediately after the `try` clause and works its way down the program's text. For each `catch` clause, Java asks: Is the exception that was just thrown an instance of the class in this clause's parameter list? If it isn't, Java skips the `catch` clause and moves on to the next `catch` clause in line; if it is, Java executes the `catch` clause and then skips past all other `catch` clauses that come with this try clause. Java goes on and executes whatever statements come after the whole `try` / `catch` statement.

In the sample code with three `catch` clauses, if `averagePerDay` is zero, the code throws an `ArithmeticException`. Java skips past the `getUserTimeline` statement and looks at the `catch` clauses, starting with the topmost `catch` clause. Here's what happens.

The topmost catch clause is for `TwitterException` instances, but dividing by zero doesn't throw a `TwitterException`. So Java marches onward to the next `catch` clause.

The next `catch` clause is for `ArithmeticException` instances. Yes, dividing by zero threw an `ArithmeticException`. So Java executes the statement `a.printStackTrace()` and jumps out of the `try` / `catch` statement.

Java executes the statement immediately after the `try` / `catch` statement, displaying the words *No longer contacting Twitter*. Then Java executes any other statements after that one.

In the sample code with three `catch` clauses, I end the chain of `catch` clauses with an `Exception e` clause. Java's `Exception` class is an ancestor of `TwitterException` and `ArithmeticException` and all the other exception classes. No matter what kind of exception your code throws inside a `try` clause, that exception matches the `Exception e` catch clause. You can always rely on an `Exception e` clause as a last resort for handling a problem.

A finally clause

In addition to tacking on `catch` clauses, you can also tack a `finally` clause onto your `try` / `catch` statement. Java's `finally` keyword says, in effect, "Execute the `finally` clause's statements whether the code threw an exception or not." For example, in the following code snippet, Java always assigns `"Finished"` to the report variable, whether or not the call to `getUserTimeline` throws an exception:

```
String report = "";

try {
  statuses = twitter.getUserTimeline(username[0]);
} catch (TwitterException e) {
  e.printStackTrace();
} finally {
  report = "Finished";
}
```

Passing the buck

Here's a handy response to use whenever something goes wrong: "Don't blame me — tell my supervisor to deal with the problem." (I should have added the Tip icon to this paragraph!) When dealing with an exception, a Java method can do the same thing and say, "Don't expect me to have a try / catch statement — pass the exception on to the method that called me."

Listing 10-12, over in Chapter 10 calls the Thread class's sleep method. Execution of the sleep method can throw an InterruptedException, which is one of Java's checked exceptions. In the listing, I show you how to surround the call to Thread.sleep with a try / catch statement. In Listing 13-6, I show you how to insert that try / catch statement inside another Java program.

Listing 13-6:   Nipping an Exception in the Bud

```
package com.allmycode.naptime;

class GoodNightsSleepA {

  public static void main(String args[]) {
    System.out.println("Excuse me while I nap.");
    takeANap();
    System.out.println("Ah, that was refreshing.");
  }

  static void takeANap() {
    try {
      Thread.sleep(10000);
    } catch (InterruptedException e) {
      System.out.println("Hey, who woke me up?");
    }
  }
}
```

In Listing 13-6, the takeANap method says "Try to sleep for 10,000 milliseconds. If your sleep is interrupted, handle it by displaying the question Hey, who woke me up?" Normally, no other thread interrupts the takeANap method's sleep. So, in Figure 13-14, the output of the code doesn't include Hey, who woke me up? (In the figure, you don't see the ten-second pause between the display of the first and second lines of output. To experience the full effect, look at the first line in Figure 13-14, pause for ten seconds, and then look at the second line.)

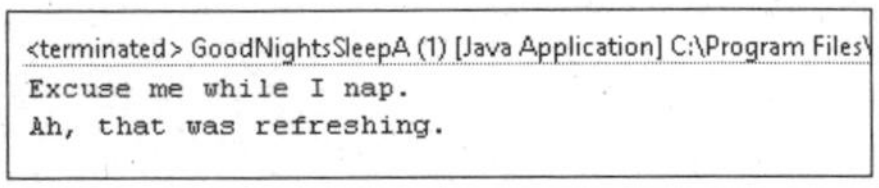

Figure 13-14:
Running
the code in
Listing 13-6.

```
<terminated> GoodNightsSleepA (1) [Java Application] C:\Program Files\
Excuse me while I nap.
Ah, that was refreshing.
```

You can get rid of the try / catch statement in the takeANap method, as long as the next method upstream acknowledges the exception's existence. To see what I mean, look at Listing 13-7.

Listing 13-7: Make the Calling Method Handle the Exception

```
package com.allmycode.naptime;

class GoodNightsSleepB {

  public static void main(String args[]) {
    System.out.println("Excuse me while I nap.");
    try {
      takeANap();
    } catch (InterruptedException e) {
      System.out.println("Hey, who woke me up?");
    }
    System.out.println("Ah, that was refreshing.");
  }

  static void takeANap() throws InterruptedException {
    Thread.sleep(10000);
  }
}
```

In Listing 13-7, the takeANap method's header contains a throws clause that passes the buck from the takeANap method to whichever method calls the takeANap method. Because the main method calls takeANap, Java insists that the `main` method contain code to acknowledge the possibility of an `InterruptedException`. To fulfill this responsibility, the `main` method surrounds the `takeANap` call with a `try` / `catch` statement.

Of course, the buck doesn't have to stop in the `main` method. You could say, "Don't blame me — tell my supervisor to deal with the problem." And then your supervisor could say, "Don't blame me — tell my supervisor to deal with the problem." The `main` method can avoid having a `try` / `catch` statement with its own `throws` clause (see Listing 13-8).

Listing 13-8: Keep Passing the Hot Potato

```
package com.allmycode.naptime;

class GoodNightsSleepC {

  public static void main(String args[])
                          throws InterruptedException {
    System.out.println("Excuse me while I nap.");
    takeANap();
    System.out.println("Hey, who woke me up?");
    System.out.println("Ah, that was refreshing.");
  }

  static void takeANap() throws InterruptedException {
    Thread.sleep(10000);
  }
}
```

If another thread interrupts this code's sleep time, the `takeANap` method passes the exception to the `main` method, which in turn passes the exception to the Java virtual machine. The Java virtual machine deals with the exception by displaying a stack trace and calling quits on your whole program. It's not the smartest way to handle a problem, but it's a legal alternative in Java.

Chapter 14

Hungry Burds: A Simple Android Game

In This Chapter

▶ Coding an Android game

▶ Using Android animation

▶ Saving data from one run to another

What started as a simple pun involving the author's last name has turned into Chapter 14 — the most self-indulgent writing in the history of technical publishing.

The scene takes place in south Philadelphia in the early part of the 20th century. My father (then a child) sees his father (my grandfather) handling an envelope. The envelope has just arrived from the old country. My grandmother grabs the envelope out of my grandfather's hands. The look on her face is one of superiority. "I open the letters around here," she says with her eyes.

While my grandmother opens the letter, my father glances at the envelope. The last name on the envelope is written in Cyrillic characters, so my father can't read it. But he notices a short last name in the envelope's address. Whatever the characters are, they're more likely to be a short name like Burd than a longer name like Burdinsky or Burdstakovich.

The Russian word for bird is *ptitsa*, so there's no etymological connection between my last name and our avian friends. But as I grew up, I would often hear kids yell "Burd is the word" or "Hey, Burdman" from across the street. Today, my one-person Burd Brain Consulting firm takes in a small amount of change every year.

Introducing the Hungry Burds Game

When the game begins, the screen is blank. Then, for a random amount of time (averaging one second), a Burd fades into view, as shown in Figure 14-1.

If the user does nothing, the Burd disappears after fading into full view. But if the user touches the Burd before it disappears, the Burd gets a cheeseburger and remains onscreen, as shown in Figure 14-2.

Figure 14-1:
A Burd
fades into
view.

Figure 14-2:
You've fed
this Burd.

After ten Burds have faded in (and the unfed ones have disappeared), the screen displays a text view, showing the number of fed Burds in the current run of the game. The text view also shows the high score for all runs of the game, as shown in Figure 14-3.

For many apps, timing isn't vitally important: For them, a consistently slow response is annoying but not disabling. But for a game like Hungry Burds, timing makes a big difference. Running Hungry Burds on an emulator feels more like a waiting game than an action game. To gain a reasonable sense of how Hungry Burds works, run the app on a real-life device.

The Hungry Burds Java code is about 140 lines long. (Compare this with one of the Android game developer's books that I bought. In that book, the simplest example has 2,300 lines of Java code.) To keep the Hungry Burds code from consuming dozens of pages, I've omitted some features that you might see in a more realistically engineered game.

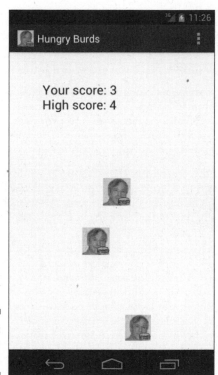

Figure 14-3:
The game
ends.

✔ **The Hungry Burds game doesn't access data over a network.**

The game's high-score display doesn't tell you how well you did compared with your friends or with other players around the world. The high-score display applies to only one device — the one you're using to play the game.

✔ **The game restarts whenever you change the device's orientation.**

If you tilt the device from Portrait mode to Landscape mode, or from Landscape mode to Portrait mode, Android calls the main activity's lifecycle methods. Android calls the activity's `onPause`, `onStop`, and `onDestroy` methods. Then it reconstitutes the activity by calling the activity's `onCreate`, `onStart`, and `onResume` methods. As a result, whatever progress you've made in the game disappears and the game starts itself over again from scratch.

For an introduction to an activity's lifecycle methods, see Chapter 5.

✔ **The game has no Restart button.**

To play the game a second time, you can press Android's Back button and then touch the game's launcher icon. Alternatively, you can tilt the device from Portrait mode to Landscape mode, or vice versa.

✔ **The screen measurements that control the game are crude.**

Creating a visual app that involves drawing, custom images, or motion of any kind involves some math. You need math to make measurements, estimate distances, detect collisions, and complete other tasks. To do the math, you produce numbers by making Android API calls, and you use the results of your calculations in Android API library calls.

To help me cut quickly to the chase, my Hungry Burds game does only a minimal amount of math, and it makes only the API calls I believe to be absolutely necessary. As a result, some items on the screen don't always look their best. (This happens particularly when the device is in Landscape mode.)

✔ **The game has no settings.**

The number of Burds displayed, the average time of each Burd's display, and the minimal length of time for each Burd's display are all hard-coded in the game's Java file. In the code, these constants are `NUMBER_OF_BURDS`, `AVERAGE_SHOW_TIME`, and `MINIMUM_SHOW_TIME`. As a developer, you can change the values in the code and reinstall the game. But the ordinary player can't change these numbers.

✔ **The game isn't challenging with the default** `NUMBER_OF_BURDS`, `AVERAGE_SHOW_TIME`, **and** `MINIMUM_SHOW_TIME` **values.**

I admit it: On this front, I'm at a distinct disadvantage. I'm a lousy game player. I remember competing in video games against my kids when they were young. I lost every time. At first it was embarrassing; in the end it was ridiculous. I could never avoid being shot, eaten, or otherwise squashed by my young opponents' avatars.

I don't presume to know what values of NUMBER_OF_BURDS, AVERAGE_SHOW_TIME, and MINIMUM_SHOW_TIME are right for you. And if no values are right for you (and the game isn't fun to play no matter which values you have), don't despair. I've created Hungry Burds as a teaching tool, not as a replacement for Super Mario.

The Project's Files

The project's AndroidManifest.xml file is nothing special. The only element you have to watch for is uses-sdk — in that element, the android:minSdkVersion attribute has the value 13 or higher. That's because the Java code calls the Display class's getSize method, and that method isn't available in Android API levels below 13.

If you have to get a layout's measurements in an app that runs in API Level 12 or lower, check the documentation for Android's ViewTreeObserver. OnPreDrawListener class.

The project's activity_main.xml file is almost empty, as shown in Listing 14-1. I put a TextView somewhere on the screen so that, at the end of each game, I can display the most recent statistics. I also add an android:id attribute to the RelativeLayout element. Using that android:id element, I can refer to the screen's layout in the Java code.

Listing 14-1:   The Main Activity's Layout File

```
<RelativeLayout xmlns:android=
    "http://schemas.android.com/apk/res/android"
  xmlns:tools="http://schemas.android.com/tools"
  android:id="@+id/relativeLayout"
  android:layout_width="match_parent"
  android:layout_height="match_parent"
  android:paddingBottom=
      "@dimen/activity_vertical_margin"
  android:paddingLeft=
      "@dimen/activity_horizontal_margin"
  android:paddingRight=
      "@dimen/activity_horizontal_margin"
  android:paddingTop=
      "@dimen/activity_vertical_margin"
  tools:context=".MainActivity" >

<TextView
```

(continued)

Listing 14-1 *(continued)*

```
        android:id="@+id/textView1"
        android:layout_width="wrap_content"
        android:layout_height="wrap_content"
        android:layout_alignParentLeft="true"
        android:layout_alignParentTop="true"
        android:layout_marginLeft="42dp"
        android:layout_marginTop="34dp"
        android:text="@string/nothing"
        android:textAppearance=
            "?android:attr/textAppearanceLarge" />

    </RelativeLayout>
```

In the `res` directory of my Hungry Burds project, I have ten `.png` files — two files for each of Android's generalized screen densities, as shown in Figure 14-4.

For a look at Android screen densities, see Chapter 8.

Each `burd.png` file is a picture of me. Each `burd_burger.png` file is a picture of me with a cheeseburger. When Android runs the game, Android checks the device's specs and decides, on the spot, which of the five screen densities to use. (You don't need an `if` statement like the one in Chapter 8.)

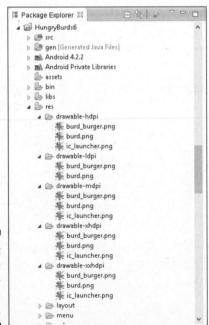

Figure 14-4:
Images in the proj-
ect's `res`
directory.

The Main Activity

The Hungry Burds game has only one activity: the app's main activity. So you can digest the game's Java code in its entirety in one big gulp. To make this gulp palatable, I start with an outline of the activity's code. The outline is in Listing 14-2. (If outlines don't work for you, and you want to see the code in its entirety, refer to Listing 14-3.)

Listing 14-2:   An Outline of the App's Java Code

```java
package com.allmycode.hungryburds;

public class MainActivity extends Activity
    implements OnClickListener, AnimationListener {

  // Declare fields

  /* Activity methods */

  @Override
  public void onCreate(Bundle savedInstanceState) {
    super.onCreate(savedInstanceState);
    setContentView(R.layout.activity_main);

    // Find layout elements

    // Get the size of the device's screen

    // Set up SharedPreferences to record high scores
  }

  @Override
  public void onResume() {
    showABurd();
  }

  /* Game methods */

  void showABurd() {
    // Add a Burd in some random place
    // At first, the Burd is invisible

    // Create an AlphaAnimation to make the Burd
    // fade in (from invisible to fully visible).
    burd.startAnimation(animation);
  }

  private void showScores() {
    // Get high score from SharedPreferences
```

(continued)

Listing 14-2 *(continued)*

```
      // Display high score and this run's score
    }

    /* OnClickListener method */

    public void onClick(View view) {
      countClicked++;
      // Change the image to a Burd with a cheeseburger
    }

    /* AnimationListener methods */

    public void onAnimationEnd(Animation animation) {
      if (++countShown < NUMBER_OF_BURDS) {
        showABurd(); // Again!
      } else {
        showScores();
      }
    }

}
```

The heart of the Hungry Burds code is the code's game loop, as shown in the following example:

```
public void onResume() {
  showABurd();
}

void showABurd() {
  // Add a Burd in some random place.
  // At first, the Burd is invisible ...

  burd.setVisibility(View.INVISIBLE);

  // ... but the animation will make the
  // Burd visible.

  AlphaAnimation animation =
      new AlphaAnimation(0.0F, 1.0F);
  animation.setDuration(duration);
  animation.setAnimationListener(this);
  burd.startAnimation(animation);
}

public void onAnimationEnd(Animation animation) {
  if (++countShown < NUMBER_OF_BURDS) {
    showABurd(); // Again!
```

```
  } else {
    showScores();
  }
}
```

When Android executes the onResume method, the code calls the showA-
Burd method. The showABurd method does what its name suggests, by
animating an image from alpha level 0 to alpha level 1. (Alpha level 0 is fully
transparent; alpha level 1 is fully opaque.)

In the onCreate method, you put code that runs when the activity comes
into existence. In contrast, in the onResume method, you put code that runs
when the user begins interacting with the activity. The user isn't aware of the
difference because the app starts running so quickly. But for you, the developer, the distinction between an app's coming into existence and starting to
interact is important. In Listings 14-2 and 14-3, the onCreate method contains
code to set the layout of the activity, assign variable names to screen widgets,
measure the screen size, and prepare for storing high scores. The onResume
method is different. With the onResume method, the user is about to touch
the device's screen. So in Listings 14-2 and 14-3, the onResume method displays something for the user to touch: the first of several hungry Burds.

When the animation ends, the onAnimationEnd method checks the number
of Burds that have already been displayed. If the number is less than ten,
the onAnimationEnd method calls showABurd again, and the game loop
continues.

By default, a Burd returns to being invisible when the animation ends. But
the main activity implements OnClickListener, and when the user touches
a Burd, the class's onClick method makes the Burd permanently visible, as
shown in the following snippet:

```
public void onClick(View view) {
  countClicked++;
  ((ImageView) view).setImageResource
                        (R.drawable.burd_burger);
  view.setVisibility(View.VISIBLE);
}
```

The code, all the code, and nothing but the code

Following the basic outline of the game's code in the previous section,
Listing 14-3 contains the entire text of the game's MainActivity.java file.

Listing 14-3: The App's Java Code

```java
package com.allmycode.hungryburds;

import java.util.Random;

import android.app.Activity;
import android.content.SharedPreferences;
import android.graphics.Point;
import android.os.Bundle;
import android.view.Display;
import android.view.Menu;
import android.view.View;
import android.view.View.OnClickListener;
import android.view.animation.AlphaAnimation;
import android.view.animation.Animation;
import android.view.animation.Animation.AnimationListener;
import android.widget.ImageView;
import android.widget.RelativeLayout;
import android.widget.RelativeLayout.LayoutParams;
import android.widget.TextView;

public class MainActivity extends Activity
    implements OnClickListener, AnimationListener {

  final int NUMBER_OF_BURDS = 10;
  final long AVERAGE_SHOW_TIME = 1000L;
  final long MINIMUM_SHOW_TIME = 500L;
  TextView textView;
  int countShown = 0, countClicked = 0;
  Random random = new Random();

  RelativeLayout relativeLayout;
  int displayWidth, displayHeight;

  SharedPreferences prefs;
  SharedPreferences.Editor editor;

  /* Activity methods */

  @Override
  public void onCreate(Bundle savedInstanceState) {
    super.onCreate(savedInstanceState);
    setContentView(R.layout.activity_main);

    textView = (TextView) findViewById(R.id.textView1);
    relativeLayout = (RelativeLayout)
        findViewById(R.id.relativeLayout);

    Display display =
        getWindowManager().getDefaultDisplay();
    Point size = new Point();
```

```
    display.getSize(size);
    displayWidth = size.x;
    displayHeight = size.y;

    prefs = getPreferences(MODE_PRIVATE);
    editor = prefs.edit();
}

@Override
public boolean onCreateOptionsMenu(Menu menu) {
    getMenuInflater().inflate(R.menu.main, menu);
    return true;
}

@Override
public void onResume() {
    super.onResume();
    countClicked = countShown = 0;
    textView.setText(R.string.nothing);
    showABurd();
}

/* Game methods */

void showABurd() {
    long duration =
        random.nextInt((int) AVERAGE_SHOW_TIME)
        + MINIMUM_SHOW_TIME;

    LayoutParams params = new LayoutParams
                    (LayoutParams.WRAP_CONTENT,
                     LayoutParams.WRAP_CONTENT);

    params.leftMargin =
        random.nextInt(displayWidth) * 7 / 8;
    params.topMargin =
        random.nextInt(displayHeight) * 4 / 5;

    ImageView burd = new ImageView(this);
    burd.setOnClickListener(this);
    burd.setLayoutParams(params);
    burd.setImageResource(R.drawable.burd);
    burd.setVisibility(View.INVISIBLE);

    relativeLayout.addView(burd);

    AlphaAnimation animation =
        new AlphaAnimation(0.0F, 1.0F);
    animation.setDuration(duration);
    animation.setAnimationListener(this);
    burd.startAnimation(animation);
```

(continued)

Listing 14-3 *(continued)*

```
  }

  private void showScores() {
    int highScore = prefs.getInt("highScore", 0);

    if (countClicked > highScore) {
      highScore = countClicked;
      editor.putInt("highScore", highScore);
      editor.commit();
    }

    textView.setText("Your score: " + countClicked +
                     "\nHigh score: " + highScore);
  }

  /* OnClickListener method */

  public void onClick(View view) {
    countClicked++;
    ((ImageView) view).setImageResource
                            (R.drawable.burd_burger);
    view.setVisibility(View.VISIBLE);
  }

  /* AnimationListener methods */

  public void onAnimationEnd(Animation animation) {
    if (++countShown < NUMBER_OF_BURDS) {
      showABurd();
    } else {
      showScores();
    }
  }

  public void onAnimationRepeat(Animation arg0) {
  }

  public void onAnimationStart(Animation arg0) {
  }
}
```

Random

A typical game involves random choices. (You don't want Burds to appear in the same places every time you play the game.) Truly random values are difficult to generate. But an instance of Java's Random class creates what appear to be random values (*pseudorandom* values) in ways that the programmer can help determine.

For example, a `Random` object's `nextDouble` method returns a `double` value between 0.0 and 1.0 (with 0.0 being possible but 1.0 being impossible). The Hungry Burds code uses a `Random` object's `nextInt` method. A call to `nextInt(10)` returns an `int` value from 0 to 9.

If `displayWidth` is 720 (which stands for 720 pixels), the call to `random.nextInt(displayWidth)` in Listing 14-3 returns a value from 0 to 719. And because `AVERAGE_SHOW_TIME` is the `long` value 1000L, the expression `random.nextInt((int) AVERAGE_SHOW_TIME)` stands for a value from 0 to 999. (The casting to `int` helps fulfill the promise that the `nextInt` method's parameter is an `int`, not a `long` value.) By adding back `MINIMUM_SHOW_TIME` (refer to Listing 14-3), I make `duration` be a number between 500 and 1499. A Burd takes between 500 and 1499 milliseconds to fade into view.

Measuring the display

Android's `Display` object stores information about a device's display. How complicated can that be? You can measure the screen size with a ruler, and you can determine a device's resolution by reading the specs in the user manual.

Of course, Android programs don't have opposable thumbs, so they can't use plastic rulers. And a layout's characteristics can change depending on several runtime factors, including the device's orientation (portrait or landscape) and the amount of screen space reserved for Android's notification bar and buttons. If you don't play your cards right, you can easily call methods that prematurely report a display's width and height as zero values.

Fortunately, the `getSize` method in Android API level 13 and higher gives you some correct answers in an activity's `onCreate` method. So, here and there in Listing 14-3, you find the following code:

```
public class MainActivity extends Activity {

  int displayWidth, displayHeight;

  public void onCreate(Bundle savedInstanceState) {

    Display display =
        getWindowManager().getDefaultDisplay();
    Point size = new Point();
    display.getSize(size);
    displayWidth = size.x;
    displayHeight = size.y;

  }

  void showABurd() {
```

```
LayoutParams params;
params = new LayoutParams(LayoutParams.WRAP_CONTENT,
                          LayoutParams.WRAP_CONTENT);
params.leftMargin =
    random.nextInt(displayWidth) * 7 / 8;
params.topMargin =
    random.nextInt(displayHeight) * 4 / 5;

}
```

An instance of Android's `Point` class is basically an object with two components: an x component and a y component. In the Hungry Burds code, a call to `getWindowManager().getDefaultDisplay()` retrieves the device's display. The resulting display's `getSize` method takes an instance of the `Point` class and fills its x and y fields. The x field's value is the display's width, and the y field's value is the display's height, as shown in Figure 14-5.

A `LayoutParams` object stores information about the way a widget should appear as part of an activity's layout. (Each kind of layout has its own `LayoutParams` inner class, and the code in Listing 14-3 imports the `RelativeLayout.LayoutParams` inner class.) A `LayoutParams` instance has a life of its own, apart from any widget whose appearance the instance describes. In Listing 14-3, I construct a new `LayoutParams` instance before applying the instance to any particular widget. Later in the code, I call

```
burd.setLayoutParams(params);
```

to apply the new `LayoutParams` instance to one of the Burds.

Constructing a new `LayoutParams` instance with a double dose of `LayoutParams.WRAP_CONTENT` (one `LayoutParams.WRAP_CONTENT` for width and one `LayoutParams.WRAP_CONTENT` for height) indicates that a widget should shrink-wrap itself around whatever content is drawn inside it. Because the code eventually applies this `LayoutParams` instance to a Burd, the Burd will be only wide enough and only tall enough to contain a picture of yours truly from one of the project's `res/drawable` directories.

The alternative to `WRAP_CONTENT` is `MATCH_PARENT`. With two `MATCH_PARENT` parameters in the `LayoutParams` constructor, a Burd's width and height would expand to fill the activity's entire relative layout.

A `LayoutParams` instance's `leftMargin` field stores the number of pixels between the left edge of the display and the left edge of the widget. Similarly, a `LayoutParams` instance's `topMargin` field stores the number of pixels between the top edge of the display and the top edge of the widget. (Refer to Figure 14-5.)

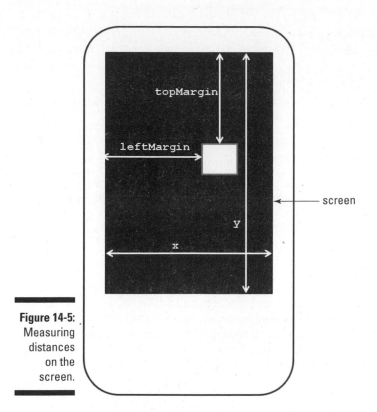

Figure 14-5:
Measuring
distances
on the
screen.

In Listing 14-3, I use random values to position a new Burd. A Burd's left edge is no farther than ⅞ths of the way across the screen, and the Burd's top edge is no lower than ⅘ths of the way down the screen. If you don't multiply the screen's width by ⅞ (or some such fraction), an entire Burd can be positioned beyond the right edge of the screen. The user sees nothing while the Burd comes and goes. The same kind of thing can happen if you don't multiply the screen's height by ⅘.

The fractions ⅞ and ⅘, which I use to determine each widget's position, are crude guesstimates of a portrait screen's requirements. A more refined app would carefully measure the available turf and calculate the optimally sized region for positioning new Burds.

Constructing a Burd

Android's `ImageView` class represents objects that contain images. Normally, you put an image file (a `.png` file, a `.jpg` file, or a `.gif` file) in one of your project's `res/drawable` directories, and a call to the `ImageView` object's `setImageResource` method associates the `ImageView` object with the image file. In Listing 14-3, the following lines fulfill this role:

```
ImageView burd = new ImageView(this);

burd.setImageResource(R.drawable.burd);
```

Because of the `R.drawable.burd` parameter, Android looks in the project's `res/drawable` directories for files named `burd.png`, `burd.jpg`, or `burd.gif`. (Refer to Figure 14-4.) Android selects the file whose resolution best suits the device and displays that file's image on the `ImageView` object.

The statement

```
burd.setVisibility(View.INVISIBLE);
```

makes the Burd be completely transparent. The next statement

```
relativeLayout.addView(burd);
```

normally makes a widget appear on the user's screen. But with the `View.INVISIBLE` property, the Burd doesn't show up. It's not until I start the code's fade-in animation that the user begins seeing a Burd on the screen.

Android has two kinds of animation: view animation and property animation. The Hungry Burds code uses view animation. An object's `visibility` property doesn't change when a view animation makes the object fade in or fade out. In this chapter's example, a Burd starts off with `View.INVISIBLE`. A fade-in animation makes the Burd appear slowly on the screen. But when the animation finishes, the Burd's `visibility` field still contains the original `View.INVISIBLE` value. So normally, when the animation ends, the Burd simply disappears.

When the user clicks on a Burd, Android calls the `onClick` method in Listing 14-3. The `onClick` method's `view` parameter represents the `ImageView` object that the user clicked. In the body of the `onClick` method, the statement

```
((ImageView) view).setImageResource
                    (R.drawable.burd_burger);
```

assures Java that `view` is indeed an `ImageView` instance and changes the picture on the face of that instance from a hungry author to a well-fed author. The `onClick` method also sets the `ImageView` instance's visibility to `View.VISIBLE`. That way, when this Burd's animation ends, the happy Burd remains visible on the user's screen.

Android animation

Android has two types of animation:

✔ **View animation:** An older system in which you animate with either tweening or frame-by-frame animation, as described in this list:

- *Tweening:* You tell Android how an object should look initially and how the object should look eventually. You also tell Android how to change from the initial appearance to the eventual appearance. (Is the change gradual or sudden? If the object moves, does it move in a straight line or in a curve of some sort? Will it bounce a bit when it reaches the end of its path?)

  With tweening, Android considers all your requirements and figures out exactly how the object looks *between* the start and the finish of the object's animation.

- *Frame-by-frame animation:* You provide several snapshots of the object along its path. Android displays these snapshots in rapid succession, one after another, giving the appearance of movement or of another change in the object's appearance.

  Movie cartoons are the classic example of frame-by-frame animation even though, in modern moviemaking, graphics specialists use tweening to create sequences of frames.

✔ **Property animation:** A newer system (introduced in Android 3.0, API Level 11) in which you can modify any property of an object over a period of time.

With property animation, you can change anything about any kind of object, whether the object appears on the device's screen or not. For example, you can increase an `earth` object's average temperature from 15° Celsius to 18° Celsius over a period of ten minutes. Rather than display the `earth` object, you can watch the way average temperature affects water levels and plant life, for example.

Unlike view animation, the use of property animation changes the value stored in an object's field. For example, you can use property animation to change a widget from being invisible to being visible. When the property animation finishes, the widget remains visible.

The Hungry Burds code uses view animation, which includes these specialized animation classes:

✔ `AlphaAnimation`: Fades into view or fades out of view

✔ `RotateAnimation`: Turns around

✔ ScaleAnimation: Changes size

✔ TranslateAnimation: Moves from one place to another

In particular, the Hungry Burds code uses AlphaAnimation.

The statement

```
AlphaAnimation animation =
    new AlphaAnimation(0.0F, 1.0F);
```

creates a fade-in/fade-out animation. An alpha level of 0.0 indicates complete transparence, and an alpha level of 1.0 indicates complete opaqueness. (The AlphaAnimation constructor expects its parameters to be float values, so I plug the float values 0.0F and 1.0F into the constructor call.)

The call

```
animation.setAnimationListener(this);
```

tells Java that the code to respond to the animation's progress is in this main activity class. Indeed, the class header at the top of Listing 14-3 informs Java that the HungryBurds class implements the AnimationListener interface. And to make good on the implementation promise, Listing 14-3 contains bodies for the methods onAnimationEnd, onAnimationRepeat, and onAnimationStart. (Nothing happens in the onAnimationRepeat and onAnimationStart methods. That's okay.)

The onAnimationEnd method does what I describe earlier in this chapter: The method checks the number of Burds that have already been displayed. If the number is less than ten, the onAnimationEnd method calls showABurd again, and the game loop continues.

Shared preferences

When a user finishes a game of Hungry Burds, the app displays the score for the current game and the high score for all games. (Refer to Figure 14-3.) The high score display applies to only one device — the device that's running the current game. To remember the high score from one run to another, I use Android's *shared preferences* feature.

Android provides several ways to store information from one run of an app to the next. In addition to using shared preferences, you can store information in the device's SQLite database. (Every Android device has SQLite database software.) You can also store information in an ordinary Linux file or on a network host of some kind.

Here's how you wield a set of shared preferences:

✔ **To create shared preferences, you call the activity's** `getShared`
`Preferences` **method.**

In fact, the `getSharedPreferences` method belongs to Android's
`Context` class, and the `Activity` class is a subclass of the `Context`
class.

In Listing 14-3, I call `getSharedPreferences` in the activity's `on`
`Create` method. The call's parameter, `MODE_PRIVATE`, tells Android
that no other app can read from or write to this app's shared preferences. (I know — there's nothing "shared" about something that no
other app can use. But that's the way Android's terminology works.)

Aside from `MODE_PRIVATE`, the alternatives are described in this list:

- `MODE_WORLD_READABLE`: Other apps can read from these
  preferences.

- `MODE_WORLD_WRITEABLE`: Other apps can write to these
  preferences.

- `MODE_MULTI_PROCESS`: Other apps can write to these preferences even while an app is in the middle of a read operation. Weird
  things can happen with this much concurrency. If you use `MODE_`
  `MULTI_PROCESS`, **watch out!**

You can combine modes with Java's bitwise *or* operator (|). A call such as

```
getSharedPreferences(
    MODE_WORLD_READABLE | MODE_WORLD_WRITEABLE);
```

makes your preferences both readable and writable for all other processes.

✔ **To start adding values to a set of shared preferences, you use an
instance of the** `SharedPreferences.Editor` **class.**

In Listing 14-3, the `onCreate` method makes a new editor object. Then,
in the `showScores` method, I use the editor to add (`"highScore"`,
`highScore`) to the shared preferences. Taken together, (`"high`
`Score"`, `highScore`) is a *key/value pair*. The *value* (whatever number
my `highscore` variable holds) is the actual information. The *key* (the
string `"highScore"`) identifies that particular piece of information.
(Every value has to have a key. Otherwise, if you've stored several different values in your app's shared preferences, you have no way to retrieve
any particular value.)

In Listing 14-3, I call `putInt` to store an `int` value in shared preferences.
Android's `Editor` class (an inner class of the `SharedPreferences`
class) has methods such as `putInt`, `putFloat`, `putString`, and `put`
`StringSet`.

✔ **To finish adding values to a set of shared preferences, you call the editor's** `commit` **method.**

In the `showScores` method in Listing 14-3, the statement `editor. commit()` does the job.

✔ **To read values from an existing set of shared preferences, you call** `getBoolean`, `getInt`, `getFloat`, **or one of the other get methods belonging to the** `SharedPreferences` **class.**

In the `showScores` method in Listing 14-3, the call to `getInt` takes two parameters. The first parameter (the string `"highscore"`) is the key that identifies a particular piece of information. The second parameter (the `int` value 0) is a default value. So when you call `prefs. getInt("highScore", 0)`, the following applies:

- If `prefs` has no pair with key `"highscore"`, the method call returns 0.

- If `prefs` has a previously stored `"highscore"` value, the method returns that value.

It's Been Fun

This chapter has been fun, and this book has been fun! I love writing about Android and Java. And I love hearing from readers. Remember that you can send e-mail to me at `java4android @allmycode.com`, and you can reach me on Twitter (`@allmycode`) and on Facebook (`/allmycode`).

Occasionally, I hear from a reader who says something like this: "If I read your whole book, will I know everything I have to know about Java?" The answer is always "No, no, no!" (That's not only one "no." It's "no" times three.) No matter what topic you study, there's always more to learn. So keep reading, keep practicing, keep learning, and, by all means, keep in touch.

Part V
The Part of Tens

Enjoy an additional Part of Tens chapter from *Java Programming for Android Developers For Dummies* online at www.dummies.com/extras/java programmingforandroiddevelopers.

In this part . . .

- ✔ Preventing mistakes
- ✔ Mining the web for more information

Chapter 15

Ten Ways to Avoid Mistakes

"**T**he only people who never make mistakes are the people who never do anything at all." One of my college professors said that. I don't remember the professor's name, so I can't give him proper credit. I guess that's my mistake.

Putting Capital Letters Where They Belong

Java is a case-sensitive language, so you really have to mind your *P*s and *Q*s — along with every other letter of the alphabet. Here are some concepts to keep in mind as you create Java programs:

✔ Java's keywords are all completely lowercase. For instance, in a Java `if` statement, the word *if* can't be *If* or *IF*.

✔ When you use names from the Java Application Programming Interface (API), the case of the names has to match what appears in the API.

✔ You also need to make sure that the names you make up yourself are capitalized the same way throughout the entire program. If you declare a `myAccount` variable, you can't refer to it as `MyAccount`, `myaccount`, or `Myaccount`. If you capitalize the variable name two different ways, Java thinks you're referring to two completely different variables.

For more info on Java's case-sensitivity, see Chapter 5.

Breaking Out of a switch Statement

If you don't break out of a switch statement, you get fall-through. For instance, if the value of roll is 7, the following code prints all three words — win, continue, and lose:

```
switch (roll) {
case 7:
  System.out.println("win");
case 10:
  System.out.println("continue");
case 12:
  System.out.println("lose");
}
```

For the full story, see Chapter 8.

Comparing Values with a Double Equal Sign

When you compare two values with one another, you use a double equal sign. The line

```
if (inputNumber == randomNumber)
```

is correct, but the line

```
if (inputNumber = randomNumber)
```

is not correct. For a full report, see Chapter 6.

Adding Listeners to Handle Events

You want to know when the user clicks a widget, when an animation ends, or when something else happens, so you create listeners:

```
public class MainActivity extends Activity
   implements OnClickListener, AnimationListener {
 ...
 public void onClick(View view) {
   ...
 }
 public void onAnimationEnd(Animation animation) {
   ...
 }
```

When you create listeners, you must remember to set the listeners:

```
ImageView widget = new ImageView(this);
widget.setOnClickListener(this);
...
AlphaAnimation animation =
    new AlphaAnimation(0.0F, 1.0F);
animation.setAnimationListener(this);
...
```

If you forget the call to setOnClickListener, nothing happens when you click the widget. Clicking the widget harder a second time doesn't help.

For the rundown on listeners, see Chapter 11.

Defining the Required Constructors

When you define a constructor with parameters, as in

```
public Temperature(double number)
```

Java no longer creates a default parameterless constructor for you. In other words, you can no longer call

```
Temperature roomTemp = new Temperature();
```

unless you explicitly define your own parameterless Temperature constructor. For all the gory details on constructors, see Chapter 9.

Fixing Nonstatic References

If you try to compile the following code, you get an error message:

```
class WillNotWork {
  String greeting = "Hello";

  public static void main(String args[]) {
      System.out.println(greeting);
  }
}
```

You get an error message because `main` is static, but `greeting` isn't static. For the complete guide to finding and fixing this problem, see Chapter 9.

Staying within Bounds in an Array

When you declare an array with ten components, the components have indexes 0 through 9. In other words, if you declare

```
int guests[] = new int[10];
```

you can refer to the `guests` array's components by writing `guests[0]`, `guests[1]`, and so on, all the way up to `guests[9]`. You can't write `guests[10]`, because the `guests` array has no component with index 10.

For the latest gossip on arrays, see Chapter 12.

Anticipating Null Pointers

This book's examples aren't prone to throwing the `NullPointer Exception`, but in real-life Java programming, you see that exception all the time. A `NullPointerException` comes about when you call a method on an expression that doesn't have a "legitimate" value. Here's a cheap example:

```
public class ThrowNullPointerException {

  public static void main(String[] args) {
    String myString = null;
    display(myString);
```

```
    }

  static void display(String aString) {
    if (!aString.contains("confidential")) {
      System.out.println(aString);
    }
  }
}
```

The `display` method prints a string of characters only if that string doesn't contain the word *confidential*. The problem is that the `myString` variable (and thus the `aString` parameter) doesn't refer to a string of any kind — not even to the empty string (`""`).

When the computer reaches the call to `aString.contains`, the computer looks for a `contains` method belonging to `null`. But `null` is nothing. The `null` value has no methods. So you get a big `NullPointerException`, and the program comes crashing down around you.

To avoid this kind of calamity, think twice about any method call in your code. If the expression before the dot can possibly be `null`, add exception-handling code to your program:

```
try {
  if (!aString.contains("confidential")) {
    System.out.println(aString);
  }
} catch (NullPointerException e) {
  System.out.println("The string is null.");
}
```

For the story on handling exceptions, see Chapter 13.

Using Permissions

Some apps require explicit permissions. For example, the app in Chapter 13 talks to Twitter's servers over the Internet. This doesn't work unless you add a `<uses-permission>` element to the app's `AndroidManifest.xml` file:

```
<uses-permission android:name=
    "android.permission.INTERNET"/>
```

If you forget to add the `<uses-permission>` element to your `Android Manifest.xml` file, the app can't communicate with Twitter's servers. The app fails without displaying a useful error message. Too bad!

The Activity Not Found

If you create a second activity for your app, you must add a new `<activity>` element in the app's `AndroidManifest.xml` file. For example, the Android app in Chapter 12 has two activities: `MainActivity` and `MyListActivity`. Eclipse automatically creates an `<activity android:name=".Main Activity"` element, but you have to type your own element for the `MyListActivity`:

```
<activity android:name=".MyListActivity">
    <intent-filter>
        <data android:scheme="checked" />
    </intent-filter>
</activity>
```

If you don't add this `<activity>` element, Android can't find the `MyListActivity` class, even though the `MyListAcitivity.java` file is in the app's Eclipse project directory. Your app crashes with an `ActivityNotFoundException`.

And that makes all the difference.

Chapter 16

Ten Websites for Developers

This chapter lists ten useful and fun websites. Each one has resources to help you use Java more effectively. And as far as I know, none of these sites uses adware or pop-ups or other grotesque programs.

This Book's Websites

For all matters related to the technical content of this book, visit `www.all mycode.com/Java4Android`.

For business issues (for example, "How can I purchase 100 copies of *Java Programming For Android Developers For Dummies?*"), visit `www.dummies. com/extras/javaprogrammingforandroiddevelopers`.

The Horse's Mouth

Oracle's official website for Java is `www.oracle.com/technetwork/java`.

Consumers of Java technology should visit `www.java.com`.

Programmers and developers interested in sharing Java technology can go to `www.java.net`.

For everything an Android developer needs to know, visit `developer. android.com`.

Finding News and Reviews

For articles by the experts, visit the InfoQ site: www.infoq.com.

For discussions by everyone (including many very smart people), visit JavaRanch at www.javaranch.com.

Everyone's Favorite Sites

No geekworthy list of resources would be complete without Slashdot and SourceForge.

Slashdot's slogan ("News for nerds, stuff that matters") says it all.

By all means, visit slashdot.org.

The SourceForge repository (at sourceforge.net) houses more than 200,000 free, open source projects.

Check it out!

Index

About the Author

Barry Burd received a master of science degree in computer science at Rutgers University and a PhD in mathematics at the University of Illinois. As a teaching assistant in Champaign-Urbana, Illinois, he was elected five times to the university-wide List of Teachers Ranked As Excellent By Their Students.

Since 1980, Dr. Burd has been a professor in the Department of Mathematics and Computer Science at Drew University in Madison, New Jersey. When he's not lecturing at Drew University, Dr. Burd leads training courses for professional programmers in business and industry. He has lectured at conferences in the United States, Europe, Australia, and Asia. He is the author of several articles and books, including *Java For Dummies*, *Beginning Programming with Java For Dummies*, and *Android Application Development All-in-One For Dummies*, all from Wiley.

Dr. Burd lives in Madison, New Jersey, with his wife and two kids (both in their 20s and mostly on their own). In his spare time, he enjoys being a workaholic.

Dedication

For

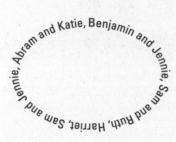

Jennie, Abram and Katie, Benjamin and Jennie, Sam and Ruth, Harriet, Sam and Jennie,

Acknowledgments

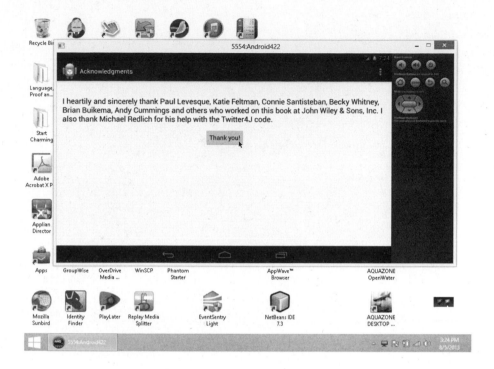

Publisher's Acknowledgments

Acquisitions Editor: Constance Santisteban

Senior Project Editor: Paul Levesque

Copy Editor: Becky Whitney

Technical Editor: Brian Buikema

Editorial Assistant: Annie Sullivan

Sr. Editorial Assistant: Cherie Case

Project Coordinator: Kristie Rees

Cover Image: ©iStockphoto.com/scanrail

Apple & Mac

iPad For Dummies,
5th Edition
978-1-118-49823-1

iPhone 5 For Dummies,
6th Edition
978-1-118-35201-4

MacBook For Dummies,
4th Edition
978-1-118-20920-2

OS X Mountain Lion
For Dummies
978-1-118-39418-2

Blogging & Social Media

Facebook For Dummies,
4th Edition
978-1-118-09562-1

Mom Blogging
For Dummies
978-1-118-03843-7

Pinterest For Dummies
978-1-118-32800-2

WordPress For Dummies,
5th Edition
978-1-118-38318-6

Business

Commodities For Dummies,
2nd Edition
978-1-118-01687-9

Investing For Dummies,
5th Edition
978-0-470-90545-6

Personal Finance
For Dummies,
7th Edition
978-1-118-11785-9

QuickBooks 2013
For Dummies
978-1-118-35641-8

Small Business Marketing Kit
For Dummies,
3rd Edition
978-1-118-31183-7

Careers

Job Interviews
For Dummies,
4th Edition
978-1-118-11290-8

Job Searching with
Social Media
For Dummies
978-0-470-93072-4

Personal Branding
For Dummies
978-1-118-11792-7

Resumes For Dummies,
6th Edition
978-0-470-87361-8

Success as a Mediator
For Dummies
978-1-118-07862-4

Diet & Nutrition

Belly Fat Diet For Dummies
978-1-118-34585-6

Eating Clean For Dummies
978-1-118-00013-7

Nutrition For Dummies,
5th Edition
978-0-470-93231-5

Digital Photography

Digital Photography
For Dummies,
7th Edition
978-1-118-09203-3

Digital SLR Cameras &
Photography For Dummies,
4th Edition
978-1-118-14489-3

Photoshop Elements 11
For Dummies
978-1-118-40821-6

Gardening

Herb Gardening
For Dummies,
2nd Edition
978-0-470-61778-6

Vegetable Gardening
For Dummies,
2nd Edition
978-0-470-49870-5

Health

Anti-Inflammation Diet
For Dummies
978-1-118-02381-5

Diabetes For Dummies,
3rd Edition
978-0-470-27086-8

Living Paleo For Dummies
978-1-118-29405-5

Hobbies

Beekeeping
For Dummies
978-0-470-43065-1

eBay For Dummies,
7th Edition
978-1-118-09806-6

Raising Chickens
For Dummies
978-0-470-46544-8

Wine For Dummies,
5th Edition
978-1-118-28872-6

Writing Young Adult Fiction
For Dummies
978-0-470-94954-2

Language &
Foreign Language

500 Spanish Verbs
For Dummies
978-1-118-02382-2

English Grammar
For Dummies,
2nd Edition
978-0-470-54664-2

French All-in One
For Dummies
978-1-118-22815-9

German Essentials
For Dummies
978-1-118-18422-6

Italian For Dummies
2nd Edition
978-1-118-00465-4

Available in print and e-book formats.

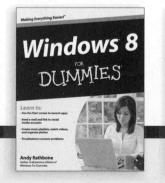

Math & Science

Algebra I For Dummies,
2nd Edition
978-0-470-55964-2

Anatomy and Physiology
For Dummies,
2nd Edition
978-0-470-92326-9

Astronomy For Dummies,
3rd Edition
978-1-118-37697-3

Biology For Dummies,
2nd Edition
978-0-470-59875-7

Chemistry For Dummies,
2nd Edition
978-1-1180-0730-3

Pre-Algebra Essentials
For Dummies
978-0-470-61838-7

Microsoft Office

Excel 2013 For Dummies
978-1-118-51012-4

Office 2013 All-in-One
For Dummies
978-1-118-51636-2

PowerPoint 2013
For Dummies
978-1-118-50253-2

Word 2013 For Dummies
978-1-118-49123-2

Music

Blues Harmonica
For Dummies
978-1-118-25269-7

Guitar For Dummies,
3rd Edition
978-1-118-11554-1

iPod & iTunes
For Dummies,
10th Edition
978-1-118-50864-0

Programming

Android Application
Development For
Dummies, 2nd Edition
978-1-118-38710-8

iOS 6 Application
Development For Dummies
978-1-118-50880-0

Java For Dummies,
5th Edition
978-0-470-37173-2

Religion & Inspiration

The Bible For Dummies
978-0-7645-5296-0

Buddhism For Dummies,
2nd Edition
978-1-118-02379-2

Catholicism For Dummies,
2nd Edition
978-1-118-07778-8

Self-Help & Relationships

Bipolar Disorder
For Dummies,
2nd Edition
978-1-118-33882-7

Meditation For Dummies,
3rd Edition
978-1-118-29144-3

Seniors

Computers For Seniors
For Dummies,
3rd Edition
978-1-118-11553-4

iPad For Seniors
For Dummies,
5th Edition
978-1-118-49708-1

Social Security
For Dummies
978-1-118-20573-0

Smartphones & Tablets

Android Phones
For Dummies
978-1-118-16952-0

Kindle Fire HD
For Dummies
978-1-118-42223-6

NOOK HD For Dummies,
Portable Edition
978-1-118-39498-4

Surface For Dummies
978-1-118-49634-3

Test Prep

ACT For Dummies,
5th Edition
978-1-118-01259-8

ASVAB For Dummies,
3rd Edition
978-0-470-63760-9

GRE For Dummies,
7th Edition
978-0-470-88921-3

Officer Candidate Tests,
For Dummies
978-0-470-59876-4

Physician's Assistant Exam
For Dummies
978-1-118-11556-5

Series 7 Exam
For Dummies
978-0-470-09932-2

Windows 8

Windows 8 For Dummies
978-1-118-13461-0

Windows 8 For Dummies,
Book + DVD Bundle
978-1-118-27167-4

Windows 8 All-in-One
For Dummies
978-1-118-11920-4

e **Available in print and e-book formats.**

Take Dummies with you everywhere you go!

Whether you're excited about e-books, want more from the web, must have your mobile apps, or swept up in social media, Dummies makes everything easier .

Dummies products make life easier!

- DIY
- Consumer Electronics
- Crafts
- Software
- Cookware
- Hobbies
- Videos
- Music
- Games
- and More!

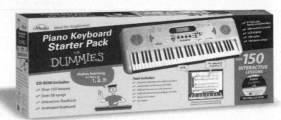

For more information, go to **Dummies.com**® and search the store by category.

For Dummies is a registered trademark of John Wiley & Sons, Inc.